# Contents

# 7   World Order Perspectives   247

# 8   New World, New Worldviews?   302

# Preface

This book introduces students to the major foreign policy worldviews that have competed for public attention since the end of World War II—(1) cold war containment, (2) reassertionism, (3) neorealism, (4) neo-isolationism, (5) radical and Marxist approaches, and (6) world order perspectives. Underlying this volume is a firm conviction that understanding competing worldviews is essential for undergraduates, and especially for those undergraduates who will never move beyond introductory courses in international politics or foreign policy.

Worldviews are the very foundations from which scholars, journalists, and policy makers think about issues of war and peace, and for that reason alone they deserve attention. But there are other significant rewards for students as well. By comparing competing worldviews, students become more attuned to the underlying assumptions beneath the positions people take on current foreign policy issues. In addition, students learn a great deal about the history of American foreign policy, and they become well acquainted with the intellectual tools of trade—the assumptions, concepts, analogies, metaphors, "lessons of history," and "stock nations" and "stock characters" that are incessantly bandied about. Finally, by working through exemplary statements of the major foreign policy worldviews, students are forced to examine critically and better ground their own philosophies of foreign policy.

Chapter 1 discusses the nature of worldviews and explores their impact upon perceptions of international trends and events. In addition, the chapter contains an analytical framework that students can use to compare and assess the readings that comprise the bulk of the text.

The substantive chapters all begin with analytical overviews, and the selections that follow are framed with comments and questions, many of which require students to consider issues that cut across worldviews. The essays by William Odom, "How to Handle Moscow," and Robert Mueller, "Enough Rope: The Cold War was Lost, Not Won," for example, were explicitly chosen to reveal how proponents of different worldviews come to vastly different conclusions about identical events—in this case, the radical changes in Soviet foreign policy under Mikhail Gorbachev. Comprehension Checkpoint sections ask students to define terms, answer questions, and complete activities that will assist them to interact with the readings. Lists of leading proponents of each worldveiw provide a guide to the people students might see on television, while listings of appropriate journals and magazines will make students aware of the rich variety that exists in magazines of opinion and scholarly journals. Each chapter concludes with a carefully selected annotated bibliography.

Analyzing and evaluating the essays contained in this anthology are difficult tasks for professionals, let alone students. In fact, after I shared a copy of my table of contents with William Maynes, the editor of *Foreign Policy*, he wrote in his return letter that "it looks like a stimulating collection of articles." Then he half-teasingly added, "The students should be appropriately confused when they get through all of them." In part, Maynes is right. Dealing with opposing points of view is difficult, and frequently confusing, for many students. But at the same time, my own students feel a sense of empowerment as they read and analyze the essays contained in this book.

In my own teaching, I have found that requiring students to buy a good newspaper and read not the news, but the editorials, columns, and "Op Ed" essays is immensely helpful when teaching about worldviews. These opinion pieces invariably reflect different worldviews. Thus, the "theories" studied in class come alive when people like Tom Wicker, Anthony Appel, William Safire, and George Will address current issues. Students also see see a sense of relevance when the authors they read in class turn up as authors on Op Ed pages. Finally, when students are required to read opinions and commentary about the news, they are motivated to read the news stories on the front pages.

As the cold war fades into history, we need to direct our students' attention to the subject of worldviews as much as ever. Not only must we ask what lessons can be derived from the worldviews that have competed in the past, but we must also decide upon the basic conceptions that will guide the nation in the new era that is emerging. To address this latter issue, the concluding chapter contains an introductory overview and a sampling of essays that reflect the major worldviews that are now emerging. As the readings in this chapter reveal, there are great continuities between current assessments and the worldviews that competed during the cold war era.

Anyone who compiles a reader like this must address the question of whether worldviews really matter. Obviously, there is never a one-to-one correspondence between the worldviews underlying presidential administrations and the foreign policies they implement. As Coral Bell, a political scientist, has instructed us well, there is always a gap, and sometimes a vast gap, between the "declaratory" signals and the "operational" behavior of administrations.[1] Domestic political considerations, the power, interests, and positions of other nations, bureaucratic politics and inertia, cost calculations, a lack of appropriate means, and sheer prudence—all of these factors, alone or in combination, lead to those frequent gaps between rhetoric and behavior.

But the existence of this gap does not mean that worldviews or "philosophies of foreign policy" can be ignored. How decision makers view the world determines the agendas of nations and the ways in which those agendas will be

---

[1]See for example, *The Reagan Paradox* (New Brunswick, NJ: Rutgers University Press, 1989), especially Ch. 1.

tackled. In addition, how we evaluate both the rhetoric and operational policies of various administrations depends upon our own worldviews.

This book would not have been possible without the help of many people. I am deeply grateful to the following for reading and commenting upon parts of the manuscript: Beverly Bimes-Michalak, W.G.P.; Terri L. Bimes, Associate, The Freeman Company, Washington, D.C.; Dr. Robert Bresler, Professor of Political Science, Pennsylvania State University, Harrisburg Campus; Dr. Robert C. Gray, Professor of Government, Franklin and Marshall College; Dr. Keith Shimko, Professor of Political Science, Purdue University; Dr. Jerome Slater, Professor of Political Science, SUNY at Buffalo. I also wish to thank the following reviewers for HarperCollins: Larry Elowitz, Georgia College; John Gilbert, North Carolina State; Carroll McKibbin, California Polytech; Dean Minix, University of Houston—Downtown; Steven Poe, North Texas State; and Kenneth Thompson, University of Virginia; as well as Lauren Silverman, Editor, College Division, HarperCollins.

Special thanks also go to several of my students. As a summer Hackman Fellow, David Murray, class of '90, joined me in countless hours of reading and discussing scores of essays on American foreign policy. David Keller, class of '91, and Todd Marshall, class of '92, proofread the entire draft manuscript.

In addition to reading and commenting on portions of the manuscript, my daughter, Sarah Michalak, spent hours gathering information and filling out first drafts of permission forms. My son David joined me for two very long days of cutting and pasting—for which he gained a Nintendo game of his choice.

Finally, this text would never have appeared without the editorial assistance of Jeanette Ninas Johnson, who turned my manuscript into the book before you, and the invaluable help and unflappable good cheer of Rose Musser, Secretary to the Department of Government at Franklin and Marshall College.

Responsibility for whatever follows is, of course, mine alone.

*Stanley J. Michalak, Jr.*

# Chapter
## *1*

# Worldviews and the Analysis of Foreign Policy

**Was it wise for President Bush to rush American troops to Saudi Arabia after the Iraqi invasion of Kuwait?**

**Should the United States continue its economic sanctions against South Africa?**

**What can the United States do to reduce hunger in Africa?**

**Should the United States continue to provide for the defense of Japan now that the cold war has ended?**

*F*or many people, the answers to these questions can be found in gathering information. "Once you have the facts, you'll know what to do." We have heard that message repeated by teachers and TV ads alike ever since we were children. In addition, our attentiveness to facts has been reinforced by the so-called "knowledge explosion" and "the information revolution." Facts that we learned yesterday are supposedly out of date today, and in their place are new mounds of facts waiting to be mastered. So entrenched is our national "facto-mania" that many of us think of education in quantitative rather than qualitative terms—more educated people know more facts, and they are quicker at finding even more facts whenever they need them.

Given our national preoccupation with facts, it should not be surprising that many people see foreign policy questions as questions of information. We disagree on issue X because one or both of us has not done enough reading and research. Experts are experts because they have more facts or information. The government should have the benefit of the doubt on foreign policy issues because our officials have access to facts that the average citizen does not and, frequently, cannot know.

From this perspective, foreign policy analysis involves breaking up "big questions" into a bundle of smaller factual questions. Consider, for example, a question that was widely debated at the end of the 1980s—whether or not the United States should tighten its economic sanctions against South Africa. The answer to that "large" question presumably lay in answers to a series of smaller factual questions. What was the extent of existing sanctions, and what had been their impact? What items were not banned, and how vital were those items to South Africa? If America tightened its sanctions, would other countries be supportive or would they profit from new markets created by the tightened American sanctions? What impact would tighter sanctions have had upon the United States? What costs would they have had for U.S. corporations and their workers?

Obviously, facts are essential in analyzing foreign policy questions and, all too frequently, the nation's welfare suffers because foreign policy decisions have to be made on the basis of incomplete, imperfect, or unknowable information. But most foreign policy disputes stem not from differences about the facts but from differences in underlying worldviews that give different meanings to the same sets of facts. Acting like filters, these underlying worldviews allow some issues to pass through our mental nets while keeping others outside. And once inside our net, worldviews envelop issues with contexts that establish their meaning and relate them to other issues.

The responses of Jimmy Carter and Ronald Reagan to the *Global 2000 Report* provide a striking illustration of the impact that worldviews can have on people's perceptions of foreign policy questions. *Global 2000* resulted from President Carter's request for a study of the "probable changes in the world's population, natural resources, and environment through the end of the century."[1] Painting an ominous ecological future, the report predicted that

> if present trends continue, the world in 2000 will be more crowded, more polluted, less stable ecologically, and more vulnerable to disruption than the world we live in now. . . . Barring revolutionary advances in technology, life for most people on earth will be more precarious in 2000 than it is now—unless the nations of the world act decisively to alter current trends.[2]

To President Carter, these words were a call to action. In establishing an interagency task force to seek ways to arrest these trends, President Carter stated that "among the most urgent and complex challenges before the world today is the projected deterioration of the environment and resource base. Unless nations of the world take prompt, decisive action to halt the current trends," he continued, "the next twenty years may see a continuation of serious food and population problems, steady loss of croplands, forests, plants and animal species, fisheries, and degradation of the earth's resources."[3]

Since 1980 was an election year, the press asked President Carter's challenger, Ronald Reagan, for his opinion of the *Global 2000 Report*. Reagan's response? He scoffed; things were probably not all that bad. Reagan claimed that if American farming techniques were used on all the tillable land on the globe, "the earth could support a population of 28 billion people."[4] What explains the different responses of Carter and Reagan? Not the facts contained in the report, but the worldviews within which the facts were defined and evaluated.

In order to think critically about foreign policy issues, one must examine the underlying worldviews that define problems and that set criteria for evaluating policy alternatives. By looking beneath the surface arguments on specific issues, we can construct intellectual scaffoldings that allow us to compare, contrast, and evaluate the fundamental bases from which differences over specific issues arise in the first place. To understand debates over particular foreign policy issues, one must be well grounded in the nature and substance of alternative worldviews—what they are, what they consist of, how they are structured, and how solidly they are grounded.

## THE CONTEMPORARY DEBATE AMONG COMPETING WORLDVIEWS

Throughout much of our past, the American people were in fundamental agreement about the strategy and tactics of their nation's foreign policy. From Washington's farewell address until our entry into World War I, America stood aloof from the quarrels in Europe, and after that war it quickly lapsed back into its traditional policy of isolationism.

After World War II, Americans settled into a bipartisan consensus behind a foreign policy of cold war containment. But with the war in Vietnam that consensus dissolved, and, for the rest of the cold war, the American public witnessed a "war of competing worldviews"—worldviews that differed radically about what international trends and events threatened the national interest, what our foreign policy agenda should have been, and how we should have secured the items on that agenda. While the end of the cold war at the turn of the 1990s may have deprived the nation of its foreign policy sextant,[5] the issues in the post-Vietnam debate provide a firm foundation for evaluating the new worldviews that are emerging before the public. In fact, strong continuities exist between the assessments and arguments that are being made today and those that were made in the last decade of the cold war.

The issues that decision makers will confront in the post–cold war era are fairly easy to enumerate—changing configurations of power and interests in Central Europe, instability and unrest in the Soviet Union, the continuance of long-standing regional conflicts that are losing their cold war components, the rise of new expansionist powers such as Hussein's Iraq, the frictions of an increasingly interdependent world economy, and growing environmental problems stemming from industrial growth in both the developed and developing countries. A consensus on how to interpret and deal with these issues, however, will not come easily, if it comes at all.

Thus, the nation is again at a turning point in its foreign policy. According to Jeane Kirkpatrick, "[This] is the first time since 1939 that there has been an opportunity for Americans to consider what we might do in a world less constrained by political and military competition with a dangerous adversary."[6]

Such considerations, in fact, are filling the pages of newspapers, magazines, scholarly journals, and books. As citizens, each of us must sort through this new debate and decide which of the newly competing worldviews is best for the nation.

The chapters that follow present extensive statements of the major worldviews that have competed for public allegiance since the end of World War II. In addition, the final chapter presents examples of the major alternatives that are now vying for public support. Once you understand the components of these worldviews as ideal types, you will become better able to locate and understand the views of participants in foreign policy debates over particular issues. While no one will hold all of the tenets of an ideal type, most individuals will fall closer to one worldview than any other.

## THE STRUCTURE AND FUNCTIONS OF WORLDVIEWS

Scholars in the fields of intellectual history, sociology, social psychology, and cognitive psychology have contributed much to our understanding of the nature of worldviews and their impact upon foreign policy decision making. The fundamental contribution of all these disciplines has been the revelation that how we perceive things, and whether in fact we perceive them at all, stems from underlying mental structures. Walter Lippmann noted this characteristic of our thinking as early as 1922 in his pioneering work, *Public Opinion:* "We notice a trait which marks a well known type and fill in the rest of the picture by means of the stereotypes we carry in our heads."[7] Seven years later, the German sociologist Karl Mannheim began publishing his ground-breaking research on underlying "styles of thought" that shaped the ways in which German conservatives and liberals viewed the world and responded to particular political questions.[8]

At first, sociologists saw styles of thought as ideologies or rationalizations tied largely to underlying economic interests,[9] but in recent decades, psychologists have found that in all aspects of life underlying mental structures govern not only what we perceive, but how we respond to what we perceive. According to cognitive psychologists, people are categorizers and labelers. As psychologist Susan Fiske puts it, "A person draws on organized prior knowledge to aid in the understanding of new information. A new person, event, or issue," she writes, "is treated as an instance of an already familiar category."[10] Once such "things" are categorized, we understand or comprehend them by looking at the attributes of the categories into which they have been placed. Comprehension, then, is a matching process; we match what we are now perceiving with categories of past perceptions that are stored in memory.

For example, many people have in their minds a category called Third World countries, which includes a set of *descripters*—a rich but tiny ruling class; widespread poverty; hunger, primitive housing, and vast urban slums; and low levels of industrialization. Once a person categorizes a country as a developing one, she will attribute to that nation all of the characteristics that already exist in her own "ideal" category. In fact, once a person categorizes a nation as a Third World country, she may even cease to examine it at all and just assume that all of the descripters in her own ideal type apply to it. In addition to sets of descripters, categories frequently contain *scripts* which cue responses to items so classified. Thus, a "Third World country" category might include such scripts as "provide foreign aid," "promote human rights," or "support democratic movements."

Psychologists have also found that if a person perceives a case that does not fit all of the descripters, she might either ignore the discrepancies altogether or minimize them. Only rarely will a person challenge the accuracy of her existing category and seek to refine it or create a new one. People tend to be "cognitive misers," as political scientist Robert Jervis puts it. But if a person is attuned to looking for differences and variations, she might revise the attributes of her category or create two categories. For example, having read about the great industrial development of countries such as South Korea, Taiwan, and Singapore, a person might create two categories of Third World countries: (a) rapidly industrializing Third World countries and (b) traditional Third World countries. If placing Mexico or North Vietnam into one of these two categories were difficult, the person might create a third category.

Categories are great economizers in our daily lives; in fact, we could not function effectively without them. They order our lives by lending quick predictability to our daily experience. To cite a trivial example, when we go to a restaurant, we know immediately what to do when the waiter comes to the table; we are not surprised if he asks us if we want cocktails, and we know how to respond; we know the meaning of *à la carte;* and we know how much we should tip.

Worldviews develop from our experience and our learning—learning obtained from "the air," from snippets we hear and read about, and from our formal education. Formal education, critical thinking, and feedback allow us to examine, to refine, and to test the validity of the categories that we use to organize and to respond to the world about us.

Of special relevance to students of foreign policy are three aspects of the sets of categories that we use to order our experiece—scripts, metaphors, and "stock characters" or "stock nations."[11] Psychologist Robert Abelson defines a script as a "set of vignettes" that explains the underlying causes of something we observe and prescribes an action that should be taken in a particular situation.[12] Scripts allow us to see events "in familiar contexts rather than in isolation, with great savings in computational efficiency and apparent 'understanding.' "[13]

Perhaps the most widely shared script in the field of international politics is "the Munich script." If citizens and students know only one script relevant to international politics, it will undoubtedly be the Munich script, which includes (1) *a dictator's demand* for some territorial change, (2) *an explanation* that attributes such demands to an insatiable desire for expansion, (3) a "lesson" that conciliatory responses in such situations only lead to further demands, and (4) *a prescription* that, in such situations, one should be firm, and, if necessary, use force to "teach" the dictator a "lesson"—that demands and threats of force do not work.

In Chapter 2, you will see how quickly and how directly President Truman drew upon this script in formulating a response to the North Korean invasion of South Korea. More recently, many people have drawn upon this script in making judgments about President Bush's response to the Iraqi subjugation of Kuwait. Former Secretary of State Alexander Haig drew directly upon the Munich analogy to underscore his perception of the stakes in the Kuwait crisis. According to Haig,

> the appeasement of Saddam Hussein, like that of his forebears in the 30s, would favor a greater crisis later and enlarge Iraq's capability to prevail in such a crisis. Saudi Arabia, Jordan, the United Arab Emirates, possibly Egypt, surely Israel, would be drawn one by one into either submission or conflict.
>
> After an Iraqi victory in the gulf, it is all too easy to foresee the U.S. and Israel standing together against a hostile Iraq-led Arab world.[14]

*Metaphors* involve the use of analogies to describe, explain, or predict international events. Perhaps the most widely known foreign policy metaphor is the domino theory which predicted that if South Vietnam "fell" to "Communism," all of Southeast Asia, if not more, would quickly follow. But other metaphors abound as well. People who write about foreign policy frequently try to make the actions of nations comprehensible by talking about balances of power and power vacuums, games, and races. In the early years of his presidency, Harry Truman guided his diplomatic encounters with Joseph Stalin by imagining that he and the Soviet dictator were playing poker.[15]

Worldviews also contain categories of *stock characters* or *stock nations* that attribute personality characteristics and typical behaviors to political leaders and nations. In the field of foreign policy, the cast of stock characters includes the democratic reformer, the right wing dictator, the revolutionary nationalist, the enemy, the puppet, the proxy, and the client. In dealing with other nations, leaders base their expectations of and behavior toward other leaders on the descripters of the stock characters that they attribute to those leaders, especially in the initial stages of contact.

Perceiving Chinese Communist leaders as enemies, John Foster Dulles refused to shake hands with Chinese Foreign Minister Chou En Lai at the Geneva Conference in 1954. When President Nixon sought to end the nation's policy of isolating China, his first act upon arriving in that country was to shake the hand of Chou En Lai. Nixon saw in this handshake a symbolic way of showing the Chinese leadership that they were no longer perceived as enemies.

In his early months as president, Harry Truman attributed to Joseph Stalin the character of Missouri political boss Tom Pendergast. Pendergast ran his political machine on a set of precepts that Truman referred to as "the code of the politician." Central to this code was an obligation to carry out agreements freely made and publicly acknowledged. When Stalin failed to follow this "code of the politician" by refusing to hold free elections in Poland and other East European countries, Truman became very angry. That Stalin may never have heard of the

Missouri boss and his code did not seem to matter to Truman. While Truman was expecting Stalin to behave as a stock character in boss Pendergast's political machine, Secretary of State James Byrnes was attributing to Soviet Foreign Minister V. Molotov the stock character of a "horse trading" member of the U.S. Senate. When Molotov did not behave as such a U.S. senator would, Byrnes placed him into another stock category, that of a diabolical enemy who could never be trusted.[16]

When Mikhail Gorbachev's behavior began to deviate markedly from past Soviet leaders, analysts and officials sought to "make sense" out of the Soviet leader's actions by finding the "right" label or stock character to attribute to him—a stock characterization that would make his actions comprehensible and provide a basis for responding to his moves. Given the Soviet president's unorthodox behavior, the wide range of characterizations should not have been surprising—"a dedicated Communist," "a closet Social Democrat," "an extremely clever power-seeking Machiavellian," "a good dictator," "a Zen genius," "a Communist pope," "a Soviet Martin Luther," and "a Soviet Franklin Delano Roosevelt."

Political scientists have begun to study how such stock characterizations affect the behavior of diplomats. After surveying a sample of American foreign service officers, Martha Cottam identified seven "stock countries" that were shared by these diplomats, and she compiled the typical attributes of each. In a follow-up study of negotiations over gas and oil prices, she found that how American negotiators classified Mexico as a stock country significantly affected their definitions of the negotiating situation, their expectations, and their strategies in bargaining with Mexican officials.[17] In his book, *Perception and Behavior in Soviet Foreign Policy*, Richard Hermann uncovered seven "stock countries" in the writings and speeches of Soviet writers and officials—the enemy, the barbarian (a category used to define the Chinese), the degenerate, the ally, the dependent ally, the child, and the satellite.[18]

From such collections of categories, people "make sense" out of the trends and events that take place in the world around them. These collections of categories define problems, they cue and limit responses to those problems, and they create expectations. In fact, debates over foreign policy questions can be seen as debates about the nature and the adequacy of the underlying sets of categories that people impose upon the world.

Individuals vary vastly in the quantity and quality of the sets of categories that make up their worldviews. They also vary in the extent to which these sets of categories are implicit or explicit, examined or unexamined. Researchers have repeatedly warned against worldviews that are sparse in categories, attributes, scripts, metaphors, analogies, and stock characters. Since our perceptions and inferences are driven not by "reality out there" but by the categories in our own mind, worldviews that allow for finer distinctions might enable us better to comprehend external events and actions.

Cognitive psychologists have also found that people vary greatly in their styles of information processing—in fact, an *explicit* awareness about the difference between seeing and perceiving marks the sophisticated thinker. More simple information processors seldom explore multiple definitions of problems or multiple explanations for their causes. They also tend to look for evidence that confirms their perceptions, and they tend to end their searching and assessing relatively quickly. Evidence that does not fit the worldviews of more simple information processors tends to be ignored, unperceived, or forced to fit into existing categories. Incongruous information seldom serves as a trigger for gathering more information, refining categories, or rethinking the perception of a problem. When worldviews containing only a few categories are wedded to simple information-processing components, growth, development, and refinement may not take place.

In novel situations, complex information processors frequently become highly aware of their cognitive processes. They will look for different ways of defining a problem, they will look for multiple causal explanations, develop competing hypotheses, think explicitly about what information would test their hypotheses, look for inconsistencies or anomalies, tend to be slow and cautious, and be much more tentative or provisional about the conclusions they reach.

Cognitive psychologists have studied differences between novices and experts in solving similar problems, and as one would expect, experts are both quicker and better in defining, assessing, and processing incoming stimuli from the external environment.[19] Experts possess more chunks of knowledge, and that knowledge is organized into treelike structures that link concepts into patterns. Because they have a vast array of categories, scripts, and metaphors, experts have a larger stock of categories against which to test their perceptions.

Thus, when presented with stimuli, experts recall more information and the information recalled is better organized. Inconsistent information or information that "doesn't fit" has a much greater impact on the expert than the novice. In fact, experts are more likely to look actively for inconsistencies when matching perceptions and categories. In her studies of political perceptions, psychologist Susan Fiske also found that experts tended to be less ideological and less partisan than novices.

Before we decide to leave the world to the experts, a few warnings are in order. Even the best experts can become entrapped in what the late Princeton University Professor Harold Sprout referred to as "intellectual jails." According to Sprout, experts frequently become encased in theoretical frameworks or worldviews that prevent them from observing events and trends from any other perspective. In such cases, the cognitive processing component of their worldviews reverts to that of a novice despite the vast amount of content that such experts may possess.

This tunnel vision of experts was revealed sharply in a simulation conducted by political scientists Michael Shapiro and G. Matthew Bonham.[20] Shapiro and Bonham asked three groups of experts to respond to an identical scenario—the placement of nuclear weapons in Syria by the Soviet Union. The experts in international politics viewed the scenario in terms of the East-West conflict; the experts in comparative politics responded to the scenario by examining the kinds of regimes in the region and the relations among them; the Middle East specialists attempted to illuminate the scenario by examining historical forces operating in the Middle East.

# WORLDVIEWS AND THE ANALYSIS OF FOREIGN POLICY

The chapters that follow present writings from four mainstream and two non-mainstream worldviews, while the final chapter sketches out what appear to be the main contending worldviews for the post–cold war era. The mainstream worldviews include *cold war containment, reassertionism, neorealism,* and *neo-isolationism. Cold war containment* framed our response to the Soviet challenge in the late 1940s, and it enjoyed wide, bipartisan support until the war in Vietnam. With the collapse of that consensus in the mid-1960s, three world-views vied for public allegiance:

1. *The reassertionist worldview,* which characterized the foreign policy of the Reagan administration and most closely resembled cold war containment;
2. *The neorealist worldview,* which undergirded the foreign policies during the first three years of the Carter administration and later served as a basis from which critics attacked the Reagan and Bush administrations;[21]
3. *The neo-isolationist worldview,* which was critical of both reassertionism and neorealism and called for strategic disengagement—a withdrawal from all the military commitments the United States had undertaken since the end of World War II.

Mainstream worldviews are worldviews that encase the parameters of debate for the vast majority of the American people and their political leaders. Fifteen years ago, neo-isolationism might not have been included as a mainstream worldview, but, during the 1980s, essays presenting neo-isolationist positions appeared in such mainstream publications as *Foreign Policy, Foreign Affairs,* and *Harper's.* With the end of the cold war, some former reassertionists have moved close to the neo-isolationist position, as have some former neorealists.

The non-mainstream worldviews are the *radical/Marxist worldview* and the *world order perspective.* These worldviews are non-mainstream in two senses. First, they have not gained the allegiance of any significant political groups in the nation; thus, they are, in fact, at the margins of the national political debate. However, on college and university campuses, these non-mainstream worldviews frequently have articulate advocates. Secondly, each of these worldviews rejects some major tenet held by advocates of mainstream views. Radicals and Marxists, for example, view the United States as a major cause of the injustice, poverty, and arms spending that exists in most of the developing world. World order proponents believe that the nation-centered approach of mainstream spokesmen is ill conceived and unlikely to insure the nation's long-run security and standard of living.

Each of the six worldviews provides a different set of perceptual lenses through which the world can be viewed and organized. These sets of lenses classify events and trends as threatening or nonthreatening; they identify nations as friends, allies, competitors, enemies, puppets, or neutrals; they highlight "lessons" learned from the past; they contain working assumptions about how the international system works; and from these lessons and assumptions, scripts are derived that cue appropriate strategies and tactics for dealing with different kinds of states and events.

The differences among competing worldviews stem from different classifications of identical events, trends, and nations—different classifications that lead to different scripts and "lessons" that stem from different metaphors and readings of history, and even different readings of the same history. What makes foreign policy analysis especially difficult is that people seldom argue openly about their categories of thought or the assumptions upon which their arguments are based. Instead, arguments about foreign policy issues contain mixtures of assumptions, scripts, metaphors, and lessons of history, which are all too frequently heaped upon further unstated assumptions.

In the chapters that follow, your analysis will begin by placing the content of the selections into a common set of categories that will profile the substance of each worldview. As soon as even two worldviews are placed into a common framework, areas of agreement and disagreement will immediately become apparent, and the task of assessment and evaluation will have begun.

The questions that follow will allow you to organize a worldview into a coherent, analytical framework. In terms of assessment and evaluation, proponents of various worldviews frequently criticize the assumptions and assessments of other worldviews. Consequently, a great deal of critical material can be gleaned from selections by the advocates themselves. In addition, there is a wealth of scholarly studies that subject different worldviews to critical scrutiny. Some of the most important critical studies are included in the chapters that follow, and others are noted in the annotated bibliographies.

## PROFILING A FOREIGN POLICY WORLDVIEW: SOME FUNDAMENTAL QUESTIONS

The following questions will allow you to profile a foreign policy worldview. In addition, each of these questions provides a personal agenda for research and thought. To make sense of American foreign policy issues and to ground our own worldviews in reason, each of us must have a defensible answer to the questions that follow.

1. **What is the foreign policy agenda?** What items should be at the top of the agenda for American foreign policy makers—the creation of a new world order based upon international law, social justice, and the peaceful settlement of disputes; the promotion of American values of freedom and enlightened capitalism; the maintenance of the global balance of power; the abolition of nuclear weapons from the face of the earth; the enhancement of

human rights and self-determination; or cleaning up the environment? Obviously, no nation has only one aim or interest. Nor does every nation have the resources to do everything it would like to do. But each worldview does have its own set of priorities for the nation's foreign policy agenda.

2. **Why this agenda?** What is the rationale for the agenda of a particular worldview? Why should those items be at the top of the agenda rather than others? The rationale of any agenda will lie in a mixture of judgments about the nation's interests and perceptions about how the international system works.

3. **What assumptions underlie the worldview?** The foundation of any worldview lies in the assumptions upon which it rests. Different assumptions drive different agendas and different policy proposals on changing international issues. For example, disagreements over arms control policies during the 1980s rested upon different assumptions about Soviet aims, ambitions, and credibility. More recently, differences over President Bush's actions in the Persian Gulf have turned in part upon assumptions about what Hussein and others, namely Japan and our Western European allies, would have done if the United States had not gone to the United Nations and sent hundreds of thousands of troops to Saudi Arabia. If the assumptions upon which a worldview are based prove faulty or incorrect, the strategies and policy proposals that derive from them may be unproductive or even counterproductive. Thus, examining the evidence upon which fundamental assumptions rest is a vital step in analysis and evaluation. But assumptions about what? The following questions tap those issues that have driven people into different worldviews since the end of World War II.

a. *What are the fundamental axes of conflict in the international system and how do they affect the United States?*

## The Era of Isolationism: Conflict, Yes; American Involvement, No

During most of its history, the United States was able to ignore the perils of international politics. The Monroe Doctrine, in fact, was designed precisely to ensure that America could remain insulated from European power politics. Thus, through most of the nineteenth century, America pursued "manifest destiny" on the continent, "big stick" diplomacy in South America, and isolation from European power politics. At the turn of the century, the United States broke with its isolationist tradition in Asia by taking the Philippines, searching for naval bases, and seeking to preserve an "open door" in China.

During World War I, however, German submarines ended America's insulation from the European system of power politics. While the nation waged war, President Woodrow Wilson planned to build a new security system based upon his League of Nations. When the U.S. Senate refused to ratify the new organization's charter, the United States returned to its prewar isolationism. When the European system broke down during the 1930s, many still hoped that the United States could avoid being drawn into the conflicts in Europe and Asia. When the Japanese attacked Pearl Harbor and Hitler declared war on America, the die was cast, and the United States entered the most devastating war in history.

## Axes of Conflict in the Cold War Era: The Nature of the Soviet Threat

World War II left a world in ruins. Europe, in the words of Winston Churchill, was "a charnal house," and only Soviet, American, and British troops could provide order and security. Yet even before victory was declared, the Grand Alliance was falling apart. As Soviet troops advanced toward the center of Europe, it was clear that Stalin was regaining former Czarist territory and installing "friendly" governments throughout Eastern Europe.

What were the Soviets up to? What did they want, and why did they want it? And in what ways, if any, did Soviet behavior affect vital American interests? For over forty-five years, different answers to these questions have divided foreign policy makers and scholars alike.

At the core of the postwar foreign policy debates, then, were fundamental differences over the nature of the Soviet regime and the foreign policy challenge it posed for the United States. To some, the Soviet Union was a revolutionary power bent upon the creation of a world Communist state. To others, the Soviet Union was a traditional, but imperialist, great power seeking to extend its power and influence throughout the world. Those making this assumption viewed the Soviet Union's Communist ideology as an instrument or a pretext rather than a motivating force behind Soviet behavior. To still others, the Soviet Union was a defensive and reactive state whose actions were motivated largely by deeply rooted fears and insecurities—fears and insecurities that drove Soviet leaders to perceive Western foreign policies in threatening and hostile terms. Finally, there were those who perceived no Soviet threat; in fact, such people frequently saw the Soviet Union as a progressive force for social and economic justice.

Each of these perceptions rested upon its own set of assumptions, examples, and readings of history. Assessing the degree to which each perception is valid is no easy task. Yet such assessments are vital because perceptions about the nature and aims of the Soviet Union significantly affect other components of foreign policy worldviews.

## Axes of Conflict in the Post–Cold War Era

During the cold war era, perceptions of the Soviet Union were central because of that regime's great power and its potential to affect significantly the global balance of power. As the Soviet threat recedes, a new debate is arising, and at the core of this new debate are assumptions about the future axes of conflict in the international system and their relationship to America's power and interests.

As in the cold war era, differing values and assumptions are leading people into different worldviews. Some believe that the United States should try to shape the evolving balances of power in Central Europe and Asia, while others believe that we can sit back and allow matters to take their course. Some people believe that the United States cannot live in a disorderly world of regional wars and instabilities; others, of course, reject this view. Finally, there are those who believe that power politics has become obsolete, replaced by economic might and competition.

### b. What are the sources and significance of instability and unrest in the Third World?

Since the end of the colonial era, foreign policy worldviews have all had to address the unrest, instability, and economic underdevelopment in the Third World. During the cold war era, there were those who attributed much of this unrest and instability to the Soviet Union. In their opinion, the Soviets fanned domestic unrest in order to isolate the West from strategic materials and vital geopolitical positions. Others, however, attributed this unrest to age-old ethnic or tribal controversies, difficulties in meeting sharply rising expectations, and the inevitable social strains that accompany economic growth and development.

How observers viewed the sources of this instability frequently determined their policy responses. Those who saw Soviets as the cause of unrest frequently favored supporting authoritarian allies when they were under siege, as in Vietnam and El Salvador. Those who believed that the forces of unrest were largely indigenous, frequently favored a hands-off policy in revolutionary situations and assumed that postrevolutionary elites would be guided by interests rather than ideology. At the same time, they also believed that instability and revolutionary conflict might be lessened by American policies that favored human rights, increased foreign aid, and promoted reforms in the international economic order that would provide greater income for developing countries.

In the post–cold war era, the Soviet Union has abandoned the field of competition in the Third World, and differences among proponents of various worldviews now turn on the *significance* of such instability for America's interests. Thus, some who favored Ronald Reagan's policy of competing with the Soviet Union in the Third World are now asking whether it any longer matters who rules in Nicaragua, Angola, Cambodia, Afghanistan, or Ethiopia.[22] Different responses to President Bush's actions in the Middle East also reflected different perceptions about the significance of the Iraqi invasion of Kuwait. Supporters of the president feared that Hussein might gain control over a significant portion of the world's known reserves of oil. Skeptics pointed out that the effect of such control would be much more threatening to the West Europeans and Japanese than to the United States. Skeptics also argued that the laws of economics would "discipline" Hussein just as they disciplined earlier OPEC leaders such as the Shah of Iran and the elites of Saudi Arabia, Kuwait, and the United Arab Emirates.

### c. How tightly interrelated is the international system?

Proponents of different worldviews also disagree on the extent to which events or actions in one part of the globe might spill over into other areas. Some believe that peace is indivisible—that unchallenged acts of aggression will only lead to further aggression and that forces of change can sweep across whole areas. Others believe that the spillover effects of forces, movements, and unchallenged acts of aggression depend upon the particulars in any situation.

Such differences were at the base of disagreements over the domino theory during the war in Vietnam. In that particular case, the spillover effect was nonexistent beyond the confines of Indochina. On the other hand, the "fall" of Poland and Hungary quickly led to the collapse of the Soviet bloc in Eastern Europe and threatened other parts of the Soviet empire both internally and externally.

In the post–cold war era, views on the interrelatedness of international events and actions will be crucial determinants of foreign policy worldviews. In fact, one reason President Bush acted so quickly in response to the Iraqi invasion of Kuwait was to deter other possible aggressors in the world. In the president's opinion, our failure to respond quickly would have sent an open invitation to other potential Husseins.

In reflecting upon all of these questions, you might wonder why analysts make assumptions about questions that appear to be matters of fact? The answer lies in the complexity of the subject matter. Since the evidence for answering the questions raised above is unclear or mixed, people must make *assumptions* about the *directions* in which the answers lie. As you read the selections in this book, write down the answers that various authors provide for questions a, b, and c and note the evidence that they present. However, do not be surprised if you find little evidence in support of the answers. Many proponents frequently assume or take for granted the answers to these questions.

4. **What is the cast of characters?** What major stock characters or stock nations recur in the writings that reflect a particular worldview? How accurate are the characteristics attributed to various persons or nations? In comparing these characterizations, note how different worldviews attribute different stock characteristics to the same individuals and nations. Ask yourself what accounts for such differences and try to decide which characterizations are more accurate. Also, note differences in the nature and variety of stock characters that comprise different worldviews.

5. **What metaphors define the world, and what lessons of history are drawn from that world?** Because reality is infinite, metaphors and analogies help to make the world comprehensible. Some worldviews draw heavily on *competitive metaphors* such as chess and races, while others draw on *cooperative metaphors*. In addition, worldviews vary in their readings of history. Consequently, the "lessons of history" that drive particular worldviews must be assessed in light of the situations for which they are and are not appropriate. As you read the selections in this book, note how different worldviews have their own sets of historical events that guide and shape the meaning given to particular issues.

6. **What scripts or policy proposals recur in the writings of advocates of the worldview?** In addition to defining our problems and shaping how we think about them, worldviews also provide us with strategies, scripts, and policy proposals to solve those problems. Some worldviews emphasize the importance of force or threats of force; others emphasize diplomatic measures.

Again, patterns will appear both within and among worldviews. Strategies, scripts, and policy proposals are frequently related to the assumptions about the nature of the international system and how that system works.

7. **What is your assessment of the worldview?** After you have profiled a worldview, reflect upon the answer to the above question and the evidence upon which this answer rests. Do you accept the tenets of the worldview? If so, why? If not, why not? By studying the worldviews of the cold war era, we can learn about the mistakes and successes of the past. We can also become better able to assess the debate among post–cold war worldviews.

## A WORLDVIEW PROFILE

The next two pages consist of a Worldview Profile Form. Xerox multiple copies of these pages and use them to take notes on each of the worldviews that follow. You might want to pretest your own worldview by filling in your answers to these items. In this way, you can see how your worldview changes or remains the same as you read the selections in this text.

# WORLDVIEW PROFILE FORM

1. Top items on the foreign policy agenda:

2. Rationale for the agenda:

3. Major assumptions and support for them:

   a. Axes of international conflict and their significance for the United States:

   b. Sources, nature, and significance of instability and unrest in the Third World:

   c. The interrelatedness of the international system:

4. Major stock characters or stock nations:

5. Major metaphors, analogies, and "lessons of history":

6. Major strategies, scripts, and policies:

7. My assessment:

# THE GAP BETWEEN WORLDVIEWS AND POLICIES

While worldviews always affect the evaluation of policies pursued by different presidents, there will always be gaps between the worldviews of policy makers and the policies they pursue. For example, John F. Kennedy announced in his inaugural address that the United States would "pay any price, bear any burden, meet any hardship, support any friend, oppose any foe to assure the survival and success of liberty." Yet, within weeks after making his pronouncement, the young president sought to negotiate a face-saving settlement in response to Communist advances in Laos. Three months later, when the CIA-sponsored Cuban invasion force ran aground in the Bay of Pigs, Kennedy decided not to use American power to rescue it or support it in any way. To cite another example, political scientist Coral Bell has dwelled at length upon the vast gap between the "declaratory signals" of the Reagan administration and the actual policies it followed in issue areas ranging from arms control to terrorism.[23]

The reasons for such gaps lie in limited resources, the constraints of public and congressional opinion, trade-offs between domestic and foreign priorities, disagreements with allies, the potential costs and risks of various policy alternatives, and simple prudence. Since these factors will never disappear, one can always expect a gap between the worldviews and foreign policies of presidential administrations.

But the existence of this gap does not mean that worldviews or "philosophies of foreign policy" can be ignored. How decision makers view the world determines the agendas of nations and the ways in which they seek to tackle those agendas. In addition, how we evaluate both the rhetoric and operational policies of various administrations depends upon our own worldviews.

## FOR FURTHER READING

Crabb, Cecil V. *Policy Makers and Critics: Conflicting Theories of American Foreign Policy.* New York: Praeger Publishers, 1976. According to its author, this excellent book seeks "to focus attention upon a dimension of contemporary American foreign policy that . . . often tends to be neglected—the underlying principles, values, and assumptions guiding American behavior abroad." Although pre-Carter, pre-Reagan, and pre-Bush, this book contains clear discussions of major postwar worldviews along with critical comments that are as appropriate to the mid-1990s as they were when Crabb wrote this book in the mid-1970s.

Fiske, Susan T. "Schema-Based Versus Piecemeal Politics: A Patchwork Quilt, but Not a Blanket of Evidence," in Richard R. Lau and David O. Sears. *Political Cognition.* Hillsdale, NJ: Lawrence Erlbaum Associates, 1986, pp. 41–42. A psychologist explains how people process information by placing people, events, or issues into more or less developed categories or schemas.

Holsti, Ole. "Cognitive Process Approach to Decision Making." *American Behavioral Scientist,* Vol. 20, No. 1 (September–October 1976), pp. 11–32. Holsti briefly and clearly explains and assesses the major psychological approaches to the study of foreign policy decision making.

Jervis, Robert. *Perception and Misperception in International Politics*. Princeton, NJ: Princeton University Press, 1976. A pioneering and now classic study on the role of perception and worldviews in foreign policy decision making.

Lau, Richard R. and David O. Sears (eds.). *Political Cognition*. Hillsdale, NJ: Lawrence Erlbaum Associates, 1986. A volume of essays that explains and evaluates cognitive approaches to the study of political perception and decision making.

Larson, Deborah Welch. *Origins of Containment: A Psychological Explanation*. Princeton, NJ: Princeton University Press, 1985. A study of the cognitive processes of W. Averell Harriman, Harry Truman, James Byrnes, and Dean Acheson. Larson's first chapter provides an excellent overview of the contributions of cognitive psychologists to our understanding of foreign policy worldviews.

Little, Richard and Steve Smith (eds.). *Belief Systems and International Relations*. New York: Basil Blackwell, 1988. A theoretical discussion of the problems involved in studying belief systems along with some excellent case studies on Thatcher and the Falkland Islands, the foreign policies of Carter and Reagan, the belief system of Harry Truman, and that of British Prime Minister Harold Macmillan.

May, Ernest. *'Lessons' of the Past: The Use and Misuse of History in American Foreign Policy*. New York: Oxford University Press, 1972. A short and highly readable book of case studies illuminating the role of misperception in the making of foreign policy.

Shapiro, Michael and G. Matthew Bonham. "Cognitive Process and Foreign Policy Decision-Making." *International Studies Quarterly*, Vol. 17, No. 2 (June 1973), pp. 147–74. The essay cited in the text studied the responses of different experts to an identical scenario.

Smoke, Richard. "The 'Peace' of Deterrence and the 'Peace' of the Antinuclear War Movement." *Political Psychology*, Vol. 5, No. 4 (1984), pp. 741–48. Smoke outlines two worldviews or "universes of discourse" for dealing with the problem of world peace—the deterrence, or trust in arms, worldview and the abolitionist, trust in disarmament, worldview. He then examines the fact that "they begin from such fundamentally different assumptions that they talk past each other." Smoke provides an excellent analysis of the basic assumptions that separate these two worldviews.

Sylvan, D. and S. Chan (eds.). *Foreign Policy Decision-Making: Perception, Cognition, and Artificial Intelligence*. New York: Praeger Press, 1984. A collection of articles exploring and evaluating the contribution of cognitive psychology to understanding foreign policy decision making.

Tetlock, Phillip E. "Policy-Makers' Images of International Conflict." *Journal of Social Issues*, Vol. 39, No. 1 (1983), pp. 67–86. Psychologist Tetlock asks the following question: "Do policy-makers often rely on excessively simplistic or inaccurate [worldviews] of the international scene?" His answer is, "This is indeed the case." Given this starting point, Tetlock discusses the psychological factors that lead to oversimplified worldviews—personality variables, "lessons of history," groupthink, and crisis-induced stress. This essay is an excellent introduction to the nature and function of worldviews.

# NOTES

1. Gerald Barney, Study Director, *The Global 2000 Report to the President* (Washington, DC: Government Printing Office, 1980), p. iii.
2. *Ibid.*, p. 1.
3. *Public Papers of the President, Jimmy Carter, 1980–81, Vol. II*, p. 1417.
4. Quoted in *Science*, November 28, 1980, pp. 88–89.
5. See C. W. Maynes, "America without the Cold War," *Foreign Policy*, 79 (Spring 1990), pp. 3–26.
6. Jeane Kirkpatrick, "A Normal Country in a Normal Time," *The National Interest*, 21 (Fall 1990), p. 40.
7. Walter Lippmann, *Public Opinion* (Toronto, Ontario: Collier-Macmillan, 1922), p. 59.
8. Karl Mannheim, *Essays on Sociology and Social Psychology* (London: Routledge & Kegan Paul Ltd., 1953). See especially Part I.
9. This, of course, was one of Marx's contributions, but Mannheim also saw ideas in this light. See, for example, his *Ideology and Utopia* (New York: Harcourt Press, 1936).
10. Susan T. Fiske, "Schema-Based Versus Piecemeal Politics: A Patchwork Quilt, but Not a Blanket of Evidence," in Richard R. Lau and David O. Sears, *Political Cognition* (Hillsdale, NJ: Lawrence Erlbaum Associates, 1986), pp. 41–42.
11. The following discussion is taken largely from Deborah Larson, *The Origins of Containment* (Princeton, NJ: Princeton University Press, 1985), Ch. 1.
12. Robert P. Abelson, "Psychological Status of the Script Concept," *The American Psychologist*, Vol. 36, No. 7 (July 1981), p. 717.
13. *Ibid.*, p. 116.
14. Alexander M. Haig, Jr., "Gulf Analogy: Munich or Vietnam?," *The New York Times*, December 16, 1990, p. A19.
15. See Deborah Larson, *The Origins of Containment*, Chs. 3 and 4.
16. The role of stock characterization in the diplomatic activities of Truman and Byrnes is analyzed in Deborah Larson, *The Origins of Containment*, Chs. 3 and 4.
17. Martha Cottam, *Foreign Policy Decision Making: The Influence of Cognition* (Boulder, CO: Westview Press, 1986), Chs. 2, 3, 4.
18. Richard Hermann, *Perception and Behavior in Soviet Foreign Policy* (Pittsburgh, University of Pittsburgh Press, 1985).
19. See, for example, S. Fiske *et al.* "The Novice and Expert: Knowledge Based Strategies in Political Cognition," *Journal of Experimental Social Psychology*, Vol. 19 (1983), pp. 381–400.
20. M. Shapiro and G. Bonham, "Cognitive Process and Foreign Policy Decision Making," *International Studies Quarterly*, Vol. 17 (1973), pp. 147–74.
21. The terms "reassertionism" and "neorealism" are drawn from Richard Feinberg's excellent book, *The Intemperate Zone* (New York: W.W. Norton, 1983). Feinberg used the term "reassertionism" to characterize the foreign policy worldview of the Reagan administration and its supporters. He used the term "neorealism" to characterize some aspects of the Carter administration's foreign policy and to define a worldview from which many criticized the policies of the Reagan administration. These terms later became commonly used in foreign policy discourse. As used in this book, neorealism does not refer to the theory of political analysis that is an outgrowth of political realism. For neorealism as a mode of inquiry see Robert O. Keohane, ed., *Neorealism and Its Critics* (New York: Columbia University Press, 1986).

22. Neoconservative supporter Nathan Glazer raises such questions in his "A Time for Modesty," *The National Interest*, 21 (Fall 1990), pp. 31–35.
23. See Coral Bell, *The Reagan Paradox: U.S. Foreign Policy in the 1980s* (New Brunswick, NJ: Rutgers University Press, 1989).

# Chapter
## 2

# Cold War
# Containment

When Franklin Delano Roosevelt took America into World War II, he had no intention of replacing America's traditional policy of isolationism with balance of power politics. Like other internationalists, Roosevelt shared the isolationists' disdain for spheres of influence, exclusive alliances, and unilateral uses of force. In place of the equally discredited policies of isolationism and balance of power politics, Roosevelt sought to build a new international order based upon principle rather than power.

The principles that Roosevelt had in mind were clearly set forth in his Atlantic Charter, which he persuaded the British and the Soviets to sign in the late summer of 1941. By signing the charter, the members of the Grand Alliance committed themselves to the following principles:

First, their countries seek no aggrandizement, territorial or other;

Second, they desire to see no territorial changes that do not fully accord with the freely expressed wishes of the peoples concerned;

Third, they respect the right of all peoples to choose the form of government under which they will live; and they wish to see sovereign rights and self-government restored to those who have been forcibly deprived of them.

As the war drew to a close, however, it was clear that Stalin and Churchill were behaving more in accord with the principles of balance of power politics than with the principles embodied in the Atlantic Charter. Stalin was building a sphere of domination in Eastern Europe, and Churchill was seeking to contain the Russians as far east as possible. In addition, the British prime minister was also trying to hold on to his nation's weakening empire.

As the Soviets implanted puppet governments in Poland, Romania, and Bulgaria, the Truman administration quickly lost hope for a new world order based upon the principles of the Atlantic Charter. In fact, by the summer of 1945, the alliance that FDR had worked so hard to solidify was on the verge of collapse. American and Soviet leaders were deadlocked on almost every postwar issue.

But what could be done? Given the power vacuum in Europe, isolationism appeared untenable; the Soviets could march to the shores of Brittany in a matter of weeks if American forces left the continent. On the other hand, going to war with the Soviet Union was also unthinkable. By the end of the war, Russian prestige was at its apex in America, and the war-weary American people insisted on "bringing the boys back home." At the same time, a negotiated settlement that recognized the Soviet-imposed regimes would make a mockery of the principles of the Atlantic Charter. Yet, as the Truman administration quickly found out, words and economic diplomacy did little to make Stalin accede to American principles in Eastern Europe.

What did the Soviets want and why did they want it? What were America's interests and how could they be secured? These questions preoccupied decision makers during the last six months of 1945. In February of 1946, George Kennan provided a convincing set of answers to these questions in a "long cable" that he sent to the State Department from his post as counselor at the American Embassy in Moscow. In the July 1947 issue of *Foreign Affairs*, the career diplomat also presented his ideas to the American public in an essay entitled "The Sources of Soviet Conduct." Given Kennan's highly placed position in the federal government at that time, the author of the essay was given the pseudonym of Mr. X.

Kennan's assessment was a sobering one. Because of ideology and circumstance, he explained, the leaders in the Kremlin had "no abstract love of peace and stability [and] no real faith in the possibility of a permanent happy coexistence of the Socialist and Capitalist worlds."[1] According to Kennan, Marxist ideology painted the United States and Britain as implacable enemies of the Soviet regime, and Soviet leaders took their ideology seriously. Circumstances also hindered good relations between the United States and the Soviet Union. The Soviets actually needed foreign enemies, Kennan argued, in order to legitimize the oppressive and extractive regime that they had placed upon their people. The diplomat's assessment was ominous: The Soviets were expansionistic, and their hostility to the West was inherent in their ideology and their situation. No matter what America did, the Soviets would continue to be hostile. Thus, reconciliation and friendly relations were impossible.

At the same time, Kennan also noted that the Soviets were neither incautious nor reckless. Since their ideology promised ultimate victory, Soviet leaders could afford to be prudent in their pursuit of a Communist world. No Soviet leader, he argued, would risk lightly all that their revolution had attained since 1917. Accordingly, Kennan concluded that

the Kremlin is in no ideological compulsion to accomplish its purposes in a hurry. The very teachings of Lenin himself require great caution and flexibility in the pursuit of Communist purposes . . . . Thus, the Kremlin has no compunction about retreating in the face of superior force. And being under the compulsion of no timetable, it does not get panicky under the necessity for such retreat. Its political action is a fluid stream which moves constantly, wherever it is permitted to move, toward a given goal. Its main concern is to make sure it has filled every nook and cranny available to it in the basin of world power.[2]

Thus, Kennan sought to dash any hope that the United States could "convert" the Soviets and implant American ideals in places where the nation had, at best, limited influence. "In these circumstances," Kennan wrote, "it is clear that the main element of any United States policy toward the Soviet Union must be that of a long-term, patient but firm and vigilant containment of Russian expansive tendencies."[3] Kennan counseled what Franklin Roosevelt had hoped to avoid, namely, the entry of America into the rough and tumble of balance of power politics.

## THE AXIOMS OF COLD WAR CONTAINMENT

The hallmarks of the containment worldview were the perception of an inherently expansionist Soviet Union, a requirement for American action, a prescription for policy makers, and a set of justifying scripts and assumptions.

By the summer of 1945, Communist governments were in power in Poland, Romania, Bulgaria, Albania, and Yugoslavia, and Communist parties were in significant positions of power in Hungary and Czechoslovakia. In addition, the Communist parties in France and Italy were large, strong, and popular. In Greece, China, and Vietnam, Communist forces were also seeking power. By the end of 1945, Stalin was demanding a revision of both Turkish borders and the Montreux Convention governing the Turkish straits. In nearby Iran, Russian troops were supporting pro-Soviet rebels who were demanding "autonomy" for the northern province of Azerbaijan. When Stalin continued his demands on Turkey in 1946 and Soviet troops failed to leave Iran, President Truman and some of his closest advisers concluded that "the Soviets were on the march."[4]

If communism was on the march, its conquests would probably be easy ones if America retreated into isolationism. The defeat of Germany and Japan and the devastation of the victors in Europe and Asia left a bipolar world beset with power vacuums and tottering colonial empires. Given an expansionist Soviet Union with seemingly unlimited global ambitions, only the United States had the power to keep Europe and Asia free from Soviet domination.

The prescription for policy makers was articulated by Kennan and practiced by Truman: The United States would attempt to contain the Soviets through policies of deterrence, defense, economic aid, and, if necessary, military action. Truman's firmness and a show of the flag in the eastern Mediterranean had three results: Stalin gave up his territorial demands on Turkey, he dropped his insistence on changes in the Montreux Convention, and he withdrew his troops from northern Iran. When he did the latter, support for the Azerbaijani rebels collapsed.

In February 1947, the British government informed the Truman administration that it could no longer afford to support the Greek government in its struggle against Communist insurgents who were aided by the Communist governments of Yugoslavia, Albania, and Bulgaria. Six weeks later, Truman asked Congress to provide funds to support the Turkish economy and to enable the Greek government to defeat the Communist guerrillas. In announcing his Truman Doctrine, the feisty president implied that much more was at stake than the two countries targeted for American aid. He told the Congress that

> at the present moment in world history nearly every nation must choose between alternative ways of life. The choice is too often not a free one. . . .
>
> I believe that it must be the policy of the United States to support free peoples who are resisting attempted subjugation by armed minorities or by outside pressures.[5]

Several months later, the United States unveiled its Marshall Plan, which, from 1948 to 1952, provided over $13 billion dollars to foster economic recovery and political stability in sixteen European countries. This sum approximated $80 billion in 1990 dollars. Shortly thereafter, the United States began building its political-military alliances—NATO, ANZUS, the OAS, SEATO—which were designed to deter probes by the Soviet Union or its allies. When deterrence failed in Korea, the United States went to war.

As a worldview, cold war containment was short on categories and distinctions. Most nations were placed in one of two stock categories—friendly, democratic, and peace-loving countries or Communist-totalitarian, aggressive countries. For the fallen countries of Eastern Europe, there was a "captive-nation category," where alien, totalitarian rule was imposed upon democratic and peace-loving peoples. The analogies and scripts of the containment worldview were also few. Two past events preoccupied decision makers: *the Munich crisis*, where the democracies gave in to Hitler's territorial demands in Czechoslovakia and *the Spanish Civil War*, where Germany and Italy supported fascist forces against a democratic government while the democracies looked the other way.

The scripts of the containment worldview were drawn from the hard school of the 1930s. The positive script was a simple one: Potential aggressors had to be deterred by clear warnings that force would be met with counterforce and by military arsenals that gave credibility to such warnings. As Harry Truman put it, "Only one language do [the Russians] understand—'How many divisions have you?'"[6] The negative script was equally simple: Negotiations and negotiated settlements do not work with expansionist totalitarian governments. The assumptions underlying these scripts were equally simple—no country was too far away to be written off to aggressors; peace was indivisible; appeasement merely whets the appetite of aggressors while demoralizing allies at the same time.

President Truman articulated these lessons in recounting his thoughts after the North Korean attack on South Korea in June 1950:

> In my generation, this was not the first occasion when the strong had attacked the weak. I recalled earlier instances: Manchuria, Ethiopia, Austria. I remembered how each time the democracies failed to act it had encouraged the aggressors to keep going ahead. Communism was acting in Korea just as Hitler, Mussolini, and the Japanese had acted ten, fifteen, and twenty years earlier. I felt certain that if South

Korea was allowed to fall Communist leaders would be emboldened to override nations closer to our shores. If the Communists were permitted to force their way into the Republic of Korea without opposition from the free world, no small nation would have the courage to resist threats and aggression by stronger Communist neighbors. If [the North Korean attack on South Korea] were allowed to go unchallenged it would mean a Third World War, just as similar incidents had brought on the Second World War.[7]

Despite its dearth of categories, scripts, and assumptions, the containment worldview arose in a world that fit fairly well its perceptions and assessments. The Soviet Union was ruthlessly ruled by one man, and members of the international Communist movement seemed as controlled by this man as inanimate pieces on a chessboard. Soviet strategy, while cautious, was unceasing—probing here, creating unrest there. The postwar world was a world of ruins. With the exception of the Soviet Union, all the former great powers of Europe and Asia were laid waste.

Only the United States possessed the power to contest and contain the Soviets. Each crisis, each probe, and each insurrection was perceived as a "test" for the United States. If the Soviets gained a string of victories beyond Eastern Europe, many feared that resistance to Communist forces, both domestic and external, might collapse in Western Europe and in the colonial areas. If the United States failed to contain the Soviets and to maintain the world balance of power, World War III might not be far behind.

## TWO VIEWS OF CONTAINMENT

While cold war containment enjoyed widespread, bipartisan support, the consensus behind it masked two different groups of supporters. One group consisted of political realists who saw the Soviet-American conflict in traditional balance of power terms. Despite the picture drawn in "The Sources of Soviet Conduct," Kennan was one such realist. In his position as the first deputy for foreign affairs at the National War College, Kennan instructed the nation's rising officer corps in the fundamentals of balance of power politics. With the publication of his *Politics Among Nations* in 1948, Professor Hans Morgenthau placed political realism and balance of power politics firmly within the center of the academic community. Morgenthau's text, which is still widely used in courses in international politics, educated generations of graduate and undergraduate students in the tenets of political realism. Other leading exponents of the realist tradition were foreign service officers Louis Halle and Charles Burton Marshall, the theologian Reinhold Niebuhr, and political scientists Kenneth W. Thompson and Robert Osgood.

The hallmarks of political realism were *interests, nationalism,* and *balances of power* as opposed to the *ideals, internationalism,* and *communal systems of power* that were embodied in the Charter of the United Nations. For realists, policies and proposals were to be judged by their *consequences* rather than the motives or abstract principles that led to their creation. In fact, realists downplayed the impact of abstract ideological or moral principles in the international arena. According to realists, the Communist threat stemmed not from the ideology of Marxism-Leninism, but from the military might of the Soviet state. And the threat of that power had to be met not with American rhetoric or ideals, but with countervailing American power.

But what were America's interests? Where was America to apply containment? Was Kennan really asking the nation to become a global policeman when he proposed "a policy of firm containment ... at every point where [the Soviets] show signs of encroaching upon the interest of a peaceful and stable world"? And, if coexistence were impossible, as Kennan suggested, how long would the nation have to persist in its policy of containment?

Many, if not most, readers of Kennan's essay inferred that he proposed using military force to meet Soviet thrusts everywhere. But as the historian John Lewis Gaddis has made clear, Kennan had a much more limited conception of American interests, and he proposed a three-stage strategy for securing those interests. The first stage involved rebuilding the balance of power by developing self-confidence in those nations threatened by Soviet expansionism. The means to this end were the restoration of viable economies in Western Europe and Japan, the integration of West Germany into Western Europe, and the protection of the Middle East.

Once these weights in the world balance of power were restored, Kennan proposed reducing the Soviet Union's ability to project influence beyond its borders by exploiting tensions between Moscow and the international Communist movement. As a realist, Kennan believed that national interests were more influential than ideologies in determining the behavior of nations. Thus, he predicted that the Soviet empire would fragment as it expanded, and he believed that the United States had significant, although limited and indirect, leverage to hasten that fragmentation.

The third stage of Kennan's strategy involved the "modification, over time, of the Soviet concept of international relations with a view to bringing about a negotiated settlement of outstanding differences."[8] Kennan believed that the creation of a stable balance of power, the fragmentation of the Communist movement, and internal social and economic problems would force Soviet leaders to confront their frustrations and alter their foreign policy goals and strategies. Time and frustration, he predicted, would force the Soviet drive for expansion to "mellow." At that time, a negotiated settlement of outstanding issues between the Soviets and the West could be worked out. How long would all of this take? Kennan predicted ten to twenty years.

A second group supporting cold war containment saw the Soviet-American conflict in ideological and moral terms. For them, containment was not so much about national interests and balances of power, as about defending freedom and promoting self-determination and democracy throughout the world. In their opinion, a world laid waste by war required the United States to act as a trustee for Western civilization against a predatory, godless tyranny. Despite Kennan's warnings, some members of this group saw Stalin as Hitler and were determined that America would not repeat the mistakes of Britain under Neville Chamberlain.

Members of this second group, which included Republican Senator Arthur Vandenberg, Secretary of the Navy James Forrestal, and President Eisenhower's Secretary of State, John Foster Dulles, perceived the Soviet threat in ideological terms, and they sought to prevent both the rise and expansion of Communism. Their reaction to Communism was similar to Edmund Burke's response to Jacobinism after the French Revolution of 1789. According to Burke:

> I never thought we could make peace with the [Jacobin] system; because it was not for the sake of an object that we pursued in rivalry with each other, but with the system itself, that we were at war. As I understood the matter, we were at war not with its conduct, but with its existence; convinced that its existence and its hostility were the same.[9]

Thus, the threat was not merely Soviet imperialism but Communism anywhere. As recently as 1989, Owen Harries, the editor of *The National Interest*, reflected the view of this group concisely when he wrote that "since the 1940s the central purpose of the foreign policy of the United States has been the global containment of communism."[10]

Cold war containment, then, was supported by people who adhered to one of two quite distinct worldviews, as the following summary reveals:

|  | Burkean cold warriors | Political realists |
| --- | --- | --- |
| The Challenge | The spread of Communism | Soviet imperialism |
| The Goal | Containment and rollback of Communism | Containment of Soviet imperialism |
| The Means | Create alliances with non-Communist nations | Build a stable balance of power |
| Nature of the international system | Tightly coupled/domino theory Regional conflicts/largely Soviet inspired | Not tightly coupled/no domino theory Regional conflicts largely indigenous |

In the late 1940s and early 1950s, the differences between these two groups were obscured because they were largely academic. Communism was monolithic and centrally directed by Stalin. And while Stalin's successor, Nikita Khrushchev, was a reformer both at home and within the Soviet bloc, he was a formidable cold warrior who supported wars of liberation in the Third World. With the exception of Yugoslavia, the Communist camp appeared united well into the early 1960s. Also, through the 1950s, the world was, in fact, largely bipolar, and America's allies in Europe and Asia were still rebuilding from the devastation of World War II. Finally, the struggle for the Third World did not really begin until the late 1950s and the early 1960s.

Thus, Kennan supported our intervention in Greece and our decision to fight in Korea. To do nothing might have led to despair in Britain, Western Europe, and Japan, the three great centers of world power. Both groups also supported the Marshall Plan. When the Soviets obtained the ability to produce atomic bombs, an increase in conventional military forces seemed necessary to both camps. While Kennan bristled when our policies were presented to the public in Burkean terms, he also knew that the American public would hesitate to support proposals that smacked of interests, spheres of influence, and balances of power.

But words and distinctions do make a difference. Containing Communism and containing the Soviet Union are not the same. Maintaining a stable balance of power required less than containing Communism or defending all non-Communist regimes. Soviet imperialism and civil wars between local Communists and non-Communists were also different. The pursuit of America's interests would not always mean that the nation was promoting its ideals of freedom and self-determination, as we were to learn in China, South Korea, Vietnam, Iran, El Salvador, and Nicaragua.

The differences between the Burkeans and realists emerged as the war in Vietnam intensified, and the two groups split apart. Those who adhered to the Burkean view became reassertionists, while those who adhered to the European realist view became neorealists.

# The Selections

## 1. George F. Kennan
### *The Sources of Soviet Conduct*    July 1947

George Kennan's Mr. X article is one of the most important documents in the history of American foreign policy. In this essay, Kennan answers the following questions: What do the Soviets want? Why do they want it? How should the United States respond and why? In addition to noting Kennan's answers, ask yourself what *evidence* Kennan presents in support of his answers.

Immediately after the publication of Kennan's essay, the distinguished political columnist Walter Lippmann wrote a series of columns critical of containment as a strategy. What possible problems or weaknesses do you see with Kennan's assessment and his containment strategy? After you make your own assessment, read Lippmann's columns, which were later published as a book under the title *The Cold War: A Study in Foreign Policy*.

Two decades after the Mr. X article appeared, Kennan claimed that readers had misread his essay as a call for *military* containment. What he was really proposing, he said, was the use of nonmilitary instruments of diplomacy to effect containment. This misinterpretation, Kennan claimed, led to an overmilitarization of America's postwar containment policies. Do you agree with Kennan about the nature of his proposal? Finally, many of Keenan's predictions about what would happen if the Communist party lost its grip on the country are chillingly prescient in the second-to-last paragraph on pages 35-36.

[Section I has been omitted.]

# II

So much for the historical background. What does it spell in terms of the political personality of Soviet power as we know it today?

Of the original ideology, nothing has been officially junked. Belief is maintained in the basic badness of capitalism, in the inevitability of its destruction, in the obligation of the proletariat to assist in that destruction and to take power into its own hands. But stress has come to be laid primarily on those concepts which relate most specifically to the Soviet regime itself: to its position as the sole truly Socialist regime in a dark and misguided world, and to the relationships of power within it.

The first of these concepts is that of the innate antagonism between capitalism and Socialism. We have seen how deeply that concept has become imbedded in foundations of Soviet power. It has profound implications for Russia's conduct as a member of international society. It means that there can never be on Moscow's side any sincere assumption of a community of aims between the Soviet Union and powers which are regarded as capitalist. It must invariably be assumed in Moscow that the aims of the capitalist world are antagonistic to the Soviet regime, and therefore to the interests of the peoples it controls. If the Soviet government occasionally sets its signature to documents which would indicate the contrary, this is to be regarded as a tactical maneuver permissible in dealing with the enemy (who is without honor) and should be taken in the spirit of *caveat emptor*. Basically, the antagonism remains. It is postulated. And from it flow many of the phenomena which we find disturbing in the Kremlin's conduct of foreign policy: the secretiveness, the lack of frankness, the duplicity, the wary suspiciousness and the basic unfriendliness of purpose. These phenomena are there to stay, for the foreseeable future. There can be variations of degree and of emphasis. When there is something the Russians want from us, one or the other of these features of their policy may be thrust temporarily into the background; and when that happens there will always be Americans who will leap forward with gleeful announcements that "the Russians have changed," and some who will even try to take credit for having brought about such "changes." But we should not be misled by tactical maneuvers. These characteristics of Soviet policy, like the postulate from which they flow, are basic to the internal nature of Soviet power, and will be with us, whether in the foreground or the background, until the internal nature of Soviet power is changed.

This means that we are going to continue for a long time to find the Russians difficult to deal with. It does not mean that they should be considered as embarked upon a do-or-die program to overthrow our society by a given date. The theory of the inevitability of the eventual fall of capitalism has the fortunate connotation that there is no hurry about it. The forces of progress can take their time in preparing the final *coup de grâce*. Meanwhile, what is vital is that the "Socialist fatherland"—that oasis of power which has been already won for Socialism in the person of the Soviet Union—should be cherished and defended by all good Communists at home and abroad, its fortunes promoted, its enemies badgered and confounded. The promotion of premature, "adventuristic" revolutionary projects abroad which might embarrass Soviet power in any way would be an inexcusable, even a counterrevolutionary act. The cause of Socialism is the support and promotion of Soviet power, as defined in Moscow.

This brings us to the second of the concepts important to contemporary Soviet outlook. That is the infallibility of the Kremlin. The Soviet concept of power, which permits no focal points of organization outside the Party itself, requires that the Party leadership remain in theory the sole repository of truth. For if truth were to be found elsewhere, there would be justification for its expression in organized activity. But it is precisely that which the Kremlin cannot and will not permit.

The leadership of the Communist Party is therefore always right, and has been always right ever since in 1929 Stalin formalized his personal power by announcing that decisions of the Politburo were being taken unanimously.

On the principle of infallibility there rests the iron discipline of the Communist Party. In fact, the two concepts are mutually self-supporting. Perfect discipline requires recognition of infallibility. Infallibility requires the observance of discipline. And the two together go far to determine the behaviorism of the entire Soviet apparatus of power. But their effect cannot be understood unless a third factor be taken into account: namely, the fact that the leadership is at liberty to put forward for tactical purposes any particular thesis which it finds useful to the cause at any particular moment and to require the faithful and unquestioning acceptance of the thesis by the members of the movement as a whole. This means that truth is not a constant but is actually created, for all intents and purposes, by the Soviet leaders themselves. It may vary from week to week, month to month. It is nothing absolute and immutable—nothing which flows from objective reality. It is only the most recent manifestation of the wisdom of those in whom the ultimate wisdom is supposed to reside, because they represent the logic of history. The accumulative effect of these factors is to give to the whole subordinate apparatus of Soviet power an unshakable stubbornness and steadfastness in its orientation. This orientation can be changed at will by the Kremlin but by no other power. Once a given party line has been laid down on a given issue of current policy, the whole Soviet governmental machine, including the mechanism of diplomacy, moves inexorably along the prescribed path, like a persistent toy automobile wound up and headed in a given direction, stopping only when it meets with some unanswerable force. The individuals who are the components of this machine are unamenable to argument or reason which comes to them from outside sources. Their whole training has taught them to mistrust and discount the glib persuasiveness of the outside world. Like the white dog before the phonograph, they hear only the "master's voice." And if they are to be called off from the purposes last dictated to them, it is the master who must call them off. Thus the foreign representative cannot hope that his words will make any impression on them. The most that he can hope is that they will be transmitted to those at the top, who are capable of changing the party line. But even those are not likely to be swayed by any normal logic in the words of the bourgeois representative. Since there can be no appeal to common purposes, there can be no appeal to common mental approaches. For this reason, facts speak louder than words to the ears of the Kremlin; and words carry the greatest weight when they have the ring of reflecting, or being backed up by, facts of unchallengeable validity.

But we have seen that the Kremlin is under no ideological compulsion to accomplish its purposes in a hurry. Like the Church, it is dealing in ideological concepts which are of long-term validity, and it can afford to be patient. It has no right to risk the existing achievements of the revolution for the sake of vain baubles of the future. The very teachings of Lenin himself require great caution and flexibility in the pursuit of Communist purposes. Again, these precepts are fortified by the lessons of Russian history: of centuries of obscure battles between nomadic forces over the stretches of a vast unfortified plain. Here caution, circumspection, flexibility and deception are the valuable qualities; and their value finds natural appreciation in the Russian or the oriental mind. Thus the Kremlin has no compunction about retreating in the face of superior force. And being under the compulsion of no timetable, it does not get panicky under the necessity for such retreat. Its political action is a fluid stream which moves constantly, wherever it is permitted to move, toward a given goal. Its main concern is to make sure that it has filled every nook and cranny available to it in the basin of world power. But if it finds unassailable barriers in its path, it accepts these philosophically and accommodates itself to them. The main thing is that there should always be pressure, unceasing constant pressure, toward the desired goal. There is no trace of any feeling in Soviet psychology that that goal must be reached at any given time.

These considerations make Soviet diplomacy at once easier and more difficult to deal with than the diplomacy of individual aggressive leaders like Napoleon and Hitler. On the one hand it is more sensitive to contrary force, more ready to yield on individual sectors of the diplomatic front when that force is felt to be too strong, and thus more rational in the logic and rhetoric of power. On the other hand it cannot be easily defeated or discouraged by a single victory on the part of its opponents. And the patient persistence by which it is animated means that it can be effectively countered not by sporadic acts which represent the momentary whims of democratic opinion but only by intelligent long-range policies on the part of Russia's adversaries—policies no less steady in their purpose, and no less variegated and resourceful in their application, than those of the Soviet Union itself.

In these circumstances it is clear that the main element of any United States policy toward the Soviet Union must be that of a long-term, patient but firm and vigilant containment of Russian expansive tendencies. It is important to note, however, that such a policy has nothing to do with outward histrionics: with threats or blustering or superfluous gestures of outward "toughness." While the Kremlin is basically flexible in its reaction to political realities, it is by no means unamenable to considerations of prestige. Like almost any other government, it can be placed by tactless and threatening gestures in a position where it cannot afford to yield even though this might be dictated by its sense of realism. The Russian leaders are keen judges of human psychology, and as such they are highly conscious that loss of temper and of self-control is never a source of strength in political affairs. They are quick to exploit such evidences of weakness. For these reasons it is a sine qua non of successful dealing with Russia that the foreign government in question should remain at all times cool and collected and that its demands on Russian policy should be put forward in such a manner as to leave the way open for a compliance not too detrimental to Russian prestige.

## III

In the light of the above, it will be clearly seen that the Soviet pressure against the free institutions of the Western world is something that can be contained by the adroit and vigilant application of counterforce at a series of constantly shifting geographical and political points, corresponding to the shifts and maneuvers of Soviet policy, but which cannot be charmed or talked out of existence. The Russians look forward to a duel of infinite duration, and they see that already they have scored great successes. It must be borne in mind that there was a time when the Communist Party represented far more of a minority in the sphere of Russian national life than Soviet power today represents in the world community.

But if ideology convinces the rulers of Russia that truth is on their side and that they can therefore afford to wait, those of us on whom that ideology has no claim are free to examine objectively the validity of that premise. The Soviet thesis not only implies complete lack of control by the west over its own economic destiny, it likewise assumes Russian unity, discipline and patience over an infinite period. Let us bring this apocalyptic vision down to earth, and suppose that the western world finds the strength and resourcefulness to contain Soviet power over a period of ten to fifteen years. What does that spell for Russia itself?

The Soviet leaders, taking advantage of the contributions of modern technique to the arts of despotism, have solved the question of obedience within the confines of their power. Few challenge their authority; and even those who do are unable to make that challenge valid as against the organs of suppression of the state.

The Kremlin has also proved able to accomplish its purpose of building up in Russia, regardless of the interests of the inhabitants, an industrial foundation of heavy metallurgy, which is, to be sure, not yet complete but which is nevertheless continuing to grow and is approaching those of the other major industrial countries. All of this, however, both the maintenance of internal political security and the building of heavy industry, has been carried out at a terrible cost in human life and in human hopes and energies. It has necessitated the use of forced labor on a scale unprecedented in modern times under conditions of peace. It has involved the neglect or abuse of other phases of Soviet economic life, particularly agriculture, consumers' goods production, housing and transportation.

To all that, the war has added its tremendous toll of destruction, death and human exhaustion. In consequence of this, we have in Russia today a population which is physically and spiritually tired. The mass of the people are disillusioned, skeptical and no longer as accessible as they once were to the magical attraction which Soviet power still radiates to its followers abroad. The avidity with which people seized upon the slight respite accorded to the Church for tactical reasons during the war was eloquent testimony to the fact that their capacity for faith and devotion found little expression in the purposes of the regime.

In these circumstances, there are limits to the physical and nervous strength of people themselves. These limits are absolute ones, and are binding even for the cruelest dictatorship, because beyond them people cannot be driven. The forced labor camps and the other agencies of constraint provide temporary means of compelling people to work longer hours than their own volition or mere economic pressure would dictate; but if people survive them at all they become old before their time and must be considered as human casualties to the demands of dictatorship. In either case their best powers are no longer available to society and can no longer be enlisted in the service of the state.

Here only the younger generation can help. The younger generation, despite all vicissitudes and sufferings, is numerous and vigorous; and the Russians are a talented people. But it still remains to be seen what will be the effects on mature performance of the abnormal emotional strains of childhood which Soviet dictatorship created and which were enormously increased by the war. Such things as normal security and placidity of home environment have practically ceased to exist in the Soviet Union outside of the most remote farms and villages. And observers are not yet sure whether that is not going to leave its mark on the overall capacity of the generation now coming into maturity.

In addition to this, we have the fact that Soviet economic development, while it can list certain formidable achievements, has been precariously spotty and uneven. Russian Communists who speak of the "uneven development of capitalism" should blush at the contemplation of their own national economy. Here certain branches of economic life, such as the metallurgical and machine industries, have been pushed out of all proportion to other sectors of economy. Here is a nation striving to become in a short period one of the great industrial nations of the world while it still has no highway network worthy of the name and only a relatively primitive network of railways. Much has been done to increase efficiency of labor and to teach primitive peasants something about the operation of machines. But maintenance is still a crying deficiency of all Soviet economy. Construction is hasty and poor in quality. Depreciation must be enormous. And in vast sectors of economic life it has not yet been possible to instill into labor anything like that general culture of production and technical self-respect which characterizes the skilled worker of the west.

It is difficult to see how these deficiencies can be corrected at an early date by a tired and dispirited population working largely under the shadow of fear and compulsion. And as long as they are not overcome, Russia will remain economically a vulnerable, and in a certain sense an impotent, nation, capable of exporting its enthusiasm and of radiating the strange charm of its primitive political vitality but unable to back up those articles of export by the real evidences of material power and prosperity.

Meanwhile, a great uncertainty hangs over the political life of the Soviet Union. That is the uncertainty involved in the transfer of power from one individual or group of individuals to others.

This is, of course, outstandingly the problem of the personal position of Stalin. We must remember that his succession to Lenin's pinnacle of preeminence in the Communist movement was the only such transfer of individual authority which the Soviet Union has experienced. That transfer took 12 years to consolidate. It cost the lives of millions of people and shook the state to its foundations. The attendant tremors were felt all through the international revolutionary movement, to the disadvantage of the Kremlin itself.

It is always possible that another transfer of preeminent power may take place quietly and inconspicuously, with no repercussions anywhere. But again, it is possible that the questions involved may unleash, to use some of Lenin's words, one of those "incredibly swift transitions" from "delicate deceit" to "wild violence" which characterize Russian history, and may shake Soviet power to its foundations.

But this is not only a question of Stalin himself. There has been, since 1938, a dangerous congealment of political life in the higher circles of Soviet power. The All-Union Congress of Soviets, in theory the supreme body of the Party, is supposed to meet not less often than once in three years. It will soon be eight full years since its last meeting. During this period membership in the Party has numerically doubled. Party mortality during the war was enormous; and today well over half of the Party members are persons who have entered since the last Party congress was held. Meanwhile, the same small group of men has carried on at the top through an amazing series of national vicissitudes. Surely there is some reason why the experiences of the war brought basic political changes to every one of the great governments of the west. Surely the causes of that phenomenon are basic enough to be present somewhere in the obscurity of Soviet political life as well. And yet no recognition has been given to these causes in Russia.

It must be surmised from this that even within so highly disciplined an organization as the Communist Party there must be a growing divergence in age, outlook and interest between the great mass of Party members, only so recently recruited into the movement, and the little self-perpetuating clique of men at the top, whom most of these Party members have never met, with whom they have never conversed, and with whom they can have no political intimacy.

Who can say whether, in these circumstances, the eventual rejuvenation of the higher spheres of authority (which can only be a matter of time) can take place smoothly and peacefully, or whether rivals in the quest for higher power will not eventually reach down into these politically immature and inexperienced masses in order to find support for their respective claims? If this were ever to happen, strange consequences could flow for the Communist Party: for the membership at large has been exercised only in the practices of iron discipline and obedience and not in the arts of compromise and accommodation. And if disunity were ever to seize and paralyze the Party, the chaos and weakness of Russian society would be revealed in forms beyond description. For we have seen that Soviet power is only a crust concealing an amorphous mass of human beings among whom no independent organizational structure is tolerated. In Russia there is not even such a thing as local government. The present generation of Russians have never known spontaneity of collective action. If, consequently, anything were ever to occur to disrupt the unity and efficacy of the Party as a political instrument, Soviet Russia might be changed overnight from one of the strongest to one of the weakest and most pitiable of national societies.

Thus the future of Soviet power may not be by any means as secure as Russian capacity for self-delusion would make it appear to the men in the Kremlin. That they can keep power themselves, they have demonstrated. That they can quietly and easily turn it over to others remains to be proved. Meanwhile, the hardships of their rule and the vicissitudes of international life have taken a heavy toll of the strength and hopes of the great people on whom their power rests. It is curious to note that the ideological power of Soviet authority is strongest today in areas beyond the frontiers of Russia, beyond the reach of its police power. This phenomenon brings to mind a comparison used by Thomas Mann in his great novel *Buddenbrooks*. Observing that human institutions often show the greatest outward brilliance at a moment when inner decay is in reality farthest advanced, he compared the Buddenbrook family, in the days of its greatest glamour, to one of those stars whose light shines most brightly on this world when in reality it has long since ceased to exist. And who can say with assurance that the strong light still cast by the Kremlin on the dissatisfied peoples of the western world is not the powerful afterglow of a constellation which is in actuality on the wane? This cannot be proved. And it cannot be disproved. But the possibility remains (and in the opinion of this writer it is a strong one) that Soviet power, like the capitalist world of its conception, bears within it the seeds of its own decay, and that the sprouting of these seeds is well advanced.

# 2. President Harry S. Truman
## *The Truman Doctrine*    March 12, 1947

Harry Truman's request for aid to Greece and Turkey can be viewed as the public or political statement of our containment policy. Like Kennan's Mr. X article, the Truman Doctrine has provided later presidents with a rationale for

America's support of governments under siege by insurgent revolutionary forces. Lyndon Johnson drew upon the Truman Doctrine to justify the war in Vietnam, and Ronald Reagan used it to justify his support for the government of El Salvador.

In this address, Truman states the four hallmarks of the containment worldview—the centrality of the Soviet challenge, a requirement for American action, a prescription for policy makers, and a script to justify that action. Be sure that you can identify each. As you read this speech, note the ways in which Truman's presentation of the containment strategy differs from Kennan's presentation. What do you think accounts for these differences?

Some scholars and commentators have criticized the Truman Doctrine for making an "open-ended" commitment to support any country besieged by insurgent forces. Is this a valid criticism? If so, how might Truman's address have been redrafted?

*Mr. President, Mr. Speaker, Members of the Congress of the United States:*
The gravity of the situation which confronts the world today necessitates my appearance before a joint session of the Congress.

The foreign policy and the national security of this country are involved.

One aspect of the present situation, which I present to you at this time for your consideration and decision, concerns Greece and Turkey.

The United States has received from the Greek Government an urgent appeal for financial and economic assistance. Preliminary reports from the American Economic Mission now in Greece and reports from the American Ambassador in Greece corroborate the statement of the Greek Government that assistance is imperative if Greece is to survive as a free nation.

I do not believe that the American people and the Congress wish to turn a deaf ear to the appeal of the Greek Government.

Greece is not a rich country. Lack of sufficient natural resources has always forced the Greek people to work hard to make both ends meet. Since 1940, this industrious, peace loving country has suffered invasion, four years of cruel enemy occupation, and bitter internal strife.

When forces of liberation entered Greece they found that the retreating Germans had destroyed virtually all the railways, roads, port facilities, communications, and merchant marine. More than a thousand villages had been burned. Eighty-five percent of the children were tubercular. Livestock, poultry, and draft animals had almost disappeared. Inflation had wiped out practically all savings.

As a result of these tragic conditions, a militant minority, exploiting human want and misery, was able to create political chaos which, until now, has made economic recovery impossible.

Greece is today without funds to finance the importation of those goods which are essential to bare subsistence. Under these circumstances the people of Greece cannot make progress in solving their problems of reconstruction. Greece is in desperate need of financial and economic assistance to enable it to resume purchases of food, clothing, fuel and seeds. These are indispensable for the subsistence of its people and are obtainable only from abroad. Greece must have help to import the goods necessary to restore internal order and security so essential for economic and political recovery.

The Greek Government has also asked for the assistance of experienced American administrators, economists and technicians to insure that the financial and other aid given to Greece shall be used effectively in creating a stable and self-sustaining economy and in improving its public administration.

The very existence of the Greek state is today threatened by the terrorist activities of several thousand armed men, led by Communists, who defy the government's authority at a number of points, particularly along the northern boundaries. A Commission appointed by the United Nations Security Council is at present investigating disturbed conditions in northern Greece and alleged border violations along the frontier between Greece on the one hand and Albania, Bulgaria, and Yugoslavia on the other.

Meanwhile, the Greek Government is unable to cope with the situation. The Greek army is small and poorly equipped. It needs supplies and equipment if it is to restore authority to the government throughout Greek territory.

Greece must have assistance if it is to become a self-supporting and self-respecting democracy.

The United States must supply this assistance. We have already extended to Greece certain types of relief and economic aid but these are inadequate.

There is no other country to which democratic Greece can turn.

No other nation is willing and able to provide the necessary support for a democratic Greek government.

The British Government, which has been helping Greece, can give no further financial or economic aid after March 31. Great Britain finds itself under the necessity of reducing or liquidating its commitments in several parts of the world, including Greece.

We have considered how the United Nations might assist in this crisis. But the situation is an urgent one requiring immediate action, and the United Nations and its related organizations are not in a position to extend help of the kind that is required.

It is important to note that the Greek Government has asked for our aid in utilizing effectively the financial and other assistance we may give to Greece, and in improving its public administration. It is of the utmost importance that we supervise the use of any funds made available to Greece, in such a manner that each dollar spent will count toward making Greece self-supporting, and will help to build an economy in which a healthy democracy can flourish.

No government is perfect. One of the chief virtues of a democracy, however, is that its defects are always visible and under democratic processes can be pointed out and corrected. The government of Greece is not perfect. Nevertheless it represents 85 percent of the members of the Greek Parliament who were chosen in an election last year. Foreign observers, including 692 Americans, considered this election to be a fair expression of the views of the Greek people.

The Greek Government has been operating in an atmosphere of chaos and extremism. It has made mistakes. The extension of aid by this country does not mean that the United States condones everything that the Greek Government has done or will do. We have condemned in the past, and we condemn now, extremist measures of the right or the left. We have in the past advised tolerance, and we advise tolerance now.

Greece's neighbor, Turkey, also deserves our attention.

The future of Turkey as an independent and economically sound state is clearly no less important to the freedom-loving peoples of the world than the future of Greece. The circumstances in which Turkey finds itself today are considerably different from those of Greece. Turkey has been spared the disasters that have beset Greece. And during the war, the United States and Great Britain furnished Turkey with material aid.

Nevertheless, Turkey now needs our support.

Since the war Turkey has sought additional financial assistance from Great Britain and the United States for the purpose of effecting that modernization necessary for the maintenance of its national integrity.

That integrity is essential to the preservation of order in the Middle East.

The British Government has informed us that, owing to its own difficulties, it can no longer extend financial or economic aid to Turkey.

As in the case of Greece, if Turkey is to have the assistance it needs, the United States must supply it. We are the only country able to provide that help.

I am fully aware of the broad implications involved if the United States extends assistance to Greece and Turkey, and I shall discuss these implications with you at this time.

One of the primary objectives of the foreign policy of the United States is the creation of conditions in which we and other nations will be able to work out a way of life free from coercion. This was a fundamental issue in the war with Germany and Japan. Our victory was won over countries which sought to impose their will, and their way of life, upon other nations.

To ensure the peaceful development of nations, free from coercion, the United States has taken a leading part in establishing the United Nations. The United Nations is designed to make possible lasting freedom and independence for all its members. We shall not realize our objectives, however, unless we are willing to help free peoples to maintain their free institutions and their national integrity against aggressive movements that seek to impose upon them totalitarian regimes. This is no more than a frank recognition that totalitarian regimes imposed upon free peoples, by direct or indirect aggression, undermine the foundations of international peace and hence the security of the United States.

The peoples of a number of countries of the world have recently had totalitarian regimes forced upon them against their will. The Government of the United States has made frequent protests against coercion and intimidation, in violation of the Yalta agreement, in Poland, Rumania, and Bulgaria. I must also state that in a number of other countries there have been similar developments.

At the present moment in world history nearly every nation must choose between alternative ways of life. The choice is too often not a free one.

One way of life is based upon the will of the majority, and is distinguished by free institutions, representative government, free elections, guarantees of individual liberty, freedom of speech and religion, and freedom from political oppression.

The second way of life is based upon the will of a minority forcibly imposed upon the majority. It relies upon terror and oppression, a controlled press and radio, fixed elections, and the suppression of personal freedoms.

I believe that it must be the policy of the United States to support free peoples who are resisting attemped subjugation by armed minorities or by outside pressures.

I believe that we must assist free peoples to work out their own destinies in their own way.

I believe that our help should be primarily through economic and financial aid which is essential to economic stability and orderly political processes.

The world is not static, and the *status quo* is not sacred. But we cannot allow changes in the *status quo* in violation of the Charter of the United Nations by such methods as coercion, or by such subterfuges as political infiltration. In helping free and independent nations to maintain their freedom, the United States will be giving effect to the principles of the Charter of the United Nations.

It is necessary only to glance at a map to realize that the survival and integrity of the Greek nation are of grave importance in a much wider situation. If Greece should fall under the control of an armed minority, the effect upon its neighbor, Turkey, would be immediate and serious. Confusion and disorder might well spread throughout the entire Middle East.

Moreover, the disappearance of Greece as an independent state would have a profound effect upon those countries in Europe whose peoples are struggling against great difficulties to maintain their freedoms and their independence while they repair the damages of war.

It would be an unspeakable tragedy if these countries, which have struggled so long against overwhelming odds, should lose that victory for which they sacrificed so much. Collapse of free institutions and loss of independence would be disastrous not only for them but for the world. Discouragement and possibly failure would quickly be the lot of neighboring peoples striving to maintain their freedom and independence.

Should we fail to aid Greece and Turkey in this fateful hour, the effect will be far reaching to the West as well as to the East.

We must take immediate and resolute action.

I therefore ask the Congress to provide authority for assistance to Greece and Turkey in the amount of $400,000,000 for the period ending June 30, 1948. In requesting these funds, I have taken into consideration the maximum amount of relief assistance which would be furnished to Greece out of the $350,000,000 which I recently requested that the Congress authorize for the prevention of starvation and suffering in countries devastated by the war.

In addition to funds, I ask the Congress to authorize the detail of American civilian and military personnel to Greece and Turkey, at the request of those countries, to assist in the tasks of reconstruction, and for the purpose of supervising the use of such financial and material assistance as may be furnished. I recommend that authority also be provided for the instruction and training of selected Greek and Turkish personnel.

Finally, I ask that the Congress provide authority which will permit the speediest and most effective use, in terms of needed commodities, supplies, and equipment, of such funds as may be authorized.

If further funds, or further authority, should be needed for the purposes indicated in this message, I shall not hestiate to bring the situation before the Congress. On this subject the Executive and Legislative branches of the Government must work together.

This is a serious course upon which we embark.

I would not recommend it except that the alternative is much more serious.

The United States contributed $341,000,000,000 toward winning World War II. This is an investment in world freedom and world peace.

The assistance that I am recommending for Greece and Turkey amounts to little more than $\frac{1}{10}$ of 1 percent of this investment. It is only common sense that we should safeguard this investment and make sure that it was not in vain.

The seeds of totalitarian regimes are nurtured by misery and want. They spread and grow in the evil soil of poverty and strife. They reach their full growth when the hope of a people for a better life has died.

We must keep that hope alive.

The free peoples of the world look to us for support in maintaining their freedoms.

If we falter in our leadership, we may endanger the peace of the world— and we shall surely endanger the welfare of this Nation.

Great responsibilities have been placed upon us by the swift movement of events.

I am confident that the Congress will face these responsibilities squarely.

# 3. NSC-7: The Position of the United States with Respect to Soviet-Directed World Communism
## March 30, 1948

NSC-7 is the foreign policy bureaucracy's first "in house" assessment of the threat from Communism. Prepared by the staff of the National Security Council, the document was designed to guide policy makers working in the area of national security policy.

When you have finished reading this document, compile a list of differences between NSC-7, Truman's address, and Kennan's essay in the following areas: (1) complexity and depth of analysis, (2) the tone of the language used, (3) images of the power and tactical competency of the Soviet Union, and (4) Burkean realist imagery.

## THE PROBLEM

1. To assess and appraise the position of the United States with respect to Soviet-directed world communism, taking into account the security interests of the United States.

## ANALYSIS

2. The ultimate objective of Soviet-directed world communism is the domination of the world. To this end, Soviet-directed world communism employs against its victims in opportunistic coordination the complementary instruments of Soviet aggressive pressure from without and militant revolutionary subversion from within. Both instruments are supported by the formidable material power of the USSR and their use is facilitated by the chaotic aftermath of the war.

3. The defeat of the Axis left the world with only two great centers of national power, the United States and the USSR. The Soviet Union is the source of power from which international communism chiefly derives its capability to threaten the existence of free nations. The United States is the only source of power capable of mobilizing successful opposition to the communist goal of world conquest. Between the United States and the USSR there are in Europe and Asia areas of great potential power which if added to the existing strength of the Soviet world would enable the latter to become so superior in manpower, resources and territory that the prospect for the survival of the United States as a free nation would be slight. In these circumstances the USSR has engaged the United States in a struggle for power, or "cold war", in which our national security is at stake and from which we cannot withdraw short of eventual national suicide.

4. Already Soviet-directed world communism has achieved alarming success in its drive toward world conquest. It has established satellite police states in Poland, Yugoslavia, Albania, Hungary, Bulgaria, Rumania, and Czechoslovakia; it poses an immediate threat to Italy, Greece, Finland, Korea, the Scandinavian countries, and others. The USSR has prevented the conclusion of peace treaties with Germany, Austria, and Japan; and has made impossible the international control of atomic energy and the effective functioning of the United Nations. Today Stalin has come close to achieving what Hitler attempted in vain. The Soviet world extends from the Elbe River and the Adriatic Sea on the west to Manchuria on the east, and embraces one-fifth of the land surface of the world.

5. In addition, Soviet-directed world communism has faced the non-Soviet world with something new in history. This is the worldwide Fifth Column directed at frustrating foreign policy, dividing and confusing the people of a country, planting the seeds of disruption in time

of war, and subverting the freedom of democratic states. Under a multitude of disguises, it is capable of fomenting disorders, including armed conflicts, within its victim's territory without involving the direct responsibility of any communist state. The democracies have been deterred in effectively meeting this threat, in part because communism has been allowed to operate as a legitimate political activity under the protection of civil liberties.

6. In its relations with other nations the USSR is guided by the communist dogma that the peaceful co-existence of communist and capitalist states is in the long run impossible. On the basis of this postulate of ultimate inevitable conflict, the USSR is attempting to gain world domination by subversion, and by legal and illegal political and economic measures, but might ultimately resort to war if necessary to gain its ends. Such a war might be waged openly by the USSR with her satellites, or might be waged by one or a combination of the satellites with the avowed neutrality or disapproval of the USSR, though with her covert support. However, the Soviet Union so far has sought to avoid overt conflict, since time is required to build up its strength and concurrently to weaken and divide its opponents. In such a postponement, time is on the side of the Soviet Union so long as it can continue to increase its relative power by the present process of indirect aggression and internal subversion.

7. In view of the nature of Soviet-directed world communism, the successes which it has already achieved, and the threat of further advances in the immediate future, a defensive policy cannot be considered an effectual means of checking the momentum of communist expansion and inducing the Kremlin to relinquish its aggressive designs. A defensive policy by attempting to be strong everywhere runs the risk of being weak everywhere. It leaves the initiative to the Kremlin, enabling it to strike at the time and place most suitable to its purpose and to effect tactical withdrawals and diversions. It permits the Kremlin to hold what it has already gained and leaves its power potential intact.

8. As an alternative to a defensive policy the United States has open to it the organization of a world-wide counter-offensive against Soviet-directed world communism. Such a policy would involve first of all strengthening the military potential of the United States, and secondly, mobilizing and strengthening the potential of the non-Soviet world. A counter-offensive policy would gain the initiative and permit concentration of strength on vital objectives. It would strengthen the will to resist of anti-communist forces throughout the world and furnish convincing evidence of US determination to thwart the communist design of world conquest. It should enlist the support of the American people and of the peoples of the non-Soviet world. It would be consistent with the national objectives of the United States. This policy, in fact, would be the most effective way of deterring the USSR from further aggression. Such aggression might ultimately require the United States, in

order to sustain itself, to mobilize all of its resources against the continued threat of war, resulting in the creation of a vast armed camp within its borders. In the latter eventuality, rigid economies, regimentation and a fear psychosis might easily promote the very conditions in the United States that we are determined to eliminate elsewhere in the world. The measures adopted under a counter-offensive policy need not be inconsistent with the purposes and principles of the 0United Nations. We would continue to support the United Nations within the limits of its capabilities, and seek to strengthen it.

## CONCLUSIONS

9. The defeat of the forces of Soviet-directed world communism is vital to the security of the United States.
10. This objective cannot be achieved by a defensive policy.
11. The United States should therefore take the lead in organizing a worldwide counter-offensive aimed at mobilizing and strengthening our own and anti-communist forces in the non-Soviet world, and at undermining the strength of the communist forces in the Soviet world.
12. As immediate steps in the counter-offensive, the United States should take the following measures:
    a. Domestic
       (1) Strengthen promptly the military establishment of the United States by:
           (a) Initiation of some form of compulsory military service.
           (b) Reconstitution of the armaments industry.
       (2) Maintain overwhelming US superiority in atomic weapons. (In the event of international agreement on the control of atomic weapons this conclusion should be reconsidered.)
       (3) Urgently develop and execute a firm and coordinated program (to include legislation if necessary) designed to suppress the communist menace in the United States in order to safeguard the United States against the disruptive and dangerous subversive activities of communism.
       (4) To the extent necessary to implement (1) above, initiate civilian and industrial mobilization.
       (5) Vigorously prosecute a domestic information program, designed to insure public understanding and non-partisan support of our foreign policy.
    b. Foreign
       (1) In our counter-offensive efforts, give first priority to Western Europe. This should not preclude appropriate efforts in the case of other countries of Europe and the Middle East, which are immediately threatened by world communism and where loss of freedom would most seriously threaten our national security.

(2) Urgently adopt and implement the European Recovery Program [i.e., the Marshall Plan].

(3) Strongly endorse the Western Union and actively encourage its development and expansion as an anti-communist association of states.

(4) Work out an appropriate formula which will provide for:

    (a) Military action by the United States in the event of unprovoked armed attack against the nations in the Western Union or against other selected non-communist nations.

    (b) Initiation of political and military conversations with such nations with a view to coordination of anti-communist efforts.

(5) Assist in building up the military potential of selected non-communist nations by the provision of machine tools to rehabilitate their arms industries, technical information to facilitate standardization of arms, and by furnishing to the extent practicable military equipment and technical advice.

(6) When we have developed a program for suppressing the communist menace in the United States (12-a-(3) above), cooperate closely with governments which have already taken such action and encourage other governments to take like action.

(7) Encourage and assist private United States citizens and organizations in fostering non-communist trade union movements in those countries where that would contribute to our national security. Measures of assistance should include consideration of individual income tax deductions for that purpose.

(8) Intensify the present anti-communist foreign information program.

(9) Develop a vigorous and effective ideological campaign.

(10) Develop, and at the appropriate time carry out, a coordinated program to support underground resistance movements in countries behind the iron curtain, including the USSR.

(11) Establish a substantial emergency fund to be used in combatting Soviet-directed world communism.

(12) Make unmistakably clear to the Kremlin at an opportune time, and in an appropriate manner, United States determination to resist Soviet and Soviet-directed communist aggression so as to avoid the possibility of an "accidental" war through Soviet miscalculation of how far the Western Powers might be pushed.

(13) Effectuation of the above policies requires bi-partisan support.

# 4. Hans Morgenthau
## *The Real Issue Between the United States and the Soviet Union*                1952

The final selection by political scientist Hans Morgenthau delineates three different perceptions of the Soviet threat by drawing upon the precedent of revolutionary France. Written in 1952, Morgenthau's essay is prescient because it outlines the issues that would later define the differences between hawks and doves or reassertionists and neorealists. When you finish reading this essay, be sure you can restate the positions of Fox, Burke, and Pitt on the nature of the French threat.

In this selection, Morgenthau discusses four sources of confusion in thinking about the Soviet challenge. To what extent were these sources of confusion compounded or cleared up by Mr. X, President Truman, and NSC 7? To what extent, in fact, does Morgenthau's category of *genuine revolution* fit into the positions of Mr. X, President Truman, and NSC 7? Can you think of any reservations Morgenthau might have had about President Truman's address to the Congress or Kennan's presentation in the Mr. X article?

Do you agree or disagree with Morgenthau's assessment of the Soviet threat? What evidence supports your position?


## 1. THE THREE CHOICES

Three answers are logically possible to the question of what the issues are between the United States and the Soviet Union. One can answer that there is no real issue of a political nature separating the United States and the Soviet Union, and if only suspicion and false propaganda were eliminated, nothing would stand in the way of normal, peaceful relations. Or one can answer that the issue between the United States and the Soviet Union is that of world revolution, an objective to which the Soviet government is irrevocably committed. Or, finally, one can answer that what concerns the United States in its relations with the Soviet Union is Russian imperialism, which uses for its purposes the instrument of world revolution.

These distinctions are not mere hair-splitting. For the choice of one alternative instead of another will of necessity determine our moral and intellectual attitude toward the Soviet Union, and it is obvious that the choice of the policies to be pursued by the United States with regard to the Soviet Union must depend upon which of these three answers is chosen. If one believes that there is no real political issue, policy must concentrate either upon propaganda penetrating the Iron Curtain or upon economic aid to the countries behind it. This aid will narrow the gap in well-being between East and West, and it is this gap which is presumed to create misunderstanding and suspicion. If one believes that what confronts us as long as the Soviet government reigns in Moscow is the threat of world revolution, then there is only one way to meet that threat: extirpate the evil at its roots. If Russian imperialism is assumed to be the problem, the traditional methods of military and political policies can be employed to meet it. In the first alternative, peace can be brought to the world on the strengthened waves of the Voice of America, or can be bought by ten or twenty billion dollars. In the second alternative, the problem is not how to preserve peace but when to go to war, and the idea of a preventive war is a legitimate one. In the third alternative, military preparations must join hands with an accommodating diplomacy, and preparing for the worst while working for a peaceful settlement becomes the order of the day.

## The Precedent of Revolutionary France

The dilemma of these alternatives confronting the United States today is not a new one in the history of the Western world. It arose in the minds of British statesmen in the last decade of the eighteenth century on the occasion of the expansionist policies of revolutionary France. The three-cornered contest among three of the greatest political minds Great Britain or any other country has produced—Edmund Burke, Charles James Fox, and William Pitt—provides us with the most lucid and penetrating exposition of the problem: the expansionism of a great power which is also the seat of a universal political religion. To grasp the contemporary relevance of that debate one needs only to substitute for France, the Soviet Union; for Jacobinism, Communism; for England, the United States; for Napoleon, Stalin.

The concrete issue of that debate was the participation of Great Britain in the war that the European monarchies were waging against revolutionary France. Fox, the leader of one faction of the Whigs, believed that Great Britain was not at all threatened by France or, for that matter, by the principles of the French Revolution, which were a mere domestic concern of France, and that therefore there was no reason for Great Britain to join the coalition against France. While he detested the terror of the Jacobins, he was not willing to support a war for the purpose of eliminating Jacobinism. "He should now show," he said in the House of Commons on February 1, 1793,

> that all the topics to which he had adverted were introduced into the debate to blind the judgment, by arousing the passions, and were none of them the just grounds of war. . . . What, then, remained but the internal government of France, always disavowed, but ever kept in mind, and constantly mentioned? The destruction of that government was the avowed object of the combined powers whom it was hoped we were to join. . . . He thought the present state of government in France any thing rather than an object of imitation; but he maintained as a principle inviolable, that the government of every independent state was to be settled by those who were to live under it, and not by foreign force.

Fox summarizes his position with a statement that has in more than one respect a contemporary ring:

> He knew that he himself should now be represented the partizan of France, as he had been formerly represented the partizan of America. He was no stranger to

the industry with which these and other calumnies were circulated against him, and therefore he was not surprised; but he really was surprised to find that he could not walk the streets without hearing whispers that he and some of his friends had been engaged in improper correspondence with persons in France. If there were any foundation for such a charge, the source of the information could be mentioned. If it were true, it was capable of proof. If any man believed this, he called upon him to state the reasons of his belief. If any man had proofs, he challenged him to produce them. But, to what was this owing? The people had been told by their representatives in parliament that they were surrounded with dangers, and had been shown none. They were, therefore, full of suspicion and prompt of belief. All this had a material tendency to impede freedom of discussion, for men would speak with reserve, or not speak at all, under the terror of calumny. But he found by a letter in a newspaper, from Mr. Law, that he lived in a town where a set of men associated, and calling themselves gentlemen . . . not only received anonymous letters reflecting on individuals, but corresponded with the writers of such letters, and even sometimes transmitted their slanders to the secretary of state. He could not be much surprised at any aspersion on his character, knowing this; and therefore he hoped the House would give him the credit of being innocent till an open charge was made; and that if any man heard improper correspondence imputed to him in private, he would believe that he heard a falsehood, which he who circulated it in secret durst not utter in public.

In contrast to this position, Burke, the leader of another faction of the Whigs, finds the issue in the principles of the French Revolution. He looks on the war as a contest between two moral principles, as

the cause of humanity itself. . . . I do not exclude from amongst the just objects of such a confederacy as the present, the ordinary securities which nations must take against their mutual ambition, let their internal constitutions be of what nature they will. But the present evil of our time, though in a great measure an evil of ambition, is not one of common political ambition, but in many respects entirely different. It is not the cause of nation as against nation; but, as you will observe, the cause of mankind against those who have projected the subversion of that order of things, under which our part of the world has so long flourished, and indeed, been in a progressive state of improvement; the limits of which, if it had not been thus rudely stopped, it would not have been easy for the imagination to fix. If I conceive rightly of the spirit of the present combination, it is not at war with France, but with Jacobinism. They cannot think it right, that a second kingdom should be struck out of the system of Europe, either by destroying its independence, or by suffering it to have such a *form* in its independence, as to keep it, as a perpetual fund of revolutions, in the very centre of Europe, in that region which alone touches almost every other, and must influence, even where she does not come in contact. As long as Jacobinism subsists there, in any form, or under any modification, it is not, in my opinion, the gaining a fortified place or two, more or less, or the annexing to the dominion of the allied powers this or that territorial district, that can save Europe, or any of its members. We are at war with a *principle*, and with an example, which there is no shutting out by fortresses, or excluding by territorial limits. No lines of demarcation can bound the Jacobin empire. It must be extirpated in the place of its origin, or it will not be confined to that place. In the whole circle of military arrangements and of political expedients, I fear that there cannot be found any sort of *merely defensive plan* of the least force, against the effect of the *example* which has been given in France. That *example* has shown, for the first time in the history of the world, that it is very possible to subvert the whole frame and order of the best constructed states, by corrupting the common people with the spoil of the superior classes. It is by that instrument that the French orators have accomplished their purpose, to the ruin of France; and it is by that instrument that, if they can establish themselves in France (however broken or curtailed by themselves or others), sooner or later, they will subvert every government in Europe. The effect of *erroneous doctrines* may be soon done away; but the example of *successful pillage* is of a nature more permanent, more applicable to use, and a thing which speaks more forcibly to the interests and passions of the corrupt and unthinking part of mankind, than a thousand theories. Nothing can weaken the lesson contained in that example, but to make as strong an example on the other side. The leaders in France must be made to feel, in order that all the rest there, and in other countries, may be made to see that such spoil is no sure possession.

When the war against France had been in progress for seven years, a supporter of Fox asked Pitt, the Prime Minister and leader of the Tories in the House of Commons, what the war was all about. Was Jacobinism not dead, and was Napoleon not indifferent to the principles of the French Revolution? What, then, was Britain fighting for? Here is Pitt's reply, representing the third answer which can be given to our question.

The hon. gentleman defies me to state, in one sentence, what is the object of the war. In one word, I tell him that it is security;—security against a danger, the greatest that ever threatened the world—security against a danger which never existed in any past period of society. This country alone, of all the nations of Europe, presented barriers the best fitted to resist its progress. We alone recognized the necessity of open war, as well with the principles, as the practice of the French revolution. We saw that it was to be resisted no less by arms abroad, than by precaution at home; that we were to look for protection no less to the courage of our forces than to the wisdom of our councils; no less to military effort than to legislative enactment. At the moment when those, who now admit the dangers of Jacobinism while they contend that it is extinct, used to palliate this atrocity, this House wisely saw that it was necessary to erect a double safeguard against a danger that wrought no less by undisguised hostility than by secret machination.

## 2. THE AMERICAN CHOICE

The United States has taken all these three positions toward the Soviet Union, either simultaneously or successively. From 1917 to the entrance of the Soviet Union into the Second World War in 1941, the United States looked at the Soviet Union primarily with the eyes of Burke. It saw in it and its adherents in foreign countries a threat to the established moral and social order of the West. What the United States feared and opposed during that period of history was the Soviet Union, the instigator and mastermind of world revolution, not Russia, the great power; for as a great power Russia did not exist during that period, and its potentialities as a great power were hardly recognized by the United States.

From June 1941 to the breakdown of the Yalta and Potsdam agreements in

1946, the Soviet Union appeared to the United States as revolutionary France had appeared to Fox. The Soviet Union was considered to be no threat to the United States either as the fountainhead of world revolution or as a great imperialistic power. There was a widespread tendency to look upon the Soviet leaders as democrats at heart, somewhat ill-mannered democrats, to be sure, but democrats nevertheless, whom circumstances had thus far prevented from living up to their democratic convictions and with whom, therefore, it was possible "to get along." The Soviet Union was supposed to have lost its revolutionary fervor, and as a great power it was believed to possess enough territory to keep it satisfied, and in any case to be so weakened by the devastations of war as to be unable to embark upon imperialistic ventures even if it wanted to.

Since the breakdown of the war and postwar agreements with the Soviet Union, public opinion in the United States has gone to the other extreme and reverted to the pattern established in the years following 1917. To American public opinion the conflict between the United States and the Soviet Union appears first of all as a struggle between two systems of political morality, two political philosophies, two ways of life. Good and evil are linked in mortal combat, and the struggle can only end, as it is bound to end, with the complete victory of the forces of good over the forces of evil. The policies of the Administration, after creating and supporting this popular conception of the nature of the conflict with the Soviet Union, have sporadically and sometimes half-heartedly endeavored to counteract these popular tendencies. More particularly, some of the speeches of Mr. Acheson have emphasized the primary concern with Russian imperialism, of which Communist world revolution is a mere instrument. His speeches before the National Press Club on January 12, 1950, and at Freedom House on October 8, 1950, suggest the attitude of Pitt rather than of Fox or Burke.

A simple test will show which of these three conceptions of the East-West conflict are mistaken and which is correct. Let us suppose for a moment that Lenin and Trotsky had died in exile, the unknown members of a Marxist sect, and that the Czar were still reigning over a Russia politically and technologically situated as it is today. Does anybody believe that it would be a matter of indifference for the United States to see the Russian armies hardly more than a hundred miles from the Rhine, in the Balkans, with Russian influence holding sway over China and threatening to engulf the rest of Asia? Is anybody bold enough to assert that it would make all the difference in the world for the United States if Russian imperialism marched forward as it did in the eighteenth and nineteenth centuries, under the ideological banner and with the support of Christianity rather than of Bolshevism?

One can turn that same question around and ask whether anybody in the United States would need to be concerned about the American Communist Party if it were not a tool in the hands of the Kremlin and, hence, the vanguard of Russian imperialism. If the American Communist Party were an independent revolutionary organization, such as the anarchists were at one time and the Trotskyites are now, one could dismiss them as a coterie of crackpots and misfits, not to be taken seriously. It is the power of Russia that gives the

American Communists an importance they would not have otherwise, and their importance is that of treason, not of revolution. If American Communism disappeared tomorrow without a trace, Russian imperialism would be deprived of one of its minor weapons in the struggle with the United States, but the issue facing the United States would not have been altered in the least.

## Four Sources of Confusion

The confusion between the issue of Russian imperialism and that of Communism feeds on four sources. First, the public at large tends to view politics, domestic and international, in the simple contrast of black and white, defined in moral terms. Thus the public is always prone to transform an election contest or an international conflict into a moral crusade carried on in the name of virtue by one's own party or one's own nation against the other party or the other nation, which stands for all that is evil in the world. Secondly, this genuine and typical confusion is aggravated by Russian propaganda, which justifies and rationalizes its imperialistic moves and objectives in the universal terms of Marxist dogma. The Western countercrusade, taking the revolutionary stereotypes of Russian propaganda at their face value, thus becomes a mere counterpoise of that propaganda, its victim, unwittingly taking for the real issue what is but a tactical instrument of imperialistic policies.

The understanding of the real issue between the United States and the Soviet Union is still further obscured by the ambiguity of the terms "Communism" and "Communist Revolution" themselves. If those who proclaim Communism as the real issue have primarily Europe in mind, they have at least a part of the truth; for in no country of Europe outside the Soviet Union has Communism succeeded in taking over the government except as a by-product of conquest by the Red Army and as an instrument for perpetuating Russian power. What has been true in the past in eastern and central Europe is likely to be true for the future in all of the Western world. If the Soviet Union pursues the goal of world revolution, it can attain that goal only by conquering the Western world first and making it Communistic afterwards. In other words, Communist revolution can come to the Western world only in the aftermath of the victory of the Red Army. In the West, then, the opposition to Communism is an integral part of resistance to Russian imperialism, and to oppose Russian imperialism is tantamount to opposing Communist revolution as well.

If those who refer to Communism as the real issue have primarily the revolutions in Asia in mind, they speak of something fundamentally different. While the Communist revolution could not have succeeded and will not succeed in any European country without the intervention of the Red Army, the revolutionary situation in Asia has developed independently of Russian Communism, and would exist in some form, owing to the triumph of Western moral ideas and the decline of Western power, even if Bolshevism had never been heard of. The revolutions in Europe are phony revolutions, the revolutions in Asia are genuine ones. While opposition to revolution in Europe is a particular aspect of the defense of the West against Russian imperialism, opposition to revolution in Asia is counter-revolution in Metternich's sense, resistance to change on behalf of an obsolescent status quo, doomed to failure from the outset. The issue of revolution in Asia is fundamentally different from that in Europe; it is not to oppose revolution as a creature and instrument of Russian imperialism but to support its national and social objectives while at the same time and by that very support preventing it from becoming an instrument of Russian imperialism. The clamor for consistency in dealing with the different revolutions sailing under the flag of Communism is the result of that confusion which does not see that the real issue is Russian imperialism, and Communist revolution only in so far as it is an instrument of that imperialism.

Finally, this confusion is nourished—and here lies its greatest danger for the political well-being of the United States—by a widespread fear not of revolution but of change. The forces that in the interwar period erected the specter of Communist revolution into a symbol of all social reform and social change itself are at work again, unaware that intelligent social reform is the best insurance against social revolution. What these forces were afraid of in the interwar period was not a threat—actually non-existent—to the security of the United States emanating from the power of Russia, but a threat to the social status quo in the United States. That threat did not stem primarily from the Communist Party, nor did it arise from the imminence of Communist revolution, which in the United States has been at all times a virtually negligible contingency. In embarking upon a holy crusade to extirpate the evil of Bolshevism these forces embarked, as they do now, in actuality upon a campaign to outlaw morally and legally all popular movements favoring social reform and in that fashion to make the status quo impregnable to change. The symbol of the threat of a non-existent Communist revolution becomes a convenient cloak, as it was for German and Italian Fascism, behind which a confused and patriotic citizenry can be rallied to the defense of what seems to be the security of the United States, but what actually is the security of the status quo. The fact that such a movement, if it were ever able to determine the domestic and international policies of the United States, would jeopardize not only the security of the United States but also the domestic status quo, only adds the touch of tragic irony to the confusion of thought and action.

What makes the task of American foreign policy so difficult is not only the unprecedented magnitude of the three great revolutions of our age, culminating in the rise of the Soviet Union, but also the necessity for American foreign policy to deal with four fundamental factors that must be separated in thought while they are intertwined in action: Russian imperialism, revolution as an instrument of Russian imperialism, revolution as genuine popular aspiration, and the use of the international crisis for the purposes of domestic reaction.

Whenever we have fallen victim, not only in thought but also in action, to the oversimplification that reduces the variegated elements of the world conflict to the moral opposition of Bolshevism and democracy, our policy has been mistaken and has failed in its objectives, ideological and political. Whenever such oversimplification and confusion has counseled our actions, we have rendered ourselves powerless either to contain Russian imperialism or prevent the spread of Communism. Of such a dual disaster, born of the confusion as to what the real issue is, our China policy is the prime example.

---

## COMPREHENSION CHECKPOINT

Now that you have read the selections, fill out a Worldview Profile Form for cold war containment. If you have trouble filling in any of the items, reread the introduction and the selections. Check your results with a classmate.

What is the significance of the following?

| | | |
|---|---|---|
| Atlantic Charter | the Marshall Plan | Mr. X Article |
| the Munich Crisis | containment policy | "captive nations" |
| Edmund Burke | monolithic Communism | phony revolution |
| Truman Doctrine | Charles Fox | William Pitt |
| Spanish Civil War | political realism | Jacobinism |
| genuine revolution | bipolar world | Burkean cold warriors |
| the infallibility of | Turkish and Greek Cri- | Kennan's three-stage |
| the Kremlin | ses of 1945–46 | strategy |

### Can You Match the Following?

1._____ Communism
2._____ France
3._____ Burke
4._____ Kennan
5._____ Communist China
6._____ Stalin
7._____ Communist Poland

a. genuine revolution
b. Napoleon
c. Pitt
d. NSC-7
e. the Soviet Union
f. phony revolution
g. Jacobinism

(Answers appear on page 54.)

---

## FOR FURTHER READING

Dulles, John Foster. *War or Peace.* New York: Macmillan Company, 1950 (The 1957 edition contains a special, updated preface). A Burkean view of the Soviet-American conflict by President Eisenhower's secretary of state. The first edition of the book appeared at the height of the cold war.

Etzold, Thomas H. and John Lewis Gaddis (eds.). *Containment: Documents on American Policy and Strategy, 1945–1950.* New York: Columbia University Press, 1978. A collection of documents that reveals the official "thinking out" and construction of the nation's containment policy. The collection includes Kennan's long cable, summaries of the world situation, military plans for war with the Soviet Union, and NSC-68, which outlined a global containment policy based upon conventional forces. Many of the documents were previously classified, and some were top secret.

Gaddis, John Lewis. *Strategies of Containment: A Critical Appraisal of Postwar American National Security Policy.* New York: Oxford University Press, 1982. A brilliant discussion of the theory and practice of containment from Truman to Reagan. The second chapter draws heavily upon the development of Kennan's ideas while he served as a faculty member at the National War College.

Isaacson, Walter and Evan Thomas. *The Wise Men: Six Friends and the World They Made.* New York: Simon and Schuster, 1986. Absorbingly written biographies of the lives, careers, and interactions of six men who molded and implemented our containment policy—Dean Acheson, Charles Bohlen, Averell Harriman, George Kennan, Robert Lovett, and John J. McCloy.

Kennan, George F. *Memoirs, 1925–1950.* Boston: Atlantic Monthly Press, 1967. Kennan's own tale of his rise from a young foreign service officer to one of the nation's most influential foreign policy makers. Early chapters present an interesting picture of the day-to-day life of a foreign service officer.

Larson, Deborah Welch. *Origins of Containment: A Psychological Explanation.* Princeton: Princeton University Press, 1985. A careful and critical examination of the worldviews of four decision makers who molded and implemented our containment policy—W. Averell Harriman, Harry S. Truman, James F. Byrnes, and Dean Acheson. Larson's book is a path-breaking work in its effort to apply the research of cognitive psychologists to the making and shaping of foreign policy worldviews.

Lippmann, Walter. *The Cold War: A Study in U.S. Foreign Policy.* New York: Harper Row, 1947. This short book contains a critique of the Mr. X article and Lippmann's proposal for meeting the Soviet challenge—a negotiated withdrawal of both Soviet and American troops from Central Europe.

Morgenthau, Hans. *In Defense of the National Interest.* New York: Alfred A. Knopf, 1951. A seminal presentation of the realist interpretation of the postwar Soviet-American conflict. A good book to read in conjunction with Dulles' *War or Peace* cited above.

---

**Answers to quiz:**    1-g; 2-e; 3-d; 4-c; 5-a; 6-b; 7-f. If some of these answers perplex you, discuss them in class with your professor. Or, reread the Morgenthau selection.

---

## NOTES

1. Mr. X, "The Sources of Soviet Conduct," reprinted in *Foreign Affairs*, Vol. 64, No. 4 (Spring 1987), p. 867.
2. *Ibid.*, p. 861.
3. *Ibid.*
4. Harry S. Truman, *Year of Decisions* (Garden City, NY: Doubleday, 1955), p. 549.

5. *Public Papers of the President, Harry S. Truman 1947* (Washington, DC: Government Printing Office, 1963), pp. 176–80.

6. Harry S. Truman, *Memoirs of Harry S. Truman*, Vol. I (New York: Doubleday, 1955), p. 552.

7. Harry S. Truman, *Years of Trial and Hope* (New York: New American Library, 1956), pp. 378–79.

8. See John Lewis Gaddis, *Strategies of Containment* (Oxford: Oxford University Press, 1982), Ch. 2, "Kennan and Containment."

9. George Saintsbury (ed.), "Second Letter on a Regicide Peace," *Political Pamphlets* (New York: Macmillan, 1892), p. 84.

10. *The National Interest*, 18 (Winter 1989), p. 46.

# Chapter
# 3

# Cold War
# Reassertionism

*I*n the mid-1960s, the war in Vietnam shattered the cold war consensus and drove Lyndon Johnson from the White House. Not surprisingly, his immediate successor sought to disengage American troops from the nation's Third World commitments while restraining Soviet adventurism at the same time. Thus, early in his term, Richard Nixon announced that America would no longer provide combat forces to save non-Communist regimes threatened by "wars of national liberation." In the future, he said, American aid would be restricted to military and economic assistance. At the same time, Nixon sought to weaken Soviet support for such insurrections with a policy of detente—Soviet restraint would be rewarded with trade and other "carrots," while "sticks" would be relied upon whenever Soviet behavior conflicted with American interests.

Both of these changes were essentially changes of tactics. The containment of Communism remained the primary American objective, and support for anti-Communist allies in the Third World took precedence over human rights. Satisfying neither opponents nor supporters of the war, Nixon's policy of detente evoked little enthusiasm; in fact, the very idea of working with the Soviets on some issues while competing with them on other issues was confusing to many Americans. Into such ill-repute did the term itself fall that Nixon's successor, Gerald Ford, banished the word "detente" from the White House during the 1976 presidential campaign. But to no avail.

Ford's successor, Jimmy Carter, decided to de-emphasize Soviet-American relations except for the area of arms control. Having declared that America had shed its "inordinate fear of communism," Carter tried to build a new foreign policy consensus by creating a "post–cold war" foreign policy that focused on such items as promoting human rights, scaling back the arms race, nuclear proliferation, curtailing burgeoning arms sales in the Third World, and working with developing nations to create a new international economic order.

While Nixon pursued detente and Carter worked on his post–cold war agenda, the Soviets were adding new allies at a rate of more than one a year. During the 1970s, Angola, Mozambique, Somalia, Ethiopia, Yemen, Vietnam, Cambodia, Laos, and Nicaragua all moved into the Soviet camp. In the twenty-five years between the fall of China in 1949 and the fall of South Vietnam in 1974, only two countries, North Vietnam and Cuba, had joined the Communist camp—and these gains were more than offset by the Soviet "loss" of China in the early 1970s. Thus, measured against its past record, the Soviet gains in the era of "no more Vietnams" was both impressive and ominous to many Americans.

With the fall of the Shah, the growing strength of Cuban- and Nicaraguan-backed guerrillas in El Salvardor, and strident Soviet behavior throughout the Third World, President Carter's efforts to transcend the cold war ran aground. After the invasion of Afghanistan, Soviet-American relations quickly popped to the top of the foreign policy agenda. In his last year in office, Carter embargoed grain sales to the Soviet Union, boycotted the Olympic Games in Moscow, withdrew the SALT II treaty from the Senate, stepped up defense spending, and threatened nuclear war if the Soviets sought to deny Middle Eastern oil supplies to the West.

But Carter's turnabout came too late. In the 1980 election campaign, Ronald Reagan castigated a decade of decommitment, detente, and disengagement and called for a reassertion of America's values and its power. He pledged to redirect the nation's foreign policy back to containing Communism, and he advocated rolling back the Soviet gains of the 1970s. Carter's Republican challenger decisively defeated him, and, once again, competition with the Soviet Union became the centerpiece of the nation's foreign policy.

Ironically, the intellectual roots of Reagan's reassertionist worldview came not so much from traditional cold warriors, as from a political coterie of neoconservatives, many of whom were lifelong Democrats.[1] From the mid-1970s on, leading neoconservatives used the monthly pages of *Commentary* magazine to lambast the efforts at decommitment, detente, and disengagement undertaken by the Nixon, Ford, and Carter administrations. Along the way, they also articulated a set of reassertionist "counter-foreign policies."

The tenor and nature of this assault can be gleaned from the following sample of titles that appeared in the magazine: "Beyond Detente" (March 1977), "Why the Soviet Union Thinks It Could Fight and Win a Nuclear War" (July 1977), "Africa, Soviet Imperialism, and the Retreat of American Power" (October 1977), "Europe—The Spector of Finlandization" (December 1977), "The Psychology of Appeasement" (October 1978), "The Illusions of SALT" (September 1979), "Dictatorships and Double Standards" (November 1979), "Soviet Global Strategy" (April 1980), "After Afghanistan, What?" (April 1980), "How to Restrain the Soviets" (October 1980). In fact, not one aspect of the Carter administration's foreign policy escaped the withering criticism of *Commentary's* neoconservative writers.

While neoconservatives were not alone in their attacks upon America's post-Vietnam policies of detente and decommitment, their writings shaped a post-Vietnam worldview that would guide the policies pursued by the Reagan administration. In fact, a number of *Commentary's* authors joined the Reagan administration. Harvard Professor Richard Pipes became the top Soviet expert on the National Security Council. Jeane Kirkpatrick became Reagan's first ambassador to the United Nations. Carl Gershman worked on Kirkpatrick's team in New York. Eugene Rostow served as head of the Arms Control and Disarmament Agency.

Beyond the neoconservatives, one of the most forceful and articulate proponents of reassertionism was former President Richard Nixon—the president who initiated the policies of decommitment and detente. Six years after leaving the presidency, Nixon was portraying the conflict between the United States and the Soviet Union in apocalyptic, if not Manichean, proportions. In his 1980 book, *The Real War*, Nixon warned that Soviet leaders were seeking only one goal—"total unconditional victory [for them] and unconditional surrender for the West."[2] In his first chapter entitled "No Time to Lose" Nixon painted an ominous picture of the challenge facing the nation:

> The Soviet Union today is the most powerfully armed expansionist nation the world has ever known, and its arms buildup continues at a pace nearly twice that of the United States. There is no mystery of Soviet intentions. The Kremlin leaders do not want war, but they do want the world. And they are rapidly moving into position to get what they want.

> In the 1980s America for the first time in modern history will confront two cold realities. The first of these is that if war were to come, we might lose. The second is that we might be defeated without war. The second prospect is more likley than the first and almost as grim. The danger facing the West during the balance of this century is less that of a nuclear holocaust than it is drifting into a situation in which we find ourselves confronted with a choice between surrender or suicide—red or dead. That danger can still be averted, but the time in which we can avert it is rapidly running out.[3]

Thus, the centrality of the Soviet threat was the lodestar for reassertionists, and their cries of alarm stemmed from what they perceived as a decade of Soviet gains in the face of western passivity. According to Nixon, detente failed because a Democratic congress shackled his administration with the War Powers Act and the Clark Amendment, which prohibited American assistance to forces fighting the Soviet- and Cuban-installed government in Angola. Then, reassertionists argued, Jimmy Carter's post–cold war foreign policy merely whetted the appetites of the Brezhnev and Castro regimes.

The basis for the reassertionists' alarm lay in what they perceived as the clear goals of the Soviets' strategy—to gain control over the vital resources in key Third World countries and, thereby, gain a stranglehold over the West. A vital component of this strategy, reassertionists believed, was the ominous Soviet buildup of nuclear weapons. With nuclear superiority, reassertionists argued, the Soviets could deter any American president from escalating militarily if a confrontation occurred over the Soviets' quest for control of what Richard Nixon termed "the West's treasure houses" in southern Africa and the Middle East.

As the Soviets expanded and the West watched, reassertionists argued that others were joining the Soviet bandwagon and pursuing gratuitous anti-American foreign policies. In the United Nations, the United States was increasingly isolated and tormented, if not taunted, by an increasingly hostile Third World majority. In the economic organizations of the United Nations, a coalition of Third World and Soviet bloc nations pushed statist, international economic proposals that would lead to "automatic resource transfers" from the rich to the poor countries and would regulate the activities of multinational corporations. As reassertionists saw it, the purpose of these schemes was to bridge the gap between the rich and poor countries not by creating new wealth, but by transferring existing wealth. Many reassertionists also saw the bravado of OPEC and the anti-Americanism that followed the fall of the Shah as a direct outgrowth of American passivity through much of the 1970s.

The reassertionists' counter–foreign policy was clear and simple. Their basic political-military strategy was "containment-plus," with the plus part later to be named the Reagan Doctrine. Not only would the United States renew its commitment to contain further efforts at expansion by the Soviets and their proxies; it would also seek to roll back some of the Soviets' recently acquired gains. The decade of decommitment, detente, and disengagement would be over.

In addition, arms control agreements would no longer be viewed as ends in themselves. According to reassertionists and members of the Reagan administration, the nation did not need agreements with the Soviets to provide for its security. Disarmament negotiations would be placed on the back burner while the nation modernized its nuclear forces. The B-1 bomber would be built. Neutron bombs would be built and stockpiled. The nation would move ahead with the Trident submarine and the lethal Trident D-2 missile. Arms control proposals and treaties would be viewed against one benchmark—did they enhance the nation's security by making its nuclear retaliatory forces more secure?

President Carter's approach to human rights would also be scrapped. For reassertionists, the human rights program of the Carter administration amounted to excoriating friendly, authoritarian allies, while seeking to befriend even more repressive Marxist regimes such as Cuba, North Vietnam, and Angola. Under Reagan, the nation would befriend regimes that sought to befriend us, and it would excoriate unfriendly nations that excoriated their own people.

Finally, the United States would speak up in international forums and in bilateral relations for America's traditional political and economic values— political liberty, free enterprise, private investment, individual initiative, and the use of markets to determine prices and to allocate goods and services.

Reassertionists saw the root of the nation's foreign policy problems in a lack of will—an unwillingness to stand up to a clear and expansionist enemy; an unwillingness to stand up for the political and economic values that made America the freest and most productive nation in the history of the world; and an unwillingness to use our military power to secure our interests and our values. The target for many reassertionists was what they perceived to be a supine, if not decadent, ruling elite. When reassertionists observed policy makers in the Carter administration and their supporters within the nation's "establishment," they perceived an elite who appeased, excused, and sought to befriend the nation's enemies; an elite who felt guilty about the nation's wealth and defensive about its values; an elite who felt that the forces of history were running against them; an elite whose only solace seemed to lie in waiting for something to turn up.[4] According to Richard Nixon:

> Too many of those who should be most jealously preserving and defending what America represents have instead been paralyzed by a misplaced sense of guilt which has led them to abandon faith in their own civilization. . . .

> If America loses World War III, it will be because of the failure of its leadership class. In particular, it will be because of the attention, the celebrity, and the legitimacy given to the "trendies"—those overglamorized dilettantes who posture in the latest idea, mount the fashionable protests, and are slobbered over by the news media, whose creation they essentially are. The attention given them and their "causes" romanticizes the trivial and trivializes the serious. It reduces public discussion to the level of a cartoon strip. Whatever the latest cause they embrace— whether antiwar, antinuclear, antimilitary, antibusiness—it is almost invariably one that works against the interest of the United States in the context of World War III.[5]

With the election of Ronald Reagan, reassertionist ideas set the broad lines of the nation's foreign policy, although, as Coral Bell has made clear, there was frequently a large gap between the rhetoric of the Reagan administration and the operational policies.[6] In fact, when the reassertionist Secretary of State Alexander Haig resigned after less than a year and a half in office, his successor, George Schultz, pursued a less strident foreign policy. Thus, during much of Reagan's two terms, reassertionist appointees fought bureaucratic battles with less reassertionist appointees who were frequently drawn from the foreign service.[7] Then, toward the end of his second term in office, Ronald Reagan himself traded in his reassertionist trappings for a new rapprochement with the Soviet Union, much to the chagrin of his reassertionist supporters.

Yet the differences between the Reagan and Carter administrations were fundamental ones. The most significant difference, of course, was the Reagan administration's preoccupation with the Soviet Union. A massive military buildup imposed serious strains on the Soviet economy; the Reagan doctrine indicated that the United States would increase the Soviet Union's costs of maintaining its newly acquired client regimes in the Third World; and the SDI portended a technological race that the Soviet regime might not be capable of matching. What impact the Reagan administration's reassertionist foreign policy had in ending the cold war is highly debatable, as the selections by William Odum and Robert Mueller illustrate (see Chapter 4).

But clearly the end of the cold war had to mean the end of reassertionism— for the central objectives of reassertionists were the death of communism and the dismantlement of the Soviet empire. Where then have reassertionists gone? As Chapter 8 indicates, some, such as Jeane Kirkpatrick and Patrick Buchanan, have moved into the noninterventionist or neo-isolationist camp. For them, America's postwar foreign policy was designed to contain and defeat an expansionist, totalitarian power. Having met that challenge, they now favor a noninterventionist policy. As Jeane Kirkpatrick put it, "We have virtually no experience in protecting and serving our interests in a multipolar world in which diverse nations and groups of nations engage in endless competition for marginal advantage." Normal balance of power politics is not for such reassertionists. [8]

Other reassertionists believe that, having defeated the Soviet Union, the United States should seek to promote the principles of American democracy worldwide. Others believe that United States should play the role of a balancer against regional hegemons. Finally, some neoconservatives favor a more in-between policy, one of keeping a watchful eye on the balance of power, working with industrial and Third World democracies, and treating other nations as they treat us. [9]

# The Selections

## 5. Charles Wolf, Jr.
## *Extended Containment*                                    1983

In this essay, Charles Wolf, Jr., compares the reassertionist worldview with the "mirror-imaging" worldview that he claims undergirded the policies of the Carter administration. According to Wolf, the differences between these two worldviews reside in fundamental differences over the nature and purpose of the Soviet regime. In his call for a restoration of cold war containment, Wolf's policy proposals are reminiscent of NSC-7 (Selection 3).

In addition to using Wolf's essay to profile the reassertionist worldview, you might also reorganize it in terms of the following four questions: (1) *What is* or has been happening in the world? (2) *Why* is "it" happening? (3) *What alternate* world should the United States seek? (4) *How* should the United States get to that world? You can then examine the evidence Wolf presents and assess the validity of his answers to each of these questions. Also, after you read the selections in the next chapter, you may want to reread this essay in order to assess Wolf's presentation of the neorealist worldview.

When he wrote this essay, Wolf was the director of the Rand Corporation's research program in international economic policy.

Disputes about U.S. policies toward the Soviet Union usually focus on such specific issues as the Strategic Arms Reduction Talks (START); Intermediate-Range Nuclear Forces (INF); "two-tracks" and zero or other options in Europe; human rights and Helsinki's "basket 9"; East-West trade, credit, and technology transactions; the Yamal pipeline. Whatever the specific content of these disputes, at their heart lie two fundamentally opposing beliefs concerning the nature of the Soviet system—how it behaves and responds, and the objectives and motivations of its leaders. The oposition between these outlooks explains the contrasting positions on specific issues, as well as the general foreign policy stances, adopted by such antagonists as Walter Mondale and Ronald Reagan;

Cyrus Vance and Zbigniew Brzezinski; George Kennan and Paul Nitze; Marshall Shulman and Richard Pipes; Tom Wicker and William Safire; or *The New York Times* and *The Wall Street Journal*.

These differing beliefs are typically so strongly held as to have the properties of "cognitive dissonance": any fact that is apparently inconsistent with them is either (a) dismissed as deception and falsehood, or (b) interpreted in such a sophisticated manner as to be construed as proof rather than disproof of the maintained belief.

Because these fundamental beliefs are usually unacknowledged, or even subconscious, the specific disputes that spring from them are like the images seen by Socrates' cave dwellers: reflections of a distant reality, rather than the reality itself. Similarly, because these beliefs are highly resistant to evidence that is inconsistent with them, they rarely change. To the extent that they are deeply held yet difficult to explicate, they appear to be similar to what Michael Polanyi has referred to as "tacit knowledge."[1] Yet to the extent that those who hold the assumptions avoid or dismiss evidence that is inconsistent with them, they represent dogma rather than knowledge, tacit or otherwise.

Nevertheless, it would be refreshing to see the underlying beliefs plainly identified at the outset of a discussion of policies and policy alternatives, rather than hidden from it. At least this would help those whose minds are not already made up. It might also help those whose minds *are* made up to arrive at "second-order agreement": namely, a mutual understanding of what precisely they disagree about, and what evidence would be required by each party to alter its position.

Toward this end, I will begin by stating what seem to me to be the two main conflicting views about the nature of the Soviet system and the motivations and objectives of its leaders, views that underlie many of the disputes that arise about specific issues and policies. I will also indicate where my own predispositions lie, because this affects the new measures I shall propose later to extend U.S. containment policies. I do not mean to imply, of course, that the two sets of beliefs are the only possible ones; combinations and nuances occur. Not everybody subscribes exactly to one of the two views. Yet the two contrasting positions capture something fundamental about what separates many of the people, institutions, and organizations active in the U.S. policy community, and account to a considerable degree for the alignments that emerge on specific issues.

## MIRROR-IMAGING VS. POWER-MAXIMIZING

For convenient, if not entirely accurate, reference, I will label the two views as *mirror-imaging* and *power-maximizing*.

The mirror-imaging view of the Soviet system and its leadership holds that Soviet preoccupation with defense grows out of Russian history and culture. Admittedly, this preoccupation may border on paranoia, and consequently may take quite aggressive forms. Such manifestations, however, are considered understandable in the light of Soviet history, including the experience of Western efforts from 1917 to 1920 to abort the Bolshevik Revolution, the twenty million casualties suffered by the Soviet Union in World War II, and the virulently anti-Communist rhetoric that sometimes emanates from right-wing circles in the West. Soviet preoccupation with military strength, and the resulting priority accorded to allocating resources and technology to the military, are, in the mirror-imaging view, explained mainly by this history. But in this vision, the long-term aims of the Soviet system are much like our own: human betterment and well-being, combined with peace, prosperity, and justice. Hence, a more forthcoming U.S. foreign policy, one that combines firmness with concessions, is likely to produce over time a symmetrical rather than an exploitative response from the Soviet leadership, as well as an irenic evolution of the Soviet system.

The power-maximizing view holds that, whatever the bitter and tragic experiences of Soviet history, and whatever the philosophical and ideological antecedents of Soviet Communism, the overriding objective of the system is to maximize the political and military power of the Soviet state at home and to expand it abroad. According to the power-maximizing view, concessions made to the Soviet Union by the United States or the West, and agreements and transactions with it, are fair game for exploitation and deception by the Soviets in the interests of expanding and maximizing their power. This view denies, or at least seriously doubts, that economic and social betterment are basic goals of the Soviet system. Instead, the power-maximizing view suggests that the sacrifice of such goals will be accepted and even obscurely welcomed by Soviet leaders as a way of justifying to the Russian people the enhancement of Soviet vigilance and power in response to ubiquitous external and internal "threats."

These two views dictate contrasting dispositions toward the Soviet Union. Adherents to mirror-imaging tend to favor a policy of accommodation or, at most, of limited containment. They will be relaxed, compared with power-maximizing adherents, about the consequences of Soviet "gains" if containment does not work. After all, such gains may entail some gains for us, too. For those who view Soviet values as mirroring our own, Soviet gains may be seen as providing reassurances to the Soviets, thus easing their defensive paranoia. This in turn will enable us to live more amicably with them.

By contrast, those adhering to the power-maximizing view regard Soviet realization of gains as much closer to a "zero-sum" process: gains realized by the Soviet Union contribute to its power and thereby to its further expansion. The result works increasingly to the detriment of the United States, which is why resistance and reversal of Soviet expansion are important in this outlook.

Those who see the Soviets as power-maximizing tend to endorse the disestablishment of the Soviet empire by all prudent means. Several of the ideas I will present later reflect this disposition. By contrast, adherents of mirror-imaging tend to disagree with these ideas and the purpose to which they are addressed. For, say the mirror-imagers, Soviet gains are not really too significant. After all, these apparent gains are beset by costs and uncertainties (e.g., Poland and Afghanistan). And, if such gains do contribute to Soviet self-confidence, that may be good for us, too (i.e., mirror-imaging is a *non*-zero-sum process).

Another striking contrast between the two views lies in their divergent positions concerning nuclear deterrence.

Holders of the mirror-imaging view gravitate toward "mutual assured destruction" and "minimum deterrence" in nuclear strategy. Threatening Soviet leadership with a second-strike capability, one that can inflict huge casualties on *population and civil industry,* will, according to adherents of mirror-imaging, suffice to deter Soviet attack on the United States and (less assuredly) on our NATO allies. Why? Because these targets are held to represent the fundamental *values* that are, through mirror-imaging, attributed to Soviet leadership by reason of the fact that we ourselves adhere to them. *Countervalue* then is the name of the deterrence game, and the values implied are precisely the ones we ourselves cherish.

The opposing view suggests that power, rather than human life and well-being, is the preeminent value motivating the Soviet party and state. Hence, nuclear deterrence should rely more heavily on "counterforce" capability, or an ability to strike the military forces, bases, and command-and-control centers on which Soviet power depends. Because, according to this view, the instruments of Soviet power are the leadership's quintessential "values," *counterforce* targeting is likely to be a more effective deterrent than targeting people and civil industry. According to this position, counterforce *is* countervalue!

As I have indicated, my own position is close to the latter; this will be evident in some of the proposals I advance below for "extended containment." It is, nevertheless, important to recognize that many, and perhaps most, putative "experts" on the Soviet Union subscribe to the mirror-imaging view, as does each of the first-named members of the six paired adversaries mentioned at the outset of this essay, as well as most of our European allies.

Two brief quotations convey, rather cogently I believe, the essentials of the power-maximizing position. The first passage comes from a former professor and chairman of the Department of Civil Law at Leningrad University, Olympiad Ioffe; the second comes from Milovan Djilas, whose intimate experience with Soviet as well as Yugoslav Communism extends over four or five decades. According to Professor Ioffe:

> The consistent policy of the Soviet State is to subordinate purely economic goals to the aim of building unlimited political power . . . and the legal regulation of the Soviet economy is carefully designed to implement that policy. . . . The leadership has made the economy work splendidly as the source of its dictatorship. In this regard, Soviet economic policy has never suffered a single real failure. . . . The Soviet economy is inefficient only as a source of material wellbeing, [but] material welfare there is simply incompatible with the aims of the Soviet system. . . . What could be done . . . to improve fundamentally the Soviet economy as a source of material welfare, without simultaneously undercutting the might of the state? Given the existing political system, only one answer is possible—nothing.[2]

According to Mr. Djilas:

Soviet communism . . . is a military empire. It was transformed into a military empire in Stalin's time. Internally, such structures usually rot . . . but to avoid internal problems, they may go for expansion. The West must be strong if it wants to save peace and stop Soviet expansionism. If it is stopped, the process of rotting will go faster.[3]

As I have implied above, the power-maximizing view underlies some of the specific directions for U.S. policy that I will propose later in this essay. Of course, I cannot prove or test, in any meaningful sense, the hypothesis embodied in this perspective. A few salient considerations, however, seem to me to provide support for this view of the Soviet Union in contrast to mirror-imaging:

- While Marxist-Leninst ideology proclaims economic and social well-being for the masses as the ultimate aim of the system, the system's performance is very different. In reality, there have been much more limited rates of improvement in civilian consumption, nutrition, housing, and health than have been experienced in Western economic systems. The Soviet Union is the only industrialized country in the world in which life expectancy has decreased and infant mortality has increased in the past decade—at the same time that Soviet military power has grown enormously and expensively.
- The declared political aim of the Soviet system is to move toward a "dictatorship of the proletariat," with the working class playing a "leading role" in the process. Again, the reality is quite different: namely, dictatorship *to* the proletariat, as was blatantly illustrated by the military suppression of Poland's trade union movement beginning in December 1981.
- The social aim of Marxism-Leninism is a classless society. In reality, the system is a rigid hierarchy within each of the three dominant bureaucracies: party, government, and military. Sharp differences of power, privilege, and perquisites exist even among the controlling elites.
- In terms of economic performance (as contrasted with power maximization), the Communist system has been relatively unsuccessful. In the Soviet Union over the past decade (and prospectively over the next decade), the economy has shown declining rates of growth in real GNP, increasing capital/output ratios, declining labor productivity and total factor productivity, and only very limited improvements in personal consumption, as noted above.
- Only in one field has the system been strikingly successful: the development of military and political power. In the Sovet Union, there has been an extraordinary buildup of nuclear and conventional power, of ground forces, naval forces, and air forces. Growth of real defense spending has been sustained over the last decade at a rate slightly above that of the growth of the Soviet economy as a whole. Growth of Soviet military investment—that is, procurement of military equipment—has been substantially larger than that of the United States. In most other Com-

munist systems, too—e.g., Cuba, Nicaragua, Vietnam, North Korea—the most dramatic evidence of sustained growth is found in military forces and military production rather than in civilian economic development and betterment.

With this as background, let me turn to two ideas for extending containment in new directions. One direction is concerned with countering and reversing the expansion of the Soviet empire; the other is concerned with realistic rules for the conduct of economic relations with the Soviet Union in an environment of "extended containment." I intend these as extensions, rather than as a fundamental revamping, of containment. "Extended containment," like "extended deterrence," is not without its limits. The reasons for advocating these extensions lie in the unsatisfactory outcomes that have resulted from "limited" containment—that is, from U.S. policies that have, at their best, faced the Soviet Union with uncertainty concerning the *rate* of its expansion, not the *sign*. Extended containment, in the proposals described below, would change this by providing *competition* for gains that the Soviets have already enjoyed, as well as containment of further gains. Thus the Soviet Union would face uncertainty regarding the sign as well as the rate of expansion of its empire.

## Reversing Expansion of the Soviet Empire

The years since World War II have seen either the demise or the severe diminution of the colonial empires of the past—British, French, Japanese, and Dutch. The less formal reflections of U.S. "hegemony" in various parts of the world have also waned sharply after their transitory appearance in the 1950s and 1960s. Only the Soviet empire, despite occasional setbacks, has expanded in a sustained and substantial manner.

Is it appropriate to use the term *empire* to describe the Soviet Union's expansion?

There are, of course, three different Soviet empires: the empire "at home" (i.e., the empire that lies within the geographic boundaries of the Soviet state); the geographically contiguous part of the empire (i.e., Eastern Europe and, more recently, Afghanistan); and the empire "abroad."

The empire "at home" is the subject of Hélène Carrère d'Encausse's recent study.[4] The Soviet Union is a multinational state, consisting of fifteen distinct national republics and over sixty nationalities, twenty-three of which have populations larger than a million. The internal empire is the product of the eastward expansion of Czarist Russia during the century before the Leninist revolution. But it is the two other Soviet empires that interest us here.

In the past dozen years or so, the Soviet imperium has come to include Angola, Ethiopia, South Yemen, Vietnam, Laos, Cambodia, Benin, Mozambique, Afghanistan, Nicaragua, Syria, and Libya, in addition to its prior and continuing satellites, allies, and associates in Eastern Europe, Cuba, and, more ambiguously, North Korea. Of course, the pattern and degree of Soviet influence or control vary considerably across these countries.

The degree of Soviet control varies: it is strongest in Eastern Europe and weakest in North Korea. Nevertheless, all these nations lie within the "sliding scale" of possibilties classified by J. A. Hobson under the term *empire* in his classic study of the nineteenth-century British version.[5]

Although there have been some Soviet setbacks (e.g., Somalia, Egypt, and Indonesia), the gains and extensions of the Soviet empire have vastly exceeded its losses and retrenchments. This is not to deny that the Soviet Union is beset by serious problems in Eastern Europe and on its eastern border with China, to say nothing of its increasingly serious economic, social, and ethnic problems at home. Nor does it deny that the acquisition and expansion of the empire impose significant costs on the Soviet economy. However, the benefits to the Soviet Union resulting from the empire—the political advantages, both at home and abroad, as well as the tangible military advantages of bases and base rights in various parts of the empire—are likely to appear to the Soviet leadership quite substantial in relation to these costs. Consequently, we probably should expect continued efforts by the Soviet Union to expand its empire.

Current U.S. containment policy lacks any appropriate means to counter or reverse this trend. To reduce the Soviet empire requires a basic policy resolution, as well as the development of prudential means for implementation. This is the reason why an extension of containment that is explicitly "anti-imperialist" as well as supportive of pluralism and self-determination is needed in U.S. foreign policy. To formulate this extension requires a brief consideration of how the Soviet Union has expanded its empire in the past decade.

The dramatic expansion of the Soviet empire has been accomplished through a skillful combination of military power, political adroitness, covert operations, economic and financial support, and organizational inventiveness. It has been carried out under two broad doctrinal positions that allow ample room for adaptation to specific opportunities and circumstances: first, the doctrine of support for "wars of national liberation" from Western colonialism and imperialism; and, second, the Brezhnev doctrine of Soviet support for "fraternal states" in which Communism is threatened by efforts to undermine it.

Under these doctrines the Soviet union has successfully developed a wide range of policy instruments to expand its domain: providing trade subsidies and export credits; extending economic assistance; providing military equipment and training; furnishing airlift, sealift, logistic support, and command, control, communications and intelligence ($C^3I$) services in support of foreign operations; and developing and managing Cuban and East German allied or proxy forces for combat, internal security, and police roles abroad. In these operations Soviet combat forces have rarely been used directly, except as a last resort in such exceptional circumstances as Afghanistan.

Current U.S. containment policy is conceptually, materially, and organizationally ill-suited to contest and reverse the operational techniques—political, military, and economic—by which the Soviet Union has expanded its empire. Indeed, Soviet efforts to expand the empire have been considerably more subtle, flexible, and adroit than U.S. efforts to contain it. Use of the Rapid Deployment Force (RDF)—to look ahead—may be valuable in certain extreme contingencies, such as seizing and protecting oil production centers on the eastern or western side of the Persian Gulf, as well as ports along the Gulf. But such uses are likely to be rare. If attempts were made to use the RDF in the more likely and recurring appearances of Cuban or East German proxy forces in such ambivalent and localized contingencies as Angola, South Yemen, and Ethiopia, the result would probably be hostility abroad and the loss of political support at home. These are precisely the kinds of contingencies that have arisen in the past decade in the Caribbean and Latin America, as well as in Africa and the Middle East, and that have provided opportunities for the Soviet Union to expand its empire. Such contingencies are likely to provide similar opportunities in the next decade as well.

## Extending Containment

To extend existing U.S. containment policy, so that it confronts more realistically and effectively the realities of Soviet imperial expansion, requires a combination of new declaratory policies, reallocation of U.S. resources, organizational changes within the executive branch, altered policies for guiding the programming of military and economic assistance, and changes in the conduct of U.S. diplomacy.[6] These changes would focus principally on U.S. policies in that amorphous and heterogeneous group of countries loosely referred to as the Third World.

**Declaratory Policies**   Extended containment requires two innovations in U.S. declaratory policies. The first is a declaration of explicit and overt—yet selective, limited, and measured—support for genuine and legitimate movements within the Third World that seek to achieve liberation from Communist imperialism and totalitarianism, and that also seek to advance more pluralistic, open, and at least incipiently democratic forms of government. Achieving support both at home and abroad for such a declaratory policy requires emphasis on both the positive elements, indicating what the policy seeks to achieve, and the negative elements, plainly labeling what the policy opposes.

The anti-Communist liberation movements that we may wish to support are not likely to be ideal democracies, either in operation or in aspiration. Instead, they will usually be characterized by elements of demagogy, elitism, repression, and even brutality. These characteristics, where they occur, should be recognized and labeled for what they are. At the same time, we should emphasize the elements of openness and pluralism that differentiate the movements we might support from the Communist totalitarianism they seek to supplant. We should emphasize the positive differences in favor of these movements, while acknowledging the shortcomings that remain.[7] Like the Soviet doctrine of support for "wars of national liberation," the doctrine of support for Movements of National Liberation from Communist Imperialism (MNLCI) should be overt and explicit, and not directed principally toward covert assistance. Equally important, such support should be limited in scope and magnitude. It should be confined to selected contingencies in which the legitimacy and demonstrated capabilities of a candidate movement augur well for effective and successful utilization of the limited support to be provided. Yet the real uncertainties involved in providing such support should be explicitly recognized as part of the declaratory policy. It should be understood that implementation will entail losses as well as gains; "calculated" losses are to be anticipated. Recognition that the outcome is uncertain is essential to avoid escalation of the intentionally limited support.*

Where might such movements arise? Prospects are modest at best. The principal reason is that Communist systems accord such high priority to strengthening their surveillance and security apparatus that aborning movements seeking "national liberation" tend to be spotted early and coopted or ruthlessly crushed. The Shah's heralded and hated security system, Savak, was much less extensive and thorough for example, than Castro's "normal" state security apparatus. Under the circumstances, fledgling movements will face an uphill struggle to get started. But the start-up is a problem they must solve themselves if their prospects for survival, growth, and legitimacy are to be helped by limited and measured U.S. support. Among countries in the Soviet empire where such possibilities exist are Nicaragua, South Yemen, Mozambique, Angola, Benin, and Cuba. Genuine and legitimate movements in two or three Communist states would turn what has been a one-sided Communist-led "national liberation" arena into a more genuinely competitive one.

The Western media and the American Congress have often gone out of their way to uncover elements of legitimacy (e.g., land reform, or the reduction of exploitation and inequality) in Communist-led guerrilla movements. The Sandinista movement in Nicaragua was one example; El Salvador is another. One sign of success for the policy redirection I am proposing would be registered when the media and Congress could discern some degree of legitimacy in the anti-Communist guerrilla movements seeking national liberation from Communistic imperialism.

A second innovation in American declaratory policies would affirm a U.S. intention to collaborate with, and provide support for, certain *associated countries* whose interests converge with those of the United States in opposing the use of Communist proxy forces in the Third World, and in advancing more pluralistic and open societies in these areas. The countries that might participate in such a loose association with the United States need be no closer geographically to the areas in which their forces might operate than those areas are to the Cuban and East German forces associated with the Soviet Union.

By focusing on such associated countries, this doctrine would not exclude the possibility of collaboration with our traditional NATO allies in activities

---

*Anticipation of losses creates an obvious temptation to proceed covertly and thereby avoid damage to U.S. prestige, a temptation that should be resisted for several reasons. One reason is that to acquire and sustain support within the United States for the policy redirection I am proposing, prior debate, including recognition of costs as well as benefits, is necessary. Without the former, the credibility of the latter will be diminished. Another reason is simply the difficulty of assuring covertness, and the high likelihood in the U.S. context that efforts to do so will backfire.

outside the NATO area as well. The aim would merely be to give greater attention to such Third World countries as South Korea, Pakistan, Turkey, Egypt, Venezuela, and Taiwan as more promising candidates for these collaborative roles than our traditional European allies.

**Reallocation of Resources**   To implement these new declaratory policies, modest reallocations of defense resources would be necessary. It would obviously be easiest if these incremental needs could be met by budget increases, but it is possible that they will need to be met within existing or planned budget levels. Underlying these suggestions is an important assumption: that the balance of forces in the strategic area (especially if a suitable basing mode for the MX can be formulated) and in the NATO theater (assuming that some INF deployment goes forward, together with suitable modernization of conventional NATO forces) is more stable and secure than is the balance in the Third World areas where the Soviet empire continues to expand. Hence, the development of a more realistic extension of containment policy requires actions that focus on these latter areas.

To implement the proposed extension and redirection of containment policy, U.S. airlift and sealift forces should be specifically earmarked to provide mobility for forces from the associated countries. If this policy is to be taken seriously, specific U.S. units should also be designated and exercised to provide resupply and logistics support, as well as $C^3I$. These earmarked forces should be configured to operate in conjunction with the Associated Country Forces (ACF), rather than with wholly American units such as the proposed Rapid Deployment Force. While these forces would presumably have joint capabilities to provide support for U.S. forces and for the ACF, specific training (including language training), as well as suitable equipment, would be needed if the operations in conjunction with the ACF were to proceed smoothly.

For implementing the declaratory policy of providing support for indigenous movements, special organizational and intelligence capabilities would be needed within the U.S. government (see below). In addition, there would be a need for light weapons designed for easy and speedy delivery by air and sea, as well as for easy maintenance and decentralized delivery and use by appropriate "liberation" movements. Provision of individually operated anti-tank and anti-aircraft weapons for Afghan freedom fighters would be an example.

None of this would obviate the need for a Rapid Deployment Force. Notwithstanding its limited utility for meeting challenges posed by expansion of the Soviet empire, the RDF retains an essential function in these contingencies: to provide a backup to deter Soviet intervention. Such forces would be deployed only in the event that Soviet forces were directly committed, or seemed likely to be. Yet even unused, the RDF would perform an invaluable role as a reassuring guarantor for the ACF; indeed, without such reassurance, the likelihood of ACF participation would be severely diminished.

**Organizational Changes**   To implement the declaratory policies and the types of operations described above would require organizational changes within the U.S. government. There is need for an organizational entity with authority to span the military services and to mobilize the multiple instruments of foreign and defense policy for the purpose of providing support for the ACF and for MNLCI.

To conduct these operations, organizational innovation is needed to provide planning and $C^3I$; to call up airlift, sealift, and logistic support; to provide military and economic aid; and, in some cases, to supply direct financial assistance. No such centralized organizational entity now exists. Instead, the required functions are spread loosely among the Departments of Defense and State and the intelligence community.

## Planning and Programming Economic and Security Assistance

Forms of U.S. economic and security assistance have typically been considered, planned, and administered separately from one another. Although there have been divergent views on this issue in the recurring debates on foreign assistance, separation between the two has been favored on various grounds. Principal among them is the view that security assistance is a direct or indirect aspect of U.S. defense preparedness, whereas economic and technical aid have a longer-term and broader relationship to U.S. foreign policy, to a brighter and more progressive image of the United States in the world, and so on.

To implement the objectives and declaratory policies advocated here—both for supporting indigenous movements and for developing an ACF—a tighter link is needed between the planning and operational responsibility for economic aid and that for security assistance. Both forms of assistance are instruments of U.S. foreign policy; they are not ends in themselves. These programs should be planned and conducted together, permitting them to be more sharply focused toward the achievement of U.S. objectives.[8]

**Diplomacy and Linkage**    The Soviet Union has repeatedly asserted that its support for wars of national liberation, and for Cuban and East German allied or proxy forces in the Third World, is entirely compatible with arms limitation negotiations and with agreements in both the strategic area and the NATO area, as well as with continued economic relations between East and West.[9]

The United States should adopt a similar stance in public and in the conduct of private diplomacy. U.S. support for indigenous movements and for the ACF should not be viewed as incompatible with the pursuit of opportunities for mutual benefit between East and West in the domains of arms limitation and of economic, financial, and technological exchanges. For the United States to conduct diplomacy in support of the extended containment policies advocated here, while at the same time maintaining a receptive stance toward other dimensions of relationships with the Soviet Union, is as difficult a task to bring off domestically as it is worthwhile internationally, especially in relations with our European allies.

F. Scott Fitzgerald once observed that the test of a first-rate intelligence is the ability to hold two opposed ideas at the same time and still retain the capacity for effective action. To create and sustain political support for a two-track policy in the domestic political environment of the United States requires first-rate leadership no less than first-rate intelligence. In principle, and in the abstract, the opportunity exists to link the two: if both tracks are cogently articulated and prudently implemented, they can provide the makings of a reasonable coalition between the Right and the Left, between conservatives and liberals. Translating the abstract into the concrete is what requires first-rate political leadership.

## Extending Containment in the Economic Realm

It is useful to distinguish three different directions for United States and Western economic policies toward the Soviet Union, although various combinations among them are also possible:

- Government subsidies to encourage East-West transactions.
- Embargoes or sanctions to cut off such transactions.
- Removing subsidies and avoiding embargoes, letting the market function to facilitate or foreclose particular transactions.

Subsidization was pursued in the 1970s by the West in the spirit of détente. This effort was notably unsuccessful in influencing Soviet behavior along the congenial lines that were hoped for by its advocates. Instead, throughout the decade the Soviets pursued an unprecedented buildup of military power, continued to expand their external empire in Angola, Nicaragua, Mozambique, Ethiopia, and South Yemen, invaded Afghanistan, and managed the suppression of Solidarity in Poland.

Both embargoes and a strict market regime would represent a restriction of East-West trade and West-East credits compared with subsidization.

Clearly, the side effects of the latter two policies are likely to differ sharply: opposition within the Western alliance to a strict market regime would be much more limited than opposition to a policy of embargoes, as was indicated by the overreaction of our European allies to the relatively short-lived embargo by the president on compressors for the Yamal pipeline.

The market regime probably comes closest to what might be termed *economic realism.* Such a policy would, on the one hand, avoid the discredited optimism of the 1970s subsidization policy, while on the other hand limit the intra-Alliance damage and the serious difficulty of implementation that would ensue if embargoes or sanctions were adopted instead.

This position may seem rather bland: advocacy of a strict market regime is like support for balanced budgets and motherhood. General support is expressed for the principle, but sharp differences emerge over specific issues. For example, the Germans argue that the loan guarantees extended to the Soviet Union by their Hermes organization do not represent inappropriate subsidies, but simply constitute a normal means of carrying on international trade. In fact, it can be shown that such guarantees really do constitute a subsidy, and the amount of the subsidy is substantial.[10] Similarly, the French say that charging the Russians an interest rate of 9.5 percent on loans connected with the Yamal pipeline did not represent a subsidy, and in any event was a higher rate than the Germans were charging!

To effect the removal of subsidies requires that certain rules of the game be established for conducting East-West economic relations. Although it is important to seek agreement on these rules with the Alliance, I will argue later that if such agreement is not forthcoming, the United States should pursue and apply the rules unilaterally. The following are examples of rules I would propose:

- No loan or investment guarantee should be available to Western lenders or investors engaged in transactions with the East unless these guarantees are extended *without* direct or indirect government underwriting.
- No concessionary interest terms should be made available to either government or commercial borrowers in the Soviet Union or in Eastern Europe. The minimum criterion for implementation of this rule should be that interest rates applying to loans to the Soviet Union and Eastern Europe should not be less than the *highest* rates charged to domestic or other foreign borrowers on loans of equivalent duration.*
- No preferential tax treatment should be accorded to either individual or corporate income derived from transactions with the Soviet Union or Eastern Europe. (The preferential tax treatment extended under the Domestic International Sales Corporation Program in the United States would have to be modified to comply with this rule.)

The purpose of such rules would be to reduce and remove the extensive network of subsidies that has undergirded economic transactions with the Soviet Union and the other countries of the Council for Mutual Economic Assistance (CMEA) over the past decade. These subsidies have contributed to the huge expansion of net West-East resource flows, totaling more than $80 billion during the 1970s. The intended result is to restrict such flows in the future to no more than what an unsubsidized market would allow. Such restrictions can help, albeit only modestly, to constrain Soviet allocation decisions, to impede the management and expansion of the Soviet empire, and possibly to bring resource pressures to bear in the longer run that will tend to reduce the Soviet military buildup. . . .

## Pluralism and Extended Containment

None of the proposals described here is incompatible with the strategy of "containment plus political action" advocated by Aaron Wildavsky—the effort to sow the seeds of pluralism in Soviet soil by means of broadcasts, cassettes,

---

*This rule assumes that the additional political, as well as economic, risk involved in loans to the Council for Mutual Economic Assistance (CMEA) countries inevitably makes such loans at least as risky as any other domestic or international loans of equivalent duration. In light of the record of delinquency, due to political and economic circumstances, in these loans in recent years, this assumption seems quite justifiable.

leaflets, and books composed and transmitted through private American groups. I endorse this approach. The attempt proposed here to develop Associated Country Forces to counter the use of Cuban and East German proxies by the Soviet Union is similarly pluralistic in aim because it extends containment in the direction of competition.

Nevertheless, while I applaud efforts to develop pluralism within the Soviet Union, I am skeptical about their effectiveness. I share the view expressed by the principal figure in Saul Bellow's *The Dean's December:*

> It was one of the greatest achievements of communism to seal off so many millions of people. You wouldn't have thought it possible in this day and age that the techniques of censorship should equal the techniques of transmission.[11]

In short, promoting pluralism in a system as tightly shackled as that of the Soviet Union is a formidable task. One should not expect too much from a Western informational barrage, although the effort is surely worth undertaking. [6,0]

## NOTES

1. Michael Polanyi, *The Tacit Dimension* (New York: Anchor, 1966), pp. 3–25.
2. Olympiad S. Ioffe, "Law and Economy in the USSR," *Harvard Law Review* (May 1982): 1591, 1625.
3. *The Wall Street Journal*, 20 October 1982, p.33.
4. See Hélène Carrère d'Encausse, *Decline of an Empire: The Soviet Socialist Republics in Revolt* (New York: Harper and Row, 1979).
5. See J. A. Hobson, *Imperialism* (New York: Gordon Press, 1975), p. 15. It is worth recalling Hobson's remark concerning the "quibbles about the modern meaning of the terms 'imperialism' and 'empire.' " Hobson's use of the term encompassed, within the British empire, areas that Britain "annexed or otherwise asserted political sway over," and he acknowledged that there is a "sliding scale of political terminology along which no man's land, or hinterland, passes into some kind of definite protectorate." A similarly elastic terminology is implied in my use of the term *empire* to refer to the various forms of political sway, influence, and "protectorate" that the Soviet Union has acquired in the past decade.
6. For a more extended discussion of some of these aspects, see my article "Beyond Containment: Reshaping U.S. Policies Toward the Third World" (pamphlet, California Seminar on International Security and Foreign Policy, Santa Monica, Calif., September 1982), pp. 1–29; and "Beyond Containment: Redesigning American Policies," *The Washington Quarterly* (Winter 1982): 107–17.
7. An example of what I have in mind is provided by the State Department's recent report to Congress, *Country Report on Human Rights Practices for 1982* (Washington, D.C.: U.S. Government Printing Office, 1983). With rare exceptions, the most egregious violations of human rights occur within Communist states. The report contrasts the more pervasive and subtle violations occurring in Communist systems with those occurring elsewhere, without thereby absolving the latter.

8. For a more complete exposition of the reasons for forging a closer link between security assistance and economic and technical aid, see my "Beyond Containment: Reshaping U.S. Policies Toward the Third World," pp. 22–25.

9. See, for example, Henry Trofimenko, "The Third World and the U.S.–Soviet Competition: A Soviet View," *Foreign Affairs* (Summer 198): 1025–27.

10. See Daniel F. Kohler and Kip T. Fisher, *Subsidization of East–West Trade through Credit Insurance and Loan Guarantees* (Santa Monica, Calif.: Rand Corporation N-1951-USDP, January 1983), pp. 43–46. For a more complete discussion of these matters, see my testimony before the Senate Committee on Foreign Relations and the Subcommittee on International Economic Policy, *Hearings on Economic Relations with the Soviet Union*, Washington, D.C., July, August, 1982, pp. 116–25, and before the Workshop of the Senate Committee on Foreign Relations and Congressional Research Service, Library of Congress, *The Premises of East–West Commercial Relations*, Washington, D.C., December 1982, pp. 142–52.

11. Saul Bellow, *The Dean's December* (New York: Pocket Books, 1982), p. 63.

# 6. Jeane Kirkpatrick
## *The Reagan Reassertion of Western Values*
### December 1981

In this essay, Jeane Kirkpatrick celebrates the Reagan victory in 1980 as "a victory for those who rejected the idea of the inevitability of America's decline." Note that Kirkpatrick reiterates many of the themes developed in Wolf's essay—the crucial importance of "moral and political will," "the massive, unprecedented, unflagging Soviet military buildup," and "an equally unprecedented [expansionist] Soviet foreign policy." Like Wolf, Kirkpatrick also attacks the "doctrinal cornerstones of detente"—the belief that "economic and cultural ties and rewards would . . . restrain Soviet expansion," and "the theory that 'weaker is better.'" In the concluding passages of this essay, Kirkpatrick outlines the alternate cornerstones of Reagan's reassertionist alternative.

A professor of political theory at Georgetown University, Dr. Kirkpatrick ventured into foreign policy issues with her essay, "Dictatorships and Double Standards," which appeared in the November 1979 issue of *Commentary* magazine. In that essay, Kirkpatrick attacked the Carter administration for abandoning friendly authoritarian allies, such as the Shah of Iran, while seeking to normalize relations with such unfriendly, totalitarian regimes as Ho Chi Minh's North Vietnam and Castro's Cuba. "Dictatorships and Double Standards" had a profound impact upon Ronald Reagan's thinking about foreign policy and ultimately led to Kirkpatrick's appointment as his administration's first ambassador to the United Nations.

The election of Ronald Reagan was a watershed event in American politics, which signaled the end of one major postwar period and the beginning of a new one.

This new period may be understood best, I think, as the third period of the postwar era. The first, which spanned two decades, began with the Soviet takeover of Eastern Europe and the subsequent creation of NATO and ended at some point in the late 1960s—probably at that moment in early 1968 when the establishment that had guided American foreign policy throughout the postwar era turned against our involvement in Vietnam. This first period has been called, for want of a better term, the period of the cold war.

Some critics of American foreign policy look back with dread and regret on the "dark years of the cold war" and express a morbid fear lest we reenter such a period. I must say that I have reservations about this view. In the context of the twentieth century, a century filled with horrors on a scale quite literally unprecedented in human history, the years of the cold war were a relatively happy respite during which free societies and democratic institutions were unusually secure. The West was united, strong, and self-assured. The United States and the democratic ethos we espoused were ascendant everywhere in the world, if not everywhere triumphant.

The circumstances in which we found ourselves during those years encouraged the expression of our national penchant for optimism, vision, and leadership. We were strong, we were prosperous. No country or group of countries could compete on equal terms with us economically or could successfully challenge our military power. Moreover, the major trends also seemed hopeful. With our help, our wartime allies and our adversaries had recovered swiftly from the war and had firmly established themselves as stable and prosperous industrial democracies. In Africa and Asia, one country after another attained independence and looked forward to the prospect of democratic development in close cooperation with the West. And in the Soviet bloc itself a series of political crises in Eastern Europe—in Hungary, in Czechoslovakia—coupled with an ideological crisis brought on by Khrushchev's denunciation of Stalin's terror gave substance to the hope that communism might indeed mellow if only we showed sufficient patience and fortitude. While we felt under no compulsion to delude ourselves about the inherently antagonistic nature of communism, we were confident that the free world—which was not at that time bracketed in derogatory quotation marks—would ultimately prevail.

All things change, or seem to. The conditions on which rested American confidence and the Western alliance seemed to many to be undermined by their own success. This sense that solutions to the problems of the postwar period were being overtaken by events clearly is present in Arthur Schlesinger's comment on the alliance in his book *The Kennedy Years:*

By 1960 the economic dependence on the United States had largely disappeared. Western Europe had been growing twice as fast as America for a decade; it had been drawing gold reserves from America; it had been outproducing America in coal. Americans were flocking across the Atlantic to learn the secrets of the economic miracle. And, at the same time, the miltary dependence had taken new and perplexing forms. If the prospect of a Soviet invasion of Western Europe had ever been real, few Europeans believed it any longer. Moreover, the Soviet nuclear achievement, putting the United States for the first time in its history under the threat of devastating attack, had devalued the American deterrent in European eyes. These developments meant that the conditions which had given rise to the Marshall Plan and NATO were substantially gone. The new Europe would not be content to remain an economic or military satellite of America. The problem now was to work out the next phase in the Atlantic relationship.

The hopes and expectations of the postwar period, as we now remember, were finally destroyed by the protracted and bitterly disillusioning conflict in Vietnam and by a sequence of political, economic, and cultural shocks that polarized our society and shattered the confidence of our ruling elites. It is not necessary to review in detail this second period in the postwar era, which began with the full emergence of the New Left in the late 1960s and ended with the defeat of Jimmy Carter and the victory of Ronald Reagan in the last election. Let us simply recall the major points.

This period, which has euphemistically been called the era of détente, was marked by the relentless expansion of Soviet military and political power and a corresponding contraction of American military and political power. It was marked as well by the rise, in what came to be called the third world, of dictators espousing anti-American and anti-Western ideologies and by the rise in Western Europe of tendencies favoring a neutralist position in world affairs. Not least, this same period saw the emergence of OPEC as a major economic power whose monopoly pricing introduced inflationary shocks throughout the world economy—most disastrously in the very "third world" countries that were presumably linked by experience and ideology with the fraternal oil-producing states.

Within the United States, an attitude of defeatism, self-doubt, self-denigration, and self-delusion—an attitude that Solzhenitsyn called "the spirit of Munich"—displaced what had been a distinctly American optimism about the world and our prospects as a nation. For a time the proponents of defeatism cultivated an air of superior optimism. We had, so it was said, liberated ourselves from the fear of communism and were therefore free to identify with the "forces of change" that were sweeping the world. According to this point of view, it was futile to try to resist these forces, and it was reckless to do so as well since the effort to hold back the tides of change would bring the wrath of the world down upon our heads. Far better, it was said, to adopt an attitude of equanimity toward what only appeared to be the decline of American power but was in fact, in this view, a process of mature adjustment to reality. Such an attitude, in the words of a top official of the last administration, was really "a sign of growing American maturity in a complex world."

The seizure of the hostages in Iran and the Soviet invasion of Afghanistan destroyed this attitude of determined equanimity as completely as the events of the late 1960s had destroyed the hopes of the first postwar period. Looked at from this persepctive, the election of Ronald Reagan was a victory for those who rejected the idea of the inevitability of America's decline. In this respect, President Reagan's election was a watershed that marked the end to a period of retreat. Similarly, the president's inauguration—endowed with unique significance by the simultaneous release of our hostages, which closed out the most humiliating episode in our history—signaled a new beginning for America.

The new period we have now entered is, I believe, an exceedingly dangerous one—perhaps the most dangerous we have faced—and its outcome is far from clear. It is not only conceivable that an affluent and technologically advanced democratic civilization may succumb to one that is distinctly inferior in the wealth and well-being of its people. This has occurred more than once in history. The decisive factor in the rise and fall of nations is what Machiavélli called *virtu*, meaning vitality and a capacity for collective action. In the battle with totalitarianism, a free society has enormous advantages of which we are all well aware. But without the political will not merely to survive but to prevail, these advantages count for naught.

We have now entered a period when the moral and political will of our nation will be tested as never before. If I am hopeful that we can meet this test, it is because of the new situation that exists as a result of Ronald Reagan's victory in the last election, as well as because of the effective causes of that victory, and because certain changes in the world have created new opportunities for our country and its allies. Still, the challenges we must face are awesome, and it is by no means a foregone conclusion that we will prevail in the tests that lie ahead.

Probably no administration in American history faced problems of foreign policy as serious, as far-flung, and as difficult as those that confronted the government of Ronald Reagan when it assumed office last January. What are euphemistically termed East-West problems had spread and intensified, and so had those called (with equal oversimplification) North-South. Further, most of the intellectual tools we had used to approach world problems had proved inadequate and had to be discarded. The massive, unprecedented, unflagging Soviet military buildup had created what Soviet theoreticians describe as a "new world correlation of forces"—which, if it does not feature Soviet military superiority, unquestionably is characterized by rough parity. It is characterized, that is, by the end of U.S. and Western military superiority.

The meaning and significance of this new correlation of forces are found not in the painstaking estimates of missiles, throw weights, tanks, and MIRVs, but in an equally unprecedented Soviet foreign policy—more menacing to the independence and peace of others than at any time since Stalin moved to swallow neighboring states in the period of the Nazi-Soviet pact. We and our friends have been reluctant to acknowledge the extent, intensity, and violence of this Soviet challenge—doubtless because it is so very unpleasant to think about and poses problems so very difficult to manage, much less to resolve.

Northern and southern and central Africa, the Middle East and Asia, Central and South America and the Caribbean, have all in the past decade become targets of Soviet-sponsored efforts at destabilization and takeover. The functional scope of Soviet expansion has enlarged alongside its expanding geographical focus: sea lanes, strategic minerals, space, and culture have become operational objects of Soviet ambition.

Menacing as they have been, Soviet strength and aggressiveness are by no means the only important problems confronting the Reagan administration— though critics often accuse us of thinking so. North-South relations have also become more troubled.

In some of the less-developed countries, separatism and fundamentalism exacerbate the problems of nation building, making it more difficult to develop national identifications and political institutions, more difficult to maintain civic peace, stable boundaries, and regional order. In many of these countries low growth or no growth, soaring energy costs, and proliferating trade barriers frustrate dreams and plans, leaving bitterness in their wake.

It has been several decades since the expectation of progress was juxtaposed to the facts of stagnation and poverty. Resignation has given way to rage. The result is new demands, new reproaches, new rights claimed, new duties assigned, creating little growth but many hard feelings. The fact that "right" to development has been promulgated during the past year at the United Nations creates no new economic growth; it does, however, lay the foundation for newly felt entitlements and resentments.

Bad as they are, the problems of Soviet expansion and the problems of instability and poverty in what even I have come at the United Nations to call the third world are at least familiar, and both have been made more difficult still by the decline of American power. But what *really* complicates the policy problems of the Reagan administration is the obsolescence of the familiar theories that have been relied on to deal with the problems.

Just as the cold war and the accompanying doctrine of limited war succumbed to the Vietnam experience, several popular theories about Soviet goals and policies were similarly disproved by the Soviet invasion of Afghanistan—among them, the two doctrinal cornerstones of détente.

The first of these cornerstones was the expectation that the proliferation of economic and cultural ties and rewards would function as incentives to restrain Soviet expansion. The main concept behind détente was the "linkage" of the military, the economic, and the political. The idea, as explained by Henry Kissinger, was "to move forward on a very broad front on many issues" in order to create many "vested interests" on both sides. That was the theory. Under that theory, unprecedented incentives were developed; yet unprecedented aggression nonetheless occurred.

A second conceptual casualty of the Carter period was the theory that "weaker is stronger"—according to which U.S. military superiority constitutes a provocation, which stimulates countermeasures and overreaction by the Soviets, leading them to ever greater arms efforts. It followed, then, according to this argument, that U.S. "restraint" in military buildup would quiet Soviet suspicions and produce reciprocal restraint. One version of this theory—that arms, being provocative, cannot produce security—is still heard. But the basic argument that U.S. restraint in military buildup would be matched by Soviet restraint has been stilled, at least for the present, by the weight of recent experience.

A third, related popular theory—the stimulus-response, frustration-aggression theory—also has fallen victim to Soviet expansionism. According to this theory, the Soviet Union behaved aggressively because it was frustrated by a sense of insecurity deriving from its relative weakness, much as an adolescent may be provoked to rebellion by frustration deriving from a sense of impotence.

The solution to aggressive behavior, then, this theory argued, lay in creating a feeling of security by eliminating the impotence.

These theories are all examples of the mirror image approach to international relations, which assumes that all "superpowers," indeed all powers, are alike in fundamental respects, that their basic motives are peaceable and decent, and that undesirable or "bad" behavior is simply a reaction to some prior condition. Thus Soviet leaders desire not superiority but parity, not conquest but security, not power but safety.

This approach is nearly irresistible to an age and to a society like ours, which regularly deny the existence of evil and explain away its manifestations as a response of the weak to the strong. As there are no bad boys, so there are no bad governments. It is only necessary, the theory argues, to change the environment in order to alter the behavior. These theories not only rest on erroneous assumptions, but also nourish a spurious sense that it is possible to control one's adversary merely by altering one's own behavior.

Because their key assumptions are rooted in popular conceptions of human psychology and behavior, these theories have widespread appeal. A massive Soviet buildup and expansionist policies on a global scale were required to break their power—even temporarily.

The intellectual situation vis-à-vis problems of development closely parallels that concerning East-West relations. The problems of the less-developed nations persist and have grown worse, but it was clear by 1980 that the theories that have guided U.S. policies were utterly inadequate to cope with those problems.

Since World War II, when most of the new nations came into being, things have not, generally speaking, moved onward and upward, fulfilling dreams of inevitable historical progress. Polities have not become stronger and more democratic, nor economies more productive, nor societies more egalitarian and participatory. Moreover, the methods that had been widely relied on failed to produce the expected or desired results. National ownership, central planning, altruistic social incentives were all once believed to be better suited to the communal spirit of the third world. But they produced bureaucracy, stagnation, and decay instead of the anticipated economic development. Determinism, socialism, and utopianism have proved no better guides to development policy than the grand theories concerning "superpower" behavior proved in dealing with the Soviet Union. One important, I believe fundamental, reason that the foreign policy of the Reagan administration seems to many to lack a comprehensive doctrine is that this administration's policy is not postulated on these conventional assumptions. We have not postulated our policy on these conventional assumptions and theories because they have become depleted and been discarded. But if we have rejected those theories, where does that leave us? Where does it leave those of us who must devise policies and make decisions?

The answer, I believe, is that both our methods and our policies must be more respectful of historical experience and more pragmatic—while never confusing historical method with historicism or pragmatism with lack of principle.

In dealing with development, for example, respect for history means taking care to note what kinds of policies have actually promoted development, growth, and increased affluence in real societies, what kinds of policies have been associated with stagnation and chaos. In dealing with Soviet and Cuban behavior, we should also begin with the facts: facts of 85,000 Soviets troops in Afghanistan, of more than 35,000 Cuban troops in Africa, of Cuban arms, advisers, and ambitions in the Middle East and Central America, the fact of SS-20s in Europe, the fact that Soviet and Cuban armies function today in Ethiopa, Angola, Yemen, and elsewhere much like the Roman legions, which maintained the rule of a distant imperial power.

Finally, a new foreign policy must begin from the equally important, irreducible fact that the Soviet empire is decaying at its center, challenged above all by Poland's insistent demands for greater freedom and autonomy, and from the fact of the exhaustion of Marxism as an idelogy capable of motivating men and women. Above all, perhaps, a new foreign policy must begin from the irreducible fact that the United States has nonnegotiable goals and non-negotiable moral commitments—and that these require our support for self-determination and for national independence, for the nurturing of regional order, for the protection of freedom wherever it exists and, within the limits of our power, skill, and opportunities, its promotion where it does not yet exist.

That being the case—that is, thus being where we begin—how do we proceed? The answer must be, I think, very carefully—remembering always that we are an open society and must honor the imperatives of that society. Speaking to this point in a discussion of the United States and the West, the distinguished historian Herbert Muller offered this advice:

> It is, above all, an open society: open politically because of its democratic processes; open intellectually because nothing—no faith whatever—is immune to inquiry and criticism; open spiritually because it is never resigned, always resolved to keep working for a better future (even if by futile efforts to restore a mythical past); open, like all modern societies, because of the very technology that is tending to regiment and standardize its life, since this also assures continuous change; and open, there-fore (lest I sound too cheerful), to horrors as well as wonders such as men hardly dreamed of before our century. A sober conclusion is that every person had better keep his eyes and ears open, and his mind closed only on the essential principles of his freedom, dignity, and responsibility.

And that, I believe, is precisely what we are trying to do in the construction and administration of this nation's foreign policy.

# 7. William E. Odom
## *How to Handle Moscow*      March 1989

Have the foreign policy initiatives of Soviet President Mikhail Gorbachev made reassertionism obsolete? In "How to Handle Moscow," William Odom argues that it was precisely the reassertionist policies of the Reagan administration that forced Gorbachev to embark upon his radical departures in Soviet domestic and foreign policy. After reading Odom's essay, be sure you can articulate why he believes that "hardline policies don't hinder reform, they help." Odom, an analyst with the Hudson Institute, presents a reassertionist's assessment of the "lessons" of diplomacy that are to be learned from the Reagan experience.

Soviet-American relations were back in the limelight last week, with Secretary of State James Baker meeting Soviet Foreign Minister Eduard Shevardnadze in Vienna. There was talk of an early Bush-Gorbachev summit.

The mood is optimistic because of the indisputable liberalization in Soviet domestic and foreign policy. And most westerners believe that a continuation of this climate of warm and conciliatory East-West relations is essential if the liberal trends are to continue.

Before it is too late, we ought to reflect on the truth or falsity of this belief by asking a simple question: Which contributes most to liberal reform in the Soviet Union: East-West detente, or East-West military and economic competition?

The record suggests that competition, not military and economic detente, gives liberal reforms a better chance in Moscow. The conventional wisdom, of course, has been the contrary: Keeping up competition hurts reform-minded elements both within the Soviet Communist Party and among the wider circles of the Soviet intelligentsia.

Every major period of East-West detente has been hailed as a new opportunity for the "liberals," or "zapadniki," in Mosocw. Strangely, the liberals have not prospered in those periods. When detente developed in U.S.-Soviet relations in the early 1970s, the liberal elements did not flourish. Their repression, begun by Brezhnev in the 1960s, continued in the 1970s. The Soviet dissident movement was quietly being decimated during the high tide of the 1970s detente. At the same time, the extensive credits and technology flowing in from the West failed to stimulate economic reforms. Nor did they have the positive effect on economic performance that Soviet leaders anticipated.

When President Reagan called the Soviet Union an "evil empire," when he accelerated the American military buildup, when he persisted in reducing the flow of high technology to the Soviet Union, he was widely condemned by observers both in the United States and Western Europe. They were convinced that his policies would block all chances of liberal change in the Soviet Union in the 1980s. Yet today we are seeing remarkable developments wholly at odds with those expectations.

How are we to account for this apparent paradox? Is the timing of the Gorbachev phenomenon purely coincidental with Reagan's hardline policies?

Many of the glasnost voices we hear in the Soviet Union today suggest that the impact of Reagan's policies have been significant. They cite poor Soviet economic performance compared to western standards. In the military competition, while the Soviets produce more weapons, they have failed to close the qualitative gap in several key areas, and they worry about many new technologies appearing in the West. The Strategic Defense Initiative is only the most spectacular example. Stealth technology is another. Who would dispute the

American deployment of medium-range missiles in Europe made the INF Treaty possible? In the case of Afghanistan, would the Soviet Union be withdrawing if there had been little or no U.S. assistance to the insurgents?

The obvious way to resolve the paradox is to admit that the conventional wisdom is wrong. Could it be that detente tends to hurt the liberal reformers in Moscow while competition helps them? Curiously, the historical record suggests that liberal reforms in Russia come only in the wake of military defeats and foreign policy setbacks. It happened in the mid-19th century, after Russia was defeated in the Crimean War; at the beginning of the 20th century, when Russia lost a war to Japan; and toward the end of World War I, when the czarist regime collapsed and the provisional government promised to elect a constituent assembly. Today it seems to be happening for the first time in the Soviet period. This historical correlation between defeat and reform should prompt us to look for a causal relationship as well.

Moscow has suffered a serious military defeat in Afghanistan. The Soviet assertive campaign to prevent the deployment of NATO medium-range missiles failed outright. While the Soviet military has done suprisingly well in the quantitative arms race, out-building the West in numbers of weapons, it has done less well in the qualitative arms race—that is, in overcoming western technological advantage. With the Reagan military buildup, the Soviet leadership found itself up against another round of competition that placed even greater strains on the stagnant Soviet economy. At the same time, East-West economic interaction declined, reducing the ameliorating effect that western aid could have on poor Soviet industrial and scientific performance.

In these circumstances, it was possible for the voices of dissident economists to raise critical questions about the very viability of the centrally planned economy. It was possible for Gorbachev to tell his Politburo colleagues, "Comrades, there is no other way but glasnost and *perestroika.*"

Most of the conditions in the Soviet economy, in science, in public health care, in agriculture, and in other sectors being criticized vociferously today were extant 10 or 15 years ago. As early as 1962, the CIA released an estimate of Soviet economic performance that indicated virtually no growth. In 1973, Prof. Abram Bergson of Harvard pointed out the negative trends in Soviet "factor productivity," suggesting that the Soviet Union would have to find a "new growth model" to avoid stagnation.

One must ask why a Gorbachev-like reform program was not initiated in the early 1970s. Why today and not then? In fact, a modest program of political and economic revitalization was launched, but it fizzled quickly. In the political sphere, an exchange of party documents was announced in 1972. Traditionally, such an exchange had been used to purge the party, to stimulate its responsiveness, to root out localism and corruption. As Pravda said at the time, it was not to be a purely "technical affair" but rather a "principled political inspection of the party's ranks." An economic reform, creating "production associations" across ministerial lines, was begun about the same time.

Why did nothing significant come from the reform program? Why did the exchange of party documents turn out to be only a "technical affair"? Why has the same fate yet to befall Gorbachev's program? To answer these questions we must imagine ourselves attending Politburo meetings and try to emphathize with the political climate.

If Gorbachev had suddenly come to power in 1973 or 1974, and if he had proposed glasnost and perestroika, citing the same objective economic and social conditions as he does today, how would his colleagues have reacted?

They would have pointed to the trends in the international correlation of forces which were moving in Moscow's favor. The United States was losing the war in Vietnam. Washington had explicitly acknowledged the Soviet Union's superpower status and signed SALT I, a treaty giving the Soviet Union a significant advantage in strategic forces. The American defense budget was declining in real terms, a steady trend since 1968. At the same time, western credits and technology were flowing into the Soviet Union faster than the economy could absorb them effectively.

In light of all these positive developments, what arguments could a reformist general secretary have used? How could he have created a sense of crisis adequate to justify bold new moves such as taking KGB pressure off the dissidents and releasing some political prisoners? Could he have vetoed the Politburo's decision to exile Solzhenitsyn in 1974? Hardly. His opponents could have easily carried the day, probably laughing him into early retirement for having such a poor understanding of the ABCs of Marxism-Leninism.

The last two decades of experience with the Soviet Union throw into serious doubt the hypothesis that detente stimulates liberal reforms in the Soviet Union. The evidence suggests the contrary. The contrary hypothesis is explicit in George Kennan's famous "Mr. X" article in 1947, and it guided U.S. "containment policy" for at least two decades. We would have to contain Soviet power until a "mellowing" (Kennan's term) of Soviet domestic politics took place. Somewhere along the way, our original understanding became muddled.

What are the implications today? That we should return to the Cold War? That we should turn up the military, economic and ideological competition? Clearly that is not the answer. But neither is "pre-emptive" detente on all fronts. That will not help the liberal reformers in the Soviet Union. If the qualitative military competition is turned down too quickly, and if massive economic aid is provided before the central planning system is forced to give way to wide use of market pricing, the trends toward liberal reform will likely be throttled.

Political detente makes sense as long as it is reciprocal. Reducing tensions that justify large military forces in the Soviet mind makes sense. Taking advantage of relaxed Soviet censorship and the pent-up desire among Soviet citizens for more contacts with the West is probably wise. Even that, however, at some point may cause a xenophobic backlash. It must, therefore, be done with care.

Quantitative arms-control agreements, limiting numbers of weapons, makes sense as long as they do not lessen our security either in objective military terms or through their political side effects. They could, for example, have the political effect of making it difficult for us to maintain our military commitments to Europe. Gorbachev's promised unilateral troop and weapons reductions, announced at the United Nations General Assembly meeting, are to be welcomed. At root, however, they probably reflect Gorbachev's recognition that winning the quantitative race while losing the qualitative arms competition is not a Soviet advantage. There is no reason, therefore, to lessen the qualitative military competition or the regional political and military competition. That pressure helps the proponents of fundamental economic reforms in Moscow.

Economic detente makes sense only on conditions, the same conditions we make for developing countries with counterproductive domestic fiscal and monetary policies. To grant large credits to the Soviet Union before a fundamental change in the pricing system has occurred almost insures that the capital will be squandered. Denial on those terms is not punishment for Moscow. It is wise advice, and it gives the liberal reformers leverage they can exploit to help carry through fundamental changes.

A return to the undiscriminating detente policy of the 1970s is a sure formula for scuttling Gorbachev's program, a program that is already in trouble. Relief for consumers and the key military-industrial sectors through unconditional liberal credits and loosened technology controls can be exploited by the conservatives to reduce the sense of urgency, the belief that there is no other way than systemic reform. Military concessions in arms-control agreements or in regional competition afford the same advantges to Gorbachev's opponents.

If Gorbachev fails—and it will take miracles for him to deal effectively with such problems as the awakening national minorities' political aspirations—we should not be discouraged or thrown off course. We will have to keep up the competition for another decade until the reformers are given another chance. The forces of history are on their side, but we can delay their success by well-intentioned, premature abandonment of the competition.

---

# COMPREHENSION CHECKPOINT

What is the significance of the following?

detente
power maximizing
Manichean conflict
political will
Reagan Doctrine
extended containment
"the spirt of Munich"

linkage
"correlation of forces"
neoconservatives
glasnost
containment-plus
wars of national liberation
Carter's post–cold war
    foreign policy

mirror-imaging
Brezhnev Doctrine
RDF
perestroika
"weaker is stronger"

Can you answer the following questions?

1. How did the foreign policies of the early Carter and early Reagan administrations differ in the following areas: (1) US-Soviet relations, (2) arms control and disarmament, (3) human rights, (4) Third World development, (5) revolutionary movements and regimes in the Third World?

2. What does Kirkpatrick mean when she writes that the Soviet invasion of Afghanistan disproved three cornerstones of detente?

3. What evidence does Odum present in support of his answer to the following question: "Which contributes most to liberal reform in the Soviet Union: East-West detente, or East-West military and economic competition?"

## Tying Everything Together: Relating Worldviews to Particular Foreign Policy Issues

In Chapter 1, the crucial importance of worldviews in shaping perceptions of particular foreign policy issues was stressed repeatedly. Given your knowledge of reassertionism, you should now be able to articulate a reassertionist response to each of the items listed below.

1. How would a reassertionist respond to the following quotation and why?

Poverty, not communism, is the principal threat in the Third World. . . . [E]very Third World revolution is not a struggle between East and West. . . . [P]overty, hunger, and repression have caused many more revolutions than Moscow and Havana combined . . . the US has managed for decades to put itself on the side of repression, corruption, and privilege in these battles, and has inevitably been on the losing side.

—Senator Gary Hart, quoted in *South*, December 1984, p. 11.

2. How would a reassertionist respond to the following policy proposals?

- to normalize relations with North Vietnam
- to disinvest from South Africa
- to negotiate an end to the civil war in El Salvador
- to increase funds for the United Nations Development Program
- to call a joint conference with the Soviet union to seek a negotiated settlement in the Middle East
- to provide low interest rates to the Soviet Union in order to subsidize farm exports
- to stay out of civil wars in the Third World
- to withdraw troops from South Korea
- to cut economic aid to U.S. allies who abuse human rights
- to pressure Israel to accept a Palestinian State

As you proceed through the text, you should compare and contrast the worldviews presented on the basis of their structures and the scripts, metaphors, and stock nations and persons they contain. Which scripts, metaphors, stock nations, and stock persons stand out in the reassertionist worldview?

## For Further Consideration

*Periodicals and journals that contain reassertionist perspectives:* The American Spectator, Commentary, The National Interest, National Review, Orbis, Policy Review, The Washington Quarterly, The Washington Times.

*Leading reassertionist scholars, authors, leaders:* Colin Gary, Alexander Haig, Michael Ledeen, Richard Nixon, Soviet scholar Richard Pipes, Norman Podhoretz, Jeane Kirkpatrick, Walter Laqueur, Edward Luttwak, William Odom, Soviet scholar Adam Ulam, Charles Wolf.

*Leading reassertionist columnists:* Jeane Kirkpatrick, Charles Krauthammer, William Safire, George Will.

# FOR FURTHER READING

Bauer, P. T. "Western Guilt and Third World Poverty," *Commentary.* (January 1976), pp. 31–38. Bauer argues that people in the West should not feel guilty about poverty in the Third World; in fact, he argues that colonialism and contacts with the West have been beneficial to developing countries. According to Bauer, poverty in the developing areas stems not from colonialism, population pressures, or a lack of capital but from socialist governments, which prevent market forces and private entrepreneurship from flourishing.

Bauer, P. T. and B. S. Yamey. "Against the New Economic Order." *Commentary.* (April 1977), pp. 25–31. Bauer and Yamey present a neoconservative critique of the assumptions underlying the proposals for a New International Economic Order.

Bauer, P. T. and John O. Sullivan. "Foreign Aid for What." *Commentary.* (December 1978), pp. 41–48. Bauer and Sullivan argue that foreign aid "unleashes a host of repercussions, damaging to economic performance and development, which can easily outweigh the marginal effect of an inflow of subsidized resources." In addition to detailing the negative effects of aid in developing countries, Bauer and Sullivan also attack the reasons frequently given for extending aid in the first place—to foster economic development, to end poverty, to redistribute wealth, to provide restitution for past evils of colonialism and neglect, and to be liked. Bauer and Sullivan argue that foreign aid has attained none of these intentions of its donors.

Brzezinski, Zbigniew. *In Quest of National Security.* Boulder, CO: Westview Press, 1988. A collection of addresses drawn from the Carter and Reagan years. Brzezinski is more moderate than most of the reassertionists on the above list. If there is a category of moderate containment, which lies between reassertionism and neorealism, it is held by Brzezinski, Henry Kissinger, and Robert Tucker.

Haig, Alexander M., Jr. *Caveat: Realism, Reagan, and Foreign Policy.* New York: Macmillan, 1984. This book contains Haig's account of his efforts to set the Reagan administration upon a reassertionist course and the obstacles he ran into from Reagan's top domestic advisers.

Kirkpatrick, Jeane. *The Reagan Phenomenon.* Washington, DC: American Enterprise Institute, 1983. Essays on the theory and practice of Reagan's reassertionism both generally and in such issue areas as human rights, Central America, the United Nations, and southern Africa.

Nixon, Richard. *1999: Victory without War.* New York: Simon and Schuster, 1988. Nixon provides an assessment of Gorbachev and presents a set of foreign policy proposals for the last decade of the century.

Nixon, Richard. *The Real War.* New York: Warner Books, 1980. This statement of the reassertionist position at the end of the Carter presidency is now a classic.

Payne, James L. *The American Threat: National Security and Foreign Policy.* College Station, TX: Lytton Publishing Company, 1981. A readable exposition of the theoretical bases of reassertionism, especially the nature and determinants of credibility, prestige, and deterrence. The book contains a wealth of case studies.

Pipes, Richard. *Survival Is Not Enough: Soviet Realities and America's Future.* New York: Simon and Schuster, 1984. A leading Russian historian presents a re-assertionist treatment of the Soviet Union—the impact of Russian history upon the Soviet state, the nature of the Soviet system and the Soviet threat, the economic and political crises facing Soviet leaders in the early 1980s, and guidelines for policies that will turn the Soviet Union from a revolutionary to a more traditional great power.

Podhoretz, Norman. *The Present Danger: Do We Have the Will to Reverse the Decline of American Power?* New York: Simon and Schuster, 1980. This short book is perhaps the most powerful statement of the reassertionist worldview that has been written. A shortened version appeared under of the same title in the March 1980 issue of *Commentary* magazine, pp. 27–40.

Revel, Jean Francois. *Why Democracies Perish.* New York: Harper & Row, 1985. In this book, a distinguished French journalist explores the reasons why "[democratic] civilization should not only be deeply convinced that it deserves to be defeated, but that it should regale its friends and foes with reasons why defending itself would be immoral and, in any event, superfluous, useless, even dangerous." An abridged version of Revel's ideas appeared in the June 1984 issue of *Commentary* under the title, "Can the Democracies Survive?"

Wildavsky, Aaron (ed.). *Beyond Containment.* San Francisco: Institute for Contemporary Studies, 1983. A collection of largely reassertionist essays. See especially the selections by Wildavsky, Seabury, Singer, and Payne. Selection 5, Charles Wolf's "Extended Containment" was taken from this book.

## NOTES

1.  For a history and overview of the neoconservative movement, see Peter Steinfels' *The Neo-Conservatives* (New York: Simon and Schuster, 1979), especially Ch. 3, "What Neo-Conservatives Believe," and Dave Gotfried and Thomas Fleming, *The Conser-*

*vative Movement* (Boston: T. Wayne Publishers, 1988), especially Ch. 4, "Revolt of the Intellectuals: The Neo-Conservatives."

2. Richard Nixon, *The Real War* (New York: Warner Books, 1980), p. 280.
3. *Ibid.* pp. 2–3.
4. Carl Gershman makes many of these points in his "The Rise and Fall of the New Foreign Policy Establishment," *Commentary* (July 1980) pp. 13–24.
5. Nixon, *The Real War*, pp. 241–42.
6. Coral Bell, *The Reagan Paradox: American Foreign Policy in the 1980s* (New Brunswick, N J: Rutgers University Press, 1989).
7. The nature, tactics, and dimensions of such battles can be gleaned from Constantine C. Menges, *Inside the National Security Council: The True Story of the Making and Unmaking of Reagan's Foreign Policy* (New York: Simon and Schuster, 1988) and Bob Woodward, *Veil: The Secret Wars of the CIA, 1981–1987,* (New York: Simon and Schuster, 1987). On the difficulties of implementing a reassertionist foreign policy, see Aleander Haig, *Caveat: Realism, Reagan, and Foreign Policy* (London: Weidenfeld & Nicolson, 1984).
8. Jeane Kirkpatrick, "A Normal Country in a Normal Time," *The National Interest,* 21 (Fall 1990), p. 40.
9. For a discussion of the post–cold war foreign policy views of leading reassertionists, see John P. Judas, "Crackup on the Right," *The American Prospect*, Number 3 (Fall 1990), pp. 30–43, and Jay Wink, "The Neo-conservative Reconstruction," *Foreign Policy*, 73 (Winter, 1988–89), pp.135–53. See also the writings of reassertionists themselves, as in the symposium, "America's Purpose Now," which appeared in *The National Interest* (Fall 1990), Number 21, pp. 26–62.

# Chapter
## *4*

# Neorealism

*T*he neorealist response to the war in Vietnam drew heavily upon the realist components of cold war containment. Consequently, the central goal for neorealism was the maintenance of the global balance of power, and the potential threat to that balance was Soviet expansion. In contrast to reassertionists, the focus for neorealism was neither the containment of Communism nor the promotion of American values. It was, instead, the protection of vital geopolitical interests, namely, the security and independence of the great industrial states of Britain, Western Europe, and Japan.

This neorealist priority for interests over ideals did not stem from an indifference to American values and ideals. Rather, it was merely an acknowledgment that nations are reluctant to sacrifice treasure and lives merely to promote their ideals abroad. As the realist-theologian Reinhold Niebuhr put it over fifty years ago, "No nation is ever true to the cause which transcends its national life if there is not some coincidence between the defense necessities of that cause and the defense requirements of the national organization."[1] Thus, the United States committed itself to the defense of democracy and self-determination in Western Europe after World War II because the independence of that area was vital to maintaining the balance of power. On the other hand, realists believed that the American people would never go to war with the Soviet Union in order to secure those same values in Eastern Europe, an area of less importance to the world balance of power.

At the core of the debate between neorealists and reassertionists was their perception of the degree of continuity between the early postwar years and the post-Vietnam era. While reassertionists focused upon the continuities, neorealists emphasized the discontinuities. In so doing, neorealists rejected two fundamental tenets of reassertionism—the centrality of the Communist challenge and the *fragility* of the world balance of power.

In stark contrast to reassertionists, neorealists argued that our postwar policy of containment had been immensely successful and that the bipolar world of the 1940s had been replaced by a less controllable, but much safer, multipolar world. For neorealists, those countries that are vital for the balance of power, the developed countries of Western Europe and Japan, had become independent, democratic, prosperous, and stable. In addition, neorealists believed that NATO remained a viable alliance with all the deterrent power it needed.

On the other hand, neorealists believed that the Soviets had netted few gains from the vast process of decolonization that took place after World War II. From the fall of China through the late 1960s, only North Vietnam and Cuba joined the Soviet camp, and the latter case surprised the Soviets as much as the Americans. Of the Soviet and Cuban gains in the 1970s, neorealists saw little cause for alarm. In their opinion, the Soviets would find their new Third World clients as intractable, costly, and unreliable as American clients frequently were.

Neorealists also believed that, given their meager economic resources, the Soviets would soon find their newly gained clients turning to the developed countries of the West for trade, aid, investment, and consumer goods. Or, if their new clients did forsake the West, as Cuba did, the Soviets would soon feel the financial costs of supporting poor and economically unviable allies. Finally, while the reassertionist Norman Podhoretz lamented that Third World nationalism was "a frail reed for us to lean upon" in stopping Soviet expansion,[2] neorealists saw such nationalism as the Soviets' Achilles heel in the developing areas.

A second factor that shaped the neorealist worldview was the rise of polycentrism within the Communist camp, a trend predicted by Kennan and Morgenthau in the late 1940s and early 1950s. According to neorealists, the nonalignment of Yugoslavia and the Sino-Soviet split meant that Communist regimes, even if they obtained power with Soviet backing, would place national interests over ideology in their dealings with other nations. And for neorealists, trends in the Communist camp from the mid-1960s on only strengthened this conviction.

Communist Albania became the most anti-Soviet regime in Eastern Europe. Romania withdrew its military forces from the Warsaw Pact, and Communist party elites in other Eastern Europe countries sought greater freedom. After Communist Vietnam invaded Communist Cambodia, Communist China invaded Communist Vietnam as a punitive measure. In "Marxist-led" Angola, Cuban troops guarded American-owned oil installations from anti-Communist forces that were supported by the Reagan administration. For neorealists, the expansion of Communism would lead to the extinction of the Communist bloc.

Given the fragmentation of the Communist coalition, noerealists believed that the United States could be far more detached when facing wars of national liberation in Third World countries. National interests, not ideologies, neorealists argued, would determine the foreign policies of all regimes, even Communist ones. As Hans Morgenthau pointed out in the early 1950s, the threat to America consisted of Soviet imperialism and "phony revolution," as in Eastern Europe. Genuine revolutions, as in China or Vietnam, could be ignored.

Given these neorealist convictions, no one should have been surprised when President Carter made the following proclamation in his commencement address to the graduating class at the University of Notre Dame in May 1977: "Being confident of our own future, we are now free of the inordinate fear of

Communism which once led us to embrace any dictator who joined us in that fear. I'm glad that's being changed."[3]

Accepting the reassertionist tenet that "capitalism works and Communism doesn't," neorealists saw the economic strength of the industrialized democracies as a significant counter to Soviet influence in the Third World. While admitting that the Third World, as a whole, contained resources of vital significance for the industrial countries, neorealists also believed that only the developed countries could supply the capital and consumer goods that would enable Third World countries to grow and develop. While Soviet military assistance might place radical or Marxist governments in power, the Soviets could offer little in terms of advice or economic assistance that would enable their clients to develop and prosper. Thus, neorealists advocated elevating economic factors over military and ideological ones.

As President Carter's statement indicates, neorealists also sought to free America of one of the most undesirable legacies of the cold war containment era policies—our attachment to anti-Communist dictators who suppressed human rights and did little to alleviate the widespread poverty within their own countries. In fact, neorealists believed that American "defeats" in places like Vietnam, Ethiopia, and southern Africa stemmed largely from American support for racist regimes and right-wing dictatorships, which bred the very conditions that led to Communist insurrections. Blanket opposition to wars of liberation, neorealists argued, perpetually put the United States on the side of repressive regimes that made a mockery of the nation's commitment to freedom and self-determination.

To decrease this mockery, President Carter initiated a human rights policy that cut American assistance to allies who abused the rights of their subjects. He quickly found out, however, that it was much easier to cut ties with objectionable regimes than to promote our values in those countries.[4] But, at the very least, neorealists favored standing aside when civil wars began in developing countries and working with the ultimate winner.

Thus, on the issue of America's response to radical and Marxist regimes in the Third World, neorealists differed fundamentally from reassertionists. For neorealists, the Reagan administration's policy of opposing and seeking to roll back radical and Marxist regimes in Nicaragua, Ethiopia, and Angola was misconceived. Such a strategy, some neorealists argued, merely served to increase Soviet influence in such countries. The Irish scholar-diplomat Conor Cruise O'Brien expressed this view well in an address at Harvard University in 1987:

> Third World Marxist nationalists may have no choice but to gravitate toward Moscow. Any Third World nationalist movement that uses Marxist language incurs the automatic hostility of Washington, soon brought to bear in modern versions of excommunication and interdict. Isolated and under pressure from the West, such movements are liable to become dependent on Moscow—Cuba and Nicaragua are the most obvious examples. And then of course the dependence itself can be used as an argument justifying the policies of isolation that proclaimed the dependence in the first place.[5]

Finally, neorealists believed that new actors and new forces required a new foreign policy agenda for the nation. Third World nations were demanding a New International Economic Order. Economic competition and protectionism were growing among the developed countries. The United States was facing rising balance of payments and trade deficits. Serious regional conflicts existed in the Middle East and southern Africa. Hunger existed in much of Africa and parts of Asia. The nuclear arsenals of the superpowers were growing ominously, and fears of nuclear proliferation were increasing as more nations gained access to plutonium-powered nuclear reactors. Terrorism was becoming chronic. Alarming data were being gathered about the environment. Still, as large as the new agenda may have appeared, neorealists believed that its seriousness was nothing compared to the stark and ominous situation that existed at the end of World War II.

According to neorealists, the United States had successfully met the great challenge of the early postwar period. The balance of power had been restored, and the Communist camp had become hopelessly fragmented. America's nuclear arsenal provided a powerful deterrent to Soviet military aggression. The liberal, postwar international economic order had been successful beyond the dreams of its founders. And, by the mid-1980s, the Soviet model for economic development was in retreat everywhere.

Unlike cold war containment and reassertionism, neorealism is replete with categories and distinctions. Instead of Soviet-controlled countries, there are varieties of Communist countries with varieties of ties to the Soviet Union. Stark bipolarity is replaced with multipolarity. The regional and local origins of conflicts are separated from their East-West components. The Munich analogy and the domino metaphor are considered inappropriate for most of the problems facing the nation. Neorealists concluded that neither the United States nor the Soviet Union could influence significantly, let alone control, the vast variety of countries in the developing world.

As Richard Feinberg put it in 1983, the United States faced a "less controllable, but safer world."[6] America's containment and its decolonization policies had resulted in a pluralistic world with independent centers of power. For neorealists, the string of Soviet victories that reassertionists railed about were victories only at the margins of world power. Neorealists also weighed Soviet victories against Soviet losses in Asia, Africa, and the Middle East. After all, neorealists asked, was not China the biggest domino to fall? In terms of economic competition, neorealists argued that the Soviet union was hopelessly outmatched not merely by the United States but by Western Europe, Japan, and, increasingly, by Korea, Taiwan, Brazil, and Mexico. Neorealists called not for complacency, but for confidence and reassurance. While utopia had not arrived, neorealists believed that America could relax and pay more attention to a new agenda that had arisen from the success of its cold war policies.

Even though the cold war is over, most neorealists believe that their fundamental beliefs are as relevant to policy makers as ever. Given the increasing pluralism and general diffusion of power, neorealists now see even less necessity for the United States to tie itself to particular Third World regimes.

Therefore, they continue to favor doing business with regimes without regard to their domestic economic and political systems. Neorealists also favor America's abstinence from taking sides in regional conflicts.

Some neorealists now believe that the United States should take the lead in strengthening multilateral institutions such as the United Nations, while others favor a more noninterventionist policy. All agree, however, that the United States should work with the developed and developing countries to maintain the health of the liberal international economic order. In fact, some neorealists believe that economic interactions will increasingly replace traditional balance of power politics in the years ahead; thus, they favor foreign policies that insure the health of the international economic order and domestic policies that enhance the nation's economic competitiveness.[7]

# The Selections

## 8. Hans Morgenthau
### *U.S. Misadventure in Vietnam*                       1968

Neorealism had its intellectual roots in realist critiques of the war in Vietnam. This selection by Hans Morgenthau illustrates well the kinds of issues raised by realist opponents of the war. In developing his argument, Morgenthau draws upon the distinctions he made in Selection 4, "The Real Issue Between the United States and the Soviet Union." In Vietnam, he argues, the United States was containing neither Russian nor Chinese imperialism. In fact, he asserts that by fighting and weakening Vietnam, the United States was actually weakening a traditional barrier to Chinese imperialism. In this essay, Morgenthau underscores the neorealist view that nationalism is a far more potent force than ideology in international politics.

The policies the United States is pursuing in Vietnam are open to criticism on three grounds: they do not serve the interest of the United States; they run counter to American interests; and the United States objectives are not attainable, if they are attainable at all, without unreasonable moral liabilities and military risks.

In order to understand the rationale underlying our involvement in Southeast Asia one must go back to the spring of 1947 when the postwar policies of the United States were formulated and put into practice—the policy of containment, the Truman doctrine and the Marshall Plan. These policies pursued one single aim by different means: the containment of communism. That aim derived from two assumptions: the unlimited expansionism of the Soviet Union as a revolutionary power, and the monolithic direction and control the Soviet Union exerted over the world Communist movement.

These assumptions, in turn, were based on empirical evidence, i.e., the policies pursued by the Soviet Union at the end and in the immediate aftermath of the Second World War. The Red Army had advanced to a distance of 100 miles east of the Rhine, and behind that line of military demarcation the Soviet Union had reduced the nations of East Europe to the status of satellites. Nothing by way of material power stood in the way of the Red Army if it were intent on taking over the nations of West Europe, all of which had been drastically weakened by the war and in some of which, such as France and Italy, large Communist parties were ready to make common cause with the "liberators" from the East.

It was against this essentially traditional military threat that the United States policy of containment was devised. Thus it partook of the rationale which since the beginning of the Republic has informed the policies of the United States with regard to Europe: the maintenance or, if need be, the restoration of the balance of power. It was for this reason that the United States intervened in two world wars on the seemingly weaker side, and it was for the same reason that it embarked on the policy of containing the Soviet Union. The Truman doctrine, itself originally applied to a specific, geographically limited emergency concerning Greece and Turkey, transformed this traditional and geographically limited commitment into a general principle of universal application by stipulating that the United States would come to the assistance of any nation threatened by Communist aggression or subversion.

The Marshall Plan served the purpose of the policy of containment in that it tried to make the nations of West Europe immune from Communist subversion and strong enough collectively to withstand Soviet aggression by restoring them to economic health. The spectacular success of the Marshall Plan had intellectual and political consequences similar to those of the policy of containment. The rationale underlying the Marshall Plan evolved into a general principle of American statecraft to be applied anywhere in the form of foreign aid.

It is against this background that one must consider the involvement of the United States in Southeast Asia. For the modes of thought and action growing from the specific European experiences of the postwar period still dominate today the foreign policies of the United States, paradoxically enough not so much in Europe as elsewhere throughout the world. The Administration consistently justifies its Asian policies by analogy with its European experiences. The United States thinks of Asia in 1968 as it thought of Europe in 1947, and the successes of its European policies have become the curse of the policies the United States is pursuing in Asia. For the problems Americans are facing in Asia are utterly different from those they successfully dealt with in Europe two decades ago, and the political world they were facing in Europe has been radically transformed.

The active involvement of the United States in Southeast Asia is a response to the Korean War. That war was interpreted by the United States government as the opening shot in a military campaign for world conquest under the auspices of the Soviet Union. In view of this interpretation, it was consistent for the United States to defend South Korea against the North Korean Communists, as it would have defended Western Europe against the Red Army had it stepped over the 1945 line of demarcation. Similarly, it was consistent for the

United States to support with massive financial and material aid the French military effort to defeat the Vietnamese Communists. When France was threatened with defeat, in 1954, it was consistent for Secretary of State John Foster Dulles and Admiral Arthur Radford, then chairing the Joint Chiefs of Staff, to recommend that President Dwight Eisenhower intervene with American airpower on the side of France. Finally, it was a logical application of this policy of containing communism in Asia to establish and support an anti-Communist regime in South Vietnam, after the division of the country in 1954. However, when the disintegration of this regime became acute (roughly from 1960 onward), the United States continued this policy of containment as though the nature of world communism had not changed since 1950 and as though the political disintegration of South Vietnam posed for the United States an issue similar to the North Korean invasion of South Korea. It was at this point that our policy went astray.

While it was plausible—even though it has proven to be historically incorrect—to attribute the outbreak of the Korean War to a world-wide Communist conspiracy, there is no historical evidence whatsoever to interpret in that manner what has happened in Vietnam since 1960. The period of history since Nikita Khrushchev's denunciation of Joseph Stalin in 1956 has been characterized by the disintegration of the Communist bloc into its national components, each pursuing to a greater or lesser degree its own particular national policy within a common framework of Communist ideology and institutions. The influence that the Soviet Union and China are still able to exert over Communist governments and movements is not the automatic result of their common Communist character, but of the convergence of national interests and of particular power relations.

## COMMUNISM IN VIETNAM

This has always been true of the Vietnamese Communists. Many of them were nationalists before they became Communists, and it was only the indifference or hostility of the West that made them embrace communism. Even under the most unfavorable conditions of war with the United States, the government of North Vietnam has been able to retain a considerable measure of independence vis-à-vis both the Soviet Union and China by playing one off against the other. The Vietnamese Communists are not mere agents of either the Soviet Union or China. The sources of their strength and their aims are indigenous and must be judged on their own merits.

This being the case, the professed United States war aim, "to stop communism" in South Vietnam, reveals itself as an empty slogan. It must be made concrete by raising the questions: what kind of communism is the United States fighting in South Vietnam? and what is the relationship of that communism to the United States interest in containing the Soviet Union and China? The answers to these questions reveal the unsoundness of American policy. The fate of communism in South Vietnam is irrelevant to the containment of Soviet or

Chinese communism since Vietnamese communism is not controlled by either of them. The United States fight against the South Vietnamese Communists is relevant only to its relations with South Vietnam, which, even if she were governed by Communists, could not affect the balance of power in Asia.

The instruments the United States is using to achieve its aim in Vietnam are three: "counter-insurgency" and "nation-building" in the South, and the bombing of the North. These instruments have failed as they were bound to fail.

# COUNTER-INSURGENCY

It is to be held as an axiom, derived from the experience of many guerrilla wars, that a guerrilla war supported, or at least not actively opposed, by the indigenous population cannot be won, short of the physical destruction of that population. In the nature of things, the guerrilla is indistinguishable from the rest of the population, and in truth the very distinction is tenuous in a situation where the guerrilla is an organic element of the social and political structure. In such a situation, everyone is in a sense a potential guerrilla. The whole population is composed of full-time guerrillas, part-time guerrillas, auxiliaries who feed, clothe and hide the combatants, make arms, build hide-outs, and carry ammunition; only a minority is permanently passive or surreptitiously hostile to the guerrillas. What the United States is facing in South Vietnam is a primitive nation-in-arms, in a war which can be won only by incapacitating the total population.

It is for this reason that "pacification," repeated time and again for almost a decade under different names and auspices, has been a consistent failure. For it is based upon the misconception that the guerrillas are an alien element within the indigenous population, who therefore can be separated from that population by an appropriate technique. A Vietnamese village is pacified only when all the men capable of bearing arms are either dead or driven away and prevented from returning. The last condition is impossible to achieve. Thus many villages have been "pacified" time and again, only to fall back under guerrilla control when the military occupation was relaxed.

In Vietnam, what makes "counter-insurgency" so futile an undertaking is the difference between the motivation of the guerrillas and that of the professional army fighting them. No professional army could have withstood the punishment Americans have inflicted on the South Vietnamese guerrillas since the beginning of 1965. It is for this reason that United States military leaders have said repeatedly that the Viet Cong were on the verge of collapse, as they would have been were they professional soldiers. But, like the Spanish and Tyrolian guerrillas fighting the armies of Napoleon, they are fanatical protagonists of an ideal—social revolution or national survival or both—and they will die rather than admit defeat. Against them fights a professional army which does its duty efficiently as well as courageously and uses "counter-insurgency" as a mechanical contrivance, a particular kind of military tactic with which to fight "unorthodox" war. Howver, guerrilla war is not just "unorthodox" in the technical, tactical sense; but different in quality from traditional war; hence, it cannot be "won" in the traditional sense.

## THE POLITICAL WAR

The United States government recognizes implicitly the truth of this analysis when it maintains that there are two wars in South Vietnam—a military war and a political war—and that victory in the latter will be decisive. In order to win that political war, the United States has embarked on a massive program of political, social and economic reconstruction in South Vietnam. It is the purpose of that program to establish the government of South Vietnam as a new focus that will attract the loyalties of the large mass of South Vietnamese who are indifferent to either side, as well as the disenchanted supporters of the Viet Cong. This program is up against three obstacles which, in the aggregate, appear insurmountable.

First, the government of South Vietnam is a military government and has remained so in spite of the democratic gloss which carefully circumscribed and managed elections have tried to put on it. The foundation of the government's power is the army, both in terms of the administrative structure and of what there is of loyal support. Yet the army is regarded by large masses of the population not as the expression of the popular will but as its enemy. This is so because of the oppressive behavior of the army toward the peasants and, more particularly, because there is reportedly no officer in the South Vietnamese army above the rank of lieutenant colonel who did not fight on the side of the French against his own people.

Second, this impression of an army fighting against its own people is reinforced by the massive presence of foreign armed forces without whom neither that army nor the government it supports could survive. Regardless of professed and actual American intention, the United States military presence, with its destructive economic, social and moral results for South Vietnam, appears to an ever increasing number of South Vietnamese as an evil to be eliminated at any price. Thus our massive visible support for the government of South Vietnam, while indispensable and, in good measure, because it is indispensable, discredits that government in the eyes of the people of South Vietnam.

Finally, the hoped for radical change in political loyalties requires radical social, economic and political reforms, especially with regard to the distribution of land. The achievement of such reforms has indeed earned the Viet Cong the allegiance of large masses of peasants. Both in its composition and policies, the government of South Vietnam represents the interests of a small group of absentee land owners and members of the urban upper middle class who would lose their economic, social and political privileges were that government really trying to counter the social revolution of the Viet Cong with radical social reforms of its own. The United States is facing here the same dilemma which has frustrated its foreign aid policies throughout the world, more particularly in the

Alliance for Progress; it is trying to achieve radical social reforms through the instrumentality of governments which have a vital interest in the preservation of the status quo.

The universally recognized weaknesses of the government of South Vietnam—corruption, inefficiency, apathy, lack of public spirit, low military performance, a staggering desertion rate—result irremediably from the nature of that government. They are not to be remedied by American appeals to the South Vietnamese government to do more for the country or to let the South Vietnamese army take over a larger share of the fighting and pacification. A government imposed on an unwilling or at best indifferent people by a foreign power to defend the status quo against a national and social revolution is by dint of its very nature precluded from doing what Americans expect it to do. That nature dooms all efforts at politically effective reconstruction.

## BOMBING OF THE NORTH

The third policy the United States is pursuing in Vietnam is the bombing of the North, to win the war in the South by interdicting the influx of men and materiel from the North, and to force the government of North Vietnam to the conference table by making it too costly for it to continue the war. Both purposes derive from a faulty perception of reality. The United States assumes that what it faces in South Vietnam is the result of foreign aggression and that there would be no unmanageable trouble in the South if only, in Secretary of State Dean Rusk's often repeated phrase, North Vietnam would leave her neighbor alone. It follows logically from this assumption that internal peace could be restored to South Vietnam if one could insulate South Vietnam from the North or compel the North to cease her assistance to the South. However, this assumption does not square with historical reality.

## SOUTHERN ROOTS OF WAR

The roots of the trouble are in the South. They were deeply embedded in the nature of the Diem regime, which combined a fierce nationalism with a totalitarian defense of the economic and social status quo. Nobody doubts that the government of North Vietnam welcomed and aided and abetted the progressive disingetration of the Diem regime. But it did not cause it, nor was its support responsible for the Viet Cong's success. When, at the beginning of 1965, the government of South Vietnam was close to defeat at the hands of the Viet Cong, according to official estimates 90 per cent of the Viet Cong weapons were of American origin and the annual infiltration from the North amounted to no more than a few thousand men, mostly of Southern origin. Only a total of a few hundred were regulars of the North Vietnamese army.

Consequently, the war could not be won by bombing the North even if the bombing were more effective.

. . . [W]hat would happen [asks General Maxwell Taylor] if Hanoi were suddenly to disappear? Suppose everything of value in the North were destroyed; we would still have over 200,000 armed guerrillas in South Vietnam who would have to be accounted for in some way. For food they could live off the land without supplies from the North. If they avoided contact with large military forces, they could husband their weapons and ammunition stocks and maintain for a long time a low level of sustained depredations and terrorist activity. If they were determined to carry on the war, if their morale did not collapse at this disaster in the North, they could conceivably remain in action for the next ten years, or the next twenty years, and we might still be tied down by this vast guerrilla force.[1]

The situation would be no different if the government of North Vietnam were suddenly to collapse and to sign our peace terms on the dotted line. Who would impose these terms on the Viet Cong, who have not been defeated in the field and who continue to draw on the support or at least the indifference of large masses of the indigenous population?

It is precisely because we have been unable to win the war in the South that we continue to assume that the source of the war is in the North and that victory can be won by bombing the North. However, the day is close at hand when everything that appears to be worth bombing will have been bombed and the war in the South will still not be won. The next logical step will be the invasion of North Vietnam; for if North Vietnam is responsible for the war, then the conquest of North Vietnam will end the war. While it will not accomplish that end, it will conjure up the likelihood of a United States military confrontation with the Soviet union or China or both. The Soviet Union has assured the United States that it will not stand idly by while the government of North Vietnam is destroyed, and China has made it clear that she will intervene, as she did in the Korean War, when a hostile army approaches her frontiers.

## A LOSING ENTERPRISE

However, if the war in the South lasts long enough, the United States has a good chance of winning it. The United States is not likely to win the war in the traditional way by breaking the enemy's will to resist, but rather by killing so many enemies that there is no one left to resist. Killing in war has traditionally been a means to a psychological end. In this war, killing becomes an end in itself. The physical elimination of the enemy and victory become synonomous. Hence, the "body count," however fictitious in itself, is the sole measure of our success.

No civilized nation can wage such a war without suffering incalculable moral damage. This damage is particularly grave since the nation can realize no plausible military or political benefit which could justify this killing for killing's sake. And it is particularly painful for a nation like the United States—founded as a novel experiment in government, morally superior to those that preceded it—which has throughout its history thought of itself as performing a uniquely beneficial mission not only for itself but for all mankind.

Why, then, is the United States evidently resolved to continue fighting a war which appears politically aimless, militarily unpromising and morally dubious? The answer is to be found in the concern for American prestige. If the United States should leave Vietnam without having won a victory, so it is argued, the credibility of its commitments throughout the world would suffer. Communist revolutions throughout the world would be encouraged, and the reputation of American invincibility would be impaired.

## CONTAINING CHINA

Not only does the containment of Vietnamese communism not further the interests of the United States but, paradoxical as it may seem, it is even detrimental to those interests. The United States has a legitimate interest in the containment of China and its involvement in Vietnam is frequently explained in terms of this interest. But Vietnamese nationalism has been for a millenium a barrier to the expansion of Chinese power into Southeast Asia. There is no patriotic Vietnamese, North or South, Communist or non-Communist, Buddhist or Catholic, who does not regard China as the hereditary enemy of Vietnam. Yet to the degree that the United States weakens Vietnam as a national entity through the destruction of her human and material resources, it creates a political, military and social vacuum into which either the United States must move in virtual permanence or into which either the Soviet Union or China will move.

What about American prestige? Its decline because of the liquidation of United States involvement in Vietnam is a matter for speculation; its drastic decline by virtue of the involvement is a matter of fact. In the eyes of most of the world, the most powerful nation on earth is trying to force a nation of primitive peasants into submission by the massive use of all the modern means of mass destruction (with the exception of biological and nuclear weapons) and it is unable either to win or to liquidate that war. The champion of the "free world" is protecting the people of South Vietnam from communism by destroying them. And in the process, the world is moved closer and closer to an unwinnable war with China, if not to the cataclysm of nuclear war. This is the image which the United States presents today to most of the outside world; in consequence its prestige has never been so low.

If the United States were to liquidate the war, the damage to its prestige would at least in some measure be repaired. The United States would show that it is wise and strong enough to admit a mistake and correct it. The liquidation of the misadventure need not affect its future policies. Commitments are not entered into or honored by way of precedent, nor do precedents initiate revolutions. For better or for worse, history does not operate like the Supreme Court of the United States (and even the Supreme Court has been known to disregard precedent for reasons of principle and prudence).

What the argument about prestige really amounts to is a concern for the prestige not of the United States but of those who are responsible for its involvement in Vietnam. But those who are responsible for the straits in which the nation finds itself today should bear the consequences of their ideological blindness and political and military miscalculations. They ought not to ask the nation to suffer for their false pride.

## NOTE

1. *Responsibility and Response* (New York: Harper & Row, 1967), p. 38.

## 9. Jimmy Carter
   ### *Power for Humane Purposes*     May 1977

Jimmy Carter's commencement address to the 1977 graduating class at the University of Notre Dame presented the outlines of a post–cold war, neorealist foreign policy. According to Carter, "historical trends" had undercut two principles of America's postwar foreign policy—"a belief that Soviet expansion was almost inevitable but must be contained and the corresponding belief in the importance of an almost exclusive alliance among non-communist nations on both sides of the Atlantic." As you read this essay, look for evidence that Carter offers in support of his assertion.

    Carter's address was also a critique of Richard Nixon and Henry Kissinger's efforts to build a post-Vietnam foreign policy upon traditional balance of power conceptions that downplayed the promotion of American values and principles. Thus, in addition to making the kinds of distinctions among Communist regimes that Morgenthau makes in the previous selection, Carter sketches out a new foreign policy agenda that closely ties American interests to the promotion of our values on such issues as human rights, world hunger, and racism in southern Africa. However, Carter found that promoting American values abroad was extremely difficult. Later neorealists, in fact, almost completely drop this aspect of Carter's neorealism. Do you think they were wise in doing so?

. . . I want to speak to you today about the strands that connect our actions overseas with our essential character as a nation. I believe we can have a foreign policy that is democratic, that is based on fundamental values, and that uses power and influence, which we have, for humane purposes. We can also have a foreign policy that the American people both support and, for a change, know about and understand.

I have a quiet confidence in our own political system. Because we know that democracy works, we can reject the arguments of those rulers who deny human rights to their people.

We are confident that democracy's example will be compelling, and so we seek to bring that example closer to those from whom in the past few years we have been separated and who are not yet convinced about the advantages of our kind of life.

We are confident that the democratic methods are the most effective, and so we are not tempted to employ improper tactics here at home or abroad.

We are confident of our own strength, so we can seek substantial mutual reductions in the nuclear arms race. And we are confident of the good sense of American people, and so we let them share in the process of making foreign policy decisions. We can thus speak with the voices of 215 million, and not just of an isolated handful.

Democracy's great recent successes—in India, Portugal, Spain, Greece—show that our confidence in this system is not misplaced. Being confident of our own future, we are now free of that inordinate fear of communism which once led us to embrace any dictator who joined us in that fear. I'm glad that that's being changed.

For too many years, we've been willing to adopt the flawed and erroneous principles and tactics of our adversaries, sometimes abandoning our own values for theirs. We've fought fire with fire, never thinking that fire is better quenched with water. This approach failed, with Vietnam the best example of its intellectual and moral poverty. But through failure we have now found our way back to our own principles and values, and we have regained our lost confidence.

By the measure of history, our Nation's 200 years are very brief, and our rise to world eminence is briefer still. It dates from 1945, when Europe and the old international order lay in ruins. Before then, America was largely on the periphery of world affairs. But since then, we have inescapably been at the center of world affairs.

Our policy during this period was guided by two principles: a belief that Soviet expansion was almost inevitable but that it must be contained, and the corresponding belief in the importance of an almost exclusive alliance among non-Communist nations on both sides of the Atlantic. That system could not last forever unchanged. Historical trends have weakened its foundation. The unifying threat of conflict with the Soviet Union has become less intensive, even though the competition has become more extensive.

The Vietnamese war produced a profound moral crisis, sapping worldwide faith in our own policy and our system of life, a crisis of confidence made even more grave by the covert pessimism of some of our leaders.

In less than a generation, we've seen the world change dramatically. The daily lives and aspirations of most human beings have been transformed. Colonialism is nearly gone. A new sense of national identity now exists in almost 100 new countries that have been formed in the last generation. Knowledge has become more widespread. Aspirations are higher. As more people have been freed from traditional constraints, more have been determined to achieve, for the first time in their lives, social justice.

The world is still divided by ideological disputes, dominated by regional conflicts, and threatened by danger that we will not resolve the differences of race and wealth without violence or without drawing into combat the major military powers. We can no longer separate the traditional issues of war and peace from the new global questions of justice, equity, and human rights.

It is a new world, but America should not fear it. It is a new world, and we should help to shape it. It is a new world that calls for a new American foreign policy—a policy based on constant decency in its values and on optimism in our historical vision.

We can no longer have a policy solely for the industrial nations as the foundation of global stability, but we must respond to the new reality of a politically awakening world.

We can no longer expect that the other 150 nations will follow the dictates of the powerful, but we must continue—confidently—our efforts to inspire, to persuade, and to lead.

Our policy must reflect our belief that the world can hope for more than simple survival and our belief that dignity and freedom are fundamental spiritual requirements. Our policy must shape an international system that will last longer than secret deals.

We cannot make this kind of policy by manipulation. Our policy must be open; it must be candid; it must be one of constructive global involvement, resting on five cardinal principles.

I've tried to make these premises clear to the American people since last January. Let me review what we have been doing and discuss what we intend to do.

First, we have reaffirmed America's commitment to human rights as a fundamental tenet of our foreign policy. In ancestry, religion, color, place of origin, and cultural background, we Americans are as diverse a nation as the world has even seen. No common mystique of blood or soil unites us. What draws us together, perhaps more than anything else, is a belief in human freedom. We want the world to know that our Nation stands for more than financial prosperity.

This does not mean that we can conduct our foreign policy by rigid moral maxims. We live in a world that is imperfect and which will always be imperfect—a world that is complex and confused and which will always be complex and confused.

I understand fully the limits of moral suasion. We have no illusion that changes will come easily or soon. But I also believe that it is a mistake to undervalue the power of words and of the ideas that words embody. In our own history, that power has ranged from Thomas Paine's "Common Sense" to Martin Luther King, Jr.'s "I Have a Dream."

In the life of the human spirit, words *are* action, much more so than many of us may realize who live in countries where freedom of expression is taken for granted. The leaders of totalitarian nations understand this very well. The proof is that words are precisely the action for which dissidents in those countries are being persecuted.

Nonetheless, we can already see dramatic, worldwide advances in the protection of the individual from the arbitrary power of the state. For us to ignore this trend would be to lose influence and moral authority in the world. To lead it will be to regain the moral stature that we once had.

The great democracies are not free because we are strong and prosperous. I believe we are strong and influential and prosperous because we are free.

Throughout the world today, in free nations and in totalitarian countries as well, there is a preoccupation with the subject of human freedom, human rights. And I believe it is incumbent on us in this country to keep that discussion, that debate, that contention alive. No other country is as well-qualified as we to set an example. We have our own shortcomings and faults, and we should strive constantly and with courage to make sure that we are legitimately proud of what we have.

Second, we've moved deliberately to reinforce the bonds among our democracies. In our recent meetings in London, we agreed to widen our economic cooperation, to promote free trade, to strengthen the world's monetary system, to seek ways of avoiding nuclear proliferation. We prepared constructive proposals for the forthcoming meetings on North-South problems of poverty, development, and global well-being. And we agreed on joint efforts to reinforce and to modernize our common defense.

You may be interested in knowing that at this NATO meeting, for the first time in more than 25 years, all members are democracies. Even more important, all of us reaffirmed our basic optimism in the future of the democratic system. Our spirit of confidence is spreading. Together, our democracies can help to shape the wider architecture of global cooperation.

Third, we've moved to engage the Soviet Union in a joint effort to halt the strategic arms race. This race is not only dangerous, it's morally deplorable. We must put an end to it.

I know it will not be easy to reach agreements. Our goal is to be fair to both sides, to produce reciprocal stability, parity, and security. We desire a freeze on further modernization and production of weapons and a continuing, substantial reduction of strategic nuclear weapons as well. We want a comprehensive ban on all nuclear testing, a prohibition against all chemical warfare, no attack capability against space satellites, and arms limitations in the Indian Ocean.

We hope that we can take joint steps with all nations toward a final agreement eliminating nuclear weapons completely from our arsenals of death. We will persist in this effort.

Now, I believe in détente with the Soviet Union. To me it means progress toward peace. But the effects of détente should not be limited to our own two countries alone. We hope to persuade the Soviet Union that one country cannot impose its system of society upon another, either through direct military intervention or through the use of a client state's military force, as was the case with Cuban intervention in Angola.

Cooperation also implies obligation. We hope that the Soviet Union will join with us and other nations in playing a larger role in aiding the developing world, for common aid efforts will help us build a bridge of mutual confidence in one another.

Fourth, we are taking deliberate steps to improve the chances of lasting peace in the Middle East. Through wide-ranging consultation with leaders of the countries involved—Israel, Syria, Jordan, and Egypt—we have found some areas of agreement and some movement toward consensus. The negotiations must continue.

Through my own public comments, I've also tried to suggest a more flexible framework for the discussion of the three key issues which have so far been so intractable: the nature of a comprehensive peace—what is peace; what does it mean to the Israelis; what does it mean to their Arab neighbors; secondly, the relationship between security and borders—how can the dispute over border delineations be established and settled with a feeling of security on both sides; and the issue of the Palestinian homeland.

The historic friendship that the United States has with Israel is not dependent on domestic politics in either nation; it's derived from our common respect for human freedom and from a common search for permanent peace.

We will continue to promote a settlement which all of us need. Our own policy will not be affected by changes in leadership in any of the countries in the Middle East. Therefore, we expect Israel and her neighbors to continue to be bound by United Nations Resolutions 242 and 338, which they have previously accepted.

This may be the most propitious time for a geniune settlement since the beginning of the Arab-Israeli conflict almost 30 years ago. To let this opportunity pass could mean disaster not only for the Middle East but, perhaps, for the international political and economic order as well.

And fifth, we are attempting, even at the risk of some friction with our friends, to reduce the danger of nuclear proliferation and the worldwide spread of conventional weapons.

At the recent summit, we set in motion an international effort to determine the best ways of harnessing nuclear energy for peaceful use while reducing the risks that its products will be diverted to the making of explosives.

We've already completed a comprehensive review of our own policy on arms transfers. Competition in arms sales is inimical to peace and destructive of the economic development of the poorer countries.

We will, as a matter of national policy now in our country, seek to reduce the annual dollar volume of arms sales, to restrict the transfer of advanced weapons, and to reduce the extent of our coproduction arrangements about weapons with foreign states. And just as important, we are trying to get other nations, both free and otherwise, to join us in this effort.

But all of this that I've described is just the beginning. It's a beginning aimed towards a clear goal: to create a wider framework of international cooperation suited to the new and rapidly changing historical circumstances.

We will cooperate more closely with the new influential countries in Latin America, Africa, and Asia. We need their friendship and cooperation in a common effort as the structure of world power changes.

More than 100 years ago, Abraham Lincoln said that our Nation could not exist half slave and half free. We know a peaceful world cannot long exist one-third rich and two-thirds hungry.

Most nations share our faith that in the long run, expanded and equitable trade will best help the developing countries to help themselves. But the immediate problems of hunger, disease, illiteracy, and repression are here now.

The Western democracies, the OPEC nations, and the developed Communist countries can cooperate through existing international institutions in providing more effective aid. This is an excellent alternative to war.

We have a special need for cooperation and consultation with other nations in this hemisphere—to the north and to the south. We do not need another slogan. Although these are our close friends and neighbors, our links with them are the same links of equality that we forge for the rest of the world. We will be dealing with them as part of a new, worldwide mosaic of global, regional, and bilateral relations.

It's important that we make progress toward normalizing relations with the People's Republic of China. We see the American and Chinese relationship as a central element of our global policy and China as a key force for global peace. We wish to cooperate closely with the creative Chinese people on the problems that confront all mankind. And we hope to find a formula which can bridge some of the difficulties that still separate us.

Finally, let me say that we are committed to a peaceful resolution of the crisis in southern Africa. The time has come for the principle of majority rule to be the basis for political order, recognizing that in a democratic system the rights of the minority must also be protected.

To be peaceful, change must come promptly. The United States is determined to work together with our European allies and with the concerned African States to shape a congenial international framework for the rapid and progressive transformation of southern African society and to help protect it from unwarranted outside interference.

Let me conclude by summarizing: Our policy is based on an historical vision of America's role. Our policy is derived from a larger view of global change. Our policy is rooted in our moral values, which never change. Our policy is reinforced by our material wealth and by our military power. Our policy is designed to serve mankind. And it is a policy that I hope will make you proud to be Americans.

# 10. Tom Farer
## *Searching for Defeat*                           Fall 1980

As Carter pursued his post–cold war agenda, the Soviet Union pursued its massive arms buildup and supported the rise and consolidation of radical Marxist regimes in Angola, Mozambique, Vietnam, Laos, Cambodia, Southern Yemen, and Nicaragua. When the Soviets invaded Afghanistan, Carter placed Soviet-American relations at the top of his foreign policy agenda. He embargoed grain sales, withdrew the SALT II treaty from the Senate, initiated a military buildup, and announced his Carter Doctrine, which threatened the use of nuclear weapons, if necessary, to prevent the oil fields of the Middle East from falling into Soviet hands. Cold War II had begun.

In the fall of 1980, Tom Farer, a professor at Rutgers Law School and President of the Inter-American Commission on Human Rights, criticized Carter for returning to the cold war agenda and ending his policy of neorealism. Farer's "Searching for Defeat" was one of the first extensive academic presentations of the principles and assumptions of neorealism. As you read this essay, be sure you can articulate why Farer's principles and assumptions led him to criticize Carter's policies in regard to Iran, Nicaragua, and Ethiopia. Also, do you agree with Farer's criticism that Carter was not neorealist enough?

From the beginning of the Cold War until Jimmy Carter arrived in Washington, the United States had a lucid, coherent policy toward the Third World, one that gradually dissipated U.S. influence there and poisoned American politics.

It was characterized by a view of the Third World as an arena of unremitting competition between the United States and the Soviet Union, and of Third World governments and people as pawns on the global chessboard. For Washington, the policy had two corollaries: first, a compelling preference for regimes that identified themselves strategically and ideologically with the United States; second, a willingness to use all the instruments of foreign policy, including force, to install and, in particular, to perpetuate such regimes.

The policy enjoyed a totalitarian grip on the hearts and minds of the American public and the foreign policy establishment. It governed the interpretation of domestic and interstate conflict, placing a Chinese, Russian, or Cuban hand behind every threat to friendly regimes and minimizing local sources of discord. It governed moral and intellectual perceptions as well. Complaisant although no doubt sincere academics elaborated the useful distinction between merely authoritarian and totalitarian regimes, and then assumed a morally anodyne equation between the former and governments that extolled capitalism and liquidated communists.

Virtually without dissent from within the grand salon of respectable opinion, the United States extended containment from its initial European venue to the entire world. There was, of course, one critical and ultimately decisive difference between the two cases. In Europe containment meant protecting well-integrated national states and consensual systems of government against alien occupation. In the Third World, however, containment could easily entail assisting one faction within a country—possibly a very ugly one—against another. Any moral qualms about a U.S. policy that called for perpetuating not a system of government but rather particular governments were eased by the comfortably paranoid assumption that Soviet, Chinese, or Cuban agents lay behind any violent threat to the status quo.

Until Vietnam, most Americans—leaders and followers alike—considered this a fine way to conduct relations with the Third World. Among other nice things it reinforced traditional sensations of U.S. omnipotence. At little apparent cost, Washington restored Shah Mohammad Reza Pahlavi to power in 1953 by helping him depose a difficult nationalist government whose political and ideological descendants the United States would love to see in power today.

Washington also extinguished a threateningly reformist government in Guatemala in 1954 and imposed a pliable tool of Western interests on the former Belgian Congo. U.S. trained and armed troops hunted down and killed Cuba's revolutionary hero, Che Guevara, in Bolivia in 1967, and crushed opposition to U.S. supported governments everywhere else in Latin America, except Cuba. Cuban exceptionalism was particularly rankling, a cruel thorn piercing the American psyche.

America's involvement in Vietnam emerged ineluctably from the womb of this policy and underlined its legal gimcrack, its moral blemishes, and its material and strategic costs. The consensus unraveled, but the policy lingered on until the mid-1970s as Secretary of State Henry Kissinger and his two presidential accomplices ordered the bombing and invasion of Cambodia, encouraged and then rewarded—with a conspicuous program of economic aid—a coup against democracy in Chile, and attempted to organize compliant anticommunist governments for Angola and Zimbabwe.

## ALTERNATIVE APPROACH

Trapped in a maze of unresolved, perhaps unrecognized contradictions, Carter himself cound neither express nor consistently implement a coherent alternative to the pre-existing orthodoxy. But he did mark a watershed in policy—foreshadowed during the Kissinger years by such congressional action as the so-called Clark Amendment that ended U.S. intervention in Angola—by bringing advocates of a consistent, alternative approach to the Third World from the shadowy frontiers of respectability into the center of power.

Supported by former Secretary of State Cyrus Vance and eccentrically personified by Andrew Young, former U.S. ambassador to the United Nations, the alternative sprang from a set of assumptions at odds with those that had guided the enthusiasts of global containment. Those assumptions were:

- that threats to the status quo in and among Third World states usually spring from volatile political, social, and economic conditions that exist independently of the Soviet-American competition;
- that transnational ideological commitments tend to be thin, inevitably subordinate to personal, group, and national interests;
- that, on the one hand, the terrible problems of economic growth and distribution and, on the other, the industrial democracies' overwhelming advantage in the deployment of markets, capital, and technology give the United States and its allies an enormous edge in East-West competition for influence in Third World states, including those run by ostensible Marxists;
- that national imperatives require Third World governments to distribute their resources through international markets;
- that the Soviet Union cannot permanently integrate Third World states into its strategic and economic system without conquering and occupying them;

- that most Third World states are of only trivial significance to the East-West strategic balance;
- that the costs of maintaining Third World regimes in power are generally disproportionate to the potential gains;
- that the costs of armed intervention either to promote or frustrate political change are high because the capacity of Third World states to resist coercion is increasing;
- that the costs of a diplomacy that relies heavily on the threat and use of force will seriously aggravate the economic difficulties and social tensions already shaking America;
- that quite independently of East-West competition, the promotion of important U.S. national interests—such as expanding markets for American exports, assuring the stable flow of essential raw materials and the development of new sources, and halting the spread of nuclear weapons—requires forms and degrees of cooperation from Third World states inconsistent with a swaggering, violent diplomacy;
- that ideas and values have material consequences and that the complex of values incorporated in the major human rights texts will therefore play a crucial orienting role for the generation coming of age in the Third World, as well as for elites in the West; and
- that the regnant image of the United States as an opponent of major Third World blocs on issues of central importance to them limits the scope of present and potential cooperation along the whole range of international issues.

Of the cluster of policies spawned by these assumptions, four stand out. First, except in very special cases, the United States would no longer equate its interests with the survival of particular regimes or automatically intervene to preserve right-wing regimes against domestic opponents, even those flaunting Marxist rhetoric and Soviet guns. Second, it would be cooler to regimes that grossly violate human rights, and it would refuse to overlook those violations simply because a regime was anticommunist.

Third, it would establish businesslike, cooperative relations with regimes of the left willing to practice nonalignment on strategic issues and to conduct their economic affairs in a manner that does not discriminate against the West. Fourth, it would treat Third World states as legitimate and significant negotiating partners in the management of the international political and economic systems and would trade balanced concessions rather than seek unilateral advantages by threatening to use force.

## THE NEW DIPLOMACY—NEOREALISM

While logically dictating a broad reorientation of policy, the assumptions—neorealism—left open profoundly contentious questions. The administration was not writing on an empty slate. Having long identified with specific, sometimes brutal regimes, how could Washington distance itself and occupy the high ground of human rights without actively assisting in undermining former intimates? And how would Washington handle relations with unpalatable regimes whose countries possessed assets genuinely important to America if the very process of violent change might endanger U.S. interests?

In the case of the member states of the Organization of Petroleum Exporting Countries (OPEC), was there any basis for accommodation not entailing very damaging American consessions? Did it then follow that an effective diplomacy might still require background indications of the will to employ coercion where other means failed?

And what would Washington do if the Kremlin adopted a high-profile interventionary diplomacy at the very moment the United Staes was relinquishing it? To encourage Soviet acceptance of low-profle competition, should the United States practice linkage politics, using trade and technology as carrots and sticks? Or could the policy ever work unless the United States were prepared to treat the Soviet Union as a legitimate and equal participant in managing global issues?

In other words, even in the case of a president personally convinced of their truth, the assumptions behind the new diplomacy left a vast, poorly explored space for creative diplomacy or fatuous fumbling. However well he coped, such a president could anticipate venomous political resistance from the densely clustered forces committed by reason of interest, emotion, or intellectual conviction to the old way of doing business in the Third World.

This resistance would be reinforced and focused by influential actors and groups who found their very particular oxen in danger of goring. Among those groups were beneficiaries of the former shah's largess, business and social cronies of former Nicaraguan President Anastasio Somoza Debayle, investors dependent on the survival of repressive regimes, industrialists specializing in certain lines of weaponry, members of the operations section of the Central Intelligence Agency, and certain ethnic constituencies.

Yet Carter never fully accepted the assumptions of the new diplomacy. Much of the president's apparent ineptitude is attributable to this uncertainty. Oscillation among premises was an understandable response to the powerful currents of domestic opinion pulling against the new diplomacy: to the dreadful uncertainties surrounding any set of foreign policies; to the Nixon administration heritage of reliance on regional hegemonies to safeguard Western interests; and to a Soviet Union able and apparently willing to follow or even enlarge the pattern of intervention woven by the United States during the preceding decades.

## DISTINGUISHING LOSSES FROM DEFEATS

A great chorus now proclaims the failure of Carter's foreign policy. Although persons of every ideological hue have enjoyed a good sneer over the president's tactical fumblings, the main burden of his prosecution is carried by characters ranging from the political center to the far right. Despite their differences on domestic issues, the members of this group are working together to drive the foreign policy of the United States back to global containment of the Soviet Union.

The message at its crudest is propagated by the man who the Rebublicans hope will lead their posse to the White House. The Soviets, Ronald Reagan reiterates without blinking, are the true authors of every disagreeable challenge to the status quo. To ignore any challenge to the status quo is to encourage the Kremlin to additional provocations.

Many more cerebral critics concede that Western interests may be threatened by forces independent of the Soviet Union, most notably by Arab oil producers. But the whole chorus, from the crudest charlatan to the subtlest intellect, unites around two grand themes: the need to back diplomacy with conspicuous threats of force and the need to sustain friendly regimes against all comers. By sharply discounting the efficacy of force and failing to back friends, they argue, Carter has dragged the country to the brink of a full-fledged calamity.

In essence, conservatives claim that Carter embraced neorealism, that the doctrine is equivalent to appeasement, and that by failing to practice a muscular diplomacy, the president has strung together a series of national defeats. The record shows, however, that Carter never resolved his ambivalence about neorealism and that its implementation is not necessarily passive or placatory. Moreover, practically all the defeats invoked by the accusers either were not defeats in any useful sense of the word or could not have been averted at any reasonable price by the use of force. Three of the most frequently cited examples—Iran, Nicaragua, and Ethiopia—illustrate nicely the void in the center of the conservative brief.

## Iran

Could a president weaned on the wit and wisdom of the late General George Patton have, unlike Carter, preserved our Pahlavian asset? In order to think about Iran with some measure of rationality, it is necessary to begin by distinguishing losses from defeats. If some extraordinary natural convulsion, such as an earthquake, devastated the oil fields of the Persian Gulf, Americans would speak of a terrible loss, but not of defeat. For defeat implies human provenance. And in the case of a superpower, it also suggests results that prudent measures might have averted.

A social eruption of incredible force and remarkable spontaneity deposed the late shah. The Ayatollah Ruhollah Khomeini and his entourage cheered and exhorted the Iranian people and improvised tactics. But ultimately, historical forces, not any one man or group, drew hundreds of thousands, finally millions of unarmed citizens into the streets to face down the shah's massed troops.

The strength and depth of this movement seem to have stunned even the shah's most frenzied American supporters. They have drawn dubious if not perverse lines of causation between Carter's tremulous appeals for human rights and the shah's eclipse. They have muttered darkly about Carterian plots to restrain the Iranian military from a last-minute restoration coup. But virtually no one has suggested that the United States should have intervened to preserve the Peacock Throne. For even the hard-liners recognize the horrendous costs and probable futility of any intervention in the face of that volcanic eruption against Pahlavi rule.

The sheer material costs of occupying a country with 35 million highly politicized people are intimidating enough. Yet even those costs might seem minor compared to the impact on American military morale, on the elementary cohesion of American society, and on the moral basis of the Western alliance. This explains why the shah's allies in the United States are reduced to cravenly vague arraignments of American policy.

But did the United States have to be so adversely affected by the shah's fall? It did not if the president had moved early in his administration to put U.S.-Iranian relations on a footing of cool, pragmatic cooperation between states with overlapping geopolitical interests. Instead, persuaded by the geopoliticians among his advisers of the shah's indispensability to the stability of the Persian Gulf, Carter brushed aside his human rights policy and proceeded to court the shah with a passion unequaled by his predecessors.

Iran was an irreversible phenomenon transformed into defeat by a president clinging, albeit without much conviction, to the premises of global containment. The United States is still paying the price for his choice and will likely continue to do so for years.

## Nicaragua

In Nicaragua, Carter—unlike the donkey in the Calvinist parable who, paralyzed by indecision, starved to death between equally succulent, equidistant bales of hay—oscillated, nibbling now at one set of premises, now at the other and often, it seemed, just wandering about dreamily.

The country's strategic insignificance, the Somoza regime's notorious marriage of cruelty and venality, and American responsibility for its birth and longevity made Nicaragua a prime target for the application of Carter's new deal on human rights. But unwilling to face the prospect of a government installed and dominated by the Sandinista guerrilla groups, Carter futilely attempted with dwarf carrots and brittle sticks to move the dictator toward reform. While Washington danced attendance on Somoza's canny maneuvers, the guerrillas catalyzed a massive popular rebellion that toppled the old order after roughly a year of bloody conflict.

Was this a defeat? In two of the senses suggested by political scientist Robert Tucker it was: The United States did not want and tried to prevent the eventual outcome; and others in the hemisphere and beyond perceived that outcome to be a U.S. defeat and an indication of a weakened U.S. position in Central America and the Caribbean.

How might defeat have been avoided? The administration might have thrown its support behind Somoza as soon as it became apparent that he was in serious trouble. An unequivocal commitment to his survival backed by a flow of weapons and military advisers might well have saved the dictator, particularly if U.S. political pressure had led other states in the region such as Panama and Cost Rica to deny arms and sanctuary to the opposition. Still, the isolation of Somoza and the desperate fury of his opponents might finally have required direct U.S. intervention to avert his collapse.

Conversely, Carter might have raced to the front of the anti-Somoza parade with an unambiguous commitment to his removal. Carter could have suspended diplomatic relations pending the formation of a representative government and declared that the people of Nicaragua by their collective resistance had withdrawn the regime's mandate to rule. Then he might have cheered from the sidelines until Somoza fled, and thus converted the appearance of defeat into one of victory. By so strong a commitment, he might in addition have precipitated an earlier loss of nerve in the Somoza camp and thereby saved Nicaragua from the final battles that cost 20,000 lives and completed the country's physical devastation.

## Ethiopia

In the early and middle years of the last decade, hard-liners on foreign policy—some of whom are now Reagan advisers—trumpeted alarms about Soviet air and naval facilities in Somalia that were said to threaten Western oil routes. The Soviet Union lost those facilities in 1977 because it opposed Somali irredentist claims to the Ogaden region of Ethiopa, which is inhabited by ethnic Somalis. Yet the same experts then announced another American defeat. For when they broke with Somalia, the Soviets embraced revolutionary Ethiopia, a strong American ally until the fall of Emperor Haile Selassie in 1974. Washington is now free to negotiate its own way into the Somali facilities for a fraction of what they cost the Soviet Union, while Moscow must spend hundreds of millions of dollars to protect its investment in Ethiopia, a country in constant danger of flying apart.

Whatever Ethiopia may be worth to the Soviet union—which is largely excluded from effective influence in almost all other significant African states—the price the United States would have had to pay to compete for influence there was grossly disproportionate to the potential gains. With the province of Eritrea on the brink of winning its war of secession and Somali armies poised to smash into Ethiopia's eastern flank, Haile Mariam Mengistu, Ethiopia's strong man, needed more from Washington than a gargantuan transfer of arms rivaling the $2 billion worth ultimately dispatched by the Kremlin. He needed more than petrol, oil, lubricants, and a small army of technicians to keep transferred equipment functioning. For a brief but crucial moment, he needed what the Cubans provided: pilots and shock troops who would hold off the Somalis and the Eritrean freedom fighters until he could marshall and deploy Ethiopia's superior manpower. And had the United States committed itself to the Ethiopian revolution by providing such massive military aid, could it then have denied Ethiopia the immense additional resources required for reconstruction and economic transformation?

Great costs were compounded by serious risks. U.S. prestige would have been tied to a small clique of officers dominated by Mengistu, who rose to his position on a pile of corpses, favored methods of social transformation likely to infuriate both conservative and liberal opinion in the United States, opposed civilian rule, and lacked an established base in any large sector of the population. Meanwhile, the Soviet Union would have remained ensconced in its Somali facilities, more secure than ever in a country now ferociously antagonistic to the United States for snatching victory from its grasp.

## POSITIVE DEVELOPMENTS

What then could people possibly mean when they speak of Ethiopia as an American defeat? In essence, they are saying that the Soviets are there in force while the United States would prefer that they were not. Thus in their view, an American defeat occurs whenever and wherever the Soviet Union intrudes against U.S. wishes, no matter what the costs of the intervention are in proportion to the gains, or what the costs of blocking the Soviets are in proportion to the potential rewards.

But this definition of defeat works both ways. If deviation from an idealized world is the measure of defeat, the Kremlin tastes it every day. For the West exerts its power and influence all over the world, a condition the Kremlin would no doubt change if only wishes could be realized without cost. The refusal to bid for overvalued assets was a triumph of strategic restraint, just as the fall of Somoza was a triumph for human rights. But according to the theology of global containment, an enemy of Moscow must be a friend of Washington, and violence practiced by opponents of left-wing states is, by definition, defensive.

These cases, which are among those most commonly cited by critics of the new diplomacy, belie the claims that the United States has experienced calamitous losses that could have been averted by an armed defense of the status quo.

Because the doctrine of global containment was ascendant throughout the 1960s and had already begun to recede in the early 1970s, one way to assess its merits is to compare the relative position of the Western alliance and the Soviet Union at the end of the 1960s with their relative positions today.

In the Western Hemisphere the situation is essentially unaltered. Almost all Latin American states and all of the major ones—including Colombia, Mexico, Venezuela, Brazil, and Argentina—remain conservative capitalist countries. Chile drifted to the left but was brutally dragged back to the right. Among the smaller states, Nicaragua has acquired a government of the left. However, it evinces no desire to follow Cuba into the Communist bloc, and the Soviet Union appears neither to anticipate nor to encourage actively such a development. Grenada with its young, mercurial government is both inconsequential and co-optable.

Moreover, there have been at least two very postive developments for the Western alliance. One is the discovery of huge, additional oil reserves here in the Western Hemisphere and hence far from the reach of Soviet power or Arab-Israeli fallout. Another is the growing capacity and will of states such as Mexico and Brazil to serve as influential actors elsewhere in the Third World. Whatever problems may exist between them and the United States, by interest and ideology they are U.S. allies on issues of first importance to East-West competition. Thus, for example, while Washington petulantly excludes itself from an active role in Angola, Brazilian diplomats encourage Angola's integration into the international capitalist system.

In sub-Saharan Africa, the West continues to enjoy economic and political pre-eminence and to absorb virtually all of the continent's mineral exports. The jury is still out on the net advantage of trading Somalia for Ethiopia. Soviet influence has decreased perceptibly in Guinea and has increased in the Congo and Angola. But the Marxist-sounding regimes of Angola and Mozambique (which has always been closer to China than to the Soviet Union) openly yearn for Western investment, and the former would apparently prefer to follow a wholly nonaligned foreign policy if it could resolve its internal difficulties. The settlement in Zimbabwe opens up that country's resources for accelerated development by Western capital. And the emergence of Nigeria as a leading oil producer experiencing rapid growth with a liberal economic model and a democratic system is a gain for Western interests.

## DEVASTATING BLOWS TO THE SOVIETS

The most important changes over the past decade have occurred in the Middle East and Asia. Egypt, by far the most important Arab country in cultural and military terms, has moved in one decade from being a virtual Soviet dependency to being one of the Third World states that is most completely integrated into the strategic and economic systems of the Western alliance. Ten years ago it sheltered the Soviet Mediterranean fleet. Today its ports and airfields and apparently even its armed forces are available to the United States for a whole range of missions, including regional intervention on behalf of friendly regimes. With Egypt's withdrawal from the Arab coalition, Israel is freer to deploy force on behalf of Western interests. These developments along with Iraq's increasing coolness toward Moscow have been devastating blows to the Soviet position.

The fall of the shah was a setback for the United States, but it was not necessarily a victory for the Soviets. Moscow enjoyed a substantial economic relationship with the shah's Iran. His successors interruptued natural gas deliveries and harshly denounced Moscow after the invasion of Afghanistan. For all the shah's grandiloquent claims, his troops were not a serious obstacle to a direct Soviet thrust against the Persian Gulf. And although successive U.S. administrations were blind to the danger, the shah's commitment to protect the gulf from revolutionary forces was as likely to precipitate a destructive conflict as to insure stability.

Asia has been the scene of three strategically important developments over the past decade: American withdrawal from the Indochina war; the emergence of India as a guarantor of a relatively decent order in South Asia and, by virtue of its enhanced national power and its amiable diplomatic relations with the Soviet Union, as a solid barrier to Soviet penetration of the region; and the transformation of relations between China and the United States.

Critics of neorealism accurately record a sharp decline in the coercive power and prestige of the United States over the past decade. They err only in assessing the causes and larger strategic consequences of that decline.

American power has declined relative to other participants in the international capitalist economic system—not only advanced industrial nations but also Third World countries such as Brazil, Mexico, Venezuela, Nigeria, and India. The enrichment of their human and material resources strengthens the system with favorable consequences for all participants, including the United States. Their strength and political maturity is the fruition of policies initiated years ago by the fathers of global containment. Restraints on American autonomy were always the foreseeable price. The United States is less powerful, but the system from which its wealth and security now spring is stronger.

The decline of U.S. military power relative to the Soviet Union is a less benign development. Globalists could argue that a president, passionately selling global containment to the American people, might have convinced them to support higher defense expenditures. However, advocates of the new diplomacy could argue that global containment's monster child, the Vietnam war, destroyed public support for an escalating budget by sowing cynicism and mutilating the U.S. economy.

The more credible position lies with the advocates of the new diplomacy. But it is only a polemical side show to the central question of whether the unavoidable enhancement of Soviet military power has been translated into major strategic gains, as most hard-liners allege. The only possible answer is that it has not. The Soviet Union has lost a few facilities here, gained a few there. It may have helped marginally to enlarge the number of regimes calling themselves Marxist. But those regimes are impoverished, increasingly disillusioned by the limits of Soviet economic assistance, and as eager as ever to sell their resources to the highest bidder.

If Soviet military prestige is high, its prestige as a model for or partner in national development has never been lower. Furthermore, by flaunting its enhanced military means, Moscow has strengthened Western political forces favoring increased defense expenditures, reduced political barriers to Japanese rearmament, and precipitated Western military assistance to China.

## NO READY ANSWERS

Because Soviet gains are so problematical, why has American prestige dropped so stunningly, creating the pervasive sense of decline that fuels the current resurgence of American jingoism? Part of the responsibility lies with those who, feeling threatened by the premises and policies of the new diplomacy, have warred against it with hysterical allegations of failure. When many of the most influential American individuals, institutions, and publications relentlessly proclaim America's supposed defeats, the U.S. public and audiences elsewhere in the world, weaned on the assumptions of global containment, are inclined to believe them.

A large measure of responsibility also lies, therefore, with the first president to doubt the premises of global containment, Jimmy Carter. For only the president has the prestige and commands the attention required to refocus fixed ideas about the national interest. And only he has the power to act consistently on new premises and in so doing progressively to validate them.

A president with the intellectual independence and political courage to embrace the new diplomacy would have made Nicaragua a victory for American policy. He would not have cozied up to the shah. Once the Iranian revolution was under way he would have advised the monarch to find refuge with some empathic tyrant. Then neither American diplomats nor U.S. prestige would be hostage to the struggle for power inside Iran.

These and the many other expressions of the new diplomacy would have been preceded and accompanied by a clear and consistent statement of the premises that lend them coherence. Standing uneasily on the same bully pulpit Theodore Roosevelt used to impose his consistent if flawed image of American interests, Carter has spoken in confusing tongues, leaving his audience prey to its fears and to his enemies.

A consistent commitment to the new diplomacy and an open, principled rejection of the premises of global containment would have established the basis for the preservation of American prestige. But the effort could not stop there. For the premises of the new diplomacy only constitute a general orientation, a cluster of presumptions refutable in particular cases. They do not provide a ready answer for every contingency. In particular, they only set broad policy guidelines for dealing with Soviet behavior in the Third World and handling Third World states that threaten Western interests.

The new diplomacy counsels against reflexive opposition to beneficiaries of Soviet assistance, whether they be established governments or rebels, except in those few countries where domestic violence threatens imperative U.S. interests. Some leftist governments may arise. But the experience of the last 20 years demonstrates that they will pursue their own interests and eventually accommodate with the West, which normally has far more to offer. Only by assuming direct physical control of the country can the Soviets prevent this.

It does not follow, however, that the United States should never guarantee a particular regime's survival. But it should do so not because the regime's opponent disparages the free market or fires Kalashnikov rifles. Rather the United States should help a government only if it is prepared to compensate U.S. assistance with a valuable concession that Washington could not obtain through the operation of international markets or if the recipients of Soviet assistance are so unrepresentative of local constituencies that, even after forming a government, they could survive only on the strength of Soviet bayonets. The United States should also support the Third World's few authentically democratic regimes, because any great alliance requires demonstrative reaffirmations of its ideological glue. It would also encourage opponents of brutal regimes, whether of the left or the right. From this perspective, Cuban aid to the Sandinistas in Nicaragua was unobjectionable, but the Soviet Union's physical conquest of Afghanistan intolerable.

## A RECIPE FOR DEFEAT

These generalizations imply several rather precise rules of the game. Each side would recognize that the other may choose to give sanctuary, advice, training, and arms to governments or their opponents. Where such aid is extended to unpopular regimes or subversives, the other superpower may make as much political capital as it can out of such involvement, but it will not treat the intervention as a basis for sanctions except in a few specified cases, such as Saudi Arabia. Regular troops may, however, be dispatched only at the request of a recognized government to resist foreign aggression, not domestic turmoil, and they must depart when the invitation is withdrawn. Neither Washington nor Moscow would be condoning intervention. They would simply be agreeing to tolerate a degree of flexibility in recognition of the fact that each country may occasionally have important and unique incentives to influence the outcome of domestic conflicts.

With far fewer nonmilitary assets to employ, the Soviets have a greater temptation to solicit influence by arming and training participants in parochial Third World conflicts. The United States can help them curb that instinct by more aggressively co-opting their erstwhile clients. The Organization for Economic Cooperation and Development in collaboration with concerned oil-producing states might even establish a fund that would offer concessional loans and investment guarantees for communist states that opt for strategic nonalignment and economic nondiscrimination and that are prepared to meet minimum humanitarian norms.

The new diplomacy would also probe the Kremlin's demand for recognition as a global actor equal to the United States. Without yielding on Afghanistan, Washington could propose formation of high-level US-USSR working groups, including representatives of the other industrial democracies, to examine possible bases for cooperative action to insure the flow of Middle East oil, facilitate a final settlement of the Arab-Israeli conflict, and accelerate the pace of change in South Africa.

As it implies distinct guidelines for U.S. competition with the Soviet Union in the Third World, neorealism also governs the instinct to coerce Third World states. Recognizing the collective sensitivity of such states to past instances of coercion and their growing power to retaliate through a variety of means, the new diplomacy requires the exhaustion of alternative remedies, the restriction of violent intervention to extreme cases, and the sanction if not of law then at least of widely recognized principles of equity. It opposes interventions that are not supported by allies, nor accepted by some prominent developing countries.

Today and in the years ahead the international system will have to cope with regimes, such as the one in Zaire, that are politically, morally, and fiscally bankrupt. Within the premises of the new diplomacy, the United States can develop norms and structures to limit the resulting injury to the larger international system, as well as to the unwilling subjects of such regimes.

Several years ago Americans might have thought that the Vietnam war, the subsequent U.S. rapprochement with China, and the exposure during the Watergate scandal of the domestic consequences of America's approach to foreign policy had finally interred global containment. Yet it has reappeared.

For a brief time, the United States enjoyed an indisputable global pre-eminence. The Vietnam war and OPEC brought a sudden realization of harsh limits on America's ability to dominate events. An adjustment of perspective does not come easily.

Defeat in other realms of policy—the persistence of poverty and racial confict, the decline of traditional industries and the dollar, inflation—has helped to fix in place a searing self-image of failure at the very time that individual Americans particularly need the satisfaction of vicarious participation in victory.

Americans are inclined to transcend a sense of personal inadequacy through identification with winners. Geographic identity with victorious sporting teams offers one source of personal fulfillment. National identity with a victorious diplomacy offers another. Foreign policy thus becomes the moral equivalent of sport, with other countries as irredeemable competitors. Cooperation spoils the game, and defeat aches. For the ultimate canon of American sporting life is that winning is not the most important thing: it is everything. But in international relations, the swaggering pursuit of triumphs torn by main force from the grasp of history, without reference to morality or cost, is a recipe for ultimate defeat or the collective destruction of the game.

## 11. Richard E. Feinberg and Kenneth A. Oye
### *After the Fall: U.S. Policy Toward Radical Regimes*                     1983

In the 1980 presidential campaign, Ronald Reagan savagely attacked Carter's neorealist foreign policies. A Reagan administration, the candidate pledged, would reassert American power and values and place Soviet expansion in the Third World at the center of its foreign policy. Unlike Carter, Reagan favored full support for such traditional dictators as the Shah of Iran, Marcos of the Philippines, and Somoza of Nicaragua. In office, Reagan scrapped Carter's human rights policies, and he provided military and economic assistance to forces seeking to overthrow the Marxist regimes in Angola, Afghanistan, and, later, Nicaragua.

In "After the Fall: U.S. Policy Toward Radical Regimes," political scientists Richard Feinberg and Kenneth Oye criticize the Reagan administration for seeking to secure interests that, in their opinion, were never really in jeopardy. According to Oye and Feinberg, reassertionists fail to comprehend two things. First, the Soviets had gained little influence with Third World radical regimes and second, the radical rhetoric of such regimes frequently belied an economic orientation toward the industrial democracies.

When you finish this essay, ask yourself how well Oye and Feinberg have rebutted the statement by former Secretary of State Alexander Haig that the 1970s were a decade in which "a bipartisan policy of failure had permitted the Soviet Union to inflict disastrous defeats on the United States at regular six month intervals." In addition, make a list of the alternative policies that Oye and Feinberg offer. Upon what key assumptions do these alternatives rest, and how valid are they?

Conventional wisdom holds that radical governments in the Third World pose a grave threat to the security and prosperity of the United States. Yet, as will be argued here, basic U.S. interests are often threatened more by the customary American response to revolutionary regimes than by the revolutionary regimes themselves.*

Since the Second World War, American policy in the Third World has aimed, appropriately, at two basic objectives. In the security realm, it has sought to limit Soviet influence; and in the economic realm, it has worked to maintain access to raw materials and markets. Contrary to common beliefs, neither interest is necessarily compromised by nationalist regimes of diverse ideological coloration. While often more troublesome than their predecessors, most of these regimes nevertheless have a vital interest in maintaining their political autonomy from the Soviet Union and engaging in mutually advantageous international economic exchange.

The American preference, which we share, for liberal democratic political systems should not prevent U.S. leaders from seeing that a broad spectrum of regimes can be reasonably congruent with American economic and security interests. Nor should the search for more effective policies to defend American interests in the post-revolutionary context be confused with the problem of dealing with revolutions in the making, a subject beyond the bounds of this essay.

Paradoxically, the United States risks its basic interests when it reflexively adopts a hostile posture toward radical and nationalist regimes, for such action may well increase the dependency of target nations on the Soviet Union and disrupt economic relations. Blind hostility toward revolutionary governments increases the likelihood of consolidation of Soviet domination and may reduce Western access to Third World economies.

There are, of course, instances in which Third World radical regimes have become captive clients of the Soviet Union. This worst-case situation usually occurs when an unpopular besieged regime must rely on Soviet aid for its own very survival. But this occasional and, by its very nature, often temporary set of conditions does not invalidate the general argument. The problem of the

---

* Some footnotes have been renumbered.

dependent post-revolutionary elite must be addressed, but it should not continue to distort American policy towards the Third World.

## A SAFER ECONOMIC WORLD

As an advanced industrial nation, the United States depends on the Third World for raw materials and export markets. The Third World provides at least half of American consumption of each of a dozen strategic materials, including tin, columbium, aluminum, and rubber. In 1980, nearly 20 percent of American production was sold abroad. The less developed countries absorbed approximately 30 percent of this total and nearly 40 percent of the manufactured goods the United States exported.

American decision-makers traditionally have assumed that this rising economic interdependence, in conjunction with decreasing American political influence in the Third World, jeopardizes American economic interests. Although conflict between established governments and insurgents can disrupt economic activity, the immediate economic consequences of revolutionary turmoil should be distinguished from the after-effects of revolutionary change. In other words, the focus should be on the degree to which the economic interests and policies of radical nationalist governments differ from those of more traditional regimes.

Both revolutionary and nonrevolutionary governments have on occasion sought to alter the terms of their relationship with the Western international economic system through the complete or partial expropriation of foreign investments, the renegotiation of mineral leases, and the threat of default on international financial obligations.[1] Although, on balance, radical states appear somewhat more likely to disrupt international economic ties, regimes of all ideological stripes appear to have an interest in maintaining access to Western markets, capital, and technology.

The less developed countries that have adopted the rhetoric of an "anti-imperialist" foreign policy—such as Algeria, Ethiopia, Grenada, Libya, Mozambique, and Nicaragua—have nonetheless continued to concentrate on cultivating their economic relations with advanced capitalist states (Table 1). Only the West can provide the food, raw materials, consumer goods, and machinery that their populations demand and that the process of development requires. To earn the foreign exchange necessary to pay for these goods, developing countries must export. They generally are unable to secure higher prices or engage in political blackmail by withholding their products from the world market, because they lack sufficient financial reserves or market power. Iran, for example, is reopening commercial and financial channels with the West. The mullahs have cancelled gas agreements with the Soviet Union, preferring instead to build a pipeline to Turkey to serve Western European customers. The National Iranian Oil Company's aggressive production and price-cutting policies suggests that the precepts of Islamic fundamentalism need not conflict with Western economic interests.

Table 1    1980 TRADE PATTERNS OF RADICAL THIRD WORLD STATES
(percentages)

| Country | Soviet Bloc | Industrial West | Developing South |
|---------|-------------|-----------------|------------------|
| Algeria | 1.9 | 93.4 | 4.6 |
| Ethiopia | 7.9 | 63.9 | 27.7 |
| Grenada | 1.3 | 55.2 | 42.3 |
| Iraq | 1.3 | 66.8 | 31.9 |
| Jamaica (Manley) | 2.1 | 64.5 | 32.9 |
| Libya | 1.2 | 83.9 | 14.9 |
| Mozambique | .3 | 55.7 | 43.8 |
| Nicaragua | .2 | 55.5 | 43.8 |
| South Yemen | 1.4 | 47.3 | 51.3 |
| Syria | 8.4 | 51.0 | 39.1 |

SOURCE: Percentages compiled from International Monetary Fund, *Direction of Trade Statistics 1981.* The Western international economic system is highly integrated, hence this table presents figures on trade with all Western nations, rather than with the United States alone.

In a world of surplus labor and scarce capital and technology, the competition for direct foreign investment is intense. The Marxist government of Angola has stationed Cuban troops near Gulf Oil operations to defend them against nominally pro-Western insurgents. Radical nationalist Guinea works in partnership with the Fria mining company. The governments of Ethiopia, Zimbabwe, and Mozambique strive, with varying degrees of success, to attract multinational investments. Even nations subjected to American economic sanctions seek investment. A high-level Cuban official argued recently that "Cuba provides the perfect climate for foreign investment—the most stable political system in Latin America, a disciplined workforce, state provision of employee benefits, no strikes, and low taxes."[2] Here, the interests of radical nationalist regimes are akin to those of newly industrializing capitalist nations or depressed areas in the United States. The Premier of Angola, the Prime Minister of Singapore, and the Governor of Michigan all compete for employment and revenue-producing investment. The plumage may vary in coloration, but the behavior cannot readily be distinguished. In short, the relationship between a regime's investment policy and its economic ideology is diminishing.

In the 1970s, lending by commercial banks became the primary avenue for capital transfer to the Third World. Socialist states from China to Cuba queued up to borrow from Western banks at commercial interest rates. As the world has become only too aware, Western bankers were more than willing to lend to Poland, Romania, and Yugoslavia. Despite today's severe credit squeeze, none of the Eastern European or radical Third World states has yet dared to default. The desire to maintain normal economic relations with the West, and the hope for future credits, compelled the revolutionary government of Nicaragua to honor the $1.6 billion in international debts it inherited. The acceptance of the hated Somoza debt by the former guerilla *commandantes* was rich in irony: an eloquent testimony to the overwhelming attractiveness and power of the international economic system.

The interest of the less developed countries in joining the international economy rests on the lack of a better alternative. Neither autarky nor "collective self-reliance" is a sufficient substitute. Third World nations may be able to replace their dependency on individual exporters and importers, and they can, to varying degrees, increase their trade with other developing states. Although such trade may be psychologically and politically satisfying, the rules governing economic interchange among developing countries merely reproduce the structures determining North-South relations.

Nor is entrance into the socialist division of labor, the COMECON system, an attractive alternative. COMECON offers some limited opportunities for market diversification, but it cannot provide a substitute for trade with the West. On the contrary, socialist states in Eastern Europe have themselves sought deeper involvement in the international economic system. Hungary, for example, already conducts half of its trade with countries outside of COMECON.

The limited involvement of the Soviet Union in the world economy leaves it without the tools that are most relevant to the Third World's major concern— economic development. Egypt, the Sudan, and Iraq became disillusioned with the Soviet Union as they discovered that friendship with the Soviets was economically unrewarding. The decline of Soviet influence in India has paralleled rising Indian dissatisfaction with Soviet technology. The Indians have elected to replace Soviet designs for large-scale power generators with West German ones, and Italian pharmaceutical technology is edging out Soviet antibiotics. Most recently, the Sandinista regime in Nicaragua has been sorely disappointed by the modest levels of economic aid offered by the Soviet Union.

Neither rhetoric nor security ties to the East have prevented radical nations from selling their production to the West or from remaining dependent upon imports from non-COMECON countries. Those nations with the requisite creditworthiness have chosen to borrow from international capital markets, and those with deposits of raw materials are doing business with multinational corporations. Revolutionary change *within* particular Third World nations does not alter the structure of the international economy. New elites have little choice but to accept the global economy of integrated financial markets, multinational corporations, and international trade flows....

## THE SOVIET THREAT AND WESTERN SECURITY

In reviewing the performance of previous administrations, former Secretary of State Alexander M. Haig declared that "... a bipartisan policy of failure had permitted the Soviet Union to inflict disastrous defeats on the United States at regular six month intervals." During the last 20 years, the argument goes, the Kremlin aggressively extended its power over Third World states. By orchestrating its military, political, ideological, and (admittedly weak) economic instruments, Moscow reduced a growing number of developing states to dependent status. Some regimes willingly became Soviet "proxies," while communist movements subverted others. The Soviet Union employed threats and force to subdue still others. Soviet influence in the Third World grew, it is argued, while that of the West declined. According to this view, the Soviet leaders are correct when they boast that the "correlation of forces" is moving in their favor. Thus, it seems to matter little that the Western economic order is more appealing to Third World leaders. The Soviets are gaining ground nonetheless.

This familiar argument rests on a misreading of the past and on an unduly pessimistic view of the future. A scoreboard of Soviet "gains and losses" would show that, at best the Soviet Union has held its own over the past two decades. Some commentators like to group countries under the dichotomies of free or communist, pro-American or pro-Soviet. Using even these crude categories, the results suggest that on balance the Soviet Union is not running away with the golden rings. On the contrary, Soviet "losses"—including China, Indonesia, Egypt, and Somalia—have been at least as significant as the much-publicized Soviet "gains" in Angola, Mozambique, Ethiopia, Afghanistan, and Southeast Asia. Soviet influence has also arguably declined in Iraq, India, and Algeria. Moscow has been able to develop and maintain true, if uneasy, client relations only where the Red Army is stationed, as in Eastern Europe and Afghanistan, or where a Third World state, like Cuba, is caught in an extremely hostile environment and is desperately dependent on Soviet military support. Elsewhere, Soviet influence has been tenuous and reversible.

The Soviet Union confronts many of the same stubborn political and economic forces that have frustrated U.S. policy toward the Third World. External powers are losing their ability to control the internal politics of Third World nations. Many analysts attributed the success of the Vietnamese communists to their ability to appropriate the banner of Vietnamese nationalism. Innumerable other instances, from the anti-Americanism and anti-Sovietism of the Islamic Republic of Iran to the 1978 plebiscite won by Chilean President Augusto Pinochet against human rights criticism from abroad, have confirmed the potency of nationalist sentiments when they are harnessed by mass movements or strong leaders. Moreover, the governments of many Third World nations have become stronger and less subject to external manipulation. Their competency and authority have grown with the recruitment of new generations of trained technocrats and managers, the enlargement of national security and intelligence forces, and the expansion of state control over the economy. Unlike in the heyday of imperialism, when a small flotilla of gunboats could manhandle an ancient civilization or conquer disorganized territories, today many Third World states wield more formidable organized power.

The nationalism that has rendered the Third World less controllable has diminished the consequences of a loss of control. Few Third World governments are likely to be irremediably captured by the Soviet Union. If provided with attractive economic incentives and a secure regional environment, most will grasp independence. Third World nations may turn left, without turning East. . . .

# LESS CONTROL—MORE SECURITY

Although the United States is increasingly unable to control events abroad or to bear the rising costs of intervention, American security and economic interests in the Third World can still be protected. But this requires that the United States distinguish between imagined and real dangers and learn to turn recent trends to advantage. Much attention has been focused, for example, on the negative developments in the Third World: its inflammatory rhetoric, its United Nations voting patterns, and its declining respect for political liberalism. Other trends are more positive and profound. A growing number of Third World leaders, including self-styled radicals, believe their interests are best served by active participation in the global economy. Their integration into a dynamic international economy has helped developing countries achieve the self-confidence and maturity they need to assert their national interests against external forces of exploitation. For their part, the Soviet leaders are adjusting poorly to these new realities.

The Reagan administration has done little better. Instead of welcoming these trends and subtly exploiting them, the Reagan administration has ignored or even tried to reverse them. Never in the postwar period has an administration given lower priority to international economic policy. Rather than responding to Soviet expansionism with a strategy based upon U.S. political and economic strengths, the administration has mirrored Soviet behavior by emphasizing military force. A wiser, more realistic policy for coping with revolutionary regimes in the Third World would elevate economics, welcome nationalism, deflate ideology, accommodate change, and defuse regional tensions.[3]

U.S. policy toward the Third World should recognize that a nation's domestic political economy does not determine its mode of participation in the international economy. Whether a nation's political institutions be authoritarian or liberal, its economy statist or decentralized, a break occurs at the shoreline of the international economy. The structure of the international economy conditions the interests of individual nations, and thereby limits the significance of variations in the form of national political economy. At the same time, the United States must do more to make the international economy function smoothly. The United States needs to help assure global liquidity, facilitate capital availability, strengthen the multilateral mechanisms for debt rescheduling, and keep trading avenues open.[4]

Economic growth by itself, of course, does not determine international political alignments. But, as states become wealthier, the Soviet Union becomes an even less attractive economic partner and subject of emulation. Global prosperity provides a continuing inducement for already independently minded regimes to remain nonaligned. Moreover, it makes regimes that are dependent on the Soviet Union but active in the world economy more likely to tread the well-worn path to non-alignment or re-alignment. As economic modernization proceeds, and as revolutionary elites become administrators and gradually are supplemented and then replaced by technocratic cadres, "anti-imperialist" fears and Marxist myths tend to fade. Of the older revolutionary regimes in the Third

World, only in Cuba has their maturation process been delayed by the diplomacy of "international solidarity." This exception is partly explained by Fidel Castro's extraordinary personality and partly by unusually extensive Soviet economic support. But, central to the explanation is the unwillingness of the United States to initiate and sustain a politics of accommodation.

A sensible strategy toward radical regimes would reinforce the ameliorating effects of international economic integration by decoupling a nation's external politico-military alignment from its polity. Regardless of their internal class structure and professed ideology, nations should not be driven to seek the protection of the Soviet Union. The United States should strive to prevent the security concerns of a radical regime from blunting its desire for autonomy and economic progress. The failure to do so in Angola and the Horn of Africa allowed Moscow easy entries. In contrast, the Lancaster accords created conditions for a nonaligned Zimbabwe.

Inadvertently, the Reagan administration's confrontational policy toward Third World radical regimes has tightened the relationship between domestic politics and external alignments. Paramilitary action against Nicaragua, belligerent rhetoric toward Grenada, acquiescence in South African incursions into Angola, and the harassment of Libya in 1981–82 may have been intended to undermine the Soviet position in the Third World, but such policies have had precisely the opposite effect.

To diminish Soviet influence, the United States should seek correct relations with most revolutionary regimes. From the perspective of such regimes, the benefits of assimilation into the Soviet empire are limited and the costs substantial. The Soviet penchant for political penetration, ideological monotheism, and conventional military intervention provides potentially dependent nations with powerful reasons to remain at arm's length. The United States should patiently exploit the inevitably emerging conflicts between the Soviet Union and radical regimes. The Soviets may make short-term gains, but time is on our side.

Finally, the containment of Soviet influence and the maintenance of an open international economic system do not fully define American concerns in the Third World. Revolutionary regimes may retain their autonomy from the Soviet Union and remain fully integrated into the international economy, and still violate the territorial integrity of neighbors or terrorize their own populations. Qaddafi's intervention in Chad and Pol Pot's gruesome genocidal actions in Camboida violate principles of self-determination and humanitarianism that Americans and the international community properly value. The appropriate American response to such actions should not be contingent on whether the violator happens to be on the right or the left. Acts of aggression and massive violations of human rights are not limited to revolutionary nationalist states, and affirmative policies directed at such actions should encompass a broader spectrum of transgressors.

Traditional American policy towards revolutionary regimes may unnecessarily compromise international norms of self-determination, human rights and American security and economic interests. As has been argued here, a policy of reflexive hostility may permit the Soviet Union to consolidate its influence over revolutionary governments and may reduce American economic access to these countries. Such a policy, if carried to the lengths pursued by the Reagan administration, directly violates the principle of self-determination and indirectly encourages threatened regimes to repress the populace. Furthermore, such a policy impedes effective collective international action in defense of self-determination and human rights. The double standard makes it more difficult to form broad-based international coalitions to defend these principles. By adopting a realistic and prudent policy towards revolutionary regimes, the United States cannot eliminate all tensions between national interests and international norms. However, movement away from the present policy of reflexive hostility would permit the United States to advance its national interests and to lay a foundation for more effective defense of these international principles.

## TOWARDS GREATER REALISM

The security policy proposed here is not novel. Many Americans have forgotten that containment, as implemented during the later 1940s, capitalized on the schism between Tito and Stalin and aimed at preventing a permanent Sino-Soviet alignment. In November 1949, Dean Acheson argued against policies ". . . to oppose the (Chinese) Communists' regime, harass it, needle it, and if an opportunity appeared to attempt to overthrow it." Instead, he supported moves ". . . to attempt to detach it from subservience to Moscow and, over a period of time, to encourage those vigorous influences which might modify it." In words that take on renewed meaning in the Reagan era, Acheson noted that this approach ". . . did not mean a policy of appeasement any more than it had in the case of Tito." It is a return to this earlier, more subtle, and patient approach to international security affairs that is needed.

The cumulative effect of American foreign policy since 1949 complicates the implemenation of such an approach. Many revolutionary elites in the Third World, particularly in Latin America, believe that an unrelenting hostility toward revolutionary change is and will remain fundamental to U.S. foreign policy. Their initial reactions upon coming to power are likely to be conditioned by fear and distrust. The interplay between the policies of radical regimes and American domestic politics creates additional problems. Political parties and candidates in this country often use Third World provocations and insults as fodder in their campaigns, and incumbents find it politically risky to exhibit the patience that a more realistic policy requires. Policies that oscillate between hostile and correct relations are unlikely to assuage the fears of radical regimes.

To sustain the strategy proposed here, an administration would have to explain its actions clearly and with one voice. If its language were ambiguous, its pronouncements divergent, or its actions contradictory, it would be overwhelmed by a confused and angry public opinion. But if it succeeded, it would place American foreign policy on a firmer, more realistic footing.

*NOTES*

1. Economic disputes are by no means limited to radical regimes. For example, consider the following actions by moderate Western-oriented governments: the Christian Democratic government of Chile (1964–1970) partially nationalized foreign copper companies; the government of Mexico imposed stringent domestic content and re-export requirements on foreign investors; and, most recently, the government of Brazil tacitly threatened to default on its foreign debts during rescheduling negotiations with commercial banks.
2. Interview by author Richard E. Feinberg.
3. For greater detail, see Richard E. Feinberg, *The Intemperate Zone: The Third World Challenge to U.S. Foreign Policy* (New York:/W. W. Norton, 1983), chapter 5, "A New Realism."
4. For a fuller discussion of suggested economic measures, see Overseas Development Council, "Global Recovery: The Contribution of the Developing Countries." Statement of the Overseas Development Council for the Williamsburg Summit, May 1983.

## 12. Robert Mueller
### *The Cold War Was Lost, Not Won*   July 1989

When Soviet Premier Gorbachev wound down the cold war and released Eastern Europe from the grip of Soviet hegemony, many conservatives argued that Reagan's reassertionism had won the cold war. In Selection 7, "How to Handle Moscow," William Odom developed this argument. In the selection that follows, University of Rochester political scientist Robert Mueller provides a neorealist rebuttal. Mueller argues that it was Carter's "appeasement," and not Ronald Reagan's reassertionism, that brought about an end to the cold war. After you have read Mueller, reread the Odom essay and make a list of the different assertions, assumptions, and facts that each employs in support of his argument. Which of the two presents the better argument?

The list of people who consider the cold war to be more or less over keeps growing. Even President Bush now says it is time to move "beyond containment" and "to integrate the Soviet Union into the community of nations." Some hard-liners still warn of a possible relapse, and their wariness is reasonable. But for now, at least, things look good: the Soviet Union appears sincere in its postrevolutionary yearning for a "quiet, normal international situation," as Mikhail Gorbachev has put it; and influential Westerners from almost everywhere along the political spectrum seem to be rooting for Gorbachev's success.

For some conservatives, one benefit of declaring the cold war over is that they can then claim to be the ones who won it. The Soviet Union's ongoing retreat, in their view, is a vindication of Ronald Reagan's eight years of aggressive opposition to communism—and, more generally, of the policy of containment that has long characerized American foreign policy and that, though less militant than the Ronald Reagan Doctrine, has often been championed by conservatives.

It is nice that the Soviet Union's redirection leaves so many conservatives in the West feeling triumphant, but the truth is that the West didn't win the cold war at all. The Soviet Union lost it. Almost all the calamities that have brought the U.S.S.R. to its present desperate condition—compelling it not only to abandon expansionism but to rethink its political and economic philosophy—have been self-inflicted. And to the extent that American policy *has* contributed to the mellowing of the Soviet Union, neither the Reagan Doctrine nor the policy of containment has been crucial. In fact, it is more nearly the case that the occasional *failures* of containment are what doomed Soviet communism.

Everyone agrees that a major cause of the Soviet Union's redirection has been the staggering failure of its bureaucratic and economic system, which stifles initiative and enshrines inefficiency and dislocation. That system, however, was the Soviets' idea, and the fact that it is now catching up with them cannot be credited to Ronald Reagan or anyone else in the United States. Similarly, the Soviets have sought to suppress, often brutally, ancient nationalisms and freedoms. The contradictions that are now emerging from that failed policy owe nothing to the West, which has always rigorously opposed it. Nor can the fact that the Soviet empire in Eastern Europe has become a severe economic drain be credited to Western policy—which, of course, strenuously opposed its formation from the beginning.

The champions of containment might concede these points but reply that the contradictions of Soviet communism have been heightened by competition with the West in the international arena. This argument is strongest as it relates to arms policy. The Soviets' vast economy-straining arms buildup is undoubtedly a reaction in part to Western defense spending. But in large part it is not. Central to the classic Soviet Communist view of the world has been an intense suspicion of, and hostility toward, the surrounding capitalist world, a suspicion that verges on paranoia. Indeed, the West tried to level or reduce arms expenditures several times—in the mid-1940s, the 1960s, and the 1970s. Each time the Soviets demonstrated that their policy was "too much is not enough." As Jimmy Carter's secretary of defense, Harold Brown, reluctantly concluded, "When we build, they build; when we cut back, they build."

Soviet ideology also has had at its center a messianic drive to undermine the capitalist enemy, and it is on this drive that containment is directly focused. As Bush has pointed out, the hope has been that if this expansionary impetus were systematically frustrated, Soviet foreign policy would eventually mellow. Accordingly, the United States has sought to counter pro-Communist movements not only in areas of highest concern, such as Western Europe, but also in such peripheral areas as Korea, Laos, and the Congo. The lesson of Munich has been applied: when a country bent on expansion gains territory, the experience only whets its appetite for more. Thus when Communist expansion has been thwarted—as in Greece in the 1940s, in Korea in the 1950s, or in Central Africa in the 1960s—the policy has been held to have been successful. When areas have fallen into the Communist camp—as in Eastern Europe in the late 1940s,

China in 1949, North Vietnam in 1954, Cuba in 1959, and portions of Laos in 1961—containment has been held to have suffered a setback.

But in fact, the less "successful" containment has been, the worse things have gotten for the Soviets. In 1975 three countries—Cambodia, South Vietnam, and Laos—fell into the Communist camp. Then, suffering from post-Vietnam syndrome, the United States went into something of a containment funk and watched from the sidelines as the Soviet Union, in what seems in retrospect remarkably like a fit of absent-mindedness, gathered a slew of Third World countries into its imperial embrace: Angola in 1976, Mozambique and Ethiopia in 1977, South Yemen and Afghanistan in 1978, Grenada and Nicaragua in 1979.

The Soviets at first were gleeful about these acquisitions; the "correlation of forces," they concluded, had decisively shifted in their direction. Ultimately, though, these gains didn't whet the Soviet appetite for more. They not only satiated the appetite for expansion but gave the expanders a case of indigestion. For almost all the new acquisitions soon became economic and political basket cases, fraught with dissension, financial mismanagement, and civil warfare. Some of this was due to the peculiar circumstances of the nations involved, but in broad terms the economic problems of the Soviet Union's client states shouldn't have surprised anyone; the Communist economic system is inherently unproductive, so a Communist overseer is not a likely savior for a Third World economy. To cap their decade-long acquisition of liabilities, in 1979 the Soviets sent troops into Afghanistan, and descended into a long period of enervating wafare there.

Charles Wolf and his colleagues at the RAND Corporation have estimated that the cost of the Soviet empire rose enormously between 1971 and 1980, from about one percent of its gross national product to nearly three percent when measured in dollars, or from under two percent to about seven percent when measured in rubles. (Wolf's "cost of empire" includes all economic and military aid, except the cost of stationing soldiers in Eastern Europe—who, Wolf assumes, would have been in uniform even if they had been in the Soviet Union. The figure also includes the cost of conducting the war in Afghanistan.) By comparison, insofar as the United States can be said to have a comparable empire, its cost—i.e., economic and military aid to foreign countries—is less than one-half of one percent of GNP.

It was just at the time when expansion was becoming a burden of almost unbearable proportions for the Soviet Union that the Reagan administration began trying to put an end to it, and even to reverse it. Reagan provided military aid to the *contras* in Nicaragua, accelerated the Carter administration's provision of aid to the Afghan resistance, and engaged in low-cost, high-profile demonstrations of military resolve, such as the Grenada invasion. All of this can be loosely described as an application of containment policy. (Strictly speaking, Nicaragua, Afghanistan, and Grenada are examples of "rollback," not containment, but during the transitional period when Communist rule in a country is still coalescing, the line between the two is somewhat fuzzy.) In this sense, containment may have contributed to ending the cold war, since the war in

Afghanistan, at least, certainly helped raise Soviet imperial costs. But that war was started and perpetuated by Afghan resentment at Soviet occupation, not by the containment strategy. The arms sent there may have deepened the damage that anti-Soviet forces could inflict, but the central dilemma for the Soviets—the reality that made the war a "running sore"—was the willingness of the rebels to fight for decades if necessary to free their country.

The key point is that the cost of maintaining the Soviet empire—which almost everyone now agrees was important in moderating Soviet ambitions—rose sharply during the de facto appeasement of the 1970s, not during the containment/rollback of the 1980s. Indeed, during the early 1980s, as Soviet expansion stopped, the costs of empire actually began declining (thanks in part to a drop in the price of oil, a commodity that the Soviet Union subsidizes heavily for its client states). Nonetheless, those costs remained high by American standards, and they continued to take a toll. The Soviet economy stagnated under the weight of foreign commitments and of its own backwardness: GNP during the 1980s grew at less than two percent annually in real terms. It was near the beginning of this stagnation that articles by Soviet academics and government advisers began expressing the fear that Nicaragua could become "another Cuba."' And they meant not what Americans mean by that phrase—a thorn in the side of the United States—but rather a bottomless pit for Soviet money. The Soviets were beginning to understand what Americans still have trouble grasping: the Red Peril was most perilous for its sponsor.

None of this is to say that containment has been a useless policy. It doubtless deserves credit for keeping some countries outside the Soviet orbit. Without a containment war in the 1950s, South Koreans would now be living as miserably as their fellow Koreans in the North. Thailand, Malaysia, and Singapore need only look to the Indochina states to see what might have happened if Communist rebels had been successful in their countries.

It could also be argued—very speculatively—that containment helped reduce the danger of a major war. If the North Koreans had been successful in 1950 in overruning the South, hawks in the international Communist movement would surely have been encouraged to consider employing the technique elsewhere. Instead, the sour experience in Korea seems to have permanently discredited such military probes; there have been no Koreas since Korea. (Most historians now agree, however, that the main impetus toward that war came from the North Koreans, not from Stalin's Kremlin, which greatly feared a wider war. Thus precipitate military action might not have been forthcoming even in the wake of a quick Korean success.) Similarly, had South Vietnam been allowed to succumb to communism in 1965, the event would have been profoundly encouraging to Communist theorists—particularly those in China—who were almost hysterically committed to the view that the United States and other Western nations were "paper tigers."

The Western policy of containment, then, has helped keep some countries free from communism, and it may have further reduced the already low post–World War II danger of major war. But insofar as it was devised to force the Soviets to face the fundamental futility of communism, it has foundered on a curious paradox. The early containment theorists were correct to conclude that Soviet communism is a singularly undesirable and pathetically flawed form of government, and they were right to anticipate that it would inevitably mellow when it could no longer avoid confronting its inner contradictions. But Soviet communism probably would have reached this point somewhat earlier if its natural propensity to expand had been tolerated rather than resisted.

---

## COMPREHENSION CHECKPOINT

What is the significance of the following?

| | | |
|---|---|---|
| Sino-Soviet split | "phony revolution | "genuine revolution" |
| counterinsurgency | radical nationalist regimes | polycentrism |
| | "a less controllable but safer world" | |

Can you answer the following questions?

1. What differences do neorealists see between containment in Europe immediately after World War II and containment in the Third World?

2. Why, according to Morgenthau, was Vietnam a mistake?

3. What does Farer mean when he claims that reassertionists fail to distinguish between losses and defeats? How does he use the examples of Iran, Nicaragua, Ethiopia, and Egypt to support his position?

4. How convincing is Feinberg and Oye's argument that Soviet gains in the 1970s had to be considered against Soviet losses? What were the gains? What were the losses?

5. What evidence can you present in support of Feinberg and Oye's position that "a wiser and more realistic policy for coping with revolutionary regimes in the Third World would elevate economics, welcome nationalism, deflate ideology, accommodate change, and defuse regional tensions"?

6. Below are several cold war axioms drawn from a set presented by J. P. Rosenberg in his essay, "Presidential Beliefs and Foreign Policy Decision-Making."[8] How would a neorealist respond to each of them?

- "Every nation that falls to Communism increases the power of the Communist bloc in the struggle with the free world."
- "Peace is indivisible. . . . Thus, any expansion of Communist influence must be resisted."
- "The preeminent feature of international politics is conflict betwen Communism and the Free World."
- "The main source of unrest, disorder, subversion, and civil war in underdeveloped areas is Communist influence and support."
- "The Third World really matters, because it is the battleground between Communism and the Free World."
- "Military strength is the primary route to national security."

## From Worldview to Particular Policy Issues

In Chapter 3, you were asked to relate the reassertionist worldview to a series of particular foreign policy issues. Below are the same issues that appeared in the previous chapter. This time, sketch out a set of neorealist responses.

1. How would a neorealist respond to the following quotation and why?

> Poverty, not Communism, is the principal threat in the Third World.... [E]very Third World revolution is not a struggle between East and West.... [P]overty, hunger, and repression have caused many more revolutions than Moscow and Havana combined.... [T]he US has managed for decades to put itself on the side of repression, corruption, and privilege in these battles, and has inevitably been on the losing side.
>
> —Senator Gary Hart, quoted in *South*, December, 1984, p.11

2. How would a neorealist respond to the following policy proposals?

- to normalize relations with North Vietnam
- to disinvest from South Africa
- to seek a negotiated settlement of the civil war in El Salvador
- to increase funds for the United Nations Development Program
- to call a joint conference with the Soviet Union to seek a negotiated settlement in the Middle East
- to provide low interest rates to the Soviet Union in order to subsidize farm exports
- to stay out of civil wars in the Third World
- to withdraw troops from South Korea
- to cut economic aid to U.S. allies who abuse human rights
- to pressure Israel to accept a Palestinian state

If you refer to your "reassertionist" answers to these questions, you will note significant differences. The source of these differences lies in the different assumptions outlined below.

## Tying Things Together

As Chapter 1 indicated, differences among worldviews reflect different agendas, values, assumptions, and categories of thought. It should not be surprising, then, that the differences between the agendas, priorities, and policy preferences of reassertionists and neorealists rest upon different sets of fundamental assumptions, especially assumptions about structure and processes of the international system. The following chart presents these differences along a set of polarities. Neorealists tend toward the left end of the polarities while reassertionists tend toward the right end. As you examine the items on this chart, try to recall the evidence that neorealists and reassertionists would present in support of their positions. In fact, you may want to review the readings in light of the polarities below.

Neorealism ————————————— Reassertionism

**1.** The Soviet Union behaves as
an imperialist great power ——————— a revolutionary great power

**2.** Soviet foreign policy is largely
reactive/defensive ————————————————— initiatory/offensive

**3.** Revolutionary instability in the Third World stems mainly from
genuine revolutionary movements ————————— Soviet proxies

**4.** Economic policies of leftist regimes in the Third World will be
determined by
national, economic interests ——————— ideological principles

**5.** Soviet gains in the Third World have been
small/offset by losses ————————————— large, accumulating

**6.** The larger the Soviet bloc grows
the weaker it becomes ——————————— the stronger it becomes

**7.** Power in the world is
fragmenting ————————————————— falling to the Soviet orbit

**8.** In any alliance or relationship among states
interests will prevail ————————————— ideology will prevail

## For Further Consideration

*Periodicals and journals* that contain neorealist points of view: *Foreign Policy, Harper's,\* International Security,\* The New Republic,\* The New York Review of Books, The Christian Century,\* World Policy Journal.\**

*Leading neorealist scholars, authors:* Tom Farer, Richard Feinberg, Stanley Hoffman, George Kennan, Anthony Lake, Charles William Maynes, Robert Mueller, Joseph Nye, Ronald Steel, Alan Tonelson, Stephen Walt.

*Leading reassertionist columnists:* Anthony Appel, Tom Wicker, Richard Cohen.

———————

\*Presents works representing other worldviews as well.

# FOR FURTHER READING

Barnet, Richard J. *Real Security: Restoring American Power in a Dangerous Decade.* New York: Simon and Schuster, 1981. Barnet, a leading radical but non-Marxist critic of American foreign policy, offers a short, incisive, and highly readable neorealist critique of the Carter years.

David, Steven R. "Why the Third World Matters." *International Security*, Vol. 14, No. 1 (Summer 1989), pp. 50–86. A reassertionist rebuttal of neorealist arguments about the minimal strategic significance of the Third World. This essay should be read after the essays by Johnson and Jentleson cited below.

Feinberg, Richard E. *The Intemperate Zone: The Third World Challenge to U.S. Foreign Policy.* New York: W. W. Norton, 1983. A well-written and well-argued book-length expansion of the points made in the Feinberg and Oye essay. Feinberg's book provides a critique of Reagan's reassertionism and Richard Nixon's book *The Real War*. New York: Warner Books, 1980.

Gibbs, David. "Does the USSR Have a 'Grand Strategy'? Reinterpreting the Invasion of Afghanistan," *Journal of Peace Research*, Vol. 24, No. 4 (1987), pp. 365–77. Gibbs presents a critique of the reassertionist position that the Soviet invasion of Afghanistan was part of a "grand strategy" to expand its military and political influence throughout the world.

Jentleson, Bruce W. "American Commitments in the Third World: Theory and Practice." *International Organization*, Vol. 41, No. 4 (Autumn 1987), pp. 667–704. A critique of reassertionist assumptions about the significance of the Third World, the interdependence of threats, the importance of keeping commitments, and the political uses of force. Jentleson bases his analysis on three case studies: Vietnam, 1950–75, Iran, 1972–79, and Lebanon, 1982–84.

Johnson, Robert H. "Exaggerating America's Stakes in Third World Conflicts." *International Security*, Vol. 10, No. 3 (Winter 1985–86), pp. 32–68. This essay provides a neorealist attack on the core assumptions of the reassertionist worldview.

Payne, Richard J. *Opportunities and Dangers of Soviet-Cuban Expansion: Toward a Pragmatic Policy.* Albany, NY: State University of New York Press, 1988. A highly readable neorealist assessment of Soviet and Cuban intervention in the Horn of Africa, Afghanistan, Nicaragua, and the Commonwealth Caribbean. A book that is filled with information.

Steel, Ronald. *Pax Americana.* New York: Penguin Books, 1970. An early realist critique of Burkean globalism and American policy in Vietnam. Steel's critique and presentation of a realist alternative is still well worth reading.

Tonelson, Alan. "The Real National Interest." *Foreign Policy*, 61 (Winter 1985–86), pp. 49–73. A short and highly readable presentation of the foundations of the neorealist worldview and a clear statement of what the nation should and should not do in the world arena.

Vance, Cyrus. *Hard Choices.* New York: Simon and Schuster, 1983. A look at the foreign policy of the Carter administration by his neorealist secretary of state. Vance's book should be read in conjunction with *Power and Principle: Memoirs of the National Security Adviser, 1977–1981* (New York: Farrar, Straus, and Giroux, 1983), the reassertionist memoir of Zbigniew Brzezinski, President Carter's national security adviser, who frequently differed with Vance.

Walt, Stephen M. "The Case for Finite Containment: Analyzing U.S. Grand Strategy." *International Security*, Vol. 14, No. 1 (Summer 1989), pp. 5–50. Walt makes the case for a balance of power strategy that focuses on Western Europe, Japan, Korea, and access to the Persian Gulf. The essay contains a table on p. 42, which compares the basic objectives and assumptions of the following worldviews among others: global containment (reassertionism), finite containment (neorealism), neo-isolationism, and world order perspectives.

## NOTES

1. Cited in Robert E. Osgood, *Ideals and Self-Interest in America's Foreign Relations* (Chicago: The University of Chicago Press, 1953), p. 383.
2. Norman Podhoretz, "The Present Danger," *Commentary* (March 1980), p. 37.
3. James Earl Carter, "The President's Commencement Address at the University of Notre Dame," *Presidential Documents*, Vol. 13, No. 22, (May 22, 1977), pp. 773–79.
4. For an insightful and well-written discussion of the domestic and foreign obstacles that confounded Carter's efforts to promote human rights, see Joshua Muravchik, *The Uncertain Crusade* (Carlsbad, CA: Hamilton Press, 1986).
5. Conor Cruise O'Brien, "The Specter of Nationalism," *Harper's* (April 1988), p. 18.
6. Richard Feinberg, *The Intemperate Zone* (New York: W. W. Norton, 1983).
7. See, for example, Theodore C. Sorenson's "Rethinking National Security," *Foreign Affairs*, Vol. 69, No. 3 (Summer 1990), pp. 1–19.
8. J. P. Rosenberg, "Presidential Beliefs and Foreign Policy Decision-Making," *Political Psychology*, Vol. 7, No. 4 (1986), p. 735.

# Chapter
## 5

# Neo-isolationism

*I*f World War II taught America anything, it was the bankruptcy of isolationism. The Japanese attack on Pearl Harbor and the collapse of British naval power in the Atlantic made one thing clear: The Atlantic and Pacific oceans were no longer the protective moats that they once were thought to be. As the distinguished political columnist Walter Lippmann told British audiences in 1952, "When the second war ended, our people were for all practical purposes unanimous in the conviction that never again would they withdraw from the organized international effort to prevent war."[1]

Yet, within two decades, notable scholars and public figures were advocating a return to isolationism. Like neorealism and reassertionism, this "new isolationism" also arose from an assessment of America's failure in Vietnam. But, unlike the other mainstream worldviews, neo-isolationism questioned the very necessity of American involvement anywhere beyond the hemisphere.

For reassertionists, a world filled with Communist and totalitarian governments would be an inhospitable place for the nation to exist. Thus, they insisted that America's security required the containment of Communism and the promotion of freedom and democracy around the world. Neorealists, on the other hand, based their conception of American foreign policy on a much more limited requirement, namely, securing the global balance of power. For them, promoting democracy and rolling back the Soviet empire were not required for America's security.

Neo-isolationists, however, concluded that neither the promotion of freedom nor the maintenance of the balance of power was necessary for America's survival and prosperity. Neo-isolationists readily admitted that *traditional isolationists* had to see that America's security was contingent upon the maintenance of the European balance of power. But in the age of nuclear weapons, they retorted, this contingency no longer existed.

Since the early 1960s, American nuclear forces have been designed to ensure that a significant number would survive even the most massive first strike. Consequently, even if America were struck by every weapon in the Soviets' nuclear arsenal, enough retaliatory weapons would survive—in the sea, the air, or hardened missile silos—to destroy the military and industrial structure of the Soviet Union. Given this "invulnerable, second strike capacity," neo-isolationists argued that no nation would ever invade or attack the United States.

According to neo-isolationists, only in a world of conventional weapons would the United States have to concern itself with balances of power on other continents. In an age of invulnerable, second strike nuclear forces, the United States could enjoy the luxury of dispensing with its allies in Europe, Asia, and the Persian Gulf—and the sooner the better for neo-isolationists. For, in their opinion, it is our foreign commitments that provide the greatest danger to our survival. Political scientist Robert Tucker noted this point as early as 1972:

> It is apparent that many people still have considerable difficulty in coming to terms with the changed structure of the American security position. . . . [N]uclear-missile weapons are still not commonly seen to invalidate conventional balance of power considerations. Thus, the statement that control of Western Europe by a hostile power would not substantially alter the threat to America's physical security continues to provoke strong opposition. Yet the fact remains that a Soviet Union in control of Western Europe would be no less vulnerable to destruction by American strategic power than it is today. Nor would America be more vulnerable to destruction by the Soviet Union than it is today. *The point cannot be made too often that to the extent security is equated with physical security, conventional balance of power calculations have become irrelevant—or very nearly so—for the great nuclear states.*[2]

For neo-isolationists, then, traditional conceptions of balance of power politics have become obsolete, and our postwar commitments to maintain the global balance of power have actually jeopardized rather than enhanced the nation's security. By threatening nuclear war in response to a Soviet invasion of Europe, Japan, or the Middle East, the nation puts its very survival at risk. While neo-isolationists admit that America's commitments to the war-torn nations of Europe and Asia were viable in the age of American nuclear superiority, they argue that those commitments had become untenable by the late 1960s. In addition, neo-isolationists claim that by the 1970s, Europe and Japan were prosperous enough to pay for and field their own defenses against the Soviet Union.

During the cold war era, the core of the neo-isolationist argument was a perception *insolvency*, a policy of commitments that were too expensive to meet with conventional forces and too ghastly to fulfill with nuclear weapons. According to Earl Ravenal:

> the high cost of our present national strategy could be tolerated, if it could be demonstrated that the cost was already more than strictly necessary to implement the strategy and if the nation found itself in comfortable fiscal circumstances. Neither is the case. Powerful critics assert . . . that even the $314 billion that the Reagan administration requested for defense in FY 1986, let alone the $289 billion that Congress finally granted, is grossly insufficient to execute the task of containing Soviet communism around the world. William Van Cleave proposed a 1986 defense budget $50 billion higher than Reagan's request. And Leonard Sullivan, Jr.'s estimate for projecting a confident conventional defense against Soviet arms envi-

sions defense authorizations reaching to 10 percent of the GNP—a budget of about $446 billion for 1987.[3]

The neo-isolationist solution to this insolvency was a policy of strategic disengagement and hemispheric defense. By drastically cutting foreign commitments, the nation could gain greater security at much lower costs, and the savings would have been substantial. By the mid-1980s, roughly two-thirds of the defense budget was allocated to the costs of maintaining our military commitments to Western Europe, Japan, and Korea—approximately $150–$175 billion for Western Europe, $40–$50 billion for Japan, and $7 billion for Korea. Moreover, with budget deficits running well over a hundred billion dollars a year, neo-isolationists noted with irony that the United States had to borrow money from the Japanese and Europeans in order to pay for the costs of preparing to defend them. Neo-isolationists also pointed to the chronic trade deficits which the United States was running with its allies—$12.5 billion with Western Europe and $52 billion with Japan in 1988.[4]

But what about Soviet expansion? On this question, neo-isolationists forthrightly acknowledged the expansionist tendencies of the Soviet Union. What was unique was their proposed response to such expansion—a policy of indifference. Earl Ravenal, for example, saw nothing in the Soviet invasion of Afghanistan that warranted a Western response. Six months after the Soviet invasion, he wrote that

> the one thing almost anyone will say about Afghanistan is that the United States cannot just sit on its hands. But why not? If Washington cannot prudently do something that is directly helpful—for example, free Afghanistan—then it should be making the least of it, not the most. And if the United States cannot defend the Persian Gulf from halfway around the world [in the event of a Soviet invasion], if all it can really do is threaten to blow up the planet, then it should be hedging against the deprivation of oil, not planning to start a world war.[5]

Like neorealists, neo-isolationists also made a distinction between Soviet imperialism and the expansion of Communism. While they would not tolerate Soviet bases in Central America, neo-isolationists saw, and still see, no threat from radical or Marxist regimes in El Salvador, Nicaragua, Panama, or even Mexico.

But would a policy of hemispheric defense leave the nation isolated or at the mercy of other powers in economic affairs? On this point, neo-isolationists based their case on probabilities. Largely accepting the views of neorealists, neo-isolationists believed that mutual dependencies between developed and developing countries and the "laws of economics" would ensure access to most of the resources the nation needs. As a backup, they proposed strategic stockpiles, conservation, and the development of domestic supplies of vital raw materials.

Neo-isolationists readily admitted that these alternatives might be more inconvenient, costly, and less efficient than relying on foreign supplies. However, they countered that such increased costs would be offset by cuts in military spending now allocated to protect foreign sources. According to Ravenal, when one factors in the military costs of defending the Persian Gulf, the cost of the oil flowing into the United States from this region comes to *between $180 and $280 a barrel!*[6]

In addition, neo-isolationists argued that an inward looking strategy would carry none of the risks involved in seeking to maintain foreign sources of supply. After President Bush rushed hundreds of thousands of American troops to the Persian Gulf in the fall of 1990, Amory and L. Hunter Lovins asked the following question, "Are we putting our kids in tanks because we didn't put them in fuel efficient cars?" After providing a "yes" answer to their question, they stated well the neo-isolationist position: "We wouldn't have needed any oil from the Persian Gulf after 1985 if we'd simply kept on saving oil at the rate we did from 1977 to 1985."[7]

According to its proponents, then, a noninterventionist foreign policy would enhance our security at greatly reduced costs. Earl Ravenal has estimated that a hemisphere-only defense posture would allow the nation to cut its defense budget by at least 40 percent. For the decade of the 1990s, he projected defense expenditures of $2.6 trillion for a noninterventionist posture as opposed to $4.1 trillion for an interventionist one.[8]

In addition to providing greater security at reduced costs, neo-isolationists believe that a hemispheric policy would allow America to escape the hard and unsettling moral choices that accompany an interventionist policy. During the cold war era, many Americans were troubled by a foreign policy that sought to defend freedom by relying upon such allies as Ferdinand Marcos of the Philippines, Chung He Park of South Korea, and the Shah of Iran. Many Americans have also felt guilty, embarrassed about, and even responsible for, covert operations abroad, plans for limited nuclear war, *apartheid* in South Africa, and the existence of hunger and poverty in many parts of the Third World.

In one fell swoop, neo-isolationism would rid the nation of such agonies; for by leaving the field of international competition, we would leave our responsibilities on that field. And having given up those responsibilities, we could return to criticizing those who pick them up, as we did during our years of isolation. With a neo-isolationist foreign policy, America could again seek to project its influence as a beacon rather than a crusader in the world. Once again, the nation would return to the precept of John Quincy Adams: "America . . . goes not abroad, in search of monsters to destroy. She is the well-wisher to the freedom and independence of all. She is champion and vindicator only of her own."

Had the cold war continued, neo-isolationism might have become a significant political force in the 1990s. Continued budget deficits combined with pressing national needs might have made cutting the nation's foreign commitments an attractive alternative to raising taxes or cutting social security benefits. How well neo-isolationism will fare in a post–cold war world of flux and movement is problematical. With the collapse of Communism in Eastern Europe and the reunification of Germany, it is not clear how many Americans will favor a foreign policy that leaves the future of Europe solely in the hands of the Europeans.

Yet, neo-isolationists force us to consider the significance of the revolution in nuclear weapons. Have nuclear weapons meant that the United States can now ignore the balances of power upon which our security has always rested in the past? Can we now be indifferent to the fate of Europe, the Middle East, Asia, and Africa as we were during the first hundred years of our republic? Neo-isolationists also force us to address the relationship between our economic interests and our military primacy. Is our superpower status necessary for the maintenance of the liberal international economic order that the nation founded during the closing years of World War II? Can the nation secure its economic interests in the world economy without its global commitments and its superpower status?

Neo-isolationists advocate neither autarky nor external insulation for the nation. In their opinion, a noninterventionist foreign policy would not entail a sacrifice of the nation's economic interests or its status in the world. Nor would the United States stop its commitment to humanitarian and cooperative programs. What today's neo-isolationists advocate is the kind of isolationism that the distinguished American historian Charles A. Beard prescribed for the nation over fifty years ago:

> This [isolationism] did not seek to make a "hermit" nation out of America. From the very beginning under the auspices of the early Republic, it never had embraced that impossible conception. It did not deny the obvious fact that American civilization had made use of its European heritages, was a part of western civilization, and had contacts with Occidental and Oriental cultures. It did not deny the obvious fact that wars in Europe or Asia "affect" or "concern" the United States. It did not mean "indifference" to the sufferings of Europe or China (or India or Ethiopia). In truth, in history, no people ever poured out treasure more generously in aid of human distress in every quarter of the globe—distresses springing from wars, famines, revolutions, persecutions, and earthquakes.
>
> With reference to such conflicts and sufferings, [isolationism] merely meant a recognition of the limited nature of American powers to relieve, restore, and maintain life beyond its own spheres of influence and control—a recognition of the hard fact that the United States, either alone or in any coalition, did not possess the power to force peace on Europe and Asia, to assure the establishment of democratic and pacific governments there, or to provide the social and economic underwriting necessary to the perdurance of such governments.[9]

# The Selections

## 13. Albert J. Beveridge
### *Pitfalls of a "League of Nations"*     1919

The following selection by the late Republican Senator Albert J. Beveridge presents the isolationist case against Woodrow Wilson's League of Nations. In announcing his opposition to American "entanglement," Beveridge was not proposing commercial, financial, or social isolation for the nation. What he opposed was America's membership in a global organization designed to maintain the peace of the world—a membership that, in his opinion, would lead to the nation's immersion in the "pathless wilderness of alien interests, or racial hatreds, [or] historic animosities." Beveridge's statement provides a bench mark against which to measure and evaluate today's neo-isolationism.

Once more let us make the inquiry as to what beneficial result can come to us from membership in any international combination whatever? Would not the inevitable consequence be that we involve ourselves in racial and historic antagonisms and complications from which thus far we have kept ourslves free? Would we not surrender every advantage which our situation on the globe, our history, our one unbroken traditional policy, and our resources afford us? Would we not place ourselves in the position of an integral, physical part of the continents of Europe and Asia?

It is said that steam and electricity have eliminated the oceans and that nations no longer are separated by water barriers. Is this true? The English Channel is now as effective a bulwark to the United Kingdom as it ever was. That narrow strip of water and a strong fleet have saved England from invasion for nearly a thousand years. From the military point of view, it would appear, then, that after all the Atlantic has not been abolished.

We are told that we must no longer be "isolated." How are we "isolated"? How have we ever been "isolated"? Not commercially. Not financially. Not socially. We have been "isolated" only in the political sense—only in the sense that we have not bound ourselves by alliance to mix up in the quarrels of others—only in the sense that we have attended to our own business. Is not that kind of "isolation" the very thing that is best for us and for the world? If so, why abandon it? Does anybody imagine that, if any European Nation were situated as we are, it would surrender its peculiar advantages?

The points that I have suggested are only a few of those involved in the present day recrudescence of the ancient scheme for a League of Nations. But do not the ones enumerated show that the international journey which we are asked to take is through an unexplored and perilous jungle?

Is it not better for the American people to advance along the highway of America's traditional foreign policy? That policy was formulated after years of thought, experience and consultation by all the wonderful company of constructive statesmen who laid the foundations of the American Nation. No such group of far-visioned men ever blessed with their wisdom any country at a given time. Call the roll of them—Washington, Hamilton, Jefferson, Adams, Madison, Marshall, and the others of that galaxy of immortals.

The foreign policy announced by Washington was the product of the combined and profoundly considered judgment of all these men. It was the only policy, foreign or domestic, on which all of them were united. On every other they disagreed. For that alone they stood as a single man. Several years after Washington formally declared this American policy, Jefferson restated it still more broadly and emphatically. Also that policy has been maintained from that day to this by every American statesman and every American political party.

For more than a hundred and thirty years the American Nation has progressed along the plain, safe course these men marked out. It has kept us from disastrous foreign entanglements and ruinous foreign complications. It has saved us hundreds of thousands of lives and hundreds of billions of dollars. Why leave it now to wander through a pathless wilderness of alien interests, racial hatreds, historic animosities?

Do not the well-being of a great people and the development of a mighty continent present problems hard enough to tax all the strength of the ablest men in the whole Republic? If the concerns of a few million people occupying a strip of seaboard engrossed all the energy, thought and time of men like "the fathers" whom I have just named, have any intellects now appeared capable of caring not only for the affairs of one hundred and ten million human beings covering an area that stretches from ocean to ocean, but also capable of adjusting all the differences of all the variegated peoples of the entire globe?

The situation of the American Nation is unique. Geographically it sits on the throne of the world. Its history is that of the evolution of a distinct, separate, and independent people. Its mission is no less than to create a new race on the earth and to present to mankind the example of that happiness and well-being which comes from progressive, self-disciplined liberty.

This was the faith of our fathers. By that faith ought we not still to abide?— the American Nation the supreme love of our hearts, the highest object of our effort and our thought—the American Nation free of hand and unmanacled of foot, marching steadily onward toward the destiny to which it is entitled by reason of its place on the globe, the genius of its people, and its orderly institutions of freedom.

## 14. Christopher Layne
### *The Real Conservative Agenda*      1985

In the following selection, political scientist and attorney Christopher Layne presents a frontal attack against the reassertionist worldview of the Reagan administration. According to Layne, the *neo*-conservative preoccupation with global containment had led Ronald Reagan away from *real* conservatism, which traditionally emphasized limited commitments abroad, balanced budgets, and small standing armies.

Although he never identifies his position as one of isolationism or neo-isolationism, Layne draws heavily upon the ideas of the isolationist Republican Senator Robert A. Taft and the increasingly neo-isolationist realist George Kennan. In addition, Layne's Marshall Plan II would have America shed its responsibilities for the defense of Western Europe and East Asia.

Layne's critique of reassertionism contains many of the points made by neoealists. However, Layne implicitly rejects the neorealist alternative when he proposes that the United States restrict its military commitments to the defense of geopolitical interests in the Western Hemisphere. As you read this selection, note points in common with Beveridge. Do you find any differences?

Pushed by a group of neoconservative intellectuals, global containment is making a comeback as the cornerstone of U.S. foreign policy. It could not happen at a worse time. The United States is running enormous budget and trade deficits, economic growth is slowing, and public support for the Reagan military build-up has all but evaporated. Global containment—recast as the Reagan Doctrine—commits the United States to resisting Soviet and Soviet-supported aggression wherever it arises; to building American-style democracies in Third World countries; and to rolling back communism by aiding anticommunist insurgencies. The Reagan Doctrine aims to create an ideologically congenial world, and it assumes that America's security requires nothing less.

It is now clear that no major challenge to this quixotic quest is likely to come from the Democrats in Congress. They are in disarray, split between the "defense Democrats," who offer a "me-too" policy of getting tough with the Soviets, and those whose outlook on national security policy still is shaped by the Vietnam syndrome—reflecting the mistaken belief that the United States can remain a global power while all but ruling out using military force to protect its vital interests abroad.

Therefore, it is up to the Republican party's real conservatives to offer an alternative to the neoconservative Reagan Doctrine. Because they are not liberals, real conservatives will not subordinate American national interests to the requirements of multilateralist internationalism. Real conservatives do not believe that the United States should sacrifice its political and economic interests to appease Western Europe and Japan. And real conservatives reject the idea that providing development aid, promoting human rights, and supporting international organizations should be major elements of U.S. foreign policy. But because they are not neoconservatives, real conservatives also reject the New Right's crusading ideological internationalism.

Real conservatives represent a tradition deeply rooted in America's political culture and history and associated with figures like Ohio Republican Senator Robert Taft, mid-century America's leading conservative voice, President Dwight Eisenhower, and realist scholar-diplomat George Kennan. As early as the late 1940s these men realized that America's strategic and economic circumstances required the United States to define its interests more realistically than the cold warriors of their day were doing and to reduce the scope of the country's overseas commitments. They knew that the United States has few vital interests in the Third World and that it is futile—and counterproductive—to try to mold the world in America's image. Most of all they knew that the pursuit of global containment imperils important political and economic goals at home not only dear to conservatives, but also vital for America's future: noninflationary growth, lower taxes, and fewer government controls over the private and economic lives of Americans.

The real conservatives' critique of global containment was prescient. But it also was premature. Thus when they challenged the emerging cold war orthodoxy, real conservatives lost the great debate of 1950–1951. They underestimated America's overwhelming military, political, and economic strength during that period, and their warnings about the limits of American power rang hollow. Moreover, their strong aversion to a crusading interventionist foreign policy was overcome by the ideological imperatives of the cold war. Because the real conservatives were intellectually discredited by their defeat in the great debate, the Eisenhower administration—though led by a real conservative president, notwithstanding his earlier military career—trimmed its sails to the political wind and embraced and extended the Truman administration's global containment policy.

But the Taft-Kennan critique of American foreign policy is unusually timely and penetrating today. The geopolitical changes of the last 35 years have finally validated their analysis. Thus the real conservatives of America's successor generation are charged with the task of rediscovering their intellectual anteced-ents and of building upon them to frame a new foreign-policy synthesis that reconciles a realistic policy of selective containment abroad with the advance-ment of conservative values at home.

Debates about foreign policy often boil down to clashes of ideas about the nature of international politics. This is especially true of the clash between real conservatives and neoconservatives, which forces Americans once again to examine the fundamental objectives of their foreign policy.

Should America attempt to contain the spread of communist ideology worldwide and try to impose democracy on repressive regimes? Or should it follow a more traditional balance-of-power policy that aims only at containing the expansion of Soviet political influence and military power in regions truly vital to U.S. national security? When should the United States intervene militarily in overseas conflict? How much can America afford to do in the world and what is the proper balance between the country's goals overseas and its domestic aspirations?

## Neoconservatives versus Real Conservatives

Real conservatives and neoconservatives are especially divided over the ques-tions of what America should do and what it can afford to do. To the extent it seriously addresses these questions at all, the Reagan Doctrine offers simple answers. Its neoconservative authors depict world politics as a Manichaean struggle between democracy and communism. Neoconservatives believe that the primary threat to the United States is ideological and that the balance of power is fragile. When combined, these two assumptions suggest that if Amer-ica fails to resist the advance of communism worldwide, its allies and neutrals will realign with the USSR.

According to the Reagan Doctrine, communist ideology per se threatens American security. Neoconservative intellectuals like Norman Podhoretz and Irving Kristol, who have given the Reagan Doctrine its conceptual un-derpinnings, stress that America is locked in an ideological struggle with com-munism rather than in a traditional great-power rivalry with the Soviet Union.[1]

Because it equates American security with an ideologically compatible world, the Reagan Doctrine is classically Wilsonian. Thus Secretary of State George Shultz frequently says that America must use its power to preserve an international environment conducive to the survival of its values, and he warns that the defeat of "democracy" by communism anywhere jeopardizes American security everywhere. Like the political scientist Michael Ledeen, writing in the March 1985 issue of Podhoretz's journal, *Commentary,* neoconservatives believe that America's task "is actively to encourage non-democratic governments to democratize and to aid democratic movements that challenge totalitarian and authoritarian regimes." Like all Wilsonians, neoconservatives justify these beliefs by arguing that the world would be peaceful and harmonious if only nondemocratic states (which are inherently bad) became democratic states (which are inherently good). This explains Shultz's insistence, in a February 1985 speech, that there is a worldwide "democratic revolution" that America must support in word and deed by standing for "freedom and democracy not only for ourselves but for others."

Superimposed on their ideological view of world politics is the neoconservatives' conviction that the balance of power is precarious and unstable and that America's overseas commitments are interdependent—which explains the fear that any failure of American resolve will erode U.S. credibility and lead to a worldwide stampede to the Soviet camp. The view that states tend to engage in what political scientist Kenneth Waltz of the University of California at Berkeley calls "bandwagoning" behavior lies behind Shultz's April 1984 statement that American credibility is itself a vital national interest that the United States must fight to preserve.

The Reagan Doctrine also holds that the Third World is the critical battleground in the war against communism. It is in Angola, Afghanistan, Cambodia, and Nicaragua that Shultz says America must halt the spread of communism. "It is in the Third World rather than in the United States or Europe," Podhoretz wrote in *Commentary* in 1981, "that Communism remains the greatest ideological menace." Consequently, the Third World is where American neoconservatives are pushing the administration, with some success, to organize an international alliance of "democratic freedom fighters." The president himself declared in February 1985: "We must not break faith with those who are risking their lives—on every continent . . . to defy Soviet-supported aggression and secure rights which have been ours since birth. Support for freedom fighters is self-defense."

Like the global containment policy of the pre-Vietnam years, the Reagan Doctrine has no obvious limits. Because it does not differentiate between what is vital and what is merely desirable, the doctrine holds that U.S. security is endangered by communism wherever it takes hold. If so, however, the United States must resist communism and defend democracy everywhere. Such a policy will make America ever more dangerously overextended. Although the administration's policies to date have been restrained, words and ideas do have consequences.

The Reagan Doctrine is a throwback to the global containment policy that characterized the cold war liberalism of Presidents Harry Truman, John Kennedy, and Lyndon Johnson. This strategy, and the Manichaean convictions on which it was based, reached its zenith in Kennedy's ringing inaugural vow in 1961 that the United States would "pay any price, bear any burden" to defeat communism around the world, and in then Secretary of State Dean Rusk's assertion that U.S. national security required nothing less than making the total international political environment ideologically safe. But if these goals ever were realistic, they certainly are not today.

Real conservatives should oppose the Reagan Doctrine on three principal grounds: In current and foreseeable circumstances it can bankrupt America; the American people wisely have no stomach for it; and it is based on a fundamental misreading of America's real interests and of the way in which countries behave.

The Reagan Doctrine calls for extending U.S. foreign commitments precisely at a time when circumstances require their reduction. Before Vietnam, U.S. hegemony was based firmly on strategic nuclear superiority and overwhelming economic muscle. Today, the former is gone and the latter is degenerating. To take one indicator, in 1945 the United States accounted for approximately one-half of world manufacturing output, and in 1953 this figure stood at a still fromidable 44.7 per cent.[2] It was during this period of economic and political predominance that America assumed the commitments to defend Western Europe, Japan and Korea, and the Mediterranean and the Middle East that have formed the core of its global strategy for the past 35 years.

By 1980, however, the United States accounted for only 31.5 per cent of world manufactures, and this share could fall to 20 per cent by the end of the century. Yet during the last 6 years U.S. commitments abroad actually have increased as America has assumed responsibilities in the Persian Gulf and Central America. As a March 1985 Congressional Research Service report entitled *U.S.-Soviet Military Balance, 1980–1985* states, "Our military force structure is inadequate to meet our formal and informal worldwide military commitments." The Reagan Doctrine, however, suggests that America will incur further obligations in the Third World.

## The Power-Interests Gap

America can balance its power and commitments in two ways: It can increase its power or reduce its commitments. The Reagan Doctrine explicitly rejects the notion of curtailing America's obligations. Former Secretary of Defense James Schlesinger told the Senate Foreign Relations Committee in February 1985: "For any great power—and most notably the protecting superpower of the West—to back away from commitments is more easily said than done. In practice, the loss in prestige may actually reduce our power more than the reduced claims on our military resources enhances that power." Therefore, Reagan Doctrine supporters must assume that the power-interests gap can be closed by increasing America's capabilities. This is extremely doubtful.

The Reagan defense program has been denounced vehemently as excessive. The administration's build-up does lack a coherent, realistic, strategic rationale, but by pre-Vietnam standards, the administration's military outlays have not been extravagant. From 1955 to 1970 defense spending stood consistently between 8 per cent and 9 per cent of gross national product (GNP)—only dipping below this range in 1965—and accounted for 40–45 per cent of annual federal outlays. In contrast, the Reagan administration's original fiscal 1986 defense proposal called for spending just under 8 per cent of GNP on the military—about 30 per cent of total federal spending.

Nevertheless, widespread perceptions that the administration's defense budgets are exorbitant and lack an overall strategic design have already killed the chances of congressional or public support for even modest real increases. Yet current spending fails to meet the country's present strategic commitments. Indeed, during Reagan's presidency, despite the administration's military build-up, the power-interests gap has widened. The country shows no signs of wanting to pay for the Reagan Doctrine.

Not only has America's international economic and political power waned, but also its domestic economy by any measure is much less robust than during the period of American hegemony. The persistent and worsening federal deficits of the past 30 years symbolize both America's decline and its current economic predicament. The deficit attests to the country's inability to set priorities and to live within its means. As the political scientist David Calleo and many others have suggested, deficits and strategic overextension really are two sides of the same coin. Taken together, they indicate that America's aspirations at home and abroad have outstripped its ability—or willingness—to pay for them.

The federal deficit endangers America's economic well-being, primarily by raising the risk of renewed runaway inflation. This is why real conservatives in the Senate, such as the majority leader, Robert Dole (R.-Kansas), and California Republican Pete Wilson, have worked so hard to achieve major deficit reductions in fiscal year 1986.

Ronald Reagan was elected in 1980 largely because of a pledge to reverse America's economic decline by cutting taxes to stimulate productivity, reducing government spending to curb inflation, and removing pervasive governmental regulations that stifled initiative and creativity. But budget deficits in the hundreds of billions of dollars now loom "as far as the eye can see" on the economic horizon, and the military build-up required to implement the Reagan Doctrine will only make matters worse. Apparently neoconservatives think that America can afford this no matter what it costs and that the country can embark on foreign-policy crusades without paying for them. Common sense says otherwise. As Senator Barry Goldwater (R.-Arizona) says, "[Y]ou can't keep pumping out money you don't have." Sooner or later America will pay for the Reagan Doctrine's almost limitless appetite for defense outlays, either with higher taxes, inflation, or both. These are not attractive options.

The United States can avoid this choice only with big cuts in government spending. Obviously, the burden of such cuts should not fall on the military budget alone. But like all advanced societies, the United States is to some degree an entitlement society, and beyond a certain point reductions in domestic spending provoke too much opposition for politicians to ignore.

Moreover, America's ability to sustain any level of strategic commitments depends on its economic strength. In a real sense the economy is the fourth branch of the armed forces. Under the Reagan Doctrine, the country would have to come very close to full mobilization to close the gap between its power and its responsibilities. The threat posed by such a policy to America's prosperity and freedom is incalculable.

Unlike past and present advocates of global containment, real conservatives have always understood this. As Taft once observed, no country "can be constantly prepared to undertake a full-scale war at any moment and still hope to maintain any of the other purposes in which people are interested and for which nations are founded."[3] Few more poignant statements of these concerns can be found than Eisenhower's April 1953 speech to the American Society of Newspaper Editors declaring that "every gun that is made . . . signifies, in the final sense, a theft from those who hunger and are not fed, and those who are cold and are not clothed."

Real conservatives have recognized that a tension always exists between the needs of an interventionist foreign policy and those of a healthy economy. Taft predicted that global containment would impose "tremendous" economic burdens and threaten the country's prosperity. Eisenhower's Secretary of State John Foster Dulles warned that large defense outlays "unbalance our budget and require taxes so heavy that they discourage incentive. They so cheapen the dollar that savings, pensions, and Social Security reserves already have lost most of their value."[4]

It was Eisenhower who put the point in sharp focus. Economic strength, he said, is the foundation of military power. Americans must be careful, Eisenhower warned, that their foreign-policy objectives do not become so ambitious that their pursuit ends up destroying what they seek to defend—the vitality and strength of America's political and economic institutions.[5] These are precisely the institutions that could be threatened by the Reagan Doctrine's version of global containment.

The all-but-evaporated public support for bigger defense budgets is only one signal that the American people want nothing to do with policies like the Reagan Doctrine. The doctrine purports to be a policy of strength and—on the declaratory level—is meant to rally the public behind the administration's defense build-up and U.S. intervention in Central America. But the more neoconservatives talk about a global anticommunist crusade, the more public anxiety they create about a possible superpower confrontation, thereby diminishing support for a policy of strength. Because the doctrine fails to set military and foreign-policy priorities, Americans know only that it will be expensive. They have difficulty seeing how this policy has made them stronger. There is a risk of what is known as mirror-imaging here: The public may become so disillusioned with the Reagan Doctrine's costs that, like the neoconservatives, it may lose the ability to distinguish between those military programs America needs and those it does not.

Moreover, the Reagan Doctrine's interventionist instincts run counter to the public's desire for noninvolvement in the rest of the world—especially in the Third World. Most Americans view the Third World as an unpleasant place: the home of corrupt regimes and equally nasty revolutionaries. U.S. intervention there, it is felt, will hurt America without helping others. Americans strongly oppose prolonged and costly military involvement in Third World countries and know that there are many more potential Vietnams than potential Grenadas. They understand that not even superpowers are omnipotent, and that the United States lacks the material, psychological, and spiritual resources to remake the world in its own image. And they remember that rhetorical excesses ("pay any price, bear any burden") can easily lead to foreign-policy excesses. Americans will be more likely to support intervention to defend the country's vital interests in Central America if they are reassured that this policy is not simply a prelude to an endless series of entanglements in faraway, insignificant lands, involving people of whom they know little or nothing.

## Paying the Price

If global containment is economially and politically beyond America's reach, how then can the United States accomplish the admittedly vital objective of containing the Soviet Union? First, by taking advantage of the natural dynamics of the international balance of power. Second, by defining its national interests more realistically.

The Reagan Doctrine implicitly assumes that the United States is not doing enough in the world. But the first objective of U.S. policy must be to compel others—namely, Western Europe and Japan—to do much more so that America can do much less.

One leading cause of America's relative decline in power is the increase in West European and Japanese economic power since the end of World War II. Yet the distribution of military responsibilities in Western Europe and Japan still reflects the conditions of 40 years ago. Japan, the world's second-ranking economic power, spends a mere 1 per cent of its GNP on defense and depends completely on the United States for its security. Taken as a unit, the economies of NATO's European members compare favorably to America's, but these countries devote considerably less of their individual GNPs to defense. More to the point, a recent Pentagon study indicates that the U.S. commitment to NATO accounts for some 58 per cent of America's own defense budget.[6]

America's early postwar policy aimed to assist Western Europe and Japan in their respective recoveries in the expectation that they could resume some semblance of their traditional international roles and relieve the United States of its global burdens. The U.S. commitment to this reconstruction—and to its corollary, multilateral free trade—made it inevitable that these countries would be strengthened at America's expense. But this was judged an acceptable price to pay because, on balance, the United States would be better off in a world where Western Europe and Japan could protect themselves. Today, America continues to pay the price for its postwar policy but is not reaping any of the benefits.

The United States should complete its historic postwar mission and devolve to Western Europe and Japan full responsibility for their own defense. What Washington needs—and what real conservatives should offer—is a sequel to the Marshall Plan. This far-sighted program helped Europe recover its economic independence. "Marshall Plan II" would build on the economic strength of Western Europe and Japan and allow them to become politically and militarily independent. To avoid leaving these countries out in the cold, the United States should set a firm timetable for a phased, long-term American withdrawal—perhaps over 10 years—coupled with an invitation to Western Europe and Japan to formulate their own postalliance defense plans. Washington would give them the assistance they needed to implement these plans. But when the transition period ended, U.S. defense commitments would terminate.

Western Europe and Japan unquestionably have the capability to defend themselves. Marshall Plan II would give them the incentive—which they will lack as long as they remain under the American umbrella—to transform their resources into real military power. Marshall Plan II may or may not lead to the pentagonal balance of power of which former President Richard Nixon and his secretary of state, Henry Kissinger, once spoke. But for this new U.S. policy to work these countries need only become strong enough to act as credible regional counterweights to the Soviet Union. This they easily can do.

The older generation of American policymakers—accustomed to U.S. hegemony—is temperamentally unable to contemplate the measures required to balance U.S. commitments and resources. However, because it is the first group of Americans in this century to experience something other than American omnipotence in world politics, the successor generation is more prepared to undertake the major strategic reorientation needed to bring about this balance.

Marshall Plan II also would be opposed on the ground that postalliance Europe would fall under the Kremlin's control. But here American and European Atlanticists join with many neoconservatives in fundamentally misperceiving the nature of world politics. States tend to balance—not to jump on band wagons. As the Princeton University political scientist Stephen M. Walt wrote in the Spring 1985 issue of *International Security:*

> Threatening states will provoke others to align against them. Because those who seek to dominate others will attract widespread opposition, status quo states can take a relatively sanguine view of threats. Credibility is less important in a balancing world because one's allies will resist threatening states out of their own self-interest, not because they expect others to do it for them. Thus the fear that allies will defect declines. Moreover, if balancing is the norm *and* if statesmen understand this tendency, aggression is discouraged because those who contemplate it will anticipate resistance.

Indeed, history provides many examples of balancing behavior. In the nuclear era, China has balanced against the menacing and proximate power of the Soviet Union by entering into an informal strategic entente with the United States. During the era of U.S. hegemony, Charles de Gaulle's France maximized its independence by moving away from the United States and edging slightly toward the Soviet Union. But in the late 1970s and early 1980s, the shift of the strategic nuclear balance toward Moscow caused Paris to tilt back toward Washington.[7] Benito Mussolini's Italy, in fact, is recent history's only major example of "bandwagoning," and all Europeans know the price his country paid.

West Europeans have strong reasons for exploiting U.S. fears that they will jump on Moscow's bandwagon if America withdraws from the Continent. They find the Atlanticist status quo comfortable. But surely Western Europe's leaders are smart enough to realize that weak states that align themselves with strong states are at the mercy of the stronger powers. Moreover, Europe's diplomatic history is the history of the balance of power. Before World War I, European states balanced against Germany's drive for continental hegemony, and they coalesced against Charles V of the Holy Roman Empire, Louis XIV of France, Napoleon I, and Adolf Hitler. Indeed, the revival of the Western European Union, recent efforts to improve Franco-West German defense cooperation, and various West European proposals for an independent West European nuclear force suggest that Western Europe already is thinking about its strategic posture in a postalliance world.

There is a small risk that Western Europe might choose to join the USSR's bandwagon after a U.S. withdrawal. But the United States runs a much greater risk in refusing to think about life after NATO. Although many leaders choose to deny it, the evidence of NATO's progressive, inevitable decay is overwhelming. Unlike their elders, successor generation real conservatives do not have a romanticized view of the Western alliance. Because geopolitical circumstances change, alliances never last forever. NATO is unraveling because Western Europe and America have very different perceptions of the Soviet threat and because they are divided by major, deepening divergences of their principal political, strategic, and economic interests.

In these circumstances, America's willingness to maintain its commitment to Western Europe is bound to diminish—especially as Americans become more fully aware of the nuclear dangers and economic costs of this commitment. At the same time, Western Europe's restlessness with America's dominance is growing, and West European countries are increasingly asserting their independence from the United States. Paradoxically, the tensions that result from trying to preserve the façade of alliance unity offer Moscow its best chance to permanently damage U.S.-West European relations.[8]

The emergence of a postalliance world can either strengthen or weaken the United States: It all depends on how America gets there. A managed transition like Marshall Plan II will maximize the likelihood of a positive outcome. An ostrich-like policy that lets events run their course on the assumption that NATO will last forever will make the reverse more likely. Wise leadership does not resist the inevitable; it seeks to turn the inevitable to its own advantage.

## Criteria for Intervention

Balancing the ends and means of U.S. policy also requires the United States to define more realistically its goals for the Third World. The United States has few tangible interests in the Third World that compel military or even extensive political involvement. There is no Third World region or country whose loss would decisively tip the superpower balance against America—including the Persian Gulf, whose oil is vital only to Western Europe and Japan, and whose defense would be handled by these countries under Marshall Plan II. The

United States is not economically dependent on Third World markets. And its current reliance on Third World raw materials can be minimized by diversifying sources of supply, by stockpiling, by developing synthetic replacements, and by using natural substitutes.

Instead, U.S. involvement in the Third World flows mainly from intangible concerns. Americans often fear that their failure to step into Third World conflicts will lead to Soviet gains. This is the price Americans pay for regarding the world as both politically and ideologically bipolar. This perspective rules out the existence of marginal areas and depicts international politics as a zero-sum game in which a single setback will inevitably have repercussions elsewhere.

The Reagan Doctrine in fact creates a self-fulfilling prophecy by failing to distinguish vital from secondary interests. When Washington says a particular outcome would be a defeat—or that U.S. interests in some part of the world are "vital"—others believe it. Thus the doctrine's rhetoric presents the country with two equally bad alternatives in the Third World: using American power to prevent political changes defined as "unacceptable," or accepting the unacceptable—with consequent damage to U.S. credibility. A wise foreign policy does not paint policymakers into corners like this.

America's avowed ideological interest in containing communism and supporting democracy also motivates U.S. involvement in the Third World. It is unclear whether neoconservatives actually believe—as did Rusk—that the United States can be secure only when its total international environment is safe. But it is clear that they believe—as the University of Maryland political scientist George Quester wrote in *Foreign Policy* 40 (Fall 1980)—that "the politics of Minnesota would also work in Burma or Kenya or Cuba or Algeria." But the question arises: How much are Americans prepared to pay to bring this about?

Any such attempt probably will prove costly and ultimately futile. In a world torn by political, social, and religious upheaval and by Third World nationalism, violence is endemic and conflicts usually intractable. Thus Third World interventions by outside powers recently have run into major troubles: America in Vietnam, the Soviet Union in Afghanistan, the United States and Israel in Lebanon. Both superpowers' inability to influence events in the Persian Gulf war illustrates the same point.

Because nationalism runs so high in the Third World, superpower intervention is resented, and its costs usually exceed the benefits. Although Americans find it difficult to accept, most states want to increase their independence from both superpowers, and an overly active U.S. policy in the Third World may have the perverse effect of pushing developing countries toward Moscow. Regardless of whether the Reagan Doctrine really seeks to impose American values on the Third World, crusading American rhetoric convinces other countries that America intends to do so, and they feel threatened. "Certainly," as Taft observed, "however benevolent we might be, other people simply do not like to be dominated, and we would be in the same position of suppressing rebellions by force in which the British found themselves during the nineteenth century."[9]

Ironically, despite Third World fears of U.S. domination, America execises virtually no control over "friendly" developing countries or over anti-Soviet "freedom fighters." They may be allies, but they are peculiar allies, because they are no more committed to liberal democratic values than are their Marxist opponents. It is naive to imagine that American political values could flourish in countries that have no indigenous democratic traditions and that lack the social, cultural, and economic institutions upon which the U.S. democratic structure rests. America's continuing search for a "third force" between the totalitarians and authoritarians of the Left and the Right is unavailing. Political pluralism in the Third World is not promoted by America's choosing among equally unsavory groups whose brutality is distinguishable only by whether it is used to hold power or to seize it.

U.S. interests may be threatened by Third World conflicts. But the United States is not threatened by the spread of communism per se. As became apparent when Josip Broz Tito's Yugoslavia broke with the Kremlin, and again when China and the USSR split, nationalism can impel even communist governments to follow anti-Soviet policies. It is other countries' foreign policies, not their domestic systems, with which the United States must be concerned. The impact on U.S. interests of communism's advance into a particular place depends, as Kennan noted, on such questions as whether and to what extent a region's loss would augment Soviet strength and shift the balance of power.[10] Also pertinent is whether America's historical involvement in the threatened area is so deep that a U.S. setback could justifiably damage American credibility; whether U.S. intervention would be necessary to force Moscow to recognize the legitimacy of U.S. geopolitical interests; and how important the threatened area is to the security of the American homeland.

But in his *Memoirs*, Kennan also pointed out that the existence of a threat to American interests is "only the beginning, not the end, of the process" of deciding whether to plunge into the Third World. Kennan—and more recently, Secretary of Defense Caspar Weinberger, in a widely noted November 1984 speech to the National Press Club—set out similar criteria on which such a decision must turn. Above all, American troops and resolve should never be used as a substitute for the troops and resolve of others.

## The Central America Debate

The difference between the neoconservative and the real conservative approaches to America's Third World policy is illustrated by the debate over U.S. Central America policy. Central America is no more hospitable a theater for direct U.S. military involvement than is the rest of the Third World. Yet the United States has a strong interest in maintaining a favorable political and strategic environment in neighboring areas. Moreover, a stable superpower relationship requires each superpower to respect the other's critical sphere of influence. The Soviets are not likely to show such respect, however, unless America so compels them by assertively defending U.S. interests.

Although the loss of Central America would not decisively affect America's core security, America does have important strategic interests in the Caribbean Basin, such as Mexican and Venezuelan oil, the Panama Canal, and the Caribbean sea-lanes. Moreover, America's strategic position obviously would be less comfortable if Mexico turned pro-Soviet. Taken individually, none of these interests is vital enough to justify direct U.S. military involvement. But taken collectively, they are.

Still, Americans must be clear on what does and does not justify U.S. military intervention in Central America. Neoconservatives, until recently at least, have not decided whether the Nicaraguan threat is ideological or geopolitical. If the former, the United States can accept nothing less than the Sandinistas' overthrow, and direct U.S. military intervention is very likely at some point.

Real conservatives see the threat as geopolitical: They insist that the United States cannot allow Nicaragua to become a Soviet satellite or to use force and subversion to export its revolution. But they do not believe that Washington's interests are threatened by the Sandinistas' domestic policies in and of themselves. These policies are odious, but they are Nicaraguan people's business, not America's. For real conservatives it is not necessarily the case that the United States must overthrow the Sandinistas, because they can envision the possibility of a political accommodation that would exchange an American guarantee of noninterference in Nicaragua's internal affairs for the withdrawal of all Soviet-bloc, Cuban, Libyan, and Palestine Liberation Organization military advisers from Nicaragua; the cessation of Sandinista support for Central American insurgents; and strict quantitative and qualitative limits on Nicaragua's armed forces. These terms will ensure that Nicaragua does not become a Soviet satellite.

Real conservatives recognize that war is a continuation of politics by other means and that U.S. policy must combine force and diplomacy to compel changes in Nicaraguan policies that threaten regional security. Thus the United States must support the anti-Sandinista *contra* forces and exert other forms of military and economic pressure, because, otherwise, the Sandinistas have little incentive to accommodate U.S. wishes.

Central America, however, is a special case for real conservatives. They agree with neoconservatives that Moscow should not have a free ride in the Third World and that, within well-defined limits, the United States should do what it can to make the Soviets pay for their interventions. But real conservatives also know that vital American interests are not engaged in Afghanistan, Angola, Cambodia, and similar Third World hot spots, and they are under no illusions that the anti-Soviet groups in these places are fighting for liberal democracy. Neoconservatives talk as if the contrary is true, and this is one reason that the Reagan Doctrine's implications are so disturbing. By placing so much emphasis on the "worldwide democratic revolution" and on U.S. support for anti-Soviet forces, the Reagan Doctrine may link American prestige and credibility to the outcome of these peripheral conflicts. The Reagan Doctrine forgets that in the real, balancing world there are, in fact, many areas of only marginal importance to America.

But real conservatives are realists. Although today there is nothing in the Third World other than Central America vital enough to compel U.S. military intervention, they know that circumstances can change and that some other region or country could become vitally important to the United States in the future. But before they take the United States down the interventionist road, real conservatives will recall Taft's advice: "Our people . . . cannot send armies to block a communist advance in every far corner of the world."

America's experience as a world power has been unique because for much of that time its power was unchallenged. Obviously, this no longer is true. Everywhere are the signs of a more plural international system—a system America helped create. Yet American foreign-policymakers still do not understand that the era of American predominance was an anomaly, not the historical norm. The Reagan Doctrine's neoconservative authors in particular seem to be caught in some Spielbergian time warp that has transported them back to the early 1950s. They talk as if the relative decline of American power, and Vietnam, had never occurred. They do not understand that the end of American hegemony was brought about by complex, objective geopolitical factors; it is not something that can be reversed merely by an assertion of national will.

The most critical functions of political leaders in a democratic society are to define the national agenda and to educate the public. The Reagan Doctrine's creators seemingly do not understand what the important issues are. The Republican party stands at the threshold of majority status. But power brings responsibility, and America needs an alternative to the Reagan Doctrine. It falls to real conservatives of America's succesor generation to provide it—first by changing the terms of the foreign-policy debate and then by changing U.S. foreign policy itself. The essence of a conservative policy is to preserve national strength, husband resources, and expend them wisely. The successor generation's real conservatives must carry the message that American power is finite and that not even a superpower can impose order on a recalcitrant world. The attempt can lead only to exhaustion, to dangerous overextension, and to lasting damage to the fabric of American society.

## NOTES

1. See Podhoretz, "The Future Danger," *Commentary* (April 1981).
2. Paul M. Kennedy, "The First World War and the International Power System," *International Security* 9, no. 1 (Summer 1984): 36–39.
3. *A Foreign Policy for Americans* (Garden City, N.Y.: Doubleday and Co., 1951), 68.
4. "A Foreign Policy of Boldness," *Life*, 19 May 1952, 146.
5. Quoted in John Lewis Gaddis, *Strategies of Containment* (New York: Oxford University Press, 1982), 134–136.
6. Richard Halloran, "Europe Called Main U.S. Arms Cost," *New York Times*, 20 July 1984, 2.
7. See Stanley Hoffmann, "Gaullism by Any Other Name," *Foreign Policy* 57 (Winter 1984–85).

8. These arguments are developed in Christopher Layne, "Toward German Reunification?"*Journal of Contemporary Studies* (Fall 1984), and "Ending the Alliance,"
   *Journal of Contemporary Studies* (Summer 1983).
9. Quoted in Ronald Radosh, *Prophets on the Right* (New York: Simon and Schuster,
   1975), 139.
10. Gaddis, *Strategies of Containment*, 40–42.

# 15. Earl C. Ravenal
## *An Alternative to Containment*                        1987

In this selection, Earl Ravenal argues for a foreign policy based upon the
principles of strategic disengagement, nonintervention, and self-reliance. In
addition, he presents the military strategy upon which this foreign policy
alternative would be based. After reading this excerpt, note the areas of
agreement and disagreement between Ravenal and neo-realists. Revenal also
presents and rebuts potential criticisms of the neo-isolationist strategy. How
convincing do you find Ravenal's rebuttals?*

The entailments and disabilities of containment suggest the consideration of a
major, coherent alternative. Such a policy would be one of strategic disengagement and non-intervention. In such a program, both of the cardinal
elements of the present U.S. strategic paradigm would change. Instead of
deterrence and alliance, we would pursue war avoidance and self-reliance. Our
security would depend more on our abstention from regional conflicts and, in
the strategic nuclear dimension, on finite essential deterrence.

In a program of non-intervention, the United States would defend primarily
against an umbra of direct threats to those values that are so basic that they are
part of the definition of state and society; our political integrity and the safety of
our citizens and their domestic property. Because those values are inalienable,
their defense would *ipso facto* be credible. We would also defend against a
penumbra of challenges that are indirectly threatening but are relevant because
of their weight, momentum, direction, and ineluctability. We would be looking
for a new set of criteria—decision rules, if you will—that condition and bound
our responses to future events that could be considered challenges. This definition is intensive, rather than extensive, in nature.

Nor are these rhetorical terms. As I have discussed at greater length
elsewhere,[1] our military program would be designed to defend the most restricted perimeter required to protect those core values, a much smaller
perimeter than the one the United States is now committed to defend. We
would defend against military threats directed against our homeland. That is

---

*Some footnotes have been renumbered.

not, in the first instance, an overtly geographical criterion, and deliberately not. We should not be fixated on drawing lines in the sand; rather, we should be concerned to characterize correctly the nature and import of other countries' actions, and to appreciate the characteristics of foreign events that cause us to consider them "threats." Functional criteria may be less definitive than geographical ones, but they are more important.

The concomitant of this restricted definition of American interests and of the threats to them is that the United States would encourage other nations to become self-reliant, to hedge. In fact, many foresighted countries already discount American protection in a wide range of possible cases, despite our formal obligations to come to their assistance. This does not imply that all these countries face imminent threats; simply that some are impressed more by the reality of our circumstances than by our reassurances and have drawn the appropriate conclusions.

War avoidance invokes primarily, though not exclusively, the strategic nuclear component of this counterparadigm. We will always need a strategy that discourages direct nuclear attacks on our homeland or intolerable coercion of our national political choices by nuclear threats. But today, given the parity between the nuclear arsenals of the two superpowers, our safety depends on maintaining a condition that is called crisis stability, wherein both sides have a strong incentive to avoid striking first with their nuclear weapons.

A design for nuclear stability would look like this: Since an enemy's first strike must logically be a damage-limiting attack against our nuclear forces, we should eliminate systems as they become even theoretically vulnerable to a Soviet preemptive strike. Land-based systems are inevitably vulnerable, despite the efforts of a succession of administrations to put them in multiple or closely spaced shelters (as with the MX), or to acquire a redundant and dispersed force (as with the prospective Midgetman single-warhead missiles). Instead, we should move to a dyad of strategic nuclear forces: ballistic missile submarines and bombers armed with medium-range air-launched cruise missiles. Then, to discourage further a Soviet first strike, we should not target Soviet missiles (nor does it make any strategic or moral sense to aim at Soviet cities). Rather, we should develop a list of some 3,000 military targets such as naval and air bases, concentrations of conventional forces, military logistical complexes, and arms industries that are relatively far from large civilian population centers. Finally, since nuclear war is most likely to occur through *our* escalation in the midst of conventional war, probably in Europe, or possibly in the Middle East, we must confront our attitude toward the first use of nuclear weapons. I believe we should impose upon ourselves an unconditional doctrine of no first use.

The two elements of war avoidance and self-reliance constitute a new paradigm, a principled policy of non-intervention that should be a major alternative. We would no longer consider peace to be seamless and indivisible. There might well be continuing troubles in the world, including cases where a Soviet-sponsored faction perpetrates a forcible revision of the local military balance. If we were to intervene, we might win a few rounds, as in Grenada in

November 1983. But the list of feasible interventions is far shorter than the list of desirable ones, and even shorter than the list of "necessary" ones.

But what of the expected, and frequent, charge that a non-interventionist foreign policy would lay the world open to Soviet expansion or revolutionary violence? In the last analysis, a true non-interventionist position does not depend on trust in Soviet intentions; it takes Soviet power seriously. It simply accepts the possibility of suffering some foreign losses in order to preserve the integrity of our own economy, society, and political system. Yet there are reasons, also, to doubt the unvarnished projection of a Soviet political-military windfall. These reasons depend on a more sophisticated calculus of the motives (the propensity to intervene) of a potential aggressor; on an unavoidably complex anlaysis of the course and future of the international system; and on a somewhat speculative projection of the status of Western Europe without America.

First, it is difficult to determine just how the Soviet Union would react to a non-interventionist American foreign policy. However, a potential aggressor will consider not simply the odds of victory or defeat; he must weigh whether his potential gains, minus the predicted costs of achieving them, exceed what he could achieve without attacking. That is a very different, and a much more discouraging, calculus.

Beyond that, a serious proposal of non-intervention must make some assumptions about the world—that is, the global political-military balance, specifically between the United States and the Soviet Union, and the situation in strategic regions of the world. The international system is not just an inert environment for the making of foreign policy, or so much malleable clay or putty for the designers of an active and manipulative foreign policy. The structure or design of the international system is also in important ways a determinant of foreign policy, a framework within which each nation must choose. Its characteristics are to some extent alterable by individual nations, more or less according to their power, and the United States will continue to have pre-eminent ability to set and modify those parameters through its own choices and actions. But to do so requires a further expense or effort and is arguably less efficient than a policy of operating within the parameters.

The evolving international system will offer increasing challenges and temptations, but it also will impose greater costs and risks for less ample and less secure gains, all within the social, economic, and political constraints of the domestic system, which are themselves becoming tighter and more troublesome. The world that we will confront as we move beyond the turn of the millennium will evolve further from the world that we have experienced during the past four decades, in six critical dimensions.

The first is the *high probability of troubles,* such as embargoes, expropriations, coups, revolutions, externally supported subversions, thrusts by impatient irredentist states, and calculated probes of defense perimeters; these will be neither resolved nor constructively equilibrated by some benign balance of power mechanism.

The second tendency is *increasing interdependence.* But this has a different implication from the one which proponents would recognize. Interdependence is a set of functional linkages of nations: resources, access routes, economic activities and organizations, populations, and the physical environment. These areas harbor problems that could be aggravated to the point where they became threats to the security of nations, demanding but not suggesting solutions.

The third element of the future international system is the probable *absence of an ultimate adjustment mechanism*, in the form of a supranational institution that can authoritatively police the system, dispensing justice and granting relief, especially in those extreme cases that threaten to unhinge the system.

The fourth factor is an interim conclusion of the first three: *Stabilization*, the long-range action of states to bring about conditions in the external system that enhance their security, *will take the form of unilateral interventions rather than collaborative world order.*

The fifth future condition—perhaps the most important one—is the *unmanageable diffusion of power*, beyond some ideal geometry of powerful but "responsible" states. Instead, this process is likely to proceed to a kaleidoscopic interaction of multiple political entities. By all measures of power—military (nuclear or conventional, actual or potential), economic (total wealth or commercial weight), or political (the thrust to autonomy and achievement)—there may be 15 or 20 salient states, not necessarily equal, and not necessarily armed with nuclear weapons, but potent to the point of enjoying the possibility of independent action. This diffusion of power will have several aspects. One is that limits will become evident in existing polities, and cracks will appear in existing military alliances. Another aspect of diffusion is the impracticality of military power, whether nuclear, conventional, or subconventional—quite a different matter from the absolute or relative disutility of military force.

The sixth condition that will complicate the enforcement of international order is the *incoherence of domestic support*, not just in our country but to a certain extent in all, and not just when political systems are free from external pressure, but precisely when they most need steady support. The lack of public support might not prevent intervention, but it might critically inhibit its prosecution. (This, in my view, is the enduring lesson of Vietnam.)

The net result of these tendencies is that general unalignment, as a pattern or type of international system, is likely to succeed the present multipolar balance of power, just as the balance of power succeeded the earlier regime of bipolar confrontation. This would be a world of circumscribed regional powers. Though absolute technological and military disparities might increase, there might be more equality of usable power among the present superpowers, great powers, and middle powers, including some accomplished or would-be "regional hegemones."

In the face of such a world, the policy choice for the United States is whether to attempt to control its environment, or simply to adjust. Although challenges and opportunities will arise, it will be increasingly unnecessary and undesirable for the United States to intervene in regional situations. It will be unnecessary because the very presence of either a regional hegemone or a perpetually conflicted situation will be an obstruction to the other superpower, or to any other external power. There would be less potential profit for any intervenor, making our own abstention less risky. It will be increasingly undesirable for the United States to intervene in regional situations because these situations will be messy and interminable. They will tend to be profitless, because intervention will be expensive, and results, even if achieved, will be transient.

Of course, for the United States the most important region is Europe. What would be the probable status of Europe without American protection? I would envisage a Europe that is independent politically and diplomatically and autonomous strategically, and that acts in greater military concert, though not political unity. Actually, Europe could go quite far toward defending itself without American help. It need not be "Finlandized," either in whole or in part. If the United States were to withdraw, the principal European countries would probably increase their defense spending gradually, perhaps to 5% or 6% of their gross national product. The countries of Western Europe, even if not formally united in a new military alliance, have the economic, demographic, and military resources, and the advantage of natural and man-made barriers, to defeat or crucially penalize a Soviet attack.[2]

The United States can make large cuts in its defense budget *if* and *only if* such a policy of strategic disengagement and non-intervention is adopted. We could defend our essential security and our central values with a much smaller force structure than we have now. Such a force structure would provide the following general purpose forces: 8 land divisions (6 army and 2 Marine Corps), 20 tactical airwing equivalents (11 air force, 4 Marine Corps, and 5 navy), and 6 carrier battle groups. With the addition of a dyad of nuclear forces (submarines and cruise-missile-armed bombers), this would mean manpower of 1,185,000 (370,000 army, 315,000 air force, 365,000 navy, and 135,000 Marine Corps). The total defense budget at the end of a decade of adjustment would be about $158 billion in 1987 dollars. In contrast, the Reagan administration originally requested, for 1987, 21 land divisions and 46 tactical airwing equivalents, with 14 carrier battle groups; this force requires 2,181,000 men and a budget autohrization of $312 billion.

These differences will multiply greatly unless we change our course. The way we are headed, the defense budget will be about $530 billion by 1996, and cumulative defense spending during this decade will be over $4.1 trillion. Under a non-interventionist policy, the 1996 defense budget would be 58% less, and the cumulative cost over a decade would be under $2.6 trillion.[3]

## CONCLUSION: THE SHAPE OF THE DEBATE

The case for non-intervention is not a pure prescription of a state of affairs that is inherently and universally attractive. It is prescription mingled with prediction. Non-intervention is proposed as an adjustment to the world as it is shaping up and to the constraints of our polity, society, and economy. Our national orientation should not depend entirely on whether some objective, such as containment, is worthy of our commitment. Worthy causes are not free. As in all things, there is a price to be paid, and that price has been growing higher. The multidimensional costs of containment (the specific acts and the general stance of perpetual preparedness) should be weighed against the consequences of not containing and not preparing to contain. Part of the prediction is that our country, taken as a decision-making system, will not pay those costs.

The consistent pursuit of non-intervention by this nation will entail a fundamental change in its foreign policy and national strategy. We would have to test our foreign and military policies against the harder questions about national security. In the first instance, this means distinguishing sharply between the interests of our allies and dependents and the interests of our own country. We would also have to learn to differentiate even our own interests from our security. This is not to deny that our other interests (defined in terms of the objective goals of actual individuals and organizations) are real, and mostly legitimate. It is rather to challenge the automatic notion that we must prepare to defend our panoply of interests by the use of threat of force, overt or covert, wholesale or piecemeal, through proxies or by ourselves.[4] And it is to challenge the notion that "milieu goals"—the shape and character of the international system, "balance" in general or with a particular antagonist, and even the more abstract concept of order in the system—should be assimilated into the schedule of objects that we must pursue and, by implication, defend. Sometimes, in the typical inflated and debased political rhetoric of our time, these more abstract and generic milieu goals are disguised as more immediate, even vital, security interests. But "vital" should be reserved for those truly supreme interests that derive so strictly from our identity as a nation that they could not credibly be alienated, even by an official expression.

When put up against these more stringent criteria, most interests are alienable, in the sense that we can choose not to defend them against all kinds of threats. We can draw back to a line that has two interacting and mutually reinforcing characteristics: credibility and feasibility—a line that we *must* hold, as part of the definition of our sovereignty, and that we *can* hold, as a defensive perimeter and a strategic force concept that can be maintained with advantage and within constraints over the long haul.

Such a national strategy would not, admittedly, maximize gross American "interests" in the world. But it would be designed to optimize the net interests of American society in the world, in terms of the value of these interests measured against the costs (and costs disguised as risks) of defending them. Ultimately, we may have to settle for less than we would like—even for less than we think we need.

## NOTES

1. See Earl C. Ravenal, *Defining Defense: The 1985 Military Budget* (Washington, D.C.: Cato Institute, 1984).

2. See the more ample treatment of this point in Earl C. Ravenal, *NATO: The Tides of Discontent* (Berkeley, Cal.: University of California, Institute of International Studies, 1985).

3. These figures, based on official Pentagon estimates for the first five years, assume, for the five-year period 1992–1996, 4% inflation plus 2% real annual increases. My alternative assumes, for the entire period 1987–1996, 4% inflation only, with my prescribed cuts taken over a 10-year period.

4. As in the case of the Persian Gulf, some national interests cost more to defend than they are worth. See the analysis in Earl C. Ravenal, "Defending Persian Gulf Oil," *Intervention*, Fall 1984, and "The Strategic Cost of Oil," testimony before the Subcommittee on the Panama Canal and the Outer Continental Shelf, Committee on Merchant Marine and Fisheries, U.S. House of Representatives, 27 June 1984.

# 16. Stephen D. Krasner
## *Neo-isolationism and Structural Change* 1989

In this essay, Stanford University political scientist Stephen Krasner develops the case for neo-isolationism. As you read this selection, look for areas of agreement and disagreement between Layne, Ravenal, and Krasner. After you finish reading this selection, create your worldview profile. To what extent do you accept or reject neo-isolationism?

The city of Mainz has the largest carnival celebration in the Frankfurt area. More than 100 groups participated in the 1989 parade. There were marching bands replete with glockenspiels, equestrian groups, and a few satirical political floats dealing with such issues as the degradation of the environment, the use of hormones in cattle and changes in Germany's public health system. All of the groups were private with two exceptions: marching bands from the American armed forces. In the parade there was no representation from Germany's military, or from the military of other European countries, or, for that matter, from any other governmental entity. The only other representatives of the state in evidence were local German police and American military police.

The deep and continuing commitment of the United States to the defense of Western Europe, including the stationing of large numbers of American troops overseas, has become part of the landscape of the modern world, taken for granted in its general topography if not its specific appearance. For almost 40 years, the United States has garrisoned troops on foreign soil, an historically unprecedented commitment. For almost as long, American strategic doctrine has been based on extended deterrence—on the threat to annihilate the Soviet Union with nuclear weapons should it attack Western Europe.

While the aggregate resource capabilities of the United States remain formidable, its relative power position has eroded since the late 1940s. This erosion has been nowhere more dramatic than in the area that is most relevant for America's global military strategy: nuclear weapons. Yet there has been no corresponding change in fundamental American commitments. These commitments now exceed American capabilities. This imbalance has created a less stable nuclear balance because of the inherent ambiguities of extended deterrence. It has exaggerated the importance of military strength as opposed to economic performance in a world in which the basic success of American values will depend more on the latter than the former. The interests of the United States would be better served by a strategy based on neo-isolationism, which would result in a relative decline in American defense expenditures, the withdrawal of American troops from Europe and the rejection of extended deterrence as an explicit doctrine. Neo-isolationism would not imply a withdrawal from global involvement. Cooperation among the advanced industrialized democracies would continue, especially in the economic realm, but policy would be based on shared interests, not on American dominance.

Unfortunately, an incongruence between capabilities and commitments does not in any automatic way lead to a change in state policy. It is difficult for political leaders to assess relative power. Policy-makers can be trapped by past actions: bureaucracies established to implement policy and rhetoric used to build public support can constrain future options. The implications of new configurations of power may become clear only in a crisis, as they did for Britain in August 1914, when it became evident that troops would be committed on the continent of Europe even though Britain had no formal treaty obligations, and for the Soviet Union in June 1941, when Germany's invasion made it painfully obvious that the pact with Hitler could not guarantee Soviet security.

Realism, as a theoretical paradigm, provides a master variable for understanding international relations: the distribution of power among states. Anaylsis of international relations, however, involves two enterprises that are in tension—explanation and prescription. If explanations were always perfectly accurate, policy choices would be obvious and prescriptions would be superfluous. Realism often fails to explain adequately particular developments because, absent a crisis that shatters ambiguity about systemic constraints, statesmen are trapped by their own cognitive limits and by the institutional and rhetorical detritus of the decisions made by their predecessors. As a prescriptive doctrine, as opposed to an explanatory framework, realism aims to reveal strains and contradictions generated by the incongruity between power and commitments, and to suggest more stable and viable policies. Contemporary American security policy, especially participation in NATO and extended deterrence, illustrates not only the stresses between commitments and capabilities, but also the tensions between explanation and prescription that are inherent in all major social science theories.

## CHANGING POWER CONFIGURATIONS

When American commitments to Europe and its other allies were first made, they were consistent with both domestic sentiments in the United States and Europe and the distribution of power in the international system. Twice in the 20th century the United States had been drawn into European wars. Historical experience provided an incentive to maintain a balance on the continent of Europe. Moreover, the erstwhile potential adversary, the Soviet Union, espoused a doctrine that was both universalistic (and therefore imminently expansionist) and profoundly alien to American liberalism's commitment to democracy and capitalism.

Europe's postwar democracies welcomed American commitments. For Great Britain they represented a deepening of the special relationship, for France a continuation of the wartime alliance. For West Germany, integration into a large military alliance was the only strategic option; unilateralism was not attractive within Germany, nor would it have been acceptable to the other countries of Western Europe or the United States. Even divided, Germany was still a formidable power and the memory of the First and Second World Wars could not simply be erased.[1]

The alliance system was also congruent with the distribution of power that defined the structure of the international system. The Second World War had truncated and divided Germany, creating a very different structural situation than the one that had existed in 1939 or 1914. Because of geographic proximity, and perhaps ideological differences as well, the Soviet Union rather than the United States was the major threat to Western Europe.

The countries of Western Europe, however, could not defend themselves. Their economies were still in disarray. The British failed to develop nuclear weapons during the Second World War and did not explode their first atomic bomb until 1952.[2] In aggregate terms, the resource base of the United States far exceeded that of any other country. While it was deficient in terms of conventional ground forces in comparison with the Soviet Union, the United States held a substantial preponderance of nuclear weapons and associated delivery systems during the first two decades of the alliance. As long as the Soviets lacked the ability to launch a major nuclear strike against the United States, extended deterrence remained highly credible. The United States could in effect say, "You attack Western Europe and we will destroy you; and remember, there isn't much that you can do to us." Hence, the structural condition of the postwar world made the United States a very attractive partner.

Over the last 40 years, structural conditions have changed. Western Europe has recovered from the devastation of the Second World War. Its aggregate economic output approximated that of the United States by the early 1970s and surpassed that of the United States in the 1980s.[3] Great Britain and France have nuclear weapons. The largest European countries—Britain, France, West Germany and Italy—have the material, technological and scientific resources to create or enlarge their national nuclear arsenals. Even though these countries, taken individually, could not match the military capability of the United States or the Soviet Union, they are capable of fielding very substantial armed forces.

Moreover, in the nuclear age, many of the relationships that could be drawn between population size, industrial capacity and military power have eroded. The possession of nuclear weapons, and not too many at that, gives even a relatively small country the ability to decimate a much larger adversary regardless of what metric is used to determine whether a country is large or small.

Western Europe is also capable of fielding a conventional army that could, within a coherent alliance, challenge any force that could be put in the field by the Soviet Union. The population of the Western European members of NATO is 30 percent larger than that of the Soviet Union. The total population of Warsaw Pact countries is slightly higher than that of NATO, excluding the United States and Canada, but it is not evident that the countries of Eastern Europe would be reliable allies for the Soviet Union in the event of a major conventional war with the West. In the 1980s, the number of active personnel in the armed forces of the members of NATO, excluding the United States, has varied between 65 and 75 percent of the number of individuals in the active armed forces of the Soviet Union. The per capita GNP of Eastern Europe is about half that of the more prosperous countries of Western Europe.[4]

Moreover, Europe as a whole could create a formidable integrated strategic force. International structure, ideology and history would each provide incentives for the creation of such a force. Physical proximity alone causes the Soviet Union to be the most obvious military threat to Western Europe. As Stephen Walt has demonstrated in his recent work, balancing rather than bandwagonning is the prevalent response to an external threat, if such a threat reflects both power capabilities and perceptions of aggression.[5] In a similar vein, Barry Posen has argued that military strategy is driven by the distribution of power rather than the organizational imperatives or domestic politics.[6] A realist perspective suggests that the long-standing American fear of Finlandization is misplaced. Power considerations reveal that the most likely West European response to a withdrawal of the American nuclear guarantee would be the development of greater indigenous capabilities rather than an effort to reach some compromise with the Soviet Union.

The imperatives of international power are reinforced by ideology and history. Western Europe has a strong commitment to democracy and, as a result of NATO, extensive experience in military cooperation. The European Community (EC) has become revitalized as a result of the push for a unified market in 1992 and perhaps even more, from the discussion of political integration. Democracy has spread in Europe to the Iberian peninsula and to Greece. One aspect of the 1992 integration is a substantial capital transfer from the wealthier to the poorer areas of the EC: Portugal, Spain, Ireland and Greece. Each of these countries will receive resources equivalent to those of the Marshall Plan. These resources are designed not simply to ease the transition to an integrated market but also to reinforce the legitimacy of democracy. The commitment to democracy will make the Soviet Union unattractive as military or political leader of any kind.

Finally, NATO itself has provided the countries of Western Europe with extensive experience in military cooperation. The United States has obviously been the major partner in this effort. But NATO could provide the Europeans with a model for developing a more integrated nuclear and conventional force should the United States abandon extended deterrence. Thus, consideration of realpolitik, ideology and bureaucratic experience all suggest that if confronted with a withdrawal of the American nuclear umbrella, the European Community, or some subset of major countries, could devlop an integrated military force of a sufficient size and sophistication to serve as a credible deterrent against Soviet attack.

The Soviet threat itself will not disappear regardless of internal changes in the Soviet Union. Despite the overall economic difficulties made so obviously visible by Gorbachev's *glasnost'*, the Soviet Union has developed and maintained a nuclear force equal to that of the United States. The size of the Soviet economy will continue to make it a potential threat to its neighbors regardless of specific military postures that are adopted in the future. In a Europe with a divided Germany, the Soviet Union will remain the most formidable potential adversary. Moreover, there is no indication that the domestic political structure in the Soviet Union will move toward what the West would regard as democratic. Fundamental power and ideological considerations point to a world in which Western Europe and the Soviet Union will have to balance against each other, all the more so in the absence of any active American role in Europe.

# EXTENDED DETERRENCE, ARMS CONTROL AND THE ALLIANCE

Basic deterrence is based on a threat that leaves something to chance. For deterrence to work, a potential aggressor must believe that retaliation could occur after an attack has been launched, even though, in the case of nuclear weapons, the rationale for retaliation disappears. The primary challenge for policy-makers is making the threat of retaliation a credible one—to convince one's adversary that an attack on one's homeland is very likely to elicit a response in kind. It is indeed not very far fetched to imagine that Soviet or American leaders might be upset enough to retaliate against a strike by their nuclear adversary, even if their own society had already been crippled or even annihilated.[7]

The threat to retaliate is less credible, however, when the initial attack is not against the homeland of the superpower but rather against one of its allies. Soviet leaders would have to believe that the Americans would be more likely to retaliate against an attack on some target in the United States than against an attack on Western Europe. Given the Soviet ability to launch a devastating second strike against the United States, the American nuclear guarantee to Europe is less credible than it was in the 1950s when the basic policies of the Western alliance were first formulated and the Soviets lacked adequate delivery systems. The contemporary configuration of power, therefore, makes the whole concept of extended deterrence even more problematic than it was in the past. The answer to the question first posed by the French in the late 1950s—Would the United States give up Washington for Paris?—is by no means self-evident.

The entire debate about the appropriate course for American strategy can be seen as an effort to resolve this credibility problem.[8] For example, the 300,000 American troops in Germany are regarded not just as a conventional fighting force but as a tripwire that guarantees American commitment to the defense of Europe. One way to enhance credibility is to raise the threshold at which strategic nuclear weapons would be employed. Hence there is a continual emphasis on increasing the conventional capability of NATO forces, a position that American policy-makers have forcefully presented to their European counterparts.[9] There has also been pressure to introduce tactical nuclear weapons, even though this might erode the salient distinction between nuclear and non-nuclear weapons, a distinction that cannot be made on the basis of destructive capability alone. The more conventional forces and tactical nuclear weapons there are, the more capable NATO would be to counter a Soviet strike without employing strategic forces based outside of Europe. Therefore, according to this logic, it is less likely that the Soviets would be tempted into aggressive action in a gamble that the United States would *not* give up Washington for Paris.

The political tensions generated by relying on nuclear forces for deterrence have been revealed with particular clarity by the recent conflict over modernizing the Lance short-range missile. The basic problem for Germans is that what is tactical for the United States is strategic for Germany. If short-range missiles are ever employed, they would land on German territory. It is not just Chancellor Kohl's domestic political difficulties that provoked tensions within NATO; rather it is the strategy of flexible response, which results in American decision-makers playing a major role in determining how an attack on Europe should be deterred. For the leaders of Europe this is a peculiar situation, especially given the fact that if deterrence fails it is their citizens, and not those of the United States, that would initially bear the brunt of suffering.

The effort to make extended deterrence more credible has motivated the ongoing debate about American nuclear strategy, a debate that is both obtuse and probably has little or no effect on the behavior of decision-makers, even if it fuels expenditure levels for weapons. So long as the United States had clear dominance, that is, so long as the Soviets lacked second strike capability, the doctrine of massive retaliation made sense. Soviet and European leaders had to take very seriously the American commitment to launch a devastating nuclear strike against the Soviet Union in the event that major American allies were attacked. Once the Soviets achieved nuclear parity, massive retaliation became less credible and the United States adopted the doctrine of flexible response along with arcane distinctions among theater, intermediate and strategic nuclear weapons, between counterforce and counter-value attacks, and between defensive and offensive strategies.

Many of these distinctions do not make sense. The most salient distinction in the area of weapons is between the nuclear and non-nuclear weapons, not among various classes of nuclear arms. Likewise, the distinction between counterforce and counter-value strategies is so blurred that it is almost meaningless. A counterforce attack against the United States or the Soviet Union would result in very large civilian casualties. One estimate places the number of civilian deaths between 12 and 27 million for the United States and between 15 and 32 million for the Soviet Union as a direct result of blast, fire and radioactive fallout. Several million additional deaths could reuslt from social breakdown, disease and famine. It is not clear that the leaders of the United States or the

Soviet Union would be able to actually distinguish between a counterforce and counter-value attack.[10]

Aside from a kind of wistful longing for a past, in which the United States could actually defend itself from attack, the incentive for the Strategic Defense Initiative (SDI) is fueled by the desire to make extended deterrence more credible. Unless, however, a defense is almost perfect, the damage wreaked by a nuclear attack would be devastating. A failure rate of 1 percent would result in more than 100 nuclear weapons striking the United States in a full scale Soviet attack. Any system would be very complex and there would be no way of realistically testing its reliability. Yet the need to make extended deterrence more credible creates an incentive for the United States to claim that it could defend against a Soviet strike, even though such a claim could never be substantiated and the development and deployment of an SDI program would be costly in terms of both material and human resources.

Given the contemporary distribution of power, the most logically compelling resolution to the problem of extended deterrence would be to eliminate this strategic option entirely. The French *force de frappe* is an effort to do exactly that. If the Soviet Union were confronted with the threat of a devastating second strike from the countries of Western Europe acting alone rather than in concert with the United States, the issue of trading Washington for Paris would never be raised in the first place. One rationale for the bizarre growth of nuclear weapons, with both sides now capable of delivering more than 10,000 warheads, would disappear; an important factor impelling this growth has been the American need to enhance the credibility of extended deterrence and the Soviet desire to maintain numerical parity with the United States. Without the credibility problems of extended deterrence, negotiated or unilateral reduction in arms would be more easily accomplished.

At the very least, such reductions would decrease financial strains on the United States and the Soviet Union. They could also make the world a less dangerous place. Given the devastation of nuclear weapons, anything even close to full scale nuclear war is not likely to be the result of rational calculation, at least not rational calculation in which individual and societal survival, as opposed to say serving God, is part of the preference function of decision-makers. If a nuclear exchange does occur between the East and the West, it is more likely to be the result of some cognitive or technical failure.[11] The possibility for such failures is positively related, although not necessarily in a linear fashion, to the number and complexity of weapons systems. Thus, arms control, which would be easier to achieve without the problem of extended deterrence, could make the world a safer place even though the knowledge of nuclear weapons, and therefore their existence, could never be erased.

A reduction in the overall level of weapons as a result of American withdrawal, arms control and an increase in European capabilities must, however, be balanced against the dangers of nuclear proliferation. Great Britain and France have already opted for some degree of nuclear independence from the United States. The presence of the American umbrella, however, discouraged proliferation in Europe in general and the development of German nuclear weapons in particular.

For some Europeans and Americans, the umbrella resolved at least part of the German problem. This concern with Germany is, however, misplaced. The German problem was not spawned by the particular national character or values of Germans (values that have, in any event, radically changed since World War II) but rather by the structural position of Germany in Europe. The unification of Germany under Bismarck coupled with Germany's rapid economic growth, beginning in the last part of the 19th century, created an inherently unstable situation in the center of Europe. Germany was a menace to its neighbors, but it was never powerful enough to peacefully change the character of the international system, that is, to alter boundaries and sources of influence.[12] The German problem was resolved by the Second World War which parcelled off people and territory to Poland and which divided, albeit not equally, what remained of Germany. Theoretically, an independent German nuclear force would not be any more of a threat to the other countries of Western Europe than the French force is now. Moreover, if the United States withdrew from the defense of Europe, the likelihood of an integrated European force would increase.

It is important to note that the situation in Asia is more complicated. The Second World War did not fundamentally change the structural power configuration in Asia. Japan lost some overseas colonies and part of the Kurile islands, but its basic resouce base was not changed. The structural problem in Asia is not the Soviet threat to Japan, but rather the threat of a powerful, rearmed Japan to the rest of East Asia. The presence of American forces has allowed Japan to limit its military, a fact which makes Japanese economic penetration of the area less menacing. While an American withdrawal from Europe would be stabilizing, an American withdrawal from Asia would be destabilizing. The American presence in East Asia, however, can be maintained with limited naval forces rather than land armies, a posture that is more consistent with a less imperial orientation, although not with isolationism as it is conventionally understood.[13]

In sum, a realist perspective suggests that the United States ought to adopt a neo-isolationist policy. According to this approach, the relative decline of American power via-à-vis Soviet military and Western European economic and technological capabilities should lead to a decline in relative American defense expenditures and a withdrawal of American troops from Europe. It is likely that such a scenario would result in more concerted European balancing behavior against the Soviet Union, including more formidable European conventional and nuclear capability, either national, international or even transnational; and a more stable international environment because of the elimination of the inherent ambiguities of extended deterrence. A world in which Europe assumed the responsibility for its own defense, either collectively or individually, would be safer than the current environment that encourages the multiplication of weapons systems among those states within the nuclear club, even if it discourages proliferation to those states without nuclear capabilities. In Asia, the

United States would have to maintain some military presence, not because the Japanese could not defend themselves against the Soviet Union, but because the smaller states of East Asia would find a re-armed Japan extremely threatening, as would China. A neo-isolationist policy would be more congruent with the present distribution of international capabilities, rather than the distribution that existed in the early 1950s. . .[14]

A fundamental change in American strategy would refocus the attention of American policy-makers. For 40 years the major concern of American leaders has been the Soviet Union, and military and security concerns have driven economic ones. In the 1950s and 1960s, the economic policies adopted by the United States were designed to increase the economic well-being of Europe and Japan. The United States tolerated restrictive trade policies in both areas and, in the case of Japan, accepted restrictions on direct foreign investment as well. The United States encouraged the creation of the Common Market in Europe, even though it was bound to divert trade from the United States.

The United States has scarcely been able to develop anything resembling an industrial policy, except in the area of defense—where it has funded extensive research activities and blocked the foreign acquisition of defense-related industries. These policies had some positive economic effects in the 1950s when military technology could be converted to commercial uses. Such conversions, however, have become increasingly difficult because the miltary uses of high technology demand extremely reliable components under exceptional environmental conditions, while most commercial applications occur in much more benign circumstances. The Strategic Defense Initiative has soaked up not only material, but also human resources.

Yet, the future of the United States and the values for which it stands are much more likely, in the contemporary international environment, to be affected by the economic vibrancy of the United States than by its military power and commitments. Communism has failed not because Marxist doctrine is illogical, or because the Soviet Union lagged in military resources, or because the system was internally repressive, but because socialism as it has been practiced in the Soviet Union has not been able to provide a level of material well-being that is anything like that found in the advanced industrialized market-economy countries. When Khrushchev said in the late 1950s that communism would "bury" capitalism in a symbolic sense, he was taken seriously. No Soviet leader could expect the same reaction today.

Economic resources have always been the foundation upon which military power was built, but in the modern world material prosperity has become something even more. It is the universal metric, the measure by which the success of different forms of social organization are measured. Most of the world's peoples are not predisposed to accept the American version of individualism, democracy and capitalism because their own national values are much more strongly oriented toward one kind of collectivity or another. In most countries, national identity is a matter of ethnicity rather than, as it is in the United States, a matter of political beliefs. What makes an American is not race or language but rather a commitment to a Lockean liberal creed.[15] The values that are cherished by America will not prevail simply because they are inherently attractive (although some form of individual freedom must be innately appealing) or because they complement other national value structures.

Most of the peoples of the world are, however, entranced by a high economic performance or quality of life. The future of American values, their external appeal and internal vigor, now depends more on the attainments of the American economy than on the power of the American military. Nuclear weapons have made the world a much more stable place, and this stability would be enhanced by a policy of neo-isolationism. A faltering of the American economy would make American values less captivating. It is not Soviet nuclear weapons, but Japanese economic prowess that ought to be the fundamental concern of American policy-makers.

Contracting America's overblown defense commitments would not necessarily increase economic growth rates, but it would allow a reallocation of resources, both human and material, and encourage a refocussing of the attention of central decision-makers as well. Alas, history does not provide much evidence that the leaders of empires are prescient enough to understand the changing structure of the international environment or, if they are so discerning, bold and wise enough to formulate a vision that is both externally viable and internally acceptable.[16]

## *NOTES*

1. For one discussion of the forming of NATO and the integration of Germany, see William Park, *Defending the West: A History of NATO* (Brighton, England: Wheatsheaf Book, 1986), pp. 7–20.
2. David N. Schwartz, *NATO's Nuclear Dilemmas* (Washington, D.C.: The Brookings Institution, 1983), pp. 26–31.
3. Figures from OECD, *National Accounts 1960–1986* Vol. 1 Main Aggregates (Paris: OECD 1988).
4. Population data from figures in *World Bank Atlas 1986* (Washington, D.C.: World Bank, 1986). Figures on active armed forces can be found in the International Institute for Strategic Studies, *The Military Balance*, various years. Data on GNP comparisons between the East and West are offered in Paul Marer, *Dollar GNPs of the U.S.S.R. and Eastern Europe* (Washington, D.C.: World Bank, 1985), pp. 114–115.
5. Stephen M. Walt, *The Origins of Alliances* (Ithaca, NY: Cornell University Press, 1987). See also Walt's article in this issue of the *Journal of International Affairs*, pp. 4–7.
6. Barry Posen, *The Sources of Military Doctrine* (Ithaca, NY: Cornell University Press, 1984).
7. For the initial discussion of the threat that leaves something to chance see Thomas C. Schelling, *The Strategy of Conflict* (Cambridge, MA: Harvard University Press, 1960). For a critique of the concept of nuclear deterrence see Jonathan Schell, *The Fate of the Earth* (New York: Knopf, 1982).
8. Earl C. Ravenal, *NATO: The Tides of Discontent* (Berkeley, CA: Institute for International Studies, University of California, 1985), pp. 1, 11.

9. Peter H. Langer, *Transatlantic Discord and NATO's Crisis of Cohesion* (Washington, D.C.: Pergamon-Brassey's, 1986), p. 5.

10. Frank Von Hippel et al., "Civilian Casualties from Counterforce Attacks," *Scientific American 259*, No. 3 (September 1988): 41–42.

11. Bruce Blair, *Strategic Command and Control* (Washington, D.C.: The Brookings Institution, 1985) discusses the development of one scenario in which the complexities of weapons systems could lead to inadvertent escalation.

12. For an elaboration of the structural argument concerning Germany's role in Europe see David Calleo, *The German Problem Reconsidered* (Cambridge, England: Cambridge University Press, 1978).

13. I am indebted to Michael Mandelbaum for suggesting this line of argument, although I am sure that he would not want to be held responsible for the use to which it has been put in this essay.

14. The sampling of elite opinion conducted by Holsti and Rosenau demonstrates that at least some American leaders consider neo-isolationism to be an attractive policy. See Ole R. Holsti and James N. Rosenau, *American Leadership in World Affairs: Vietnam and the Breakdown of Consensus* (Boston, MA: Allen and Unwin, 1984). For an important recent statement of the need to equate capabilities and policies see Robert Gilpin, *War and Change in World Politics* (New York: Cambridge University Press, 1981).

15. The best exposition of this extraordinary situation remains Louis Hartz, *The Liberal Tradition in America* (New York: Hartcourt Brace, 1955).

16. For the difficulties of Britain in the 19th century see Aaron Friedberg, *The Weary Titan* (Princeton, NJ: Princeton University Press, 1988), and for a more general discussion Gilpin (1981).

## COMPREHENSION CHECKPOINT

What is the significance of the following?

| | |
|---|---|
| foreign policy insolvency | autarky |
| Marshall Plan II | "real conservatives" |
| ideological internationalism | Reagan Doctrine |
| power interests gap | dyad |
| "milieu goals" | extended deterrence |
| Finlandization | massive retaliation |
| flexible response | invulnerable second strike nuclear forces |

Can you answer the following questions?

1. In his critique of an interventionist foreign policy, Ravenal wrote the following in selection 15: "The lack of public support might not prevent intervention, but it might critically inhibit its prosecution. (This, in my view, is the enduring lesson of Vietnam.)" Have events since 1987, when these words were written, proven Ravenal right or wrong?

2. What does Krasner mean when he claims that "the contemporary configuration of power . . . makes the whole concept of extended deterrence even more problematic than it was in the past?" What possible solutions to this problem exist?

3. Ravenal may be right when he argues that the American public will refuse to support long and costly interventions abroad, but consider the neo-isolationist alternative. If the United States adopts a policy of strategic disengagement, weaker Third World states might quickly become victims or hostages of stronger or more ambitious regional powers such as Qaddafi's Libya, Hussein's Iraq, or even South Africa.

- Are the American people really willing to see the weak fall prey to strong, ambitious, and perhaps anti-Western rulers?
- Are the American people really willing to allow areas containing important economic resources to fall into the hands of such forces?

4. If your answers to the previous questions were "yes," consider the following. If America adopts a policy of nonintervention, other nations might begin to intervene in regional disputes to protect *their* vital interests. Would Americans really have been indifferent if 300,000 German or 300,000 German, British, and French forces had been sent to the Middle East in response to the Iraqi conquest of Kuwait? Or, would Americans remain indifferent if Japan rearmed and sent a military occupation force to secure the oil of Indonesia?

5. Krasner's essay was written before the collapse of Communism in eastern Europe and the reunification of Germany. What effect do these two events have on Krasner's argument in favor of neo-isolationism, which assumed a "truncated and divided" Germany?

6. Refer to the chart presented on page 135 to illuminate the differences between neorealists and reassertionists. Use this chart to indicate how neo-isolationists differ from reassertionists; then, indicate the differences between neo-isolationists and neorealists. Finally, use this chart to indicate what Layne sees as the difference between real conservatives and neoconservatives.

## From Worldview to Particular Policy Issues

In the previous two chapters, you were asked to relate the reassertionist and neorealist worldviews to a series of particular foreign policy issues. Below are the same issues that appeared in those chapters. This time, sketch out a set of neo-isolationist responses.

1. How would a neo-isolationist respond to the following quotation and why?

Poverty, not communism, is the principal threat in the Third World. . . . [E]very Third World revolution is not a struggle between East and West. . . . [P]overty, hunger, and repression have caused many more revolutions than Moscow and Havana combined. . . . [T]he US has managed for decades to put itself on the side of repression, corruption, and privilege in these battles, and has inevitably been on the losing side.

—Senator Gary Hart, quoted in *South*, December, 1984, p. 11

2. How would a neo-isolationist respond to the following policy proposals?

- to normalize relations with North Vietnam
- to disinvest from South Africa
- to seek a negotiated settlement of the civil war in El Salvador
- to increase funds for the United Nations Development Program
- to call a joint conference with the Soviet Union to seek a negotiated settlement in the Middle East
- to provide low interest rates to the Soviet Union in order to subsidize farm exports
- to stay out of civil wars in the Third World
- to withdraw troops from South Korea
- to cut economic aid to U.S. allies who abuse human rights
- to pressure Israel to accept a Palestinian state

3. If you refer to your reassertionist and neorealist answers to these questions, you will again note significant differences. How do differences in placement on the chart presented in question 5 account for the differences on these particular issues?

## For Further Consideration

*Periodicals and journals* that present or have presented neo-isolationist points of view: *Foreign Policy, Foreign Affairs, Harpers, The New Republic, The National Interest,* publications of the CATO Institute.

*Leading neo-isolationist scholars, authors:* Earl Ravenal, Christopher Layne, Ted Galen Carpenter, Stephen Krasner, Peter Schraeder.

# FOR FURTHER READING

Adler, Selig. *The Isolationist Impulse.* New York: The Free Press, 1957. A now classic history of isolationism in the twentieth century.

Beard Charles A. *A Foreign Policy for Americans.* New York: Alfred A. Knopf, 1940. One of the nation's most distinguished and influential historians presents and evaluates "three conceptions of foreign policy which now appear in competition for possession of the American mind"—continental Americanism, imperialism, and internationalism. As late as 1940, Beard argued in favor of an isolationist policy of continental Americanism.

Chase, Stuart. *The New Western Front.* New York: Harcourt, Brace and Company, 1939. A plea for America to stay out of the coming war in Europe. Chase was a leading liberal writer and economist during the years between World War I and

WW II. He attempts to make his case by demonstrating the irrationality of European power politics and by showing how the United States could continue to prosper economically if its trade were restricted to the Western Hemisphere. His conclusion: "When war comes . . . we do not have to be dragged in (p. 187)." This well-written book provides an excellent introduction to the isolationist worldview in the interwar period.

Hoover, Herbert. *40 Key Questions About Our Foreign Policy.* Scarsdale, NY: The Updegraff Press Ltd., 1952. A collection of addresses, letters, and statements by former President Hoover, which reject America's postwar internationalism and call for a return to a hemisphere-first policy.

Krauthammer, Charles. "Isolationism, Left and Right: From McGovern to Weinberger, an Old Tradition Finds New Voices." *The New Republic* (March 4, 1985) pp. 18–25. An interesting article in which Krauthammer accuses many liberal Democrats and conservative Republicans of having adopted a posture that would lead to the same results as a traditional policy of isolationism—namely, an unwillingness to engage in unilateral uses of force to secure particular American interests abroad.

Laqueur, Walter. *Neo-Isolationism and the World of the Seventies.* Peru, IL: Library Press, 1972. A short critique of post-Vietnam neo-isolationism by a leading reassertionist. Laqueur directs much of his criticism at Robert Tucker's *A New Isolationism,* which is cited below.

Lepgold, Joseph and David Garnham. "Is There a Case for Strategic Disengagement?" *The Political Science Reviewer,* Vol. 15 (Fall 1985), pp. 337–57. Two political scientists critically assess the writings of neo-isolationist Earl Ravenal. Well worth reading.

Lippmann, Walter. *Isolation and Alliances.* Boston: Little, Brown/Atlantic Monthly, 1952. A critique of both isolationism and Wilsonian internationalism along with some proposals for resolving the Soviet-American conflict in Europe. The book is based upon a series of lectures that Lippmann delivered at Oxford, Cambridge, and the University of London.

Osgood, Robert Endicott. *Ideals and Self-Interest in America's Foreign Relations.* Chicago: The University of Chicago Press, 1953. A fascinating and very readable history of the clash between internationalists and isolationists during the interwar period. Because Osgood places this clash within the context of the debate between political realism and political idealism, the treatment is as analytical as it is descriptive.

Ravenal, Earl C. "Containment, Intervention, and Strategic Disengagement." In *Containing the Soviet Union,* edited by T. L. Deibel and J. L. Gaddis, pp. 184–207. New York: Pergamon-Brassey's International Defense Publishers, 1987. Selection 16 was excerpted from the last third of this essay. The first two sections, however, are well worth reading. In the first section, Ravenal argues that the Reagan administration's policy of global containment was insolvent. In the second section, he rejects all of the alternatives to global containment—moderate containment, detente or condominium, a New Yalta, or a world order approach.

Ravenal, Earl C. "Doing Nothing." *Foreign Policy,* No. 39 (Summer 1980), pp. 28–40. A penetrating neo-isolationist critique of reassertionism and neorealism in light of their responses to the Soviet invasion of Afghanistan. Ravenal criticizes Carter for dropping his noninterventionist posture and suddenly embracing an "ordinate fear of communism." Ravenal's proposed response to the Soviet invasion is clearly set out in the title of the essay.

Ravenal, Earl C. *Never Again: Learning from America's Foreign Policy Failures.* Philadelphia: Temple University Press, 1978. A critical evaluation of the strategies open to America in the aftermath of Vietnam and a plea for the neo-isolationist alternative which Ravenal labels "strategic disengagement."

Taft, Robert A. *A Foreign Policy for Americans.* New York: Doubleday, 1951. Isolationist Senator Robert A. Taft was a leading Republican contender for his party's nomination for president in 1952. This short book is critical of Truman's attempt to meet the Soviet challenge by placing large numbers of American conventional forces abroad. Taft proposes a temporary "internationalist" policy that would have relied upon U.S. air power to deter Communist expansion, extended economic and military assistance to threatened countries, and joined with Britain in an alliance to maintain control of sea and air power.

Tucker, Robert. "Isolation and Intervention." *The National Interest,* No. 1 (Fall 1985), pp. 16–25. A brilliant evaluation of the three mainstream worldviews covered in this anthology by one of the nation's leading writers on American foreign policy. Tucker's essay is, in part, a response to the Krauthammer essay cited above. Essential reading.

Tucker, Robert. *A New Isolationism.* New York: Universe Books/Potomac Associates, 1972. A well-written discussion of the prospects for a new isolationism. Tucker knocks down many straw men that are frequently used to oppose isolationism. He presents a strong case for retrenchment.

Walt, Stephen M. "Two Cheers for Containment: Probable Allied Responses to American Isolationism." In *Collective Defense Versus Strategic Independence,* edited by Ted Galen Carpenter. Lexington, MA: Lexington Books, 1989. A neorealist critique of the neo-isolationist worldview. Well worth reading.

## NOTES

1. Walter Lippmann, *Isolation and Alliances: An American Speaks to the British* (Boston: Little, Brown and Company), 1952.
2. Robert Tucker, *A New Isolationism: Threat or Promise* (New York: Universe Books, 1972), p. 120. Italics supplied.
3. Earl C. Ravenal, "An Alternative to Containment," *Policy Analysis No. 94,* CATO Institute, Washington DC (November 25, 1987) p. 2.
4. These figures are from Alan Tonelson, "A Manifesto for Democrats," *The National Interest,* 16 (Summer 1989), p. 46.
5. Earl Ravenal, "Doing Nothing," *Foreign Policy,* 39 (Summer 1980), p. 32.
6. Earl C. Ravenal, "The Case for Adjustment," *Foreign Policy,* 81 (Winter 1990–91), p. 9.
7. Amory B. Lovins and L. Hunter Lovins, "Make Fuel Efficiency Our Gulf Strategy," *New York Times,* December 3, 1990.
8. Earl C. Ravenal, "The Requisites of Containment," a paper presented to the conference, "Collective Security or Strategic Independence? Alternative Strategies for the

Future," sponsored by the CATO Institute, Washington, DC, December 2–3, 1987, p. 49. These projections were made, of course, before the initiatives of Soviet President Mikhail Gorbachev reduced tensions and spurred cutbacks in American defense spending.

9. Beard, Charles A., *A Foreign Policy for Americans* (New York: Alfred A. Knopf, 1940), pp. 151–52. Beard used the term "continentalism" for "isolationism."

# Chapter
## 6

# The Radical Worldview

*A*ccording to radicals, maintaining freedom and promoting self-determination have never been among the fundamental objectives of American foreign policy. While these goals have been proclaimed frequently by political leaders from Harry Truman to George Bush, radicals argue that such proclamations have been rationalizations for the nation's true objective—making the world safe for corporate capitalism. According to radicals and Marxists, America is the center of a vast neocolonial empire welded together by a worldwide structure of domination and repression. Protecting corporate investments abroad, ensuring that corporate capital can expand as widely in the world as possible, containing political forces that would assert national control over their own economies, and ensuring that corporations have access to cheap labor and raw materials—these, radicals argue, are the true goals of America's foreign policy.

The radical worldview gained a significant place in academic and elite discussions of foreign policy during the war in Vietnam. As mainstream scholars and policy makers argued about strategy and tactics, radical scholars sought deeper explanations for America's debacle in Vietnam. Ranging in ideology from Marxism and neo-Marxism to politically progressive non-Marxism, radical scholars directed their attention to the economic underpinnings of American diplomacy. As radical scholars examined America's postwar foreign policies from this perspective, they noted a persistent pattern of opposition, not merely to Soviet imperialism and Communism, but also to radical nationalism. And, as they delved back into decision making during World War II, radicals concluded that the postwar international economic order was explicitly designed to ensure that American corporations would have free reign to invest, trade, and compete all over the globe.

While mainstream commentators portray America as a reluctant and reactive entrant into the world arena, radicals read the same history as an effort by American elites to create a new world order under American tutelage. This postwar quest for world hegemony, radicals argue, was pursued with a two-sided strategy. The negative side comprised the containment of "Communism," which included opposition to even non-Communist regimes that questioned

America's conception of a legitimate international economic order. The positive side involved the restoration of capitalism in the war-torn nations of Europe and Asia and the maintenance of a liberal international economic system—a system that the Soviet Union could either accept or be excluded from.

Based upon their research, radical scholars concluded that there was much more to American diplomacy during World War II than the defeat of the Axis military forces. In their opinion, an equally important diplomatic objective was the elimination and containment of any obstacle to a liberal, capitalist, international economic order. Thus, Roosevelt's opposition to European colonialism stemmed not from a love of freedom or self-determination, but from a desire to enlarge the areas in which American corporate capital could trade and invest. America's opposition to Stalin's creation of a security buffer in Eastern Europe stemmed not from a concern for free elections and self-determination, but from a fear that Stalin might supplement his political sphere with a closed economic sphere. Finally, the United States also sought to weaken, if not eliminate, radical and leftist forces in Western Europe that might challenge America's global economic plans.

According to historian Gabriel Kolko, "In China, Italy, Greece, France, and Eastern Europe there were in varying degrees real or disguised civil wars taking place at the very time of the war against Germany and Japan."[1] A major aim of American decision makers, radicals argue, was to ensure that the left did not seize power in those countries liberated by the United States.

In the victorious postwar period, America continued to pursue policies that were designed to maintain a liberal international economic order. From this perspective, the purpose of the Marshall Plan was not merely to contain Soviet imperialism but to restore capitalism in Western Europe and to undercut the powerful socialist and Communist forces in France and Italy. In Greece, the Truman Doctrine kept in power a regime that accepted America's economic hegemony but that was also, as Richard Barnet put it, "not only repressive but hopelessly corrupt."[2]

In 1953, President Dwight Eisenhower authorized the Central Intelligence Agency to help overthrow the nationalist but non-Communist Iranian government of Mohammed Mossadeq, which had nationalized British oil companies. During 1954, the CIA organized Guatemalan forces that overthrew a freely elected government that had nationalized unused lands of the United Fruit Company. After the coup, the successor regime of Castillo Armas returned the lands to the United Fruit Company and paid for the costs of the CIA operation as well. Dictatorship and repression returned to Guatemala, and the standard of living stagnated. From facts such as these, radicals unearthed an economic side of American foreign policy, a side that placed support for U.S. corporate interests and the maintenance of a liberal international economic order at the heart of the nation's diplomacy.

The founding work in the postwar radical tradition was William Appleman Williams' *The Tragedy of American Foreign Policy*, which appeared in 1959.[3] The thesis of Williams' work was a simple one. With the closing of the frontier and the industrialization of America, full employment could no longer be maintained within the nation's traditional *laissez-faire* framework. The explosive social unrest that accompanied capitalism could only be met, Williams argued, in one of two ways—through domestic programs that would regulate capital and redistribute wealth or through the pursuit of foreign outlets that would absorb those surplus American goods that could not be consumed at home.

Williams' thesis was a novel and provocative one: In the mid-1890s, America's economic and political elites decided to "export" the nation's domestic problems through an "open door" foreign policy that would create a world that was "safe" for the export of America's surpluses and the expansion of its corporate capital. The bulk of Williams' book sought to document the consistency with which the United States pursued its open door policies during World War I, during the alleged "isolationist" interwar years, during World War II, and during the postwar era.

When Williams' book first appeared, it received little notice. But, during the war in Vietnam Williams' work gave rise to a series of detailed studies that sought to document the open door thesis. In 1965, Lloyd Gardner's *Economic Aspects of New Deal Diplomcay* argued that FDR pursued an open door policy as a means of alleviating the domestic effects of the Great Depression.[4] Three years later, Gabriel Kolko published his 626-page book, *The Politics of War*, which sought to document the centrality of open door objectives in America's wartime diplomacy with Britain, the Soviet Union, France, and the Resistance forces in allied countries.[5] In 1966, David Horowitz argued in his *Free World Colossus*[6] that America's postwar containment policies were designed not to promote freedom and self-determination, but to keep the world safe for corporate capital.

By the late 1960s, the radical worldview had marshalled a formidable challenge to mainstream scholarship on American foreign policy. *The Tragedy of American Diplomacy* had attained the status of a classic. Walter LaFeber's *America, Russia, and the Cold War, 1945–1966* was one of the most widely used in college courses on foreign policy and diplomatic history.[7] In contrast to mainstream writers on the history of the cold war, LaFeber sought to demonstrate that America's postwar policies had little to do with either the Soviet Union or Communism. "Washington officials," LaFeber wrote, "assumed that foriegn policy grew directly from domestic policy; American actions abroad did not respond primarily to the pressures of other nations, but to political, social, and economic forces at home."[8] Other radical works, such as Harry Magdoff's *The Age of Imperialism*[9] and Gabriel Kolko's *The Roots of American Foreign Policy*,[10] were also read widely in courses in American foreign policy and international politics.

Works by radical scholars also formed the intellectual basis for the foreign policy positions of the Students for a Democratic Society (SDS), which shaped much of "the new left" movement that arose on college campuses. In *Containment and Change*,[11] the definitive statement of the SDS position on foreign policy, Carl Ogelsby and Richard Schaull drew almost exclusively from the works of radical scholars. Within the professional associations, radical economists, political scientists, and sociologists created their own "caucuses" in order to challenge mainstream members of their disciplines. And indeed, radicals did provide a significant challenge to orthodox scholars. In the field of foreign policy, radical scholars such as William Appleman Williams, Gabriel Kolko, David Horowitz, and the not-so-radical revisionist, Gar Alperovitz, forced mainstream scholars to reexamine the origins of the cold war and the course of the Soviet-American conflict.[12]

Marxist and radical scholars perceive a clear pattern to American foreign policy: *capitalism leads to imperialism which leads to interventionism which leads to militarism.* American corporations require outlets for their surplus products and capital; this requirement leads to a foreign policy of imperialism that seeks to "open doors" and maintain a world free for the movement of goods and capital. Challenges to this open door policy by other nations or by indigenous forces seeking economic self-determination require intervention, as in Iran, Guatemala, Cuba, and Vietnam. Deterring and meeting such "challenges" or "threats" require militarization.

From this pattern stems the tragedy of American diplomacy that Williams refers to in the title of his book. In order to secure the needs of corporate capitalism, the United States had to negate the values and ideals that it sought to promote in the world. According to Williams:

> By the time of World War I . . . the basic dilemma of American foreign policy was clearly defined. Its generous humanitarianism prompted it to improve the lot of the less fortunate peoples, but that side of diplomacy was undercut by two other aspects of its policy. On the one hand, it defined helping other people in terms of making them more like Americans. This subverted the ideal of self-determination. On the other hand, it asserted and acted upon the necessity of overseas economic expansionism for its own material prosperity. But by defining such expansion in terms of markets for American exports and control of raw materials for American industry, the ability of other peoples to develop and act upon their own patterns of development was further undercut.[13]

But what about Soviet imperialism? To radical scholars, the Soviet Union was a convenience rather than a threat. Every radical work on the origins of the cold war draws the same conclusion: The Soviet-American confrontation stemmed largely from the unwillingness of the United States to tolerate a postwar world based upon any principle other than the open door. According to Williams:

> The popular idea that Soviet leaders emerged from the war ready to do aggressive battle against the United States is simply not borne out by the evidence. . . . [While the Soviets sought to establish an understanding with the United States] they never defined such an understanding on the basis of abandoning Russian influence in eastern Europe or acquiescing in each and every American proposal just because it emanated from Washington. But neither did they emerge from World War II with a determination to take over eastern Europe and then embark on a cold war with the United States.[14]

Radical scholars also reject the notion that radical or Marxist regimes become puppets or pawns of Soviet geopoliticians. In fact, by cutting off relations with radical regimes and by supporting counterrevolutionary forces, it is America, radicals argue, that forces such countries into the "Soviet orbit." Thus, America's opposition to radical regimes is largely self-induced. According to political scientist, Michael Parenti:

> There [is no] evidence that once a revolution succeeds, the new leaders place the interests of their country at the disposal of Moscow. As noted earlier, just about every socialist country including the USSR has tried to keep its options open and has sought friendly diplomatic and economic relations with the United States.[15]

According to radicals, a major strength of their worldview lies in its ability to explain what appear to be ironies, mistakes, or anomalies in other worldviews—America's intervention against freely elected democratic regimes such as Arbenz's Guatemala, Mossadeq's Iran, and Allende's Chile; its support for repressive dictatorships throughout the Third World; its demand for free elections in Nicaragua, but not in Saudi Arabia or Iran; its opposition to radical regimes that provide the economic and social justice that America preaches; and its military assistance and training programs in countries that have no foreign enemies, as in much of Latin America. Radicals also believe that their worldview provides compelling explanations for the existence of widespread poverty in resource-rich developing countries and foreign aid programs that seldom reach the poor.

In response to former UN Ambassador Jeane Kirkpatrick's argument that traditional dictatorships are always preferable to totalitarian or Marxist dictatorships, Jeff McMahan makes the following retort:

> In Kirkpatrick's paradigmatic totalitarian states, one does not find the same extremes of wealth and poverty, opulence and squalor, that she admits exist in her traditional authoritarian states. Nor does one find anything like the same levels of unemployment. In Cuba, her archetype of Third World totalitarianism, malnutrition and preventable infectious diseases have been virtually eradicated, and the infant mortality rate has been lowered, while the literacy rate has been dramatically increased. The same process is occurring in Nicaragua. By contrast, in most of the authoritarian states in Latin America vast numbers of people remain illiterate and continue to be plagued by malnutrition and a host of preventable diseases, even though many of these countries have economies stronger than those of Cuba and Nicaragua.[16]

For radicals, the United States is a nation that preaches democracy but supports dictatorships. It is a nation that preaches self-determination but intervenes whenever self-determination runs counter to corporate capitalism. It is a nation that preaches social and economic justice but supports repression.

Radicals also point to the double standard that American leaders apply to Communist and non-Communist regimes in the developing areas. Writes Jeff McMahan, "While for years the [Reagan] administration persistently berated the Sandinistas in Nicaragua for failing to hold elections, it has been perfectly satisfied with the absence of elections in such countries as Chile, South Korea, and Pakistan, or with bogus elections such as those in Turkey, Guatemala, and the Philippines."[17]

Radicals are also quick to point out that American presidents have seldom levelled America's formidable powers against repressive allies. According to Michael Parenti, "If Reagan hated tyranny enough to invade and attempt to overthrow the presumable tyrannical Sandinistas of Nicaragua, one might wonder why he never moved against Chile, South Africa, Indonesia, Zaire, Paraguay, Turkey, and a host of other terribly repressive regimes."[18]

The radical perspective fundamentally challenges the central beliefs and assumptions of mainstream worldviews. Not surprisingly, the work of radical scholars has reaped a host of critical responses, some of which are included in the readings and in the annotated bibliography that follows. So far, no decisive winner has emerged from this debate. Thus, mainstreamers continue as they were, frequently ignoring radical arguments and scholarship. And radicals do the same.

With the end of the cold war, one test of contending positions should be apparent. Mainstreamers have continually argued that strategic, and not economic, factors have determined American behavior in the Third World. If they are right, the end of the cold war should mean much less American intervention against radical Third World regimes. If, on the other hand, the radicals are right, we can expect the United States to continue to intervene against regimes that threaten vital resources, nationalize American property, default on international debt obligations, or support radical insurgent forces in neighboring countries.

On this simple test, radical scholar Michael Klare would argue that the radicals have won hands down. According to Klare, Bush's response to the Iraqi conquest of Kuwait has set America's role for the post–cold war era, "the role of the global gendarme." "The message, to friends and enemies alike," Klare writes, "is that *Americans are willing to risk their lives to insure the security of our friends and allies* [Klare's italics]." This policy, Klare concludes, amounts to sacrificing the lives of our young men to ensure the steady supply of oil and other raw materials that our allies need in order to compete with us more effectively.[19]

As of this writing, the final word is not in on the conflict in the Persian Gulf nor on the precedent it will set. America's quick and decisive military victory against Suddam Hussein may pave the way for similar ventures in the future. On the other hand, the intractable problems posed by Kurdish and Shiite separatism in the postwar period might dampen an interventionary impulse. However, how America acts in an age without a Soviet competitor may tell us much about the validity of the radical critique of American foreign policy.

# The Selections

*The selections that follow present essays by proponents and critics of the radical worldview. As you read these selections, try to sketch out a worldview profile and make a separate list of the major propositions that make up the radical worldview. When you read the rebuttal essay, try to assess how compelling and valid the counter arguments are.*

## 17. Michael Parenti
### *U.S. Intervention: More Foul than Foolish*
#### 1984

In this selection, Michael Parenti places the responsibility for the lack of democracy and development in much of the Third World upon the shoulders of the United States. According to Parenti, the reasons given for America's opposition to the expansion of Communism and to such regimes as Cuba, Vietnam, Nicaragua, and Grenada are largely fictitious. Do you agree or disagree?

Why is the United States government hostile toward Nicaragua? Why does it support counterinsurgency in El Salvador, Guatemala and numerous other countries? Why did it invade Grenada? Is it because our leaders want to save democracy? Or is our national security threatened? I shall try to show that the arguments given to justify US policies are false ones. But this does not mean the policies themselves are senseless. American intervention may seem "wrong-headed" but in fact, it is fairly consistent and often successful. It may not be serving the interests of other peoples, nor of the American people, but it serves well those who know how to be well served.

Our leaders would have us believe they support counterrevolution in Nicaragua because the Sandinista government is opposed to democracy. Jeane Kirkpatrick defended the US-supported Contra invasion as an "effort to bring them to elections." But our government voiced no such urgent demand for western style parliamentarism during the fifty years that the Somoza dictatorship plundered and brutalized the Nicaraguan nation. Nor today does the Reagan administration call for democracy in any of the US-backed dictatorships around the world (unless one believes the electoral charade in El Salvador qualifies as "democracy").

If anything, successive American administrations have worked hard to *subvert* constitutional governments, helping to overthrow Arbenz in Guatemala, Jagan in British Guyana, Mossadegh in Iran, Bosch in the Dominican

Republic, Sukarno in Indonesia, Goulart in Brazil, and Allende in Chile. And let us not forget how the United States assisted the militarists in overthrowing democratic governments in Greece, Uruguay, Bolivia, Pakistan, Thailand and Turkey. Given this dreadful record, it is hard to believe that the CIA has trained, armed and financed an expeditionary force of Somocista thugs and mercenaries out of a newly acquired concern for human rights in Nicaragua.

In defense of the undemocratic way the US goes about saving democracy, our policymakers argue: "We cannot always pick and choose our allies. Sometimes we must support unsavory right-wing authoritarian regimes in order to prevent the spread of far more repressive totalitarian communist ones." This, of course, was the sophistry that made Jeane Kirkpatrick famous. But surely, the degree of repression cannot be the criterion guiding White House policy, for the United States has supported some of the worst butchers in the world: Batista, Somoza, the Shah, Salazar, Marcos, Pinochet, Zia, Evren, and even Pol Pot. In the 1965 Indonesian coup, the military slaughtered 500,000 people, according to the Indonesian chief of security (*New York Times*, December 21, 1977), but this did not deter the US from assisting in that takeover nor from maintaining cozy relations with the same Jakarta regime that now perpetrates genocide in East Timor.

US leaders and the business-owned mainstream press describe "Marxist rebels" in countries like El Salvador as motivated by a lust for conquest. Our leaders would have us believe that revolutionaries do not seek power in order to eliminate hunger; they simply hunger for power. But even if this were true, why would that be cause for opposing them? Washington policymakers have never been bothered by the power appetites of Jeane Kirkpatrick's moderate authoritarian torturers.

In any case, it is not true that leftist governments are more repressive than rightwing fascist ones. The political repression of small numbers of counterrevolutionaries within Nicaragua and Cuba has been mild and limited, indeed minor as compared to the widespread and massive terror and butchery perpetrated by the Somosa and Batstia regimes before the revolutions in those countries. The revolutionary government in Angola treats its people a lot more gently than did the colonizing thugs from Portugal.

Furthermore, in a number of countries successful social revolutionary movements have brought a net *increase* in individual freedom and human life. They provided jobs and education for the unemployed and illiterate. They used economic resources for social develoment rather than for corporate profit. They overthrew brutal reactionary regimes, ended foreign exploitation, and involved large sectors of the populace in the task of rebuilding their countries.

## WHO THREATENS WHOM?

US policymakers also argue that rightwing governments, for all their deficiencies, are friendly toward us, while communist ones are belligerent and therefore a threat to our security. But, in truth, every Marxist or left-leaning country, from a great power like the Soviet Union to a small power like Vietnam to a mini-power like Grenada (under the New Jewel Movement), has sought friendly diplomatic and economic relations with the United States—as do the Sandinista leaders of Nicaragua. These governments do so not necessarily out of love and affection for Washington, but because of something firmer—their desire to live in a world without war and to enjoy the mutual advantages of trade and friendship. Every one of the existing socialist and emerging revolutionary countries have made it clear that their economic development and political security would be much better served if they could enjoy good relations with Washington.

If our government justifies its own hostility toward leftist governments on the grounds that they are hostile toward us, what becomes of the justification when they try to be friendly? When a newly established revolutionary regime threatens our cold warriors with friendly relations, this does pose a problem. The solution is (1) to heap criticism on the new government for imprisoning the butchers, assassins and torturers of the old regime and for failing to institute middle-class, western capitalist, electoral party politics, then (2) denounce it as a threat to our peace and security, then (3) harass, destabilize and impose economic sanctions, then (4) attack it with counterrevolutionary surrogate forces or, if necessary, with US troops. Long before the invasion, the targeted country responds with angry denunciations of US policy. It moves closer to other leftist nations and attempts to build up its military defenses in anticipation of a US sponsored attack. These moves are taken by our officials and media as evidence of the smaller country's antagonism toward us, and as justification for the policies that evoked such responses.

Yet it is difficult to demonstrate that small countries like Grenada and Nicaragua are a threat to US security. We remember the cry of the hawk during the Vietnam war. "If we don't fight the 'Viet Cong' in the jungles of Indochina, we will have to fight them on the beaches of California." The image of the Vietnamese getting into their PT boats and crossing the Pacific to invade our West Coast was ludicrous. The image of a tiny ill-equipped Central American Army driving through Mexico and across the Rio Grande in order to lay waste to our land is equally ludicrous. The truth is, the Vietnamese, Cubans, Grenadians, and Nicaraguans have never invaded the Unites States; it is the United States that has invaded Vietnam, Cuba, Grenada and Nicaragua, and it is our government that continues to try to isolate, destabilize and in other ways threaten these countries.

When all other arguments fail, there is always the Russian bear. According to our cold warriors these small leftist countries and insurgencies threaten our security because they are extensions of Soviet power. Behind the little Reds there stands the Giant Red Menace. Evidence to support this global menace thesis is sometimes farfetched. Recall how President Carter and National Security Advisor Brzezinski suddenly discovered a "Soviet combat brigade" in Cuba in 1979—which turned out to be a noncombat unit that had been there since 1962. This did not stop President Reagan from announcing in 1983 to a joint session of Congress: "Cuba is host to a Soviet combat brigade."

Last year, in a nationally televised speech, Reagan pointed to satellite photos that revealed the menace of three Soviet helicopters in Nicaragua. Sandinista officials subsequently noted that the helicopters could be seen by anyone arriving at Managua airport without having to climb into a satellite and, in any case, posed no military threat to the United States. Also ludicrous was the way the President's imagination transformed a Grenadian airport, built to accommodate direct tourist flights, into a killer-attack Soviet forward base, and a 20-foot deep Grenadian inlet into a potential Soviet submarine base. Similarly today, President Reagan justifies US intervention in Lebanon and, indirectly, the Israeli imperialist occupation of Southern Lebanon, as a necessary measure to stave off the Syrians who supposedly have become puppets of the Soviet Union.

We are told that the Salvadoran rebels are puppets of the Nicaraguans who are puppets of the Russians. In truth, there is no evidence that Third World peoples take up arms and embark upon costly revolutionary struggles because some sinister ringmaster in Moscow or Peking cracks the whip. Revolutions are not push-button affairs; they evolve only if there exists a reservoir of hope and grievance that can be galvanized into popular action. Revolutions are made when large segments of the population take courage from each other and stand up to an insufferable social order. People are inclined to endure great abuses before risking their lives in confrontations with vastly superior armed forces. There is no such thing as a frivolous revolution, nor one initiated and orchestrated by a manpulative cabal residing in a foreign capital.

Nor is there evidence that once the revolution succeeds, the new leaders place the interests of their country at the disposal of Moscow. As noted earlier, just about every socialist country including the USSR has tried to keep its options open and has sought friendly diplomatic and economic relations with the United States.

Why then are we in Nicaragua—and El Salvador and Guatemala? Is it just an outgrowth of our deeply conditioned anticommunist ideology? Are our leaders responding to the public's longstanding phobia about the Red Menace? Certainly many Americans are anti-communist but this sentiment does not translate into a demand for overseas interventionism. Quite the contrary: a recent Washington Post/ABC News poll shows that, by a 6 to 1 ratio, our citizens oppose any attempt by the United States to overthrow the Nicaraguan government. By more than 3 to 1 they reject Reagan's proposed increase of military aid for the Salvadoran government's war against leftist guerrillas. A substantial majority believe that "becoming too entangled in Central American problems in an attempt to stop the spread of communism" is "a greater danger to the United States" than the spread of communism itself. By more than 2 to 1 the public says that the greatest cause of unrest in Central America is not subversion from Cuba, Nicaragua and the Soviet Union but "poverty and the lack of human rights in the area." Far from galvanizing our leaders into interventionist actions, popular opinion has been one of the few restraining influences.

(There is no denying, however, that opinion can sometimes be successfully manipulated by jingoist ventures. The invasion of Grenada is such a case. Feeling violated and vulnerable after the tragic and ignominious loss of 241 Marines in Lebanon, many people responded positively when the Reagan administration—two days after the attack on the Marines—came up with a quick, easy, low-cost "win" in Grenada. For some Americans this reaffirmed the feeling that we were not weak and indecisive, not sitting ducks to some foreign prey. By a bare majority the public supported the invasion, accepting the view propagated by the media and official representatives that the administration, in one stroke, had performed a humanitarian rescue of medical students, saved democracy from the New Jewel Movement, and prevented a Soviet-Cuban conquest of the entire Caribbean region.

In sum, various leftist states do not pose a military threat to US security, want to trade and live in peace with us, and are a lot less abusive and more helpful toward their people than the fascist regimes they replaced. In addition, US leaders have shown little concern for freedom in the third world, and have actually helped subvert democracy in a number of nations. And popular opinion generally opposes interventionism by lopsided majorities. What then motivates US policy and how can we think it is not confused and contradictory?

## WHO IS THREATENED, AND WHY

The answer is, Marxist and other leftist states *do* pose a real threat, not to the United States as a national entity, nor to the American people as such, but to the corporate and financial interests of our country, to Exxon and Mobil, Chase Manhattan and First National, Ford and General Motors, Anaconda and US Steel, and to capitalism as a world system.

The problem is not that revolutionaries accumulated power but that they *use* power to pursue substantive policies that are unacceptable to US ruling circles. What bothers our political leaders (and generals, investment bankers and corporate heads) is not the left's supposed lack of *political* democracy but its attempt to construct *economic* democracy, to use capital and labor in a way that is inimical to the interests of multinational corporatism.

A *New York Times* editorial (March 30, 1983) refers to "the undesirable and offensive Managua regime," and the danger of seeing "Marxist power ensconced in Managua." But what specifically is so dangerous about "Marxist power"? What is undesirable and offensive about the Managua government? What has it done to us? What has it done to its own people? Is it the literacy campaign? the health care and housing programs? the attempt at rebuilding Managua, at increasing production or achieving a more equitable distribution of land and food? In large part, yes. Such reforms, even if not openly denounced by our government do make a country suspect because they are symptomatic of an effort to erect a new and competing economic order in which the prerogatives of wealth and corporate investment are no longer secure, and the land, labor and resources are no longer used primarily for the accumulation of corporate profits.

US leaders and the business-owned press would have us believe they oppose the Nicaraguan government because it closed an opposition newspaper for a week and forcibly relocated some Indian tribes and failed to hold elections. In fact, the rightwing newspaper, *La Prensa*, now operates with more freedom than ever, policies toward the Miskito Indians have greatly improved; and elections are scheduled, complete with autonomous opposition parties, for November 1984. But the US remains as hostile as ever, for the real grievance US ruling elites hold toward the Sandinistas is that they are building a society that benefits the land and the people—the very land and people capitalism needs to exploit if it is to continue to exist.

The bullies in Washington come closer to their true complaint about Nicaragua when they condemn the Sandinistas for interfering with the prerogatives of the private sector. Similarly Henry Kissinger came close to the truth when he defended the fascist overthrow of the democratic government in Chile by noting that when forced to choose between saving the economy or saving democracy, we must save the economy. Had Kissinger said, we must save the *capitalist* economy, it would have been the whole truth. For under Allende, the danger was not that the economy was collapsing (although the US was doing its utmost to destabilize it and thus undermine the Allende government). The real threat was that the economy was *changing*, away from capitalism and toward socialism, albeit in limited ways.

US officials say they are *for* change just as long as it is peaceful and not violently imposed. Indeed, economic elites may sometimes tolerate very limited reforms, learning to give a little in order to keep a lot. But judging from Chile, Guatemala, Indonesia, and a number of other places, they have a low tolerance for changes, even peaceful ones, that molest the existing class structure and threaten the prerogatives of corporate and landed wealth.

To the rich and powerful it makes little difference if their interests are undone by a peaceful transformation rather than a violent upheaval. The *means* concerns them much less than the *end* results. It is not the "violent" in violent revolution they hate; it is the "revolution." (They seldom actually perish in revolutions and the worst of them usually manage to make it to Miami, Madrid, Paris or New York.) They dread socialism the way the rest of us might dread poverty and hunger. So, when push comes to shove, the wealthy classes of Third World countries, with a great deal of help from the corporate-military-political elites in our country, will use fascism to preserve capitalism while claiming they are saving democracy from communism.

A socialist Nicagargua, as such, is not a threat to the survival of world capitalism. The danger is not socialism in any one country but a socialism that is spreading. Multinational corporations are just that, multinational. They need the world, or a very large part of it, to exploit, and to invest and expand in. There can be no such thing as "capitalism in one country." The domino theory may not work as automatically as its more fearful proponents claim, but who can deny there is a contagion, a power of example and inspiration, and sometimes even direct encouragement and assistance from one revolution to another.

If revolutions arise from the sincere aspirations of the populace, then it is time the United States identify itself with these aspirations, so liberal critics keep urging. They ask: "Why do we always find ourselves on the wrong side in the Third World? Why are we always on the side of the oppressor?" Too bad the question is treated as a rhetorical one, for it is deserving of a response. The answer is that right-wing oppressors, however heinous they be, do not tamper with, and give full support to, private investment and profit, while the leftists pose a challenge to that system.

There are those who say we must "learn from the communists," copy their "techniques" and thus win the battle for the hearts and minds of the people. But can we imagine the ruling interests of the United States abiding by this? Drive out the latifundio owners and sweatshop bossers; kick out the plundering corporations and nationalize their holdings; imprison the militarists and torturers; redistribute the land; use capital investment for home consumption or hard currency exchange instead of cash-crop exports that profit a rich few; install a national health insurance program; construct schools, hospitals and clinics; mobilize the population for literacy campaigns and for work in publicly owned enterprises. If we did all this we would do more than defeat the communists and other revolutionaries, we would have carried out their programs. We would have prevented revolution only by bringing about its effects—thereby defeating the very goals of US ruling-class policies.

US policymakers say they cannot afford to pick and choose the governments they can support, but *that is exactly what they do.* And the pattern of choice is consistent through each successive administration regardless of the party or personality in office. US leaders support those governments, whatever political form they take, that are friendly toward capitalism, and oppose those governments, of whatever political form, that seek to develop a noncapitalist social order. (Occasionally friendly relations are cultivated with noncapitalist nations like Yugoslavia and China if these countries show themselves in useful opposition to other socialist nations.)

In any one instance, interventionist policies may be less concerned with specific investments than with protecting the global investment system. The United States had very little direct investment in the Soviet Union, Vietnam and Grenada—to mention three countries we have invaded over the years. What was at stake in Grenada, as Reagan said, was something more than nutmeg. It was whether we let a country develop a competing economic order, a different way of utilizing its land, labor, capital and natural resources. A social revolution in any part of the world may or may not hurt specific US corporations, but more than that it becomes a part of a cumulative threat to private enterprise in general, to the multinational capitalist system.

## THE SIGNIFICANCE OF THE LEBANON VENTURE

This consistency in US policy can be seen even in regard to Reagan's Lebanon venture. We hear that our presence there has served no purpose and that we are being senselessly drawn into a "sectarian cauldron." But US policy has a very clear purpose: to institute a right-wing Phalangist government and prevent the victory of secular leftist forces composed of the Lebanese Communist Party in alliance with radical Druse, Muslim and Nasserite nationalists, the very same progressive social forces that almost succeeded in forming a government in 1976. The US Marine "peacekeeping" contingent was poorly situated at the Beirut airport and the remaining 100 Marines and Army advisors are also vulnerable but they continue to provide an excuse for maintaining a massive US naval task force offshore. And US naval bombardments effectively turned back leftist offensives with heavy losses on a couple of occasions.

Of course, US intervention in Lebanon may not succeed, for US policy is neither infallible nor omnipotent. But this does not mean, as some news commentators have said, that the policy is "senseless" or inconsistent with overall US interests as defined by present and past administrations in Washington. The United States will support governments that seek to suppress guerrilla movements, as in El Salvador, and will support guerrilla movements that seek to overthrow governments, as in Nicaragua. But there is no confusion or stupidity about it. It is incorrect to say, "We have no foreign policy." Our policy is remarkably rational. Its central organizing principle is to make the world safe for the multinational corporations. However, our rulers cannot ask the American public to sacrifice their tax dollars and the lives of their sons for Exxon and Chase Manhattan, for the profit system as such, so they tell us that US interventions are for freedom and national security and the protection of unspecified "US interests."

Whether policymakers believe their own arguments is not the key question. Sometimes they do, sometimes they don't. Sometimes Ronald Reagan is doing his Hollywood best, as when he quavers with hypocritical compassion for the Miskito Indians, and sometimes he is sincere, as when he speaks of his longstanding fear and loathing for communist and other revolutionary countries. We need not ponder the question of whether our leaders are motivated by their class interests or by a genuine commitment to anticommunist ideology—as if these two things were in competition with each other instead of mutually reinforcing. The arguments our leaders proffer may be self-serving and fabricated, yet also sincerely embraced. It is a creed's congruity with one's material self-interest that often makes it so compelling.

In any case, so much of politics is the rational use of irrational symbols. The arguments in support of interventionism may sound and may actually be irrational and nonsensical, but they serve a rational purpose. Once we grasp the central consistency of US foreign policy we can move from a liberal complaint to a radical analysis, from criticizing the "foolishness" of our government's behavior to understanding why the "foolishness" is not random but persists over time against all contrary arguments and evidence, always moving in the same sinister direction. Once we understand the real nature of US interventionism, we will start calling it by its real name—imperialism.

## 18. Roger Burbach
### *Revolution and Reaction: U.S. Policy in*
### *Central America* 1984

Roger Burbach's critique of American foreign policy in Central America
illustrates how the radical worldview can be used to analyze current issues of
foreign policy. In reading this essay, note Burbach's critique of neorealism,
which should apply to neo-isolationism as well. Do you agree or disagree?

This conflict will not be over quickly. It will last certainly for the remainder of
this decade, and perhaps even into the next century. It is, of course, impossible
to predict the exact trajectory of the war. A year from now, U.S. troops may be
fighting in Central America. Or the United States could still be clinging to its
strategy of war overlord, in which it trains, arms, and directs the established
armies of the region, while employing a private army to wage war on the
Sandinista government in Nicaragua.

There will be ebbs and flows in the war. Temporary truces may occur, the
revolutionary forces may suffer momentary setbacks, or the opposition of the
North American people may compel the U.S. government to back off at times.
But the underlying dynamic will be one of conflict and confrontation. Even if
the guerrillas in El Salvador were to be victorious in six months, or if the anti-
Sandinista forces collapsed, Central America would not find peace. The struggle
between the forces of reaction and revolution would simply assume new forms
or shift elsewhere, to Guatemala or Honduras or even to Costa Rica.

The United States today is locked into a war in Central America. It is a war
between the forces of reaction and revolution, between a modern empire
determined to defend the status quo and the social and political forces struggling
to build a new society.

Why is this so? The fundamental reason is that Central America and parts of
the Caribbean are involved in a process of intense class conflict which will be
prolonged. This has profound implications for U.S. imperialism. As the leading
capitalist nation in the world and the hegemonic power in the Caribbean Basin,*
the United States is committed to sustaining governments and political systems
that maintain capitalist relations in the economic, political, and social spheres.
The primary thrust of the revolutionary movements, on the other hand, is aimed
at overturning the established systems of class rule and setting up governments
that bring new social and political forces into power. This battle over alternative
political and economic projects is the fundamental reason why the United States
and the revolutionary movements are locked into prolonged conflict.

---

* The Caribbean Basin is here defined as including the thirty-two countries and territories that
are located in the Caribbean sea and the Central American isthmus. Neither Mexico nor any of
the countries on the South American continent are included.

This reality can be more fully understood by looking at three concrete forces that have shaped U.S. relations with Central America and the Caribbean: (1) the particular role that the region has played in the evolution of the U.S. imperial system, (2) the extensive U.S. economic interests in the Caribbean Basin, and (3) the role of the region in the U.S. National Security State. These factors have created a tightly knit web of historic and contemporary interests that the United States can only maintain by opposing the revolutionary forces and by maintaining its strategic alliance with the local ruling classes.

## CENTRAL AMERICA IN THE U.S. EMPIRE

To understand why Central America and the Caribbean are so important to the U.S. empire, it is first necessary to understand what distinguishes the U.S. imperial system from previous empires. Beginning in the latter part of the nineteenth century, the United States broke with previous imperial systems in that it established an "informal empire," one in which it did not exercise direct territorial or colonial control.* Rather than joining in the rush for colonies in Africa and Asia as the European powers did at that time, the United States called for an "Open Door" policy vis-à-vis the underdeveloped regions of the world and used its growing economic might to penetrate the markets and societies in these regions. Subsequently adopted by other imperial powers, this system of domination has been characterized as a "neocolonial system," one in which a metropolitan country holds sway over formally independent countries and extracts economic and political benefits from this arrangement.

It was in the Caribbean Basin that the United States first consolidated its informal empire. Although the United States had staked out its claim to the region with the enunciation of the Monroe Doctrine, it was not until its victory in the Spanish-American-Cuban War in 1898 that its dreams of empire in the region became a reality. After the war, U.S. direct investments in Central America and the Caribbean mushroomed, concentrating in banana and sugar plantations, public utilities, and transportation facilities, virtually the only areas where lucrative profits were to be made.

While eschewing direct colonial rule (with the exception of Puerto Rico), the young empire often resorted to military force to assure its informal political control. Between 1900 and 1930, the United States carried out 28 military interventions in the Caribbean Basins.[1] The interventions had a variety of motives—ensuring that the governments paid their debts to U.S. investors, and generally guaranteeing that no governments came to power in the region which would challenge U.S. prerogatives. Political control may not have been formal, but it was virtually complete. Indeed, the two most infamous characterizations

---

* Great Britain actually exercised informal control over some countries in the twentieth century (particularly in South America), but the heart of its empire was built on direct territorial control.

of U.S. foreign policy—"Gunboat Diplomacy" and "Dollar Diplomacy"—aptly described U.S. activities in Central America and the Caribbean during this era.

This early period of U.S. dominance in the region laid the basis for the special role which it plays in the U.S. global empire up to this day. This is the region where the sun first rose on the U.S. informal empire, and any challenges in the region strike at the underpinnings of the entire U.S. imperial system.

## THE U.S. ECONOMIC STAKE

With the post-Second World War expansion of the United States as a world power, the Caribbean Basin seemingly receded in importance. U.S. military bases were established in Western Europe and Asia, and U.S. trade and investments burgeoned around the world. Furthermore, U.S. disinvestments in plantations and public utilities in the region made it appear that the region was of only marginal economic importance to the United States.

But the expansion of U.S. power abroad did not really diminish the importance of Central America and the Caribbean. U.S. business actually expanded in the Basin, diversifying into new areas of production. Today, agriculture, manufacturing, commerce, mining, and tourism account for $62 billion in productive investments, and another $16.9 billion is tied up in banking and financial operations in the Caribbean Basin. (These investment totals do not include Puerto Rico.) This $23.1 billion constitutes 9 percent of total U.S. investments abroad. When compared to other third world regions, these figures put the Caribbean Basin in second place in economic importance to the United States, surpassed only by the rest of Latin America (i.e., South America and Mexico).

Virtually every major corporate sector in the United States has a significant stake in the Caribbean Basin. Among the big corporate interests in Central America and the Caribbean, the Rockefellers clearly predominate, with sizable holdings in tourism, petroleum, and banking. In addition, a very large number of small firms and investors, particularly from the southern and western United States, have holdings there. For these firms, the Caribbean Basin is of singular importance. Geographic proximity enables them to use the region to test their foreign investment strategies and to lay plans for further international expansion.

Do these substantial holdings mean that the U.S. corporate community is a fundamental obstacle to the revolutionary process in the region? One school of U.S. policymakers and analysts called "neorealists" advocate a kind of "peaceful coexistence" as the best survival strategy for capitalism in the third world. They argue that U.S. corporations should be able to operate profitably even in revolutionary and socialist countries.[2] While the neorealists are correct in pointing out that the multinationals have made profitable investments in established socialist countries, it is also true that historically those same corporations have consistently tried to stop revolutions in countries where existing U.S. investments might be threatened. One need only recall the role of U.S.

corporations in overthrowing Jacobo Arbenz in Guatemala or Salvador Allende in Chile to recognize this reality.[3]

The same counter-revolutionary instincts shape the behavior of U.S. corporate interests in Central America and the Caribbean today. While some U.S. transnationals may have remained in Nicaragua after the Sandinista victory, they have made virtually no new investments (and even some disinvestments) despite Nicaragua's relatively liberal foreign investment code. This is certainly not a favorable omen for those who maintain that U.S. economic institutions can or will remain neutral in the midst of the revolutionary upheaval gripping the region.

In Central America and the Caribbean, U.S. corporations are, in fact, actively involved in trying to stop the revolutionary movements and to preserve what they regard as the best climate for investment—free-market economies. The major business organization spearheading this effort is Caribbean/Central American Action (C/CAA). Founded during the last year of the Carter administration and initially led principally by southern and western capitalists, the organization has grown rapidly in the past two years. Today it is supported by over 100 big corporations and is headed by David Rockefeller, the old stalwart of the eastern financial establishment. The C/CAA is a fervent supporter of Reagan administration policies, having endorsed the Caribbean Basin Initiative and the report of the Kissinger Commission on Central America, which calls for massive economic and military aid to the region.

What these and other programs by the business community demonstrate is that U.S. corporations are clearly an integral part of the U.S. effort to maintain capitalism in Central America and the Caribbean and to stop the revolutionary threat to that system. They want to preserve the region for capitalism in general, and as an outlet for U.S. investments in particular. Corporate capital abhors revolutionary upheaval: it disrupts the local economies and throws investment planning into chaos. Nationalist and social democratic governments are also generally opposed by corporate capital, as was demonstrated by the antagonistic behavior of many U.S. multinationals toward the Manley government in Jamaica in the mid and late 1970s.

## CENTRAL AMERICA AND U.S. NATIONAL SECURITY

In defending their aggressive actions in the region U.S. leaders do not, of course, assert that they are protecting U.S. economic interests, or that the Caribbean Basin plays a special role in the U.S. imperial system. Presidents from Eisenhower to Reagan have ultimately justified U.S. intervention by asserting that "it is the U.S. national security that is at stake."[4] This is due to the way in which the needs and interests of the U.S. empire have been wedded to the concept of national security. The merger of national and imperial interests, while characteristic of most empires, achieved a particular thrust in the United

States after the Second World War, when the United States adopted a policy of systematic opposition to the Soviet Union in particular, and toward communism and revolutionary movements in general.

In National Security Council Document No. 68, or NSC-68, drawn up in 1950, U.S. national security was explicitly tied to the demands of maintaining the U.S. system abroad. This document remains a central pillar of U.S. foreign policy to this day. As the document notes on the first page, wars and revolutions led to the collapse of five empires in the past century—the Ottoman, the German, the Austro-Hungarian, the Italian, and the Japanese—and to the drastic decline of the French and the British systems. To ensure that the United States does not meet a similar fate, the document argues that the United States cannot accept "disorder" in the world at large. Viewing the Soviet Union as the primary obstacle to U.S. interests, NSC-68 asserts that the United States must "foster a fundamental change in the nature of the Soviet system." Only by using "any means, covert or overt, violent or non-violent," to achieve its global objectives could the United States create "a successfully functioning political and economic system."[5]

This is the doctrinal basis for the East-West conflict and U.S. national security. The entire world, developed and underdeveloped, is viewed as an arena of competition between the United States and the Soviet Union. Revolutionary movements in the third world are consistently seen as part of the "Soviet challenge," even though the Soviet Union in most cases has little to do with the movements.

The vision of U.S. national security has been applied with particular ferocity in the Caribbean Basin. Here, next to the U.S. shores, any efforts to break away from the U.S. orbit have been resisted; and when breaks have occurred, as in the case of Cuba in the 1960s, the United States has conducted an incessant campaign—with military, economic, and political components—to contain or reverse these challenges. U.S. presidents as diverse as Harry Truman, John F. Kennedy, and Ronald Reagan have all acted on the explicit assumption that in order to wage the global struggle against communism, the Caribbean Basin had to be made as secure as possible.

The special importance of the region since the Cold War was launched is revealed by the frequency of U.S. military interventions. While the United States has not yet waged a massive war in the region on the scale of the Korean and Vietnamese conflicts, it is notable that no other region has suffered as many U.S. interventions in the postwar era as the Caribbean Basin. The CIA's overthrow of the government of Jacobo Arbenz in 1954, the invasion of Cuba at the Bay of Pigs in 1961, the naval blockade of Cuba during the 1962 missile crisis, the use of U.S. troops in the Canal Zone to quell political unrest in Panama in 1964, the dispatch of the U.S. marines to the Dominican Republic in 1965, the U.S.-backed counterinsurgency wars in the 1960s (particularly in Guatemala), the U.S. invasion of Grenada, the present intervention in El Salvador, and the clandestine war against Nicaragua—these are the most well-known overt or covert U.S. military operations in the Caribbean Basin. The fact that U.S. interventions of one form or another have occurred approximately once every three years reveals that the United States has actually been involved in a protracted conflict in the region, for the past three decades.

In sum, a constellation of forces is at work which make it impossible for the United States to calmly accept revolutionary governments in Central America or the Caribbean. The fact that the region has historically been at the center of the U.S. informal empire, the extensive U.S. investments in the region, and the reality that counter-revolution has been at the core of U.S. national security thinking—all these factors lock the United States in a prolonged period of conflict with the revolutionary movements and governments in the region.

## THE FUNDAMENTAL CHALLENGE

The U.S. dominance of most facets of life in Central America and the Caribbean has dramatic consequences for the revolutionary movements in the region. These movements have all been strongly conditioned by the overwhelming presence of the United States in the Basin. It is no accident that the most significant and sustained challenge to the U.S. informal empire should emerge in this region. This is where the links of informal empire are strongest, and consequently the area where contradictions between the United States and the revolutionary movements are deepest. Even more so than in Vietnam—where the historical anticolonial struggle against the French was directed against the United States only because of its military intervention relatively late in the game—the Central Americans are rebelling against decades of U.S. domination over all aspects of their society (military, economic, political, and cultural).

A brief look at the economic and social realities of the region reveals just how deep-seated the contradictions are. Economically, the countries and territories are more tightly tied to the U.S. economy than any other third world region. While other economies in Latin America, such as Mexico's and Brazil's, are also linked to the U.S. system and even have a larger absolute quantity of U.S. investments, the diversity and extensiveness of their economies gives them more room for maneuver vis-à-vis the United States.

Due to the overwhelming economic dominance of the United States, the economies in Central America and the Caribbean have never been able to develop an effective plan for regional economic integration which could have given them more clout in the global capitalist system. The consequences of this extreme dependency on the United States have been severe—the failure of the region to develop heavy industries, the reliance of U.S. imports and technology for the limited industries that did develop, and the lack of significant regional markets and regional transportation and communications systems. This legacy of dependency means that efforts to achieve balanced economic development that responds to the internal needs of the countries in Central America and the Caribbean have inevitably come into head-on conflict with the United States.

The total U.S. economic dominance of the region in turn has had profound repercussions for the social and cultural development of the region. In many ways, the Caribbean Basin is one of the most diverse regions of the world; the array of cultures, the different colonial roots of the countries, the presence of all the major ethnic groups of the world—these factors and others have combined to create a tremendous cultural diversity.

While these diverse cultures remain, they have all been strongly impacted by U.S. penetration. A prolonged assault on the region's cultures has come from an array of U.S. groups ranging from U.S. evangelical missionaries and businessmen to droves of American tourists and pop music artists. Today, in fact, if there is one characteristic that unifies the region culturally, it is the penetration of the "American way of life."

## THE IDEOLOGICAL ROOTS OF CONFLICT

Given U.S. economic and cultural domination, it is not surprising then that the revolutionary forces say their main objective is self-determination—the right of even small countries to choose their own social, economic, and political systems, and the international relations which respond to their respective needs. They intend to rupture the neocolonial system in which the United States determines the political and economic destinies of third world countries.[6]

The revolutionary forces, in fact, enunciate political principles that conflict with many of the premises that guide the U.S. system. The diverse revolutionary movements and governments that have developed in such countries as Cuba, Nicaragua, and El Salvador draw their inspiration from a political world view which is very different from that which has shaped the United States throughout its history. The United States emerged in the era of the great bourgeois democratic revolutions of the late eighteenth and early nineteenth centuries. Drawing heavily on the political philosophy of John Locke, the U.S. revolution and its founding documents stressed individual initiative and individual rights in the economic and political spheres as the basis of its political system. These "rights" were essential for the development of the new capitalist societies in the United States as well as in Western Europe. To the extent that the United States has supported revolutionary movements in other parts of the world, in Latin America in the early nineteenth century or in Africa after the Second World War, it has always been in an effort to encourage or to compel them to incorporate these principles in their political systems.[7]

The movements in Central America and the Caribbean, on the other hand, are rooted in the revolutionary traditions of the twentieth century. Driven by most dispossessed and exploited social sectors, and heavily influenced by the political philosophies of Marx and Lenin, these revolutions seek to establish political systems based on the mobilization of the masses and the redistribution of the material wealth to the most impoverished sectors of society. These revolutionary movements clearly do not intend to recognize the individual's rights to accumulate economic wealth on an extensive scale, and they want to set up political systems that break substantially with the United States in its concepts of democracy and freedom.

Such terms as "democracy" and "freedom," in fact, have an entirely different meaning in each of these social orders. In the contemporary revolutionary societies, for example, democracy is often prefaced by the word "popular," meaning that participation in the direction of society can occur in various forms and at different levels—in the factories and the fields, in the communities, in the schools, and in the government itself. The local organizations that exist in these and other areas enable people to participate in decisions that affect their daily lives. While bourgeois democratic societies, on the other hand, do have some organizations that influence local decisions (school boards, community groups, etc.), the term "democracy" is predominately identified with electoral politics: it means the right of everyone to go to the ballot box every few years, even if the majority of the populace finds it irrelevant to exercise that right. This concept of democracy is what enables U.S. interventionists to proclaim that they are protecting the "democracies" in Central America while they prop up murderous regimes that hold formal elections and tyrannize their populations.

These are the fundamental differences over political philosophies between the United States and the Central American and Caribbean liberation movements. They explain, at least on the ideological plane, why it is often as difficult for liberal Democrats as it is for Reaganite Republicans to accept the revolutionary movements. Even some of the most ardent Democratic critics of Reagan's Central American policies refer to the revolutionary movements as "totalitarian" or as "antidemocratic." These characterizations are not simply political rhetoric designed to win elections in the United States—they are terms that indicate profound differences with the political philosophy of the contemporary revolutionary movements.

## THE CHARACTER OF THE REVOLUTIONARY MOVEMENTS

The rebellion against U.S. dominance in the heart of its informal empire is perceived as even more profound a challenge to the foundations of the U.S. global power than was the Vietnam conflict. President Reagan, in spelling out the U.S. stake in the Caribbean Basin in his address to the Joint Session of Congress (April 27, 1983) asserted that if the United States lost this region, "we cannot expect to prevail elsewhere. Our credibility would collapse, our alliances would crumble, and the safety of our homeland would be put in jeopardy."[8] What in fact is being challenged is the U.S. commitment to a particular type of society formation which the United States and other dominant capitalist nations have imposed on large parts of the third world.

U.S. determination to hold onto the region explains why during much of this century the insurgencies have perforce been directed as much against the United States as against the local ruling classes. To be successful, the movements for self-determination in the region must be anti-imperialist, armed, militant, and capable of mobilizing the majority of the population to resist U.S. intervention (whether overt or covert, economic or military).

Here, even more than in other parts of the world, there is no reformist path which will enable the countries to escape from U.S. control. Governments that have challenged U.S. dominance by adopting reforms within a capitalist framework, and that have not mobilized and armed their people to resist the inevitable U.S. intervention, have had to pay the ultimate consequence, i.e., the loss of power to U.S.-backed right-wing regimes. Two striking and somewhat disparate examples of this reality are the governments of Jacobo Arbenz in Guatemala in the 1950s and of Michael Manley in Jamaica in the late 1970s.*

The genius of Fidel Castro's July 26th Movement is that it recognized from the moment it took power that the support of the Cuban people was central to the revolution and that the United States would be its implacable enemy. The old debate over whether or not Fidel Castro was a Marxist when he came to power is actually misleading.[9] The key factor to understanding the initial stages of the Cuban revolution is that the leadership of the July 26th Movement recognized that the United States would oppose its economic and political platform because it challenged U.S. dominance of the island. Accordingly, the leadership began very early on to mobilize the country's population, and to seek international alliances that would give it the capacity to thwart U.S. efforts to destroy the new government. This reality, that the United States will move directly against any government which alters the status quo and challenges its prerogatives, was mastered by the Sandinistas when they took power and it is a central lesson that all future revolutions must act upon.

## EXCEPTIONS THAT PROVE A NEW RULE?

The pervasiveness of the antirevolutionary thrust of the United States is obvious when one looks at the global U.S. response to revolutionary movements throughout the twentieth century. In countries as diverse as the Soviet Union, Cuba, China, Angola, Vietnam, the United States not only tried to prevent the revolutions from seizing power, but once they did attain power, the United States used a variety of measures and tactics in an effort to undermine or destroy the revolutionary process. In the case of the older revolutions (the USSR and China), only after a period of a decade or two, when the new revolutionary governments had demonstrated that they were firmly in power, did the United States finally accept the new reality and begin to search for ways to accommodate itself to the new governments. And as we know in the cases of Vietnam, Cuba, and Angola, the United States has yet to even recognize the existence of these revolutionary governments.

However, with the triumph of the Nicaraguan and Zimbabwean revolutions in 1979 and 1980, there were signs that the United States might break with its

---

* A bitter lesson of the 1983 Grenadian experience is that the revolutionary forces must also maintain total unity. Any divisions or splits within the revolutionary leadership will cost them popular support, which among other things will leave them immediately vulnerable to the hostile actions of the United States, with dire consequences for the revolutionary movements.

past policies. In each case the United States (specifically the Carter administration) moved quickly to recognize the new governments and to extend significant amounts of bilateral assistance. Do these cases demonstrate that at least one sector of the U.S. ruling class may be willing to enter a new epoch in its relations with revolutionary governments?

A review of specific developments in the cases of Zimbabwe and Nicaragua provides little hope that the United States is on the brink of a major shift in its historic counter-revolutionary politics. As regards Zimbabwe, the principal reason why the United States has not opposed the revolutionary process is because sub-Saharan Africa in general, and the Zimbabwe in particular, are not in what is recognized as the U.S. sphere of influence. U.S. interests, both historic and contemporary, have been quite limited in that region. Even more importantly, the United States recognizes Great Britain as the major European power when dealing with Zimbabwe. Thus when Great Britain worked out the Lancaster Agreements, which were the basis for the subsequent elections in Zimbabwe and the extensive economic aid given to the country, the United States had no real alternative but to support the results of the elections, even though the openly avowed Marxist candidate, Robert Mugabe, became the prime minister.

The case of Nicaragua is obviously more relevant for the projection of future events in the Caribbean Basin. But this case offers even less basis for hope; in fact, it demonstrates that there are irreconcilable differences between the United States and the revolutionary movements in Central America and the Caribbean. As is well known, the Carter administration extended emergency relief to the new Sandinista government, and it persuaded Congress to approve a special program for $75 million in economic assistance.

However, the main problem with viewing this as a sign that the United States will not oppose future revolutionary processes in the region is that the Carter administration was clearly trying to coopt the Sandinista revolution: It wanted to create a Nicaraguan political system in the mold of the bourgeois democratic revolutions of the eighteenth and nineteenth centuries. U.S. aid was in no way designed to facilitate a transition to socialism. Over 60 percent of the assistance went to the private sector in Nicaragua, and the Carter administration in its official statements as to why it was providing the assistance repeatedly declared that it was trying to encourage a "pluralist society," i.e., a society in which private business would have a leading role and in which there would be periodic elections similar to those in Costa Rica or Venezuela.

This program of trying to coopt the Sandinista revolution was clearly doomed to failure. Even before the Reagan administration assumed power, there were signs that relations were souring between the United States and Nicaragua. The reason for this was simple—the Nicaraguan revolution, for all its uniqueness, was cast in the general mold of the twentieth-century social revolutions. The decline of the private business sectors, the growing prominence of the militant peasant and trade unions, the clear anti-imperialist stance of the Sandinista Front, and the reality that the Sandinistas supported the revolutionary forces in El Salvador—these were the major reasons why the

Carter administration in its waning days found it increasingly difficult to accept the Sandinista government and why it even began to prepare a legal brief for the incoming Reagan administration to end U.S. aid to the Sandinista government.[10]

## THE "THIRD WAY"

Facing U.S. belligerency on the military and economic fronts, and given the overwhelming preponderance of the United States in the region, must the postrevolutionary societies inevitably join the socialist bloc countries in order to survive? Or are there important limits and restraints placed on U.S. intervention which make it possible for the countries in Central America and the Caribbean to find a "third way," a way in which the societies will not be dependent on the Soviet Union?

Due to the particular nature of the economic system it has helped develop in the region the United States has ironically created the conditions which facilitate the process of transition there. While U.S. capital (whether through transnational corporations or bilateral aid programs) has caused severe economic and social dislocations discussed elsewhere, the U.S. economic penetration of the region has also been a major force in developing a relatively modern economic infrastructure. Some of the countries in the region may be among the poorest in the Western Hemisphere but compared to other countries in the third world (particularly many Asian and sub-Saharan African societies) even these societies are in a far better position to develop their economies.

The process of imperialist-led development has also brought into existence new social forces. The emergence of urban and rural proletariats, the fact that these working classes are generally literate and have achieved a certain degree of education, the existence of peasant populations which in many cases have ample contacts with the major urban centers and are not as isolated and politically conservative as in more traditional peasant societies, and the emergence of substantial middle classes from which key leadership has emerged for the revolutionary movements—these are the social forces the United States has helped create through its economic penetration of the region, and which place the Caribbean Basin in a much better position than other third world regions to try to build a socialist society.

## THE INTERNATIONAL CONTEXT

These developments combined with changes in the global economy could enable the countries in the region to deal with the economic obstacles to building socialist socieities without totally transforming their economic infrastructure and becoming dependent on the Soviet Union. During the past twenty-five years, and particularly in the last decade, the capitalist world has, in fact, become multipolar. As U.S. hegemony and the "American Century" draws to an end, the United States is no longer able to impose its will on the other capitalist countries. Specifically, the United States cannot dictate international trading patterns, nor is it even able to control the trade of its own multinational corporations.

This is a very significant development, which gives the new revolutionary societies in the Caribbean Basin much more room to maneuver than the Cuban revolution had when it came to power in 1959. Even leading third world capitalist countries have more flexibility vis-à-vis the United States. While such countries as Brazil and Mexico are still linked economically to the United States, they, along with more maverick countries such as Libya and Algeria, have been able to exercise considerable autonomy in the international political sphere and to adopt commercial and economic policies that are opposed by the United States.

The Sandinista government during its first half decade in power has fully understood this reality. This explains why it has sought and continues to receive vitally needed international development assistance without moving into the socialist bloc. Not only have Western European countries provided aid, but third world assistance has been just as critical. Import loans from Brazil, subsidized oil from Mexico, hard currency aid from Libya, and sugar imports from Algeria—these are some of the more important and critical forms of aid Nicaragua has received from the third world. There is clearly flexibility in the global capitalist system, a flexibility and multipolarity which will facilitate the development of socialist societies in the Caribbean Basin even if the United States maintains a generally antagonistic stance toward them.

## U.S. SOCIETY AND THE TRANSITION PROCESS

While the United States is clearly the main threat to the revolutionary movements in the Caribbean Basin, it would be simplistic to write off all of U.S. society as an obstacle to the revolutionary process. Within the United States there are social forces at work which have the capacity to significantly influence the U.S. role in the Caribbean Basin. The U.S. ruling class, left to its own devices, would no doubt use every means possible to destroy the revolutionary movements and governments in the region. But it operates under severe constraints, not only internationally, but most importantly from within the United States. Opposition from the U.S. public and from Congress, for example, has been a major force limiting the Reagan administration's interventionary plans in Central America.

Public opposition to U.S. intervention in the region is not simply a transitory phenomenon which Reagan or any other president will be able to purge from the U.S. body politic by manipulating the media or by mounting an anticommunist campaign. The opposition to interventions in third world countries now has a substantial social base, particularly within the black and Hispanic communities, churches, the women's movement, the intellectual community, some trade unions, and peace, environmental, and third world solidarity activists. These movements and organizations are firmly opposed to U.S. intervention in the third world. Some have been mobilized by the fact that they are directly victimized or outraged by the injustice and irrationality of the capitalist system; others are more strongly motivated by the blatant contradictions they see between the democratic rhetoric of the United States and the actual impact that the U.S. system has on many third world countries striving for their economic and political independence.

While most of these social sectors do not articulate an anticapitalist or prosocialist perspective, they nonetheless do question the prevailing economic and political system and are groping for some new alternatives to present U.S. policies, both at home and abroad. These forces are the natural allies of the liberation movements in Central America and the Caribbean. While they will not obtain control of the U.S. government apparatus in the foreseeable future, they do have sufficient (and growing) political clout in the U.S. system to undermine the more interventionist thrusts.[11]

The existence of these internal forces will, in fact, cause U.S. policies toward the Caribbean Basin to be fairly volatile during the next decade. While the inherent tendency of the U.S. state is to destroy the revolutionary forces, the social forces mentioned above are continually operating to undermine or check that tendency. In fact, the existence of these forces explains why under a future Democratic president, there will at times be serious attempts to search for a truce with the revolutionary forces in the region. Most of the social groups listed above have historically had some influence within the Democratic Party; if that party takes power, these groups will pressure the party leadership and the executive arm of the government for real changes vis-à-vis the revolutionary movements, even though they obviously will in no way be strong enough to compel the U.S. government to come to a permanent accommodation with them.

In the coming years, however, there will be a deepening interaction between the revolutionary processes in Central America and the Caribbean and political developments in the United States. The strong cultural, social, and economic ties that exist between this country and those in Central America and the Caribbean mean that there will indeed be a "spill over" effect as the revolutions in the region gain momentum. Revolutionary successes will create new problems for the U.S. ruling elites and give new momentum to the social sectors opposed to many aspects of U.S. policies at home and abroad. Minimally, the successful revolutionary movements there will have an effect on third world peoples in the United States, particularly those whose origins are in Central America and the Caribbean. At the same time, the local ruling classes in the region, once they lose power, will continue their migration to Miami and other parts of the United States, adding to the strength of the reactionary forces in this country. In effect, successful revolutionary movements in the region will increasingly polarize the political process in the United States.

Ultimately, the successful transformation of Central America and the Caribbean is linked to a major political change in the United States, a change in the U.S. ideology of empire. Other, older imperial powers finally had to adjust, however involuntarily, to anticolonial movements and to a new concept of empire.

The United States has not yet reached this point; the fundamental concepts that drive its imperial system, however unviable, still dominate the foreign policy elites as well as the Republican and Democratic parties. The United States will have to go through a period of extended conflict with the revolutionary forces in Central America and the Caribbean before these concepts are discarded in favor of a new worldview.

## NOTES

1. William Appleman Williams, *Empire as a Way of Life* (New York: Oxford University Press, 1980), pp. 136–42.
2. Richard E. Feinberg, *The Intemperate Zone: The Third World Challenge to U.S. Foreign Policy* (New York: W. W. Norton, 1983).
3. Richard H. Immerman, *The CIA in Guatemala: The Foreign Policy of Intervention* (Austin: University of Texas Press, 1982), and NACLA, *New Chile* (New York: NACLA, 1973).
4. State Department documents released in 1984 show that President Eisenhower asserted in a National Security Council meeting in 1954 that the United States is not merely "doing business in Latin America but is fighting a war there against communism." This pronouncement was made after the CIA-sponsored invasion of Guatemala. "Latin Communism Worried Ike in 1954, Documents Reveal," *San Francisco Chronicle*, January 4, 1984.
5. National Security Council, "A Report to the National Security Council by the Executive Secretary on United States Objectives and Programs for National Security," April 14, 1950, *Naval War College Review* 27 (May–June 1975).
6. For an in-depth understanding of what self-determination means for many revolutionaries in the region see *Listen, Compañero: Conversations with Central American Revolutionaries* (San Francisco: Solidarity Publications, 1983).
7. Gene Bell-Villada, "Two Americas, Two Worldviews," MONTHLY REVIEW 34, no. 5 (October 1982): 37–48.
8. President Reagan, "Central America: Defending Our Vital Interests," U.S. Department of State, Current Policy No. 482, April 27, 1983.
9. The U.S. State Department under the Reagan administration has given a new twist to this debate. It argues that it was principally Fidel Castro's quest for personal aggrandizement which led him to adopt Marxism-Leninism. This supposedly occurred after the revolutionary victory in 1959, when Castro was looking for a system that would enable him and his "tiny elite" to remain in power indefinitely. See Elliot Abrams, Assistant Secretary of State for Human Rights, "The Cuban Revolution and its Impact on Human Rights," U.S. Department of State, Current Policy No. 518, Washington, D.C., October 6, 1983.
10. Author's interview with State Department official, mid-1981.
11. See Policy Alternatives for the Caribbean and Central America (PACCA), *Changing Course: Blueprint for Peace in Central America and the Caribbean* (Washington, D.C.: Institute for Policy Studies, 1984), a policy blueprint developed to provide the anti-interventionist forces in the United States with an alternative perspective for U.S. policy.

## 19. Kathy McAfee
### *Why the Third World Goes Hungry*    1990

In this selection Kathy McAfee, a senior writer and researcher for Oxfam
America, explores a seemingly simple question: Why does famine exist when
there is more than enough food to feed the world? Her answer lies in a radical
critique of the world's major international economic organizations, such as the
World Bank and the International Monetary Fund, as well as the trade and
"development strategies" proposed by those organizations and Western
governments. As you read this essay, note the solutions that she proposes.
How likely are they to succeed?

More of the world's people are hungry today than ever before. The World Bank
has estimated that as many as 950 million people are "chronically
malnourished": too hungry to lead active, productive lives. That's nearly one
person in five worldwide. According to United Nations figures, more than 15
million children die each year of malnutrition and related sickness. Most of
these hunger-related deaths, whether of children or adults, occur in Asia,
Africa, Latin America, and the Caribbean—the global South, or third world. It
has been calculated that food deprivation causes as many deaths in a year as
would a Hiroshima-size atomic bomb dropped somewhere in the third world
every two or three days.

Most of these deaths are needless. More than enough food is grown to feed
everyone on earth. The World Resources Institute reports that if all the food
produced were distributed equitably throughout the world, it could provide an
adequate diet for nearly six billion people—one billion more than now live on
the planet. More than half this bounty is grown in the third world. The UN Food
and Agricultural Organization has documented that food production during the
past twenty-five years has outpaced population growth in every major region
except Africa south of the Sahara desert. But those who need this food—and
who do most of the work of producing it—are often not the ones who consume
it.

Some analysts, including Lester Brown and John Young of the Worldwatch
Institute, warn that global population growth may soon begin to exceed the rate
of increase of world food production—this as the result of erosion, deforesta-
tion, and other consequences of policies and practices that undermine the
planet's capacity for producing food and fresh water. Their predictions may
prove true, but that does not mean we can solve the problem of hunger by
limiting population growth. Famine exists now, when there is food enough to
feed the world. Unless we understand why today's surplus does not reach the
needy, and until we do something about it, we will not be able to avert more
widespread starvation in any future context of scarcity. Moreover, as explained
below (point No. 7), the same factors that lead to hunger also serve to degrade
the environment in many places.

Hunger makes news during severe regional famines, when cameras portray hundreds of thousands sinking toward death. But if the existence of chronic hunger in a world of abundance is rarely acknowledged, its root causes are even less understood. News media report emergency food shipments, foreign aid grants, private and governmental loans from the developed countries, leading us to assume that by these measures the rich countries are sustaining the battered economies of the third world. The opposite is closer to the truth. In the movement of wealth around the world, far more flows *out of* impoverished countries of Africa, Asia, and Latin America and *into* the richer economies of Europe, North America, and Japan. Every year since 1986, according to an estimate by the Overseas Development Council, at least $43 billion in net financial resources has been transferred from the global South to the North. The estimate is conservative; others put the South's net loss higher.

The measurable portion of this hemorrhage is made up in large part of debt payments. UNICEF reports that in 1988 would-be developing countries had to channel $178 billion to Northern nations to meet their debt bills. The total external debt of the third world is a crushing $1.2 trillion. In 1987, low- and middle-income governments paid out $102 billion in interest alone—3.4 times the total development assistance from all aid-giving nations. Other components of the measurable flow are the profits claimed by foreign owners of third-world businesses, and the deposits by the South's elite in Northern banks.

Other resources flow unseen, like underground rivers, in the same direction; they are harder to calculate, but very real. The mineral and agricultural products transferred out of Latin America, Asia, and Africa are vital to the global economy, but the prices paid for them do not begin to reflect their practical usefulness, or the profits they make possible for shippers, processors, and speculative commodity traders in the North. So also with the value added to garments, gadgets, and other goods assembled in export processing zones of the third world; workers there earn a small fraction of the wages paid to those doing comparable factory work in the North.

Still more unseen wealth is drained from the third world by illegal or semilegal means. Corporations disguise the removal of profits through the shady accounting practices of transfer pricing; individuals add to capital flight by smuggling out hard currency into foreign bank accounts. Tremendous sums are accumulated in the North at the expense of the South through the international drug trade. Andean peasants, many of whom can no longer find an adequate income alternative to growing coca leaves, receive a tiny fraction of the immense wealth gathered by the cocaine industry bosses, who use banks and corporate fronts in U.S., Europe, and the Caribbean to launder their earnings.

Cumulatively, these massive transfers of wealth from the impoverished third world to the comparatively affluent industrialized nations constitute the most important underlying cause of third-world poverty and hunger. The poor of the third world are being integrated into a global economy in which allocation of food is determined by market criteria. It is a skewed system, as different as could be from the free and competitive model imagined by Adam Smith. In the only markets to which poor people of the third world have access, they have no control over trading terms, interest rates, investment choices, or the other rules of the game. Increasingly, those with greater control edge out those with less. The consequence is that millions of farmers are being deprived of resources they need to raise food for themselves and their communities: land, water, tools, draft animals, credit, traditional knowledge, and structures of community cohesion and support.

All this is happening in a variety of ways.

1. *The expansion of export agricultue and commercial farming.* Wealthy countries have imported products like coffee, tea, and chocolate from the third world since the days of colonialism. Imports of such tropical products are still increasing; growing still faster are imports of foods like canned fish and meat, fresh fruits and vegetables, and fibers such as cotton—all products that can be produced in temperate climates but that can be raised and harvested more cheaply (or during winter) in the third world. The rich countries are also increasing their purchases of crops such as soybeans from Brazil, peanuts from West Africa, cassava from Thailand—foods that could nourish hungry people in the countries where they are grown, but are fed instead to livestock in rich countries.

Little of the money earned by these sales goes to the primary producers. In the fertile lowlands of Central America, for instance, peasants once grew crops that provided a nutritious diet: corn, beans, melons, squash, tomatoes, and chilis. Today, cattle ranches and plantations growing export crops such as sugar, coffee, cotton, and bananas cover much of this land.

The very profitability of third-world commercial crops has hurt rather than helped the poor. It has contributed to increased prices and rents for land, and to higher costs for irrigation equipment, fertilizers, and pesticides. Subsistence farmers who cannot afford these increased costs are being displaced by commercial growers. Half the farmers in the third world have access to less than 2.5 acres, often not enough to support a family. One-third of all rural third-world households have no access to land at all. Many peasants who have lost their farms now work as laborers on the same land they once owned, often earning too little to buy enough staples for an adequate diet. Other farmers, displaced by tractors and threshing machines, can find no work at all in rural areas, and must seek jobs in the third world's swelling cities, or abroad.

2. *Government policies and aid programs that increase dependency.* In many parts of the third world, land, wealth, and political power are concentrated in the hands of an elite. Efforts by farmers to resist displacement from their land, to gain access to land through land reform or, when that fails, through land occupations, are frequently met with repression that precipitates an escalating cycle of violence. Even where the poor have broader access to land, many governments provide farm loans, irrigation, seeds, and technical assistance for cash crops, but not for subsistence farming or local and regional marketing of food crops.

Few large-scale international aid projects are designed to promote local food production, and those that are food-related often result in increased dependency. Farming methods developed in Europe and the U.S. favor the relatively few landowners who can afford fertilizers, pesticides, machinery, and fuel. Over the past three decades, moreover, the bulk of development aid has not been for farming to meet local needs but for projects like large dams, ports, and power plants, or for export crops. Much of this aid money ends up in the bank accounts of contractors and consultants from the donor nations. Often, the aid is in the form of loans, but most of these expensive projects have failed to generate enough income to pay off the loans.

3. *Structures of dependency.* Although many third-world countries became politically independent during the three decades following World War II, most remained economically subordinate. They had inherited political and economic structures established to facilitate the transfer of raw materials to the colonial powers or other industrialized countries. For example: Roads, railroads, and communications lines, where they exist, generally link interior areas to port cities, but do not run between cities and towns, or even between countries in the interior of Southern continents. The goods removed via these routes were, and still are, processed and manufactured into finished goods in the nations of the global North, or in refineries and factories owned by foreign corporations. Thus, the phases of production which add the most value to—and raise the prices of—most goods that are traded internationally take place outside the territories and economies of the South. The prices of unprocessed commodity exports—crops and minerals—have been declining; most are at a forty-five-year low. Meanwhile, these same countries must purchase finished goods—trucks, steel, factory-made consumer goods—from the industrialized countries, at constantly rising prices.

4. *Third-world debt.* During the 1960s and 1970s, Western banks and governments encouraged third-world countries to borrow billions of dollars to make up the difference between their export incomes and their import expenses. The theory was that foreign financial fueling would enable Southern countries to "take off" on their own toward industrialization. Economic growth, it was said, would generate the funds needed to repay the loans.

It didn't happen. Because of the inequities built into global systems of production and trade, the third world continued to sell cheap and buy dear. Typically, countries which borrowed once soon had to borrow again. In 1973 and again in 1978, rising oil prices contributed to a massive increase in third-world debt. Non-oil-producing countries in the South had to double or triple their borrowing just to keep their economies going at pre-1970 levels. Then—also in the late 1970s—third-world debt bills rose sharply in response to a dramatic increase in interest rates. Many commercial bank loans to Southern countries were made at "floating" interest rates. When those interest rates rise, debt bills mushroom. A 1-percent increase in interest rates automatically adds $700 million to Mexico's annual debt bill. The World Bank calculated that interest rates affecting third-world borrowers rose 30 percent in just two years (1980–1982).

As interest rates soared, debtor nations were pressed by banks and international lending agencies to take on new loans just to keep up the interest payments on their previous loans. By 1983, 79 cents of each new dollar borrowed by Latin American nations was used solely to pay interest on past loans. Two-thirds of Latin America's export earnings were being consumed by debt payments.

Under pressure from their creditors, most indebted countries have increased the volume of their exports to make up for the lower prices they receive for them. Throughout the South, governments invite investors to fell more forests, mine more mountains, plow up pastures, drain wetlands, and replace staple foods with export crops. But worldwide competition among exporters of grains, other foods, minerals, and fibers has resulted in even lower prices for these commodities, and thus in lower incomes for many farmers (including some in the United States), and a decline rather than an increase in earnings from exports by third-world nations.

5. *IMF-sponsored economic austerity.* As a consequence of their debts, many countries of the South have become subject to the economic stewardship of the International Monetary Fund (IMF) and the World Bank. Both institutions were established by the victorious industrialized nations in the aftermath of World War II. The purpose of the IMF, as established in its charter, is to promote the continuation and expansion of international trade according to "free market" principles. In line with this mandate, the IMF extends loans at close-to-market interest rates to countries faced with balance-of-trade and payments deficits. These loans are intended as short- to medium-term measures to tide countries over until they can balance their books by bringing expenditures into line with earnings.

It is customary to think of IMF's mission as a form of aid from the North to the South. More accurately, the IMF serves the international financial system and reinforces the system's underlying power relations. Thus, in practice, the IMF acts as a sort of "economic policeman" on behalf of commercial banks, Northern governments, and other international lending agencies. Indebted countries that are unable or unwilling to take IMF loans, repay them on schedule, and adopt economic policy changes acceptable to the Fund are often unable to obtain longer-term development loans, or even short-term credit to import desperately needed food, fuel, medicines, and spare parts for machinery.

IMF practices do not address the causes of third-world poverty, and IMF loans have done little to reduce overall debts. More often, they have contributed to increased debts as borrowing countries have been forced to take on loans from other sources to meet strictly enforced IMF repayment schedules and IMF-required targets for economic growth. Meanwhile, IMF austerity programs aimed at bringing about "stabilization" have severely weakened many third-world economies. As a condition of loans, the IMF requires recipient countries to adopt policies to increase their export earnings and simultaneously to reduce government spending on social services and most other programs not geared toward increasing exports. This means cuts in education, health care, nutritional programs, agricultural extension services, and environmental monitoring. Often it entails reduction or elimination of subsidies many Southern governments have used to keep food prices affordable for the poor of their nations, and thereby to keep a lid on social unrest. Many IMF programs call for devaluation of the borrowing country's currency as well. This makes the devaluing country's exports cheaper—and, in theory, more competitive—on global markets, and discourages imports by making them more expensive for the borrowing country.

But these same measures also lead to immediate and often drastic increases in the prices of food, transportation, and basic consumer goods. By making credit and imported inputs impossibly expensive while opening local markets to foreign competition, they frequently put local farms and factories out of business, adding to massive unemployment. By reducing social services, they increase the pressures on women and others who care for children, the elderly, and the infirm. In brief, IMF policies serve to shift the burden of debt repayment onto those least able to bear it, and thus to deplete the human capital on which development depends.

6. *World Bank failures.* The World Bank has come to play an even more important role than the IMF in directing the devlopment policies of Southern governments. The Bank makes longer-term loans, sometimes at lower interest rates, intended to promote economic growth and trade through private enterprise. World Bank loans are increasingly geared toward export production, both in agriculture and in low-wage industries. Before the 1980s, most World Bank loans funded the construction of roads, ports, dams, power plants, and large-scale agricultural export projects. During the past decade, Bank priorities shifted. Today, about a quarter of the Bank's loans to the South are "sectoral adjustment" or "structural adjustment" loans. These loans finance economic reprogramming that alters not only the external trade policies but also the internal economic priorities of indebted countries.

Structural and sectorial adjustment programs redirect resources away from domestic needs. They require impoverished countries to reduce taxes on the wealthy, increase taxation of the working majority, sell land and other public assets to private owners, devalue their currencies further, raise still higher the prices of transportation and many food items, keep wages low and offer tax breaks and cheap factory space and services to foreign manufacturers.

Structural adjustment programs rest on the theory that countries adopting them will be able to work their way out of debt through economic growth that will generate income to finance development and pay off debts, and, not incidentally, prevent banks in the rich countries from collapsing. In reality, largely as a consequence of structural adjustment and related export-promotion policies, more resources—food, minerals, labor power, and money—are flowing out of the third world to the wealthiest countries than ever before. Capital for local development is not accumulating but dwindling.

Structural adjustment programs are not working, even on their own terms. Their failure to promote sustainable growth and equitable development has been publicly recognized by a wide range of institutions and observers, including the UN's Economic Commission on Africa, the *New York Times*, and the U.S. Catholic Conference's administrative board in its statement on third-world debt (September, 1989). Even the World Bank's own chief economist stated in March that the bank intends to reduce its structural adjustment lending. (Its export emphasis, however, is unlikely to change.)

7. *Farming practices that damage the environment.* The pressure to increase export crops production and the lack of other ways of earning income compel growing numbers of farmers to adopt agricultural practices that undermine the long-term productivity of the land. The greatly increased use of chemical fertilizers often depletes the soil. Excessive employment of pesticides creates toxic hazards for present and future generations.

Peasants displaced from high-quality farmlands by commercial producers often have no choice but to try to raise food or cash crops on land not suitable for continuous farming. Cultivation of steep hillsides results in soil erosion. On the dry plains of Africa's Sahel, soil plowed to plant cotton and peanuts is quickly turned to dust by desert winds. In Amazonia and other moist tropical regions, thin rainforest soils that are too frequently replanted quickly lose their fertility. The same thing happens when good farm land is overcultivated, without fallow years and without replacement of organic matter removed from the soil. Under such conditions, the harder farmers work over the years, the less they get for their labor. Few would choose to farm such unfriendly fields if they had other ways to survive.

The incentive to conserve dwindles as the distance increases between those who produce food and those who control food-producing resources. Decision-makers in bank and aid agency board rooms seldom confront the consequences of their actions, which alter the lives and landscapes of millions. Neither do most reporters and financial analysts who cover these matters. Yet Northern pressure on Southern governments to produce quick cash for debt repayment virtually insures that third-world lands will not be developed or preserved in the interest of the majority.

8. *Militarization and war.* World-wide military spending has doubled over the past twenty years to more than $800 billion yearly. The amount spent every minute could feed two thousand malnourished children for a year. From 1977 to 1987 the third world's share of the global arms budget increased from 9 percent to 16 percent, draining resources that could be used to combat poverty and hunger. UNICEF has reported that third-world countries spent $145 billion in 1988 on weapons and armies.

There have been more than 130 wars since 1945, nearly all of them in the third world. These "conventional" wars have killed about 25 million people, made millions more permanent refugees, and caused incalculable damage to third-world economies and environments. Third-world militarization is a result as well as a cause of increasing hunger: many third-world governments have come to power in the wake of food riots or other forms of mass protest against falling living standards. Enforcement of adjustment programs that multiply human misery will require increased coercion, repression, and military intervention.

9. *Ethnic and religious oppression.* Conquest and exploitation of some peoples by others, long a part of human history, acquired a new dimension in

the colonial era. European powers carved what we now call the third world into colonies, creating states that did not correspond to existing political boundaries, dividing linguistic and cultural groups across arbitrary borders, and giving certain ethnic and religious groups new or greater power over others.

Where there is hunger today in the third world, all do not hunger equally. Members of oppressed castes, tribal groups, and religions often have less access to food-producing resources and government assistance, and are more likely to have to go without food. Indigenous people in Latin America and minority ethnic groups in Africa and Asia are among those who suffer most as policies to speed debt payments increase the pressure on their lands.

10. *Discrimination against women.* Although in many parts of the South women are the main food producers, more womem than men suffer from malnutrition. Though women head one out of three third-world households, and perform an estimated two-thirds of all hours worked, it is women and girls who starve most often. Four times as many malnourished children are female than male, and their mortality rate is 40 percent higher than that of boys. In many societies in times of plenty, men and boys eat first; in times of famine, women and girls may not eat at all. Nutritional anemia affects about half of all third-world women of child-bearing age, draining their strength and lessening their resistance to disease.

The effect of modernization in many rural third-world areas has been to worsen the situation of women. Commercialization of agriculture in societies where men hold land titles and money means less control by women over family resources and food distribution. Mechanization of plowing and harvesting often means a loss of income for women, since agricultural loans and technology are often made available only to men. Efforts to accumulate quick cash for debt repayments accelerate these processes.

Thus the causes of world hunger are at once multiple and unitary; that is to say, systemic. They are deeply rooted and well protected; though needless hunger is a scandal, it is a hidden one, and ending it is not seen by the elites of North or South as serving their interests.

Yet there is cause for hope: North and South, a great many Davids are confronting their respective Goliaths, and, to an extent, they are learning to collaborate across borders toward achievement of common goals: to reduce hunger, eliminate its causes, bring about sustainable, broad-based development, and achieve a more just distribution of the world's resources. Linkages are most evident in the partnerships between nongovernment organizations engaged in self-help projects in the third world and private agencies in the North that provide these projects with modest funding and people-to-people publicity and support. Examples in the U.S. include Oxfam America, Food First, the American Friends Service Committee, Grassroots International, the Unitarian Universalist Service Committee, Catholic Relief Services, Food for the Poor, and Global Exchange.

Compared with the mega-projects financed by the World Bank or U.S. AID, these projects are small in scale: a women's cooperative processing local fruit, a community's poultry-rearing project, an old cargo boat renovated to carry crops to market, to list some carried out by project partners of Oxfam America. Other projects are adopting new methods of conservation and reviving old ones, building small-scale irrigation works and better food storage facilities, organizing production and marketing co-ops, expanding women's income-generating activities: weaving, dairying, farming. They are developing literacy and skills-training programs, and making use of radio, popular theater, and creative new forms of research, education, and communication to enhance their understanding of the causes of poverty and the means of improving their lives.

The importance of such projects is partly that they provide a testing ground for development models—at their best, they embody or prefigure elements of an alternative and achievable definition of development—and partly that they are conceived and carried out by the aid beneficiaries themselves. In the process, participants strengthen their technical and leadership skills, confidence, the ability to identify problems and plan solutions.

In the context of an overall drain of resources out of the global South, even successful local projects cannot engender development by themselves. Understanding of this reality is spreading, however, and in consequence grassroots and nongovernment organizations in Asia, Africa, Latin America, and the Caribbean have begun to form regional and international organizations such as the Malaysia-based Third World Network and the women's organization, DAWN, with offices in Mexico, India, and Brazil. These, along with local, national, and regional organizations of farmers, women, workers, indigenous and minority peoples, certain scholars, and some government officials, have begun to formulate experience-based alternatives to the failing debt-financed, export-dominated model of development. Central to the goals being articulated with increasing clarity and unanimity by progressive third-world NGOs is increased food production for local and regional needs. They also hope to promote more South-South trade, closer agro-industry links, more use of local materials and skills, more control by Southern nations over the prices of their exports, greater involvement and consultation of farmers and others affected by development schemes; in a phrase, more workable and more genuinely democratic development. Needless to say, relief from the debt burden is a prior condition of progress.

For that reason, and because the "aid" policies of national governments in the North and the international lending agencies constitute the major obstacles to third-world development, local and regional groups in the South are asking citizens of wealthier nations for support. They are asking not for charity in the form of food shipments, but for change. Northern policies that require Southern governments to negotiate structural adjustment programs one by one and that enforce a strategy of exports-at-any-cost rule out alternative strategies based on self-reliance and regional cooperation. Insistence on drastic reduction of public services for the sake of meeting debt schedules saps human capital. Such policies, third-world groups contend, harm the long-term interests of the majority of citizens in the North as well as the South. Farmers who cannot sell their crops, workers who cannot earn a living wage, the growing numbers with no land or job at all cannot be good customers for Northern products. Governments that respond to the unrest of their impoverished peoples with military violence cannot be reliable allies.

As already noted, development and development education agencies in the U.S. are responding to this call by entering into new relationships with third-world groups that replace almsgiving with partnership. In addition, some environmental organizations, such as the Environmental Defense Fund, are coming to recognize that saving the natural environment is impossible if it entails destroying the livelihoods of the people who inhabit rain forests and other threatened areas. Religiously motived lobbying groups—in particular, Bread for the World—carry out extensive research on the causes of hunger and the impact of U.S. policies. Church-based organizations, under the multi-denominational umbrella of Interfaith Action for Economic Justice, are paying attention to alternative development proposals from the third world. So also are public policy organizations such as Development GAP and Policy Alternatives for the Caribbean and Central America (PACCA). And, across the country, citizens are forging links among towns, churches, and trade unions in Southern Africa and Central America and their U.S. counterparts. By supporting efforts like these, we can help the people of the South to overcome hunger and develop along their own chosen pathways. We can also help to avert ecological disasters of great consequence, and to prevent replacement of the East-West cold war by a devastating global struggle between the North and the South.

## 20. Noam Chomsky
## *Of Prussians and Traders: An Interview with Noam Chomsky*     1988

Noam Chomsky, a professor at MIT, is perhaps the nation's leading linguist. In addition, he is also a leading radical political activist. In the interview reprinted below, Chomsky provides a critique of both the United States and the Soviet Union from his unique anarchist and democratic socialist position. How would a reassertionist, neorealist, or neo-isolationist respond to Chomsky's remarks?

MULTINATIONAL MONITOR: Businesses want to trade with the Soviet Union, with Libya, with many communist and socialist countries. Do you think, with the changes in technology and the creation of a genuine world market, that there may be the beginnings of a conflict between straight business interests and the traditional American foreign policy goals of controlling foreign countries?

NOAM CHOMSKY: [That is a conflict that goes back to the origins of] imperialism. Take say, the early 1920s. There were plenty of businessmen who wanted to trade with the Russians, but the state blocked it.

In the early 1950s, there was a major split in the business community about how to deal with China. There was a group that just wanted to open up trade and commercial interchange and so on, and there was another group that wanted to take a very harsh posture and to drive them into the hands of the Russians, and ultimately, overcome them. In fact, into the late 1960s, the State Department planners still had the idea that maybe we could break up China, we could restore the old order in China.

This is the distinction between what Mike Klare once called the "Traders" and the "Prussians." Basically, you have the same goals, but there is a question as to whether to achieve the goals by economic power or whether to achieve them by violence. . . . It is a matter of tactics. . . . In the Middle East, for example, the goal has always been to maintain control over oil. Not because we need it, [but] because it is one of the ways we control our allies. By having control over the energy system, you have a big effect on the whole world system. So the question is, how do we do it?

[The two approaches are] reflected very clearly in the split between [Williams] Rogers and [Henry] Kissinger around 1970. Rogers' position was that you do it by the method of the Traders, so he was, for example, in favor of a negotiated settlement of the Arab-Israeli conflict along the lines that had very broad support at the time. Kissinger, on the other hand, thought you do it by violence, so he wanted to maintain, in fact construct an Iranian, Israeli, Saudi Arabian alliance which would pretty much control the region by force. . . .

With regard to every part of the world . . . the goals are the same. You want to insure domination. The fact that those people will trade with you is not enough. Russia will trade with you but you can't control their economic decisions. That is the problem. . . . American corporations cannot control investment decisions in the Soviet Union. They are going to go their own way. They are independent of our domination. If they want to devote their resources to domestic consumption, they will do it. They are not going to devote them to export-oriented production because that is what we want. That is the problem down to tiny, little countries. Anywhere from the Soviet Union to Grenada, it is the same problem.

MM: To what extent can the United States impose its will?

CHOMSKY: In the late 1940s the world system was extremely unusual from a historical point of view. The United States literally had 50 percent of the world's wealth. There has never been a period in human history when one country had such overwhelming domination from an economic, political and military point of view. Well, that naturally had to erode and it has eroded and now the world system is considerably more complex. There are numerous centers of power, there are rising industrial countries such as Brazil, there [is] increasing independence among the raw materials producers all over the world and that means that new groupings of powers can [form], which can challenge the decisions made by the master of the world market and can begin to move in their own direction. . . .

MM: But in what direction? Won't their choices be dictated by their own economic interests?

CHOMSKY: 'Own economic interest' is a misleading term because countries don't have economic interests, groups inside of them do and those interests may differ.

MM: Precisely, and ruling groups will be out to maximize their profits.

CHOMSKY: Not necessarily. That assumes capital domination of every country. But suppose you get a government that does what the U.S. has always feared more than most anything at all—directs resources to domestic development? . . .

Here we don't have to speculate. We can go back to high level, declassified documents, which are very explicit about this topic. . . . Take Latin America for example. As far as I know the most serious and important review of U.S.-Latin American policy was in 1954, right after the Guatemalan democracy was overthrown. NSC5432, which is U.S. policy with regard to Latin America, [is a] long comprehensive and detailed study [that] gives an anlysis of what our general policy must be towards Latin America and is very clear and explicit. It says the primary concern is what they call "nationalistic regimes," which are responsive to the demands of the masses of the population for an improvement in their low living standards and for diversification of production.

In contrast, we have to organize export-oriented production and integration into the world market, and not nationalism, not use of resources for domestic needs. They are not allowed to devote their resources to say, subsistence agriculture, but rather to export crops. . . . The way to do this [was for us] to take control of the Latin American military. Now at the time that meant fighting France and England, we had to eliminate French and British training missions which still existed in Latin America. They were of course our . . . real competitors. [I]n the future . . . the real enemies are going to be Europe, Japan and other functioning economies, not the Russians. . . .

MM: What is the economic interest now in Central America?

CHOMSKY: The economic interest is, first of all, resources and resource extraction.

MM: But the resources to be extracted in Central America are minimal on a world scale.

CHOMSKY: Yes, but this is not what counts. General Motors does not decide to give up its franchise in Tucson because that is a small percentage of its income. They fight to keep their franchise in Tucson and we fight to keep our franchise in Central America. They may not be right, but they think Central America and the Caribbean is a potential East Asia.

The only [area] of the colonial world that has developed is the Japanese area and there is a reason for that. Imperial powers are brutal, but brutal in different ways. Japanese imperialism was very brutal but in a developmentalist way. So while we were robbing our colonies, Japan was building its colonies in the presecond world war period and there was significant industrial development in Taiwan, Korea, and so on. . . .

MM: What would be the harm in letting a country like Nicaragua go its own course?

CHOMSKY: Here we come to another long standing concern of American planners which has never been abandoned. . . . That is the rational version of the domino theory. There are two versions of the domino theory. One of them is crazy. That is the version that is used to scare the public: 'They are going to land in San Francisco.'

But there is also a rational version. And the rational version is that there could be a demonstration effect. If any country can fall into the hands of nationalist leaders who devote resources to their own populations, it could very well have a demonstration effect. It could be a virus that will infect the region and even beyond. . . . What was the concern about [Salvador] Allende? They are going to be able to get the copper. It is the virus of Allende. [It] will send the wrong message to Italy, not because Chile is going to conquer Italy, but because you have a big communist party there, you have a big workers' movement, which has never been destroyed despite many efforts, and if they see that there is a possibility of developing democratic socialism, it will inspire them to try the same thing. Before you know [it], the whole system [will] erode. . . . What they care about is that you might begin to get what we have always feared, workers controlling industry, for example, and separation from the U.S.-dominated international market where the multinationals, which by now are much beyond the United States, do run the world market and their international institutions like IMF and the World Bank control it and the big powers like us exercise violence when necessary and so on. That is, a complex integrated system functioning for the benefit of elite groups, economically powerful groups in our system, and in the major capitalist countries. And if this begins to erode there is a real problem. . . . Radical democracy in the United States is a threat to the conservative world order because it can spread. It can arouse the 'wrong ideas' among other people and pretty soon our system of power and privilege will collapse. That threat still exists and it will always exist. This idea is never abandoned because it is correct. . . . People often say, 'What do we care about Grenada?' You can't imagine a place in the world of less economic significance than Grenada. Nevertheless, as soon as [Maurice] Bishop took power, it caused hysteria in Washington.

They had to destroy Grenada. It was true of Carter, it is true of Reagan. They immediately embargoed, cut off support, started running big military manuevers all over the region to try to drive them into the hands of the Russians and terrorize them and finally invaded. What do they care about Grenada? It has 100,000 people and some nutmeg. But the point is the weaker a country is, the more insignificant it is, the more dangerous it is. . . . That is why you get this hysteria about places like Grenada or Laos in the 1960s and other tiny little specks of dust—because the demonstration effect is greater when the country is weaker. And that is very rational.

MM: Does the increasing power of the world market mean that U.S. corporate interests will no longer have to be concerned about controlling countries politically?

CHOMSKY: I don't think so. There is a force toward integration of the world market and so on. But there is a corresponding feature of that: namely, the diversification of the international system which allows groupings of powers to gain a capacity to pursue a different path that they didn't have previously. And that is very threatening to those who intend and expect to dominate the world system.

There has been concern about this kind of autonomy for years. Since the late 1940s there has been a concern among the smarter planners, people like George Kennan, that eventually Japan would reconstitute itself as a dominant force. So for example, in the late 1940s when most U.S. planners were convinced on mainly racist grounds that Japan was never going to be able to export anything but toys, smarter people like Kennan, who had major power in shaping the post-war world, recognized that eventually they could be a real competitor and therefore we had to guarantee some method of control. The method he suggested, which was in fact followed, was to control their energy resources.

So Japan was allowed to reindustrialize but not to develop petrochemical and refining industries and so on. And in fact, part of our concern for controlling Middle East oil has been to insure that that lever remains in our hands. But the trouble is that is not happening anymore. Japan is beginning to set up its own independence with the oil producers and Europe might do the same thing. Here the issue is quite complex. . . . Japan separated itself from the world market and pursued its own independent development and is the only what we call Third World colonial country to have industrialized. . . .

MM: Isn't it possible though that at some point the market itself may start to provide the service of undermining popular movements without the need for more direct applications of force?

CHOMSKY: I think you can find areas where it is happening in the United States itself. Through American history it has been necessary repeatedly to use violence to prevent democracy from developing. . . . Labor unions are one of the classic ways in which isolated people who lack individual resources can join together to enter the political system. And that had to be blocked. That is one of the reasons we have such a bloody labor history. After a while, the forces of the market took over. So, in the United States you don't need censorship. Censorship is carried out by corporate media who control through market forces and shape news in their own interest.

MM: To what do you attribute the move by the socialist countries toward market organization internally and some limited opening up of their economies to the world market?

CHOMSKY: These so-called socialist countries, which have absolutely nothing to do with socialism, these kind of state bureaucracies dominating them along the Leninist model, the exact antithesis of socialism, they are highly inefficient.

They are inefficient in control of the public, they are inefficient in production and so on, and the market in fact is an efficient way of allocating resources. Markets don't have to be used for distributing benefits; that's where the problem started arising. But in determining things like resource allocation, a market is a rational system and so they will move toward those systems in the effort to increase the viability of their own elite groups. Now that is going to lead to internal tensions.

Take, for example, the Soviet Union. One of the benefits that the working class has had from the limping Soviet economy is that they don't have to work very hard. But if you start introducing incentives and market forces you [have] to work and you have to suffer. That is why industrialization was such a brutal process in the West. And it is not so clear that the working classes will be willing to accept the requisite suffering for the hope of ultimate consumption. Certainly in the West it never happened very easily. It had to be done by force. And you can't predict what will happen there, whether they can do it by force, or whether they can bring it about without force.

But industrialization has been a brutal process and I think those problems are going to arise very quickly as they shift to market techniques for allocating resources and making production decisions.

MM: Politically, how important is the way the media is organized, the actual corporate structure—who owns the newspapers, how many newspapers there are in the given town, the way the TV networks are owned and regulated?

CHOMSKY: It is very important. In the United States, you can't see it very much because . . . we are much more advanced in the departure from meaningful democracy than other countries. But elsewhere, in rather similar societies, you can see it. England is not a terribly different kind of place than we are, but up until the 1960s, England had a very lively and effective labor press. The *Daily Herald* in England . . . if I remember correctly [had] twice the subscriptions of the *London Times*, the *Financial Times* and the *Guardian* put together in the early 1960s, and in fact, the polls showed that it was more intensively read and more eagerly read by its subscribers, but it was a working class newspaper. It presented an alternative view of the world. Now it doesn't exist.

The working class newspapers have become cheap tabloids, which are sex, sports, and so on, part of the decerebration of the masses. This [did not] happen by force. The police didn't come in and close them down. It happened by market pressures. Newspapers are corporations that sell a product, namely subscribers, to buyers, namely advertisers. So a newspaper or any journal is basically a corporation selling a product to other corporations. The way you sell them is by looking at the profile.

If you want to have resources in this system, you are going to have to have advertiser support in capital. And that means for one thing you are going to have to adhere to their view of the world, but it also means that you are going to have to be oriented towards the wealthier readers with the normal advertising profiles that all of these guys run on. These factors are going to drive out an independent press. It happened in the United States a long time ago. It happened in England fairly recently and the effects are very striking. . . . When the Labor Party runs in England, it is just demolished by the entire information system. And that makes a difference.

In part, this is based on the nature of the corporate media. . . . However, in my view, it wouldn't change very much even if they were more diversified. . . .

MM: Why wouldn't it?

CHOMSKY: Because the same social forces would essentially operate. If there were, say, two newspapers or three newspapers in Boston instead of one, there would probably not be that much difference. It is some difference, you lose something, but, I must say that I don't want to underestimate it. When you cross the borders you see a big difference. Every time I got to Canada, for example, which is a very similar country, or England, or Europe, there is access to national media, national television, the press, and so on. That is unimaginable in the United States.

MM: You said that if the organization applied in the workplace in capitalism were applied in the political sphere it would be called fascist. What do you mean by that?

CHOMSKY: If you go back to an early period, take even the ideals of the enlightenment that theoretically underlay the American revolution, they were concerned with certain general human values—the right of human beings to control their lives and their own work, and in fact, to control their creative work. So a leading idea of what we today call conservatism, the enlightenment thought was that if a person works under the command of others, what the person produces may be of value or even beautiful, but the person's life is a human disgrace, it is a form of slavery. The person is a machine [was] the way they put it. And the ideals of the enlightenment worked to let people be human, and human meant in control of the decisions that affect their own lives, in particular, in control of their workplace. These discussions were all [conducted] in a period prior to factories and prior to corporate capitalism, so they [were] directed against slavery and the feudal system and serfdom. . . .

But the same ideas carry over to later developments and it means that if we are really serious about enlightment ideals, we will try to turn the productive lives of people into a democratic system that they control and where they make the decisions and where they make them in community with others. That is socialism, not what we call socialism or what the Russians call socialism, but what it meant prior to the distortion that was introduced by the anti-socialist forces of the 20th Century, including capitalism and Marxism/Leninism, all of them very hostile to socialist ideals. . . .

At the core of it is the central part of most human beings' lives, namely, their productive work and that means workers controlling industry. Just about any workplace, whether it is an office or a factory, or whatever, is a system where there is a flow of command that is centralized at the top and goes straight down to the bottom and there is nothing that goes in the other directon other than some symbols that are introduced to make people feel good sometimes.

These are very traditional ideas. They have been forgotten. What I have just been saying would not have surprised the major thinkers of enlightenment, the people we now regard as classics.

MM: There seems to be a convergence between the way the capitalist managers and the managers in the socialist countries organize the production in their factories. Is this because both have made the same ideological choice or both have personal or class interests in organizing it that way or is there also a tension with the needs of efficiency and production?

CHOMSKY: There is no evidence that it has anything to do with efficiency, and even if it did have anything to with efficiency, it would be irrelevant. . . . The distribution of power and the course of history was such that those groups who could gain their power and privilege by exerting authority over the control of production did so.

We have various forms of state capitalism in the West and various forms of military bureaucratic control in the East. They are all very much opposed to socialism. In fact, there has been a kind of hoax perpetrated on the world by the world's two leading propaganda systems since 1971. The two major propaganda systems in the world are the American one and all of its affiliates and the Soviet one. And they both like to pretend that what exists in the Soviet Union is socialism . . . and they do it for opposite reasons.

In the West we do it because we want to defame socialism by associating it with the dungeon over there. And in the East they want to do it by making their dungeon look a litte better by associating it with the deservedly positive appeal that the moral values of socialism have to working people everywhere.

MM: Where has real socialism or something approaching it actually been tried?

CHOMSKY: It has been tried here and there, but it has usually been destroyed. In fact, it has often been destroyed by the joint activity of the Soviet Union and the United States. . . . Spain is a good example. . . . The western capitalist countries and the Soviet Union combined to destroy the popular revolution in Spain. That was the main commitment on all sides and it really wasn't until the large scale popular revolution had been wiped out . . . . that they fell to fighting among one another for the rest of the loot. And that's rather typical. The Soviet Union would certainly not tolerate any socialist development anywhere, nor would we.

There [are] some similarities in the societies. They are both class structured and societies with a state management and a coordinator controlled industrial system. They obviously differ too. They don't have private control over capital the way we do, but in many respects the systems are similar in their doctrinal systems. They are mainly similar in their belief that people have to be subordinated to higher authority. It is [a] different higher authority in the two cases but subordination is accepted on both sides.

MM: You have said that totalitarian states have to control action but democracies have to control thought. Can you explain that distinction?

CHOMSKY: Totalitarian states are really more behaviorists, since they have the means of power. [They] don't want to exercise violence because it is inefficient, but they want the threat to be there and to be visible.

In a country like ours, where the state has very limited means of violence available to coerce the population, comparatively speaking, it is much more important to control what people think. And that is in fact why the United States developed so early such sophisticated systems as the public relations industry and the highly ideological corporate media.

That process is continuing, [and] its effects are very complex. . . . There is a real split developing between much of the population and the elites, including the liberal elites. There has undoubtedly been a right turn among elites, so you get what they call "neo-liberalism" and "neo-conservatism," which are dominant among elite groups. But the population has not moved in that direction. The population is moving in the opposite direction.

MM: What will be the legacy of the so-called Reagan Revolution?

CHOMSKY: In many ways, it has certain similarities to what was called the Hitler revolution. Putting aside atrocities and massacres and that sort of thing, just look at the mechanics of it. Hitler's revolution was Keynesian economics— pre-Keynes, of course—revitalizing the economy through military spending, which worked. It got Germany out of a huge depression, got people back to work, created affluence. They had restored faith in the grandeur and the glory of Germany, winning cheap victories over defenseless rivals, which gave people a big shot in the arm and aroused patriotism and restored what they called the traditional values—home, family, devotion and so on. That is all very familiar. In fact, these are the basic ingredients of what are today called, ludicrously, "conservatism" in the United States.

You take the modern conservatives, the people around Reagan, guys that are straight out of Orwell. Any conservative would turn over in his grave to hear the way the word is used, but these are people who believe in a very powerful state. That is not at all surprising, that under Reagan you have all the phenomena of lunatic Keynesianism—massive expenditures, but expenditures not for productive purposes, but for consumption and waste. Military production, after all, is a waste production from an economic point of view. . . .

So what you have is a very substantial increase in state expenditures. In fact, state expenditures [increased] under Reagan, relative to GNP, faster than in any peace-time period in history. The state intervenes massively in the economy, in the highly protected economy that they constructed. That is what the military is, a state-guaranteed market for high technology production.

Looking at it institutionally, it is . . . somewhere between lunatic Keynesianism and quasi-fascism—a big, powerful state creating a protected market, guaranteeing that the production that is done in advanced industry will have a market because the state will buy it. . . .

From the point of view of the corporate manager, you couldn't imagine anything better. It is a gift, a gift from the public for research and development and for production in a period when you cannot sell things. . . . The Reaganites have pushed that to an extreme.

## 21. Jerome Slater
### *Is United States Foreign Policy Imperialist?*

1976

Both this essay and the following one seek to rebut the radical worldview. In the first selection, political scientist Jerome Slater assesses the evidence upon which the radicals rest their case. How convincing do you find Slater's assessment?

We shall begin with a discussion of radical, neo-Marxist theories of the causes or motivations of American policy. Is the open-door policy—unrestricted access to the economies of the Third World—structurally necessary to the survival of United States capitalism, or, more generally, to the health of the economy? Some contemporary neo-Marxists, most notably Gabriel Kolko,[1] do in fact so argue, following Lenin's earlier arguments about the crucial dependence of late monopoly capitalism on overseas economic imperialism. Consider first direct overseas investment. Although the figures vary, all recent analyses demonstrate that private overseas direct investment is only about 5 percent of total investment (i.e., 95 percent of the United States direct investment is domestic), and the vast majority of that overseas investment is not in the Third World but in the advanced industrial societies of Western Europe, Japan, Canada, and Australia. The proportion of overseas investment in the Third World, then, is less than 2 percent of all United States investment, which would hardly seem critical.[2] Looked at from a different perspective, as of 1968 the income from corporate investment in the Third World was only 3–4 percent of the total income of United States corporations, and it was declining relative to income from investments in the industrial world.[3]

The figures for trade reveal the same nonessentiality of the Third World to the United States economy. Total American trade with the rest of the world is only about 7–8 percent of GNP and, once again, by far the largest and most rapidly growing proportion of that trade is not with the Third World but with the advanced contries.[4] Only in the case of strategic raw materials is the Third World *possibly* of critical importance to the American economy, and even here the situation is far from clear. For the moment the United States is increasingly dependent on overseas oil as well as other important raw materials such as copper, tin, and bauxite found in Third World countries. But (1) it is still the case that *most* of these raw materials are produced not in the Third World but in the developed countries; (2) mining the deep seabed is likely to soon further reduce United States dependence on Third World countries; and (3) pending that development most economists still argue that substitutes and alternatives to

Third World raw materials, even oil, are now or soon will be available, at costs which are higher, but not so much higher as to make Third World importations more of a necessity than essentially a convenience.[5] In any case, it is only very recently that the United States has become dependent on strategic raw materials imports from the Third World countries to any significant degree, whatever the exact magnitude of that dependence might be now and in the future, and thus the matter is entirely irrelevant to the alleged structural necessity of the open-door policy in the past.

Even if the United States economy *was* structurally dependent on access to Third World markets, raw materials, or sources of investment, would it follow that imperial *control* of the Third World is a necessity? The radical argument depends on that assumption, although it is nearly always left implicit; that is, that the choice is the stark, all-or-nothing one of imperial domination or no access at all. When made explicit, though, the assumption is demonstratively preposterous. Indeed, there seems to be a clear *inverse* relationship between "imperialism" and prosperity in the postwar period. Though of course other factors have also played important roles, it is interesting to note that the least imperial countries have had the highest overall growth rates (Japan, West Germany, Canada, the Netherlands, the Scandinavian countries—all dependent in varying degrees on interstate trade and investment), while the most imperial have done least well (France and Britain in the 1940s and 1950s; Portugal, with the lowest per capita income in Europe for the entire postwar period). Nor should this be unexpected: it is not just that the maintenance of political and military imperial control is extremely costly when there is serious indigenous opposition, but also that states perceived by the nationalist and sensitive Third World countries as imperialist, whether accurately or not, are much more likely to suffer economic retaliation than those seen as quite harmless. In case of renewed Arab-Israeli conflict, for example, the Arabs are probably more likely to cut off oil shipments to the United States than to Japan. The radical assumption is best stood on its head: *only* efforts to gain imperialist economic control, to push against a door that is already open, would be likely to provoke nationalist resentments intense enough to override economic rationality and close off American access to Third World products.

All this may be true, implicitly or explicitly concede some radical analysts, but policy makers, however inaccurately, *believe* that the health of the United States capitalist system requires an open door to the Third World economies and therefore direct political or economic control over them, and act accordingly, i.e., imperialistically.[6] While this is certainly a logical possibility and a neat theory-saver, the evidence is overwhelming that it is a wholly inaccurate description of how policy makers in fact have perceived American interests in the Third World. There is, after all, an enormous body of available material in the form of memoirs, official documents, and scholarly analyses on how American policy makers have defined the "external challenges" to the United States, in the Third World and elsewhere. It rather conclusively shows that genuine security fears; ideological anticommunism; expansionist idealism; or other political, strategic, or psychological factors have been at the roots of the United

States postwar policies, including interventionist or, if you will, "imperial" behavior.[7]

Still another variant of the neo-Marxist argument is that open-door imperialism in the Third World, while neither structurally necessary to the United States economy nor genuinely believed to be so by policy makers, *is* necessary to the largest, most powerful banks and corporations which in turn control foreign policy.[8] Both parts of this argument are quite unpersuasive. A number of scholars have demonstrated that, with the exception of the seven oil majors (to be examined below), the largest United States foreign banks and corporations are among those that are *least* dependent on the Third World, as the overwhelming proportion of their investment, sales, and profits come from the American domestic market, Europe, Japan, and Canada. And, more importantly, while it would be beyond the scope of this article to go into detail, no serious scholarship on the foreign policy-making process in the United States government supports the notion that it is controlled or in most cases even substantially influenced by the desires of "big business." Indeed, even in the case of those American-based multinational corporations which *do* have major investments in the Third World, most recent scholarship establishes that the distance between the corporations and the United States government is increasing, as both the policy makers and the corporations are coming to realize that, faced with growing nationalism, *no* interests—economic or political, private or public—are served by government involvement in corporate disputes with indigenous governments.[9]

The final variation of the neo-Marxist argument is at once the most sophisticated but also the least subject to empirical confirmation or refutation. It is not that corporations control foreign policy or that political leaders consciously seek to promote and protect corporate economic interests, but rather that all United States elites are products of American history, institutions, and class structures, and as such have internalized an overall ideology or *weltanschauung* that equates the maintenance of capitalism at home and its extension overseas—i.e., the open-door policy—with the preservation of the entire "American way of life."[10] The problem with this formulation, "sophisticated" as it may be, is that it is so broad as to be quite immune from normal tests of evidence. It is quite easy to show that American foreign policy makers since World War II have not usually defined their objectives in terms of the open-door policy, the preservation of capitalism, or, indeed, in economic terms of any kind, either in their public rhetoric or in their private correspondence, memoirs, or intragovernmental communications, but then it can be claimed that the policy makers were either concealing their "real" objectives or that their anticommunism and security fears were "ultimately," perhaps even unconsciously, rooted in the desire to preserve capitalism as an economic system.[11] Similarly, instances in which United States policy has been oriented toward the protection or promotion of American economic interests overseas are seized upon as irrefutable proof of the theory, whereas the far more numerous instances of United States passivity when confronted with economic nationalism are treated as signs of the growing subtlety of corporate capitalism, which is willing to let minor infractions on its imperial control go unchallenged in the interest of preserving "the system" as a whole.[12] Or, in another version, even intervention which is overwhelmingly counterproductive in economic terms, such as Vietnam, is explained in terms of "the empire's" need to preserve the system as a whole by supporting even "the weakest links in the chain."[13] As others have pointed out, both in the context of examining this variant of neo-Marxist theory and in discussing the nature of scientific inquiry in general, a theory so broad that it is capable of "explaining" both A and its opposite B (intervention and nonintervention, intervention that is economially productive and intervention that is economically costly), a theory that rests not on the empirical evidence considered in its entirety but on assertion buttressed only by the selected evidence that fits, is no theory at all, but simply dogma.[14]

It is not the contention of this article that economic considerations, including if you will the maintenance of an open-door for products and investment capital, do not play a significant role in the United States foreign policy, but only that such economic considerations have not been the central, dominant ones. Certainly it is obvious that the government has sought to promote trade and investment around the world and has often used its economic and political influence on behalf of such objectives. In so acting, political officials have been motivated by several factors: the belief that an open economic world is genuinely in the best interests of all states; the belief that it is beneficial to the United States economy; and the belief that one of the obligations of the government is to protect and promote the legitimate activities of its citizens abroad, at least as long as those activities do not conflict with larger policy objectives. But what is crucial are the *means* used on behalf of the open-door policy, that is, the *intensity* of the government's commitment to it or the *priority* that policy has relative to other foreign policy objectives.[15] Normally, the government has promoted the interests of private corporations by diplomacy only: verbal representations, exhortation, and bargaining. On some, but increasingly exceptional occasions, the government has gone further, making use of both positive and negative economic sanctions, through its bilateral assistance programs and its influence in international financial institutions, on behalf of private economic interests. On most occasions where the government has resorted to economic pressures, though, larger issues than mere nationalization of American property are perceived to be at stake, as in the case of economic and other actions by the United States against Cuba and the Allende government in Chile. Finally, there is *no* case in which it can persuasively be argued that Washington resorted to serious covert political action or the use of armed force on behalf of private economic interests as such. Apparent exceptions to this assertion, such as the CIA's role in the overthrow of Iran's Mossadegh following his nationalization of oil corporations in 1953, on closer inspection do not undermine the argument, for oil is the *one* foreign economic commodity perceived to be absolutely vital, not to private interests but to the United States economy as a whole. Indeed, what is particularly striking about the case of oil is that even *given* its critical importance, the government nonetheless has consistently subordinated easy and favorable access to it to other, noneconomic objectives: as many observers have pointed out, if economic rather than cold-war, ideological/moral, or domestic considerations dominated foreign policy, the United States stance in the Arab-Israeli crisis would have been very different over the last three decades.[16] So even in the single case in which one might *expect* to find economic considerations to be dominant, the reality has been different. That being so, it is hardly credible that the United States interventions in Guatemala in 1954 and the Dominican Republic in 1965 were motivated by, respectively, banana and sugar interests, rather than by ideological, cold-war, and even strategic considerations genuinely believed—whether accurately or not is irrelevant—by policy makers to be at stake in those countries.[17]

# AMERICAN EXPLOITATION OF THE THIRD WORLD?

We can now proceed directly to examine the charge that the United States, as the leading contemporary neoimperialist power, economically exploits the Third World. According to classic economic theory, free trade in an open international market is of mutual and equal benefit to rich and poor nations alike, because of the familiar principles of comparative advantage based on specialization and division of labor. However, in the real world international trade may not be truly open and based strictly on supply and demand, and the benefits may be unequally distributed. Until quite recently, it was widely accepted, even by non-Marxist and nonradical economists, that in fact the terms of trade were weighted against the Third World countries as a result of the deliberately or unconsciously exercised political and financial power of the industrialized world, for it was generally thought that at least since 1940 the prices of raw materials and other commodities exported by the Third World had steadily fallen relative to the price of manufactured goods they had no chioce but to import from the industrialized world. In actual operation the international "free trade" system, it was usually conceded, had the same disadvantages as the domestic "free enterprise" system: where not all participants have equal political and economic power, the rich do disproportionately better than the poor, or even in more extreme formulations, the poor are actually *further* impoverished. The open-door policy or economic liberalism became, in the words of two sophisticated writers, simply "the ideology of a continuing American hegemony.[18]

In the last few years, however, the accuracy of this assessment has been called into question, as it has applied to the recent past, as well as to the present and the forseeable future. A recent study, for example, concluded that *even excluding oil from the calculation,* in the last twenty-five years the prices of raw materials exported by poor countries had risen at about the same rate as the prices of imported manufactures.[19] Steven Krasner has gone even further, arguing that the Third World countries have been the relative *beneficiaries* of restrictive schemes imposed by the consuming states or their multinational corporations: "For most primary commodities, the actual prices are higher than those that would prevail in a free market. In terms of neoclassical concepts of value, *consuming states have been exploited by producing areas.*[20] As for the present and forseeable future, there is a growing consensus that as a result of the increasing scarceness of certain key raw materials and the ability of producing states to form successful cartels, not only in oil but also in other commodities (copper, tin, bauxite, and apparently more on the way), the terms of trade will increasingly shift in favor of the Third World, or at least that part of the Third World fortunate enough to control major commodities or raw materials.

Does the direct corporate investment of advanced countries in the Third World constitute exploitation, in either the absolute or relative senses of the word? According to radical critics, foreign-owned subsidiaries of multinational corporations "decapitalize" the underdeveloped countries by taking out more in profits than they put in through investment; further block local growth and industrialization by buying up smaller local firms or driving them out of business through cutthroat competition; create sudden unemployment by ruthlessly closing local subsidiaries whenever worldwide profit maximization so dictates; remove key sectors of the economy from local control; create a domestic bourgeoisie whose self-interests are tied to foreign industry rather than indigenous growth; disrupt local cultural patterns and institutions and substitute in their place the crass materialism of the West; and, in general, integrate the economies, social structure, and political institutions of Third World countries into permanently subordinate peripheral positions in the world capitalist structure.[21] Among themselves, critics may disagree on whether these alleged consequences of foreign investment are intended and stem from the deliberate governmental strategies of the advanced countries to gain political and economic domination over the Third World, or whether they are the unintended, uncoordinated by-product of private corporate greed. But there is no disagreement that the Third World is exploited by foreign investment.

Other students of foreign investment see the matter quite differently. Foreign investment is said to clearly bring with it many positive benefits. Foreign companies have the capital and the skills initially lacking in underdveloped countries to explore for, develop, produce, and market raw materials that would otherwise lie dormant for decades. In the course of doing so, they build transportation networks; employ large numbers of local people, usually at wage rates much above host country norms; build housing, schools, and hospitals; and through taxation contribute much needed foreign currency. In the manufacturing area, multinational corporations provide the managerial skills, the infusion of advanced technology, and the access to world markets that the underdeveloped countries lack.

To be sure, the multinational corporations usually make profits, sometimes very high profits, but they also take risks—the political risks of nationalization, the economic risks of failure—and without the promise of high profits they simply would not invest at all. And it is wrong to conclude that a net economic loss—exploitation—has necessarily occurred at the point at which the outflow of profits exceeds the inflow of new capital investment, for the notion of "decapitalization" ignores the value of the economic infrastructure left in place and the transfer of technology, labor, and marketing skills which have or at least should have led to continuing self-sustaining development.

Still, there are undoubtedly costs, as the critics have pointed out: the elimination of local competitors and the squeezing out of infant industries, the domination of key sectors of local economies by foreigners and the consequent difficulties of instituting national planning and economic controls when a substantial proportion of the economy is immune from such measures, the political and psychological resentments. Probably the balance of cost and advantage cannot be determined in general, but only on a case-by-case basis, depending on the indigenous context and the precise terms of the agreements negotiated between foreign investors and the host governments.[22]

What certainly is clear is that although there is considerable nationalistic rhetoric about the evils of foreign investment, most Third World countries continue to actively seek it. Nor can it be argued, á la the dependence theorists, that this simply reflects an alliance between local reactionaries and foreign exploiters, for in recent years even the most radical, nationalistic states (such as Cuba, Algeria, Peru, and even to some extent China) have sought increased foreign investment. To be sure, they have insisted on terms that do not unduly compromise national independence, but the fact that they can successfully do so certainly suggests a rather more evenly distributed balance of power between the multinational corporations and the Third World countries than the literature on "exploitation" implies.

Finally, even foreign aid is seen by many radicals as nothing more than another instrument of control and exploitation of the Third World by the capitalist countries, particularly the United States. Here the argument is that economically the aid eventually comes to be a net burden on Third World economies: repayments on past loans mount higher and higher, until they exceed new inflows of assistance. Politically, it is argued, aid serves mainly to support reactionary dictatorships and local oligarchies who block real social change and balanced economic growth, and who serve as agents of United States imperial control in the Third World.

There is no doubt that for a number of Third World countries the annual inflow of new capital assistance is less than the outflow in the form of interest on past debts, but it is clearly fallacious to conclude that this *necessarily* demonstrates that aid is harmful, for if the previous aid has been used productively it will have generated new sources of wealth out of which interest on previous debt can be repaid. And it cannot be doubted that a number of countries have in fact achieved self-sustained growth in good part because of the infusion of major amounts of foreign aid; examples are Western Europe following the Marshall Plan, Turkey, Taiwan, Brazil, and South Korea. To be sure, most of the latter countries are indeed conservative and authoritarian, but it cannot be seriously argued that United States assistance created those conditions, as opposed to the quite different proposition that aid is more likely to go to safely pro-American and therefore usually conservative regimes. Aid, we may conclude, if efficiently used, promotes overall economic growth and thus cannot be considered exploitative; economic growth, however, by no means assures democracy, social change, or even equitable distribution of the fruits of growth, but these are matters determined by indigenous policies and practices only slightly or not at all subject to outside influence.[23]

## NOTES

1. See especially Gabriel Kolko, *The Politics of War* (New York, 1968), and Joyce Kolko and Gabriel Kolko, *The Limits of Power* (New York, 1972).

2. Lincoln P. Bloomfield, *In Search of American Foreign Policy* (New York, 1974), p. 37.

3. S. M. Miller et al., "Does the U.S. Economy Require Imperialism?" *Social Policy*, September/October 1970.

4. Aron, *The Imperial Republic*, p. 164; Bloomfield, *In Search of American Foreign Policy*, p. 37.

5. For a summary of some arguments see Benjamin J. Cohen, *The Question of Imperialism* (New York, 1973), chap. 4.

6. See Julien, *America's Empire:* "There is a basic and complete agreement among U.S. [political and economic elites] . . . that the growing of the empire is indispensable to the preservation of American way of life" (p. 379). See Williams, *Tragedy of American Diplomacy*, for the most complete statement of this point of view.

7. For example, see the recently declassified famous "NSC-68", a top-secret, intergovernment document prepared by the secretaries of state and defense in 1950 to set forth the overall rationale for the United States containment policy. Throughout the report the emphasis is on the communist threat to democracy and freedom and the fundamental principles of Western civilization; no word is to be found about an "open door," the maintenance of capitalism, or, indeed, economic matters at all, except as related to the building of military and political strength. NSC-68 was published in full in *The Naval War College Review*, May/June 1975.

8. The most complete statement of this view (which derives directly from Hobson's famous analysis of nineteenth-century European colonialism), is in Harry Magdoff, *The Age of Imperialism* (New York, 1969). See also the essays by James O'Connor and Paul A. Baran and Paul M. Sweezy in K. T. Fann and D. C. Hodges (eds.), *Readings in U.S. Imperialism* (Boston, 1971).

9. The best evidence of this, of course, is the rapidly growing wave of nationalization of American private investments around the world, with the United States government reaction rarely going beyond rather *pro forma* protest. This will be discussed in greater detail below.

10. See Williams, *Tragedy of American Diplomacy*, for the most complete statement of this point of view.

11. See Bernard S. Morris, *Imperialism and Revolution* (Bloomington, Ind., 1973), who writes that where one cannot find evidence of economic motivations, as in Vietnam, "the governing class may well have concealed its economic interests behind a cloud of ideological verbiage" (p. 36).

12. For one among many examples of this approach see Anibal Quijano Obregon's essay in Julio Cotler and Richard R. Fagen (eds.), *Latin America and the United States* (Palo Alto, Calif., 1974). Quijano accounts for the recent examples of United States government nonintervention after American corporations in Latin America have been nationalized in these terms: "Since the principal imperialist state's

policy is constrained by the new forces conditioning international politics, this state must now face situations in which the mere defense of the interests of each North American imperialist firm operating in these countries could aggravate the contradictions and the political-social conflicts within these countries. This, in turn, could threaten the very existence of capitalism as a mode of production in these countries, owing either to the flaring up of nationalism that derives from these readjustments of imperialist domination, or to the triumph of revolutionary, socialist social forces. In the face of these conditions, the principal imperialist state in the hemisphere finds itself obligated to accept, or at least tolerate and adjust to, the political currents that under the banner of nationalism seek to reduce the internal social tensions of some countries, and obligated, as well, to maintain capitalism by readjusting its methods of operation and the very conditions of imperialist exploitation" (pp. 81–82).

13. Timothy Harding in Fann and Hodges, *U. S.Imperialism*, p. 14. Harry Magdoff also makes use of the "weakest link" metaphor to argue that even in Vietnam economic considerations ultimately underlay United States policy (in Owen and Sutcliffe, *Theory of Imperialism*, p. 170).

14. For similar conclusions about the neo-Marxist analyses see Tucker, *The Radical Left;* Cohen, *Question of Imperialism;* Robert Maddox, *The New Left and the Origins of the Cold War* (Princeton, N. J., 1973); James Kurth in Steven J. Rosen and James P. Kurth (eds.), *Testing Theories of Economic Imperialism* (Lexington, Mass., 1974); Ole R. Holsti, "The Study of International Politics Makes Strange Bedfellows," *American Political Science Review*, March 1974.

15. See Tucker, *The Radical Left,* for a similar argument.

16. Also, Peter Odell in *Oil and World Power* (London, 1970) has shown that in the late 1950s and early 1960s the United States government prevailed upon American oil corporations not to plot with Venezualan rightists against the Betancourt regime, even though Betancourt had put into effect substantially higher taxation of oil profits; of greater apparent importance to the government was that the Betancourt regime was considered as a possible liberal alternative to Castroism and a model for the kind of government envisioned by the Alliance for Progress. Moreover, the United States government today is *discouraging* exploitation by American oil companies of the apparently oil-rich coastal waters between China and Taiwan and South Asia, in order to avoid political conflict with the Peking government. See *The New York Times*, September 5, 1975, and Selig S. Harrison, "Time Bomb in East Asia," *Foreign Policy*, Fall 1975.

17. For discussion of the Guatemalan and Dominican interventions, see, respectively, Jerome Slater, *The OAS and United States Foreign Policy* (Columbus, Ohio, 1967), and Jerome Slater, *Intervention and Negotiations; The United States and the Dominican Revolution* (New York, 1970).

18. David P. Calleo and Benjamin M. Rowland, *America and the World Political Economy* (Bloomington, Ind., 1973), p. 242.

19. As reported in *The New York Times*, May 29, 1975.

20. "Trade in Raw Materials," in Rosen and Kurth, *Testing Theories of Economic Imperialism*, p. 195 (italics added).

21. For major criticisms of foreign investment see Frank, *Capitalism;* Sunkel in Ferguson and Weiker, *Continuing Issues in International Politics;* Crockroft et al., *Dependence and Underdevelopment;* Richard J. Barnet and Ronald E. Muller, *Global Reach* (New York, 1974).

22. For the most balanced, sophisticated treatments of the impact of foreign investment

in the Third World, see Louis Turner, *Multinational Companies and the Third World* (New York, 1973); Raymond Vernon, *Sovereignty at Bay* (New York, 1971); A. Kapoor and Phillip D. Grub (eds.), *The Multinational Enterprise in Transition* (Princeton, N. J., 1972); Charles P. Kindleberger, *American Business Abroad* (New Haven, Conn., 1969); Alfred D. Hirschman, *How to Divest in Latin America and Why* (Princeton, N. J., 1969).

23. On the question of the effects of foreign aid and more generally, the relationship between economic power and political influence, see Knorr, *Power and Wealth*.

## 22. David Horowitz
### *Nicaragua: A Speech to My Former Comrades on the Left*                    1986

In this final selection, David Horowitz focuses upon the radical's preferred alternative to traditional dictatorships—Marxist-Leninist regimes in the mold of Cuba, Angola, or North Vietnam. Author of *The Free World Colossus,* a pioneering work in the radical tradition, Horowitz explains why the failures of socialist and radical countries led him to cast off his former radical worldview.

Twenty-five years ago I was one of the founders of the New Left. I was one of the organizers of the first political demonstrations on the Berkeley campus—and indeed on any campus—to protest our government's anti-Communist policies in Cuba and Vietnam. Tonight I come before you as the kind of man I used to tell myself I would never be: a supporter of President Reagan, a committed opponent of Communist rule in Nicaragua.

I offer no apologies for my present position. It was what I thought was the humanity of the Marxist *idea* that made me what I was then; it is the inhumanity of what I have seen to be the Marxist *reality* that has made me what I am now. If my former comrades who support the Sandinistas were to pause for a moment and then plunge their busy political minds into the human legacies of their activist pasts, they would instantly drown in an ocean of blood.

The issue before us is not whether it is morally right for the United States to arm the *contras,* or whether there are unpleasant men among them. Nor is it whether the United States should defer to the wisdom of the Contadora powers—more than thirty years ago the United States tried to overthrow Somoza, and it was the Contadora powers of the time who bailed him out.

The issue before us and before all people who cherish freedom is how to oppose a Soviet imperialism so vicious and so vast as to dwarf any previously known. An "ocean of blood" is no metaphor. As we speak here tonight, this empire—whose axis runs through Havana and now Managua—is killing hundreds of thousands of Ethiopians to consolidate a dictatorship whose policies against its black citizens make the South African government look civilized and humane.

A second issue, especially important to me, is the credibility and commitment of the American Left.

In his speech on Nicaragua, President Reagan invoked the Truman Doctrine, the first attempt to oppose Soviet expansion through revolutionary surrogates. I marched against the Truman Doctrine in 1948, and defended, with the Left, the revolutions in Russia and China, in Eastern Europe and Cuba, in Cambodia and Vietnam—just as the Left defends the Sandinistas today.

And I remember the arguments and "facts" with which we made our case and what the other side said, too—the Presidents who came and went, and the anti-Communists on the Right, the William Buckleys and the Ronald Reagans. And in every case, without exception, time has proved the Left wrong. Wrong in its views of the revolutionaries' intentions, and wrong about the facts of their revolutionary rule. And just as consistently the anti-Communists were proved right.

Today the Left dismisses Reagan's warnings about Soviet expansion as anti-Communist paranoia, a threat to the peace, and a mask for American imperialism. We said the same things about Truman when he warned us then. Russia's control of Eastern Europe, we said, was only a defensive buffer, a temporary response to American power—first, because Russia had no nuclear weapons; and then, because it lacked the missiles to deliver them.

Today, the Soviet Union is a nuclear superpower, missiles and all, but it has not given up an inch of the empire which it gained during World War II—not Eastern Europe, not the Baltic states which Hitler delivered to Stalin and whose nationhood Stalin erased and which are now all but forgotten, not even the Kurile Islands which were once part of Japan.

Not only have the Soviets failed to relinquish their conquests in all these years—years of dramatic, total decolonization in the West—but their growing strength and the wounds of Vietnam have encouraged them to reach for more. South Vietnam, Cambodia, Laos, Ethiopia, Yemen, Mozambique, and Angola are among the dominoes which have recently fallen into the Soviet orbit.

To expand its territorial core—which apologists still refer to as a "defensive perimeter"—Moscow has already slaughtered a million peasants in Afghanistan, an atrocity warmly endorsed by the Sandinista government.

Minister of Defense Humberto Ortega describes the army of the conquerors—whose scorched earth policy has driven half the Afghan population from its homes—as the "pillar of peace" in the world today. To any self-respecting socialist, praise for such barbarism would be an inconceivable outrage—as it was to the former Sandinista, now *contra*, Edén Pastora. But praise for the barbarians is sincere tribute coming from the Sandinista rulers, because they see themselves as an integral part of the Soviet empire itself.

"The struggle of man against power is the struggle of memory against forgetting." So writes the Czech novelist Milan Kundera, whose name and work no longer exist in his homeland.

In all the Americas, Fidel Castro was the only head of state to cheer the Soviet tanks as they rolled over the brave people of Prague. And cheering right along with Fidel were Carlos Fonseca, Tomas Borge, Humberto Ortega, and the other creators of the present Nicaraguan regime.

One way to assess what has happened in Nicaragua is to realize that wherever Soviet tanks crush freedom from now on, there will be two governments in the Americas supporting them all the way.

About its own crimes and for its own criminals, the Left has no memory at all.

To the Left I grew up in, along with the Sandinista founders, Stalin's Russia was a socialist paradise, the model of the liberated future. Literacy to the uneducated, power to the weak, justice to the forgotten—we praised the Soviet Union then, just as the Left praises the Sandinistas now.

And just as they ignore warnings like the one that has come from Violetta Chamorro, the publisher of La Prensa, the paper which led the fight against Somoza, and a member of the original Sandinista junta—"With all my heart, I tell you it is worse here now than it was in the times of the Somoza dictatorship"—so we dismissed the anti-Soviet "lies" about Stalinist repression.

In the society we hailed as a new human dawn, 100 million people were put in slave-labor camps, in conditions rivaling Auschwitz and Buchenwald. Between 30 and 40 million people were killed—in peacetime, in the daily routine of socialist rule. While leftists applauded their progressive policies and guarded their frontiers, Soviet Marxists killed more peasants, more workers, and even more Communists than all the capitalist governments together since the beginning of time.

And for the entire duration of this nightmare, the William Buckleys and Ronald Reagans and the other anti-Communists went on telling the world exactly what was happening. And all that time the pro-Soviet Left and its fellow-travelers went on denouncing them as reactionaries and liars, using the same contemptuous terms with which the Left attacks the President and his supporters today.

The Left would still be denying the Soviet atrocities if the perpetrators themselves had not finally acknowledged their crimes. In 1956, in a secret speech to the party elite, Khrushchev made the crimes a Communist fact; but it was only the CIA that actually made the fact public, allowing radicals to come to terms with what they had done.

Khrushchev and his cohorts could not have cared less about the misplaced faith and misspent lives of their naive supporters on the Left. The Soviet rulers were concerned about themselves: Stalin's mania had spread the slaughter into his henchmen's ranks; they wanted to make totalitarianism safe for its rulers. In place of a dictator whose paranoia could not be controlled, they instituted a dictatorship by directorate—which (not coincidentally) is the form of rule in Nicaragua today. Repression would work one way only: from the privileged top of society to the powerless bottom.

The year of Khrushchev's speech—which is also the year Soviet tanks flattened the freedom fighters of Budapest—is the year that tells us who the Sandinistas really are.

Because the truth had to be admitted at last, the Left all over the world was forced to redefine itself in relation to the Soviet facts. China's Communist leader Mao liked Stalin's way better. Twenty-five million people died in the "great leaps" and "cultural revolutions" he then launched. In Europe and America, however, a new anti-Stalinist Left was born. This New Left, of which I was one of the founders, was repelled by the evils it was now forced to see, and embarrassed by the tarnish the Soviet totalitarians had brought to the socialist cause. It turned its back on the Soviet model of Stalin and his heirs.

But the Sandinista vanguard was neither embarrassed nor repelled. In 1957, Carlos Fonseca, the founding father of the Sandinista Front, visited the Soviet Union with its newly efficient totalitarian state. To Fonesca, as to Borge and his other comrades, the Soviet monstrosity was their revolutionary dream come true. In his pamphlet, *A Nicaraguan in Moscow*, Fonseca proclaimed Soviet Communism his model for Latin America's revolutionary future.

This vision of a Soviet America is now being realized in Nicaragua. The *comandante* directorate, the army, and the secret police are already mirrors of the Soviet state—not only structurally but in their personnel, trained and often manned by agents of the Soviet axis.

But the most important figure in this transformation is not a Nicaraguan at all. For twenty years, from the time the Sandinistas first arrived in Havana, they were disciples of Fidel Castro. With his blessings they went on to Moscow, where Stalin's henchman completed their revolutionary course. Fidel is the image in which the Sandinista leadership has created itself and the author of its strategy. Its politburo, the *comandante* directorate, was personally created by Fidel in Havana on the eve of the final struggle, sealed with a pledge of millions in military aid. It was Fidel who supplied the arms with which the Sandinistas waged their battles, just as he supplied the Cuban general—Zene Casals—who directed their victorious campaign (just as the Soviets supplied the general who directed Fidel's own victory at the Bay of Pigs). *Without Castro's intervention, Arturo Cruz and the other anti-Somoza and pro-democratic* contras *would be the government of Nicaragua today.*

And it was Fidel who showed the Sandinistas how to steal the revolution after the victory, and how to secure their theft by manipulating their most important allies: the American Left and its liberal sympathizers.

Twenty-five years ago Fidel was also a revolutionary hero to us on the New Left. Like today's campus radicals, we became "coffee-pickers" and passengers on the revolutionary tour, and we hailed the literacy campaigns, health clinics, and other wonders of the people's state.

When Fidel spoke, his words were revolutionary music to our ears: "Freedom with bread. Bread without terror." "A revolution neither red nor black, but Cuban olive-green." And so in Managua today: "Not [Soviet] Communism but Nicaraguan *Sandinismo*" is the formula Fidel's imitators proclaim.

Fidel's political poems put radicals all over the world under his spell. Jean-

Paul Sartre wrote one of the first and most influential books of praise: "If this man asked me for the moon," he said, "I would give it to him. Because he would have a need for it."

When I listen to the enthusiasts for the Sadinista redeemers, the fate of a hero of the Cuban revolution comes to my mind. For in the year that Jean-Paul Sartre came to Havana and fell in love with the humanitarian Fidel, Huber Matos embarked on a long windowless night of the soul.

The fate of Huber Matos begins with the second revolution that Fidel launched.

All the fine gestures and words with which Fidel seduced us and won our support—the open Marxism, the socialist humanism, the independent path—turned out to be calculated lies. Even as he proclaimed his color to be olive-green, he was planning to make his revolution Moscow red.

So cynical was Fidel's strategy that at the time it was difficult for many to comprehend. One by one Fidel began removing his own comrades from the revolutionary regime and replacing them with Cuban Communists.

Cuba's Communists were then a party in disgrace. They had opposed the revolution; they had even served in the cabinet of the tyrant Batista while the revolution was taking place!

But this was all incidental to Fidel. Fidel knew how to use people. And Fidel was planning a *new* revolution he could trust the Communists to support: he had decided to turn Cuba into a Soviet state. And Fidel also knew that he could no longer trust his own comrades, because they had made a revolution they thought was going to be Cuban olive-green.

Although Fidel removed socialists and the Sandinistas removed democrats, the pattern of betrayal has been the same.

To gain power the Sandinistas concealed their true intention (*a Soviet state*) behind a revolutionary lie (*a pluralist democracy*). To consolidate power they fashioned a second lie (*democracy, but only within the revolution*), and those who believed in the first lie were removed. At the end of the process there will be no democracy in Nicaragua at all, which is exactly what Fonseca and the Sandinistas intended when they began.

When Huber Matos saw Fidel's strategy unfolding in Cuba, he got on the telephone with other Fidelistas to discuss what they should do. This was a mistake. In the first year of Cuba's liberation, the phones of revolutionary legends like Huber Matos were already tapped by Fidel's secret police. Huber Matos was arrested.

In the bad old days of Batista oppression, Fidel had been arrested himself. His crime was not words on a telephone, but leading an attack on a military barracks to overthrow the Batista regime. Twelve people were killed. For this Fidel spent a total of eighteen months in the tyrant's jail before being released.

Huber Matos was not so lucky. Fidel was no Batista, and the revolution that had overthrown Batista was no two-bit dictatorship. For his phone call, Huber Matos was tried in such secrecy that not even members of the government were privy to the proceeding. When it was over, he was sentenced to solitary confinement, in a cell without sunlight, for *twenty-two years*. And even as Fidel buried his former friend and comrade alive, he went on singing his songs of revolutionary humanism and justice.

Milan Kundera reveals the meaning of this revolutionary parable of Huber Matos and Fidel. Recalling a French Communist who wrote poems for brotherhood while his friend was being murdered by the poet's comrades in Prague, Kundera says: "The hangman killed while the poet sang."

Kundera explains: "People like to say revolution is beautiful; it is only the terror arising from it which is evil. But this is not true. The evil is already present in the beautiful; hell is already contained in the dream of paradise. . . . To condemn Gulags is easy, but to reject the poetry which leads to the Gulag by way of paradise is as difficult as ever." Words to bear in mind today as we consider Nicaragua and its revolution of poets.

To believe in the revolutionary dream is the tragedy of its supporters; to exploit the dream is the talent of its dictators. Revolutionary cynicism, the source of this talent, is Fidel's most important teaching to his Sandinista disciples. This is the faculty that allows the *comandantes* to emulate Fidel himself: to be poets and hangmen at the same time. To promise democracy and organize repression, to attack imperialism and join an empire, to talk peace and plan war, to champion justice and deliver Nicaragua to a fraternity of inhumane, repressive, miltarized, and economically crippled states.

"We used to have one main prison, now we have many," begins the lament of Carlos Franqui, a former Fidelista, for the paradise that Nicaragua has now gained. "We used to have a few barracks; now we have many. We used to have many plantations; now we have only one, and it belongs to Fidel. Who enjoys the fruits of the revolution, the houses of the rich, the luxuries of the rich? The *comandante* and his court."

To this grim accounting must be added the economic ruin that Fidel's Marxism has wrought. Among the proven failures of the Marxist promise, this is the most fateful of all. The failure of Marxist economies to satisfy basic needs, let alone compete with the productive capitalisms of the West, has produced the military-industrial police states which call themselves socialist today. Nicaragua, with its Sandinista-created economic crisis and its massive military build-up, is but the latest example of this pattern.

Twenty-five years ago we on the Left applauded when Fidel denounced Cuba's one-crop economy and claimed that U.S. imperialism was the cause of the nation's economic plight. It seemed so self-evident. Cuba was a fertile island with a favorable climate, but U.S. sugar plantations had monopolized its arable land, and the sugar produced was a product for export, not a food for Cubans. The poor of Cuba had been sacrificed on the altar of imperialist profit. Whenever we were confronted by the political costs Castro's revolution might entail, we were confident that this gain alone—Cuba's freedom to grow food for Cubans—would make any sacrifice worthwhile. The same illusion—that the revolution will mean better lives for Nicaragua's poor—underlies every defense of the Sandinistas today.

It is nearly three decades since Cuba's liberation, and Cuba is still a one-crop economy. But the primary market for its sugar is now the Soviet Union instead of the United States. Along with this have come other economic differences as well. Cuba's external debt is now *200 times* what it was when Fidel took power. And it would be far greater if the Communist *caudillo* had not mortgaged his country to his Soviet patron. So bankrupt is the economy Castro has created that it requires a Soviet subsidy of over $4 billion a year, one-quarter of the entire national income, to keep it afloat. Before the revolution, Cubans enjoyed the highest per-capita income in Latin America. Now they are economic prisoners of permanent rationing and chronic shortages in even the most basic necessities. The allotted rations tell a story in themselves: two pounds of meat per citizen per month; 20 percent less clothing than the allotment a decade earlier; and in rice, a basic staple of Cuba's poor, *half* the yearly consumption under the old Batista regime.

The idea that Marxist revolution will mean economic benefit for the poor has proved to be the most deadly illusion of all. It is *because* Marxist economies *cannot* satisfy economic needs—not even at the levels of the miserably corrupt capitalisms of Batista and Somoza—that Marxist states require permanent repression to stifle and permanent enemies to saddle with the blame.

This is also why Castro has found a new national product to supply to the Soviet market (a product his Sandinista disciples are in the process of developing in their turn). The product is the Cuban nation itself, as a military base for Soviet expansion.

The event that sealed the contract for this development was the moment of America's defeat in Vietnam in April 1975. This defeat resulted in America's effective withdrawal from the crucial role it had played since 1945, as the guardian of the international status quo and the keeper of its peace.

To the Soviet imperialists, America's loss was an opportunity gained. In 1975 the Kremlin began what would soon be a tenfold increase in the aid it had been providing to Cuba. Most of the aid was of military intent. Toward the end of the year, 36,000 Cuban troops surfaced in Africa, as an interventionary force in Angola's civil war. Soviet aid to Cuba tripled and then quintupled as Castro sent another 12,000 Cuban troops to provide a palace guard for Ethiopia's new dictator, Mengistu Haile Mariam, who had thrown himself into the Soviet embrace with a campaign which he officially called his "Red Terror." A year after his henchmen had murdered virtually the entire graduating class of the high schools of Addis Ababa—just the most poignant of Mengistu's 100,000 victims—Fidel presented him with a Bay of Pigs medal, Cuban socialism's highest award.

Ethiopia's dictator is only one of the international heroes who regularly pass through the Cuban base to be celebrated, trained, and integrated into a network of subversion and terror that has come to span every continent of the globe. And in the Sandinista revolution Fidel's colonial plantation has produced its most profitable return: an opportunity for Moscow to expand its investment to the American land mass itself.

Nicaragua is now in the grip of utterly cynical and utterly ruthless men, exceeding even their sponsors in aggressive hostility to the United States. The Soviets may be the covert patrons of the world's terrorist plague, but not even they have had the temerity to embrace publicly the assassin Qaddafi as a "brother" the way the Sandinistas have. The aim of the Sandinista revolution is to crush its society from top to bottom, to institute totalitarian rule, and to use the country as a base to spread Communist terror and Communist regimes throughout the hemisphere.

The Sandinista anthem which proclaims the Yankee to be the "enemy of mankind" expresses precisely the revolutionaries' sentiment and goal. That goal is hardly to create a more just society—the sordid record would dissuade any reformer from choosing the Communist path—but to destroy the societies still oustide the totalitarian perimeter, and their chief protector, the United States.

Support for the *contras* is a first line of defense. For Nicaraguans, a *contra* victory would mean the restoration of the democratic leadership from whom the Sandinistas stole the revolution in the first place, the government that Nicaragua would have had if Cuba had not intervened. For the countries of the Americas, it would mean a halt in the Communist march that threatens their freedoms and their peace.

In conclusion, I would like to say this to my former comrades and successors on the Left: you are self-righteous and blind in your belief that you are part of a movement to advance human progress and liberate mankind. You are in fact in league with the darkest and most reactionary forces of the modern world, whose legacies—as the record attests—are atrocities and oppressions on a scale unknown in the human past. It is no accident that radicals in power have slaughtered so many of their own people. Hatred of self, and by extension one's country, is the root of the radical cause.

As American radicals, the most egregious sin you commit is to betray the privileges and freedoms ordinary people from all over the world have created in this country—privileges and freedoms that ordinary people all over the world would feel blessed to have themselves. But the worst of it is this: you betray all this tangible good that you can see around you for a socialist pie-in-the-sky that has meant horrible deaths and miserable lives for the hundreds of millions who have so far fallen under its sway.

---

## COMPREHENSION CHECKPOINT

What is the significance of the following?

| | | |
|---|---|---|
| Marshall Plan | Truman Doctrine | *Weltanschauugn* |
| open door policy | "informal empire" | Sandinistas |
| "gunboat diplomacy" | IMF | dollar diplomacy |
| liberal international | "bourgeois democracy" | "Prussians and |
| economic order | Reagan Doctrine | traders" |

Can you complete the tasks and answer the questions that follow?

1. Write a one-paragraph summary of the radical perspective.

2. Write a one-paragraph summary of the radical perspective on the origins of the cold war.

3. Write a one-paragraph summary of the critical points made by Slater and Horowitz.

4. The radical perspective draws upon a set of "events," scripts, and analogies that do not get much attention in mainstream writings. These incidents all involve U.S. intervention or support for counterrevolutionary forces in a series of Third World countries. Can you explain the issues involved in each of the following cases?

   | | | |
   |---|---|---|
   | Iran (1953) | Guatemala (1954) | Cuba (1961) |
   | Chile (1970–72) | Nicaragua (1981–88) | Grenada (1983) |
   | Dominican Republic (1965) | Vietnam (1961–74) | |

5. What evidence would radicals present in support of Michael Parenti's statement that "it is not true that leftist governments are more repressive than right wing fascist ones." How might Parenti respond to Horowitz's rebuttal of this assertion?

6. Can you summarize the distinctions that Roger Burbach makes between the American concept of revolution and the "twentieth-century" concept of revolution? Why does Burbach think these distinctions are significant?

7. According to Kathy McAfee, how do the liberal international economic system and its major institutions work against the poorest people in the poorest countries? How would she remove the obstacles to growth that she outlines in her essay? Finally, what does she mean by "equitable development"? How would we know it if we saw it?

8. How does Chomsky define democracy and socialism, and why does he claim that there is little of either in the U.S. or the Soviet Union?

9. Because his essay was written in 1976, Slater based his argument on statistics from the early 1970s. At that time, foreign trade amounted to 7 to 8 percent of our GNP, and 40 percent of our direct overseas investment was located in the Third World. In the late 1980s the proportion of trade to our GNP has risen to 12 percent, while the proportion of our direct foreign investment in the Third World has declined to 25 percent. At the same time, 17 percent of our corporate profits came from overseas operations in 1989. Do these changes weaken or strengthen Slater's arguments? Or would you need more figures to decide and, if so, what figures would you want?

10. How convincing do you find Jerome Slater's statement that "it is hardly credible that United States intervention in Guatemala in 1954 and the Dominican Republic in 1965 were made by, respectively, banana and sugar interests, rather than by ideological cold war and even strategic considerations, genuinely believed—whether accurately or not is irrelevant—by policy makers to

be at stake in those countries"? What evidence might a radical use in responding to this statement?

11. How might a radical respond to Slater's answer to the question, "Does the United States exploit the poor?" Which explanation would you find more convincing and why?

12. How might radicals respond to the argument that the United States should seek to avoid supporting repressive governments of both the left and the right by supporting reformist, centrist forces?

13. Even if radicals are right about what is wrong with American foreign policy and the liberal international economic order, what is their solution? How do they propose to get the United States to pursue policies that foster freedom and self-determination?

14. One implication of the radical perspective is the impossibility of a neorealist or neo-isolationist foreign policy so long as the United States remains a capitalist nation and seeks to maintain a liberal, capitalist international economic order. While America might be able to drop such rollback policies as the Reagan Doctrine, radicals imply that the United States must pursue an interventionist strategy of one sort or another. Do you agree or disagree? On what evidence does your conclusion rest?

15. Refer to the chart of reassertionist and neorealist polarities presented on page 135. Where would the radical perspective fall along the polarities, and how relevant would radicals consider the various polarities? Then, sketch out a set of radical responses to the quotation by Hart and the particular policy of proposals that follow the quotation. What similarities and differences do you find between the answers that flow from the radical and the three mainstream worldviews? What accounts for these similarities and differences?

16. Can you construct a reassertionist, neorealism, and neo-isolationist critique of the radical worldview?

## For Further Consideration

*Periodicals and journals* in the radical tradition: the *Monthly Review*, the *Multinational Monitor*, the *Nation*, the *New Left Review*, *The New World Review*. The *Journal of Peace Research*, and the *Progressive* occasionally carry essays by radicals.

*Leading radical scholars and authors:* Richard Barnet, Noam Chomsky, Lloyd Gardner, Marvin Gettleman, Fred Halliday, Gabriel Kolko, Francis Moore Lappé, Saul Landau, Sidney Lens, Harry Magdoff, Michael Parenti, James Petras, William Appleman Williams.

# FOR FURTHER READING

Barnet, Richard. *Intervention and Revolution*. New York: New American Library, 1972. A critique of America's Third World policies by a leading non-Marxist radical. At times, Barnet's positions are quite close to those of neorealism. For example, see his short critique of the Carter administration's foreign policy, *Real Security: Restoring American Power in a Dangerous Decade*, cited in Chapter 4, Neorealism.

Cohen, Benjamin J. *The Question of Imperialism: The Political Economy of Dominance and Dependence*. New York: Basic Books, 1973. In chapters IV, V, and VI, Cohen disputes the economic assumptions underlying the radical worldview.

Kolko, Gabriel. *Confronting the Third World: United States Foreign Policy, 1945–1980*. New York: Pantheon Books, 1988. Kolko, a neo-Marxist, argues that anti-Communist interventions in the Third World have merely been covers for maintaining America's hegemony and its economic domination of raw material producing nations. He writes in his conclusion that "needed changes [in the Third World] will come one way or another, but they would be immeasurably more successful, humane, and faster were US backing for their surrogates and puppets not a constant menace to those seeking to end the poverty and injustice that so blights much of mankind" [p. 297].

Lappé, Francis Moore, et al. *Betraying the National Interest*. New York: Grove Press, 1987. A short and highly readable radical, but non-Marixst, critique of American foreign aid programs.

Magdoff, Harry. *The Age of Imperialism*. New York: Monthly Review Press, 1968. An effort by a leading Marxist to document the radical worldview with a wealth of economic statistics. Magdoff's book is a revealing statistical portrait of the American corporate and financial economy and the relationship between national and international business activities.

McGowan, Pat, and Stephen G. Walker. "Radical and Conventional Models of U. S. Foreign Economic Policy Making," *World Politics* 33 (Winter 198), pp. 347–82. This essay differentiates clearly the various strands of radicalism—Marxist, neo-Marxist, and radical, but non-Marxist.

McMahan, Jeff. *Reagan and the World: Imperial Policy in the New Cold War*. New York: Monthly Review Press, 1985. A very readable and predictable neo-Marxist presentation and critique of the Reagan administration's foreign policies.

Parenti, Michael. *The Sword and the Dollar: Imperialism, Revolution, and the Arms Race*. New York: St. Martins, 1989. A short but highly readable and clear presentation of the radical critique of American foreign policy in the postwar era. Parenti begins by arguing that the differences between liberals (neorealists) and conservatives (reassertionists) are merely tactical differences over how best to secure the postwar capitalist, international economic order.

Schlesinger, Jr., Arthur. "Origins of the Cold War," *Foreign Affairs*, Vol. 46 (October 1967), pp. 22–52. A "semi-official" mainstream rebuttal to the radical explanation for the origins of the cold war by a leading liberal historian.

Tucker, Robert. *The Radical Left and American Foreign Policy*. Baltimore: The Johns Hopkins University Press, 1971. A thorough presentation and critique of the radical worldview by a leading mainstream scholar.

Williams, William A. *The Tragedy of American Foreign Policy.* New York: Dell Publishing Company, revised second edition, 1972. The classic statement of the radical worldview.

# NOTES

1. Gabriel Kolko, *The Politics of War: The World and United States Foreign Policy, 1943–1945* (New York: Random House, 1968), p. 5.
2. Richard Barnet, *Intervention and Revolution* (New York: New American Library, 1972), p. 131.
3. William Appleman Williams, *The Tragedy of American Diplomacy* (New York: Dell Publishing Co., 1962).
4. Lloyd Gardner, *Economic Aspects of New Deal Diplomacy* (London: Oxford University Press, 1965).
5. Gabriel Kolko, *The Politics of War: The World and United States Foreign Policy 1943–1945.*
6. David Horowitz, *The Free World Colossus: A Critique of American Policy in the Cold War* (New York: Hill and Wang, 1967).
7. Walter LaFeber, *America, Russia, and the Cold War, 1945–1966* (New York: John Wiley and Sons, 1967).
8. Quotation cited in Joseph M. Siracusa, *The Ameican Revisionists: New Left Diplomatic Histories and Historians* (Port Washington, NY: Kennikat Press, 1973), p. 89.
9. Harry Magdoff, *The Age of Imperialism* (New York: Monthly Review, 1969).
10. Gabriel Kolko, *The Roots of American Foreign Policy* (Boston: Beacon Press, 1969).
11. Carl Oglesby and Richard Shaull, *Containment and Change* (New York: Macmillan, 1967).
12. In addition to Williams' *Tragedy of American Diplomacy*, the major revisionist works of the origins of the cold war and the course of America's postwar foreign policies are: Gar Alperovitz, *Atomic Diplomacy: Hiroshima and Potsdam, the Use of the Atomic Bomb and the Confrontation with Soviet Power* (New York: Vintage Books, 1965), Gar Alperovitz, *Cold War Essays* (Garden City, NY: Doubleday and Co., 1970), D. W. Fleming, *The Cold War and Its Origins, 1917–1960,* 2 vols. (Garden City, NY: Doubleday and Co. 1961), Lloyd C. Gardner, *Architects of Illusion: Men and Ideas in American Foreign Policy, 1941–1949* (Chicago: Quadrangle Books, 1970), David Horowitz, *The Free World Colossus,* Gabriel Kolko, *The Politics of War: The World and United States Foreign Policy, 1943–1945,* and Walter LaFeber, *America, Russia, and the Cold War, 1945–1966.*
13. Williams, *The Tragedy of American Diplomacy,* p. 82.
14. Williams, *The Tragedy of American Diplomacy,* pp. 228–29.
15. Michael Parenti, "US Intervention: More Foul than Foolish," *New World Review,* 1984 (May–June), p. 13.
16. Jeff McMahan, *Reagan and the World: Imperial Policy in the New Cold War* (New York: Monthly Review Press, 1985), p. 107.
17. *Ibid.* p. 23.
18. Michael Parenti, *The Sword and the Dollar,* p. 88.
19. Michael Klare, "The Superpower Trip: Policing the Gulf—And The World," *The Nation,* October 15, 1990, pp. 416 and 420.

# Chapter
## 7

# World Order
# Perspectives

*A*ccording to world order proponents, the pursuit of national interests is
the pursuit of national peril. For in their opinion, ominous global trends
threaten planetary survival itself unless nations start placing international interests at the top of their foreign policy agendas. To avert a series of converging
catastrophes, world order advocates call for nothing less than a revolution in
American foreign policy—a revolution in both the nation's agenda and in the
way its elites think about national and international security.

The planetary trends that drive the world order perspective were starkly
enumerated over fifteen years ago by Richard Falk in his book, *A Study of
Future Worlds*. According to Falk,

The planet is too crowded and is getting more so.

The war system is too destructive, risky, and costly, and is getting more
so.

An increasingly large number of people live at or below the level of
subsistence.

Pressure on the basic ecosystem of the planet is serious and growing, as
is the more tangible pollution of air, water, and land.

Governing groups in many societies are repressing their own people in
an intolerable manner.

Human and material resources of the planet are wasted and depleted in
a shortsighted way, and at increasing rates.

Technologies are not adequately managed to assure planetary and
human benefit.[1]

Since the publication of Falk's book, most of these trends have continued
almost unabated. In a recent text that examines American foreign policy from a
world order perspective, political scientist Melvin Gurtov presents a similarly

ominous "Brief Report on the State of the Planet." Among the figures he cites are the following:

- Over two billion people in the Third World do not have access to clean water.
- Thirty-four countries have illiteracy rates of over 80 percent.
- By the year 2000, one billion people, or about one seventh of the planet's population, will be out of work.
- Over two billion people have incomes below $400 a year, and the societies these people live in have the world's largest and fastest growing populations.
- By the year 2000, forests in the developing countries will be reduced by one-half, top soil by one-third, and food reserves will be perilously low. These trends not only intensify the search for firewood and make hunger a way of life for the poorest peoples in the world; they also contribute to the greenhouse effect by reducing the vegetation that absorbs the carbon dioxide spewed out in the rich industrial countries.
- In 1985, world armaments expenditures had reached over $2 *billion a day* with 80 percent shared by two superpowers which already possessed enough destructive power to reproduce 5,000 World War IIs.
- Third World governments were taking three-fourths of all the arms marketed worldwide, frequently paying for them with borrowed money that neither they nor their peoples can afford.[2]

Gurtov's book had hardly filtered into college classrooms before new trends could have been added to his list. While the cold war was winding down, a new fear was arising—the spread of ghastly chemical and biological weapons to unstable and revisionist Third World states. The threat to the ozone layer, which Gurtov mentioned only in regard to nuclear war, suddenly appeared much greater than scientists had feared, provoking even Margaret Thatcher, Britian's conservative and nationalist former prime minister, to call for dramatic action by all states, especially the developed ones. The depletion of the rain forests in tropical areas was dangerously accelerating the greenhouse effect, according to some leading scientists.

As the 1990s began, the Worldwatch Institute's annual report on the *State of the World* echoed the earlier alarms:

> The trends of environmental degradation described in the previous six reports in this volume all continue unabated: Forests are shrinking, deserts expanding, and soils eroding. The depletion of the stratospheric ozone layer that protects us from ultraviolet radiation appears to have escalated. The levels of carbon dioxide and other heat trapping gases in the atmosphere continue to build in an all too predictable fashion.[3]

At the base of the world order perspective is a perception of accelerating trends that, if unchecked, portend a deteriorating state of the planet—widening gaps between the developed and developing nations, seemingly mindless spending on unproductive arms, exponential population growth accompanied by massive unemployment in the poorest of countries, unchecked environmental degradation, and nations, even great nations, increasingly vulnerable to economic, technological, and communication trends seemingly beyond their control.

According to world order advocates, these trends all point to an ironic situation—a situation where "what is plainly everybody's problem is nobody's business." And the root of this ironic situation, they claim, lies in the very system within which states conduct their business with each other—the Westphalian State System, the system that began with the Peace of Westphalian in 1648.

Under this system, each nation must seek its own security and welfare as best it can. But as each state pursues its own *national interests,* no institution looks after the *global interest,* despite the clear interconnectedness of nations in an increasingly interdependent world. To support their point about this "boomerang effect" of the pursuit of national interests, world order proponents use the analogy of the commons. According to Purdue University political scientist Louis Rene Beres:

> The nations in world politics coexist in the fashion of herdsmen who share a common pasture and who feel it is advantageous to increase the size of their respective herds. Although these herdsmen have calculated that it is in their interests to augment their herds, they have calculated incorrectly. This is the case because they have failed to consider the *cumulative effect* of their calculations, which happen to be an overgrazed commons and economic ruin.[4]

However, the significance of the world order perspective does not lie in its plans for replacing the Westphalian system with a less anarchic one. Schemes for world government are, in fact, as old, if not older, than the Westphalian State System itself.[5] What is unique in our era is the advent of global forces and weapons systems that have outrun the capacity of nation-states to deal with them and that endanger human survival itself.

In the past, the impact of destructive and frequently futile wars seldom had global dimensions. But, since the end of World War II, nuclear weapons have threatened planetary extinction, and the possession of chemical and biological weapons now threatens genocide against races and nations. In addition, as the economic self-sufficiency of nations declines, so does that ability of governments to provide for the welfare of their populations. Over the past several decades, the insularity and impermeability of nation-states have increasingly been eroded by new transnational forces that are under no one nation's control.

Multinational corporations close up shops in high-wage, developed countries and build new factories in low-wage, developing countries. Price hikes by Arab oil sheikdoms create long gasoline lines in the small towns of "middle America." Spraying DDT to end the scourge of malaria in Brazil spirals through an ecological chain that threatens to extinguish the American bald eagle whose habitat is thousands of miles away from the tip of South America. A "green revolution" in developing countries puts American farmers out of business. The use of fossil fuels, air conditioners, and seemingly inoffensive aerosol spray cans has led to ominous predictions about the future of life on earth.

More and more, global interdependence is enmeshing the fates of distant peoples whether they or their leaders like it or not. According to Richard Falk:

> On balance, the logic of Westphalia now seems unable to protect the most vital needs of humanity. It no longer provides sufficient security against attack, nor permits reasonable progress in attaining social and economic justice; it cannot protect the environment from deterioration or satisfactorily allocate and conserve the scarce minerals that will be taken from the oceans.[6]

According to Saul Mendlovitz, Rutgers University law professor and codirector of the World Order Models Project, "The nation-state system as it is presently constituted is incapable of dealing with a series of global crises." Mendlovitz predicts that unless radical changes are made in the foreign policies of major states, 40 percent of mankind will never realize the values of peace, social justice, economic well-being, ecological balance, and positive identity. "This," he concludes, "is intolerable."[7]

For world order proponents, nation-states have become obsolete. Not only are states increasingly unable to provide for the security, health, and welfare of their people, but by seeking to attain those goals through national efforts, they are ominously shortening the fuse on the time bombs that are ticking away—by polluting the air, water, and soil, by degrading the environment, by depleting nonrenewable resources, by overheating the globe, and by channelling more and more resources into weapons systems that few can afford.

For world order proponents, the conclusion is obvious: "National security" must be redefined in terms of "human security." According to Louis Rene Beres:

> The United States . . . must begin to fashion its foreign policy behavior on a new set of premises, one consonant with the constraints of planetary conditions and the exigencies of national survival. . . .

> Unless the United States . . . begins to understand that its own national interest must be defined from the standpoint of what is best for the world system as a whole, that interest will not be sustained. Instead, it will crumble along with the rest of the foreign policy edifice that is oblivious to its own self-destructive tendencies.[8]

Given this conclusion, the foreign policy agenda of world order proponents is vastly different from those proposed by reassertionists, neorealists, or neo-isolationists. The major agenda items of the world order perspective include the following:

- Drastic disarmament
- Massive programs to create full employment and sustainable development in the Third World
- Concentration on meeting basic human needs for all—food, water, housing, literacy, and basic health care
- Promotion of democracy and human rights

- Ensuring a livable environment for all
- Conservation of nonrenewable resources

Moving from a nation-centric to a global-centric foreign policy would obviously require significant changes in deeply rooted values—values that get short shrift within the current international system. Given the semi-anarchical nature of the international system, the national pursuit of security places a premium on such values as ambition, prestige, competition, elitism, amorality, hegemony, hierarchy, worst case planning, exclusive alliances, nationalism, conceptions of "them versus us," narrow definitions of security, and, ultimately, violence. In the opinion of world order advocates, all of these values— values that are deeply rooted in the world's political leaders—stand in the way of arresting ominous planetary trends and providing a decent standard of living for all the world's population.

In place of these competitive and nation-centric values, a world order foreign policy would be guided by the following: compassion, respect for diversity, harmony, "enoughness," honesty, idealism, integrity, nonviolence, service to others, trust, accountability, participation, shared power, decentralization, voluntary simplicity, basic needs, equality of opportunity and rewards, ecopolitics, the creation and following of international law, the dissolution of power blocs, and the resolution of disputes by peaceful and cooperative means.[9] According to Louis Rene Beres:

> Our goal must be nothing less than the erection of a new pattern of thinking that defines the national interest in terms of strategies that secure and sustain the entire system of states. By supplanting competitive self-seeking with cooperative self-seeking, the United States can move forward to the kind of global renaissance we so desperately need.[10]

To promote and instill these new values, world order advocates have called for a new approach to the study of international politics, an approach that is *systemic, normative,* and *futuristic.* Rather than looking at issues from national- and interest-oriented perpsectives, world order advocates propose examining issues within a normative context that evaluates policy alternatives against human and planetary values. In addition, they would monitor systemwide trends, project probable futures, and note the impact these trends and futures would have upon their preferred values. Sociologist and peace activist Robert L. Irwin sums up the world order methodology in his book, *Building a Peace System: A Book for Activists, Scholars, Students, and Concerned Citizens,* "Analysis is usually of what presently exists. Vision suggests what could come to exist in the future. Strategy is about the process of getting from the present to a desired future and implies planning of efforts overcoming obstacles."[11]

But in addition to inappropriate values, powerful elites and vested interests work against the adoption of a world order foreign policy. According to Richard Falk, "The ideal of a world community that is at the center of any approximation of [planetary] values is not a significant element of the political consciousness that guides the participation of most large-scale organizations (governments, corporations, international instiutions) in the present world order system."[12] "In general," Falk writes, "principal governmental actors will feel threatened by programs of drastic world order reform, and those reorientations of political consciousness heavily influenced by [world order] priorities."[13] Melvin Gurtov puts the problem with a simple question:

> How can the national interests of [the developed countries of the Western and Soviet blocs] be made to coincide with the global interests of humankind, when any erosion of the nation-state system will threaten those state and private interests that have, up to now, been the principal beneficiaries of the unequal global distribution of power?[14]

World order advocates have resolved this dilemma by "writing off" incumbent elites. Through carefully planned transition strategies, they seek to raise and change people's consciousness and develop a new core of "genuine leaders." This new elite would be drawn from the "oppressed segments" of societies (minorities, the poor, women, and the young) and members of counterculture groups (feminists, ecologists, greens, peace activists, members of committed religious communities).[15] According to Falk:

> In the end, transformation will depend on social forces that are unconscious bearers of new values attaining influence *and* a worldview. Hence, world order inquiry, the essence of normative international relations, needs to become attuned and receptive to the voices of the oppressed, as well as those who speak for those too weak or too poor to have a voice.[16]

Obviously, the goals and tasks set by world order advocates are monumental and complex, if not utopian. But the advocates of this worldview are neither naive nor utopian. They frankly acknowledge the challenges they face. In addition, they are quick to point to the impact that former "utopians" have made in a world of cynics—the passive resisters led by Mahatma Gandhi, the civil rights workers led by Martin Luther King, and the antiwar movement that brought an end to the war in Vietnam. Moreover, world order advocates are encouraged by the growing number of change-oriented social groups that have emerged in the past two decades—the greens in Western Europe, the supporters of a nuclear freeze in the United States, and the private, nongovernmental groups working throughout the Third World. Looking at such forces, Saul Mendlovitz sees hopeful signs. "It is clear," he writes, "that major changes are taking place in the global structures of the majority of the states of the world, including the most powerful."[17]

World order perspectives flourished in the 1970s as events and trends, some hopeful and some threatening, suggested possibilities for change within the bipolar international system. The Nixon administration disengaged from Vietnam, opened relations with China, and pursued detente and arms control with the Soviet Union. These acts, along with the postwar recovery of Western Europe and Japan and the rise of the Third World, foreshadowed a less cold war-driven international system.

At the same time, OPEC oil price rises, spiralling prices for other commodities vital to the industrialized countries, and dire predictions about the exponential depletion of nonrenewable resources spread fear among elites in the developed countries. In fact, some leaders in both the developed and developing countries believed that power was quickly falling to the developing world. At the same time, worldwide attention was also directed to environmental degradation, energy shortages, and famine in the developing areas.

In this atmosphere of fear and confusion for the developed countries, Third World nations asserted their majority status within the family of United Nations agencies. Politically, they targeted the seemingly intractable regional issues in the Middle East and Southern Africa. Economically, they demanded a New International Economic Order (NIEO), a New International Information Order (NIIO), and codes of conduct for multinational corporations, restrictive business practices, and the transfer of technology. In response to the biting rhetoric of Third World leaders, some elites in the developed countries proposed "planetary bargains," "sharing the world's product," and "a program for common survival."

The 1970s, then, were a time of great ferment, controversy, and new ideas. A new set of post–cold war issues had shot to the top of the international agenda, and the first three years of the Carter administration were largely dedicated to dealing with them. With the inauguration of the Reagan administration, the United States returned to the cold war agenda and shed the internationalist postures adopted by the Carter administration. Reagan sent Jeane Kirkpatrick to the United Nations to do battle against the Third World and the "maladies" they infused into the United Nations—double standards, politicizations, Orwellian newspeak, and collectivist schemes for regulating the world economy and redistributing the world's product. In addition, he sent strong symbolic messages to the developing nations by refusing to sign the Law of the Sea Treaty, by ignoring the Common Fund for Commodities, and by instructing his delegation to vote against the ban on infant formula adopted by the World Health Organization.

During the 1980s, world order perspectives went into eclipse. As the annotated bibliography at the end of the chapter indicates, most of the major works reflecting this worldview were written in the 1970s and the early 1980s. But with the decline of the cold war, transnational issues will increasingly fill the agenda of world politics, and on these issues, world order advocates have a great deal to say. Not surprisingly, world order essays and books are beginning to reappear, as the annotated bibliography at the end of the chapter indicates.[18]

Given the deteriorating situation presented in the quotation from the *State of the World Report*, it is not hard to see why some people exclaim that "what we need is world government." But even they may be overly optimistic. Someone surveying the world will be hard pressed to find a national government for the international system to emulate; in fact, this absence of "role models" may be precisely why some world order advocates talk about world *order* rather than world government. Thus, Richard Falk asserts that "we do not propose a transplant of national governmental structures into a global setting."[19]

Certainly, none of the governments of the larger developed or developing countries stands as a model for dealing *at the national level* with such issues as air and water pollution, energy efficiency, urban sprawl and blight, structural poverty and unemployment, waste management, and the maintenance of its infrastructure. To bring the issue close to home, could we really expect any world government to be more effective than the U.S. Congress, and is that the kind of world government we envisage?

But world government is a long way off. The real issue is whether states will move toward greater supranational governance of their affairs in general or whether they will deal with discrete global problems on an ad hoc basis. World order advocates clearly prefer the former, and their prospects for success depend upon the ability of change-oriented coalitions to place like-minded people in positions of political power. Significantly, the membership of such groups has increased phenomenally over the last twenty years both here and abroad.

Others who are more issue-oriented tend to be optimistic about an ad hoc approach. They claim that world order advocates tend to be alarmists who discount the ability of states to act when their self-interest requires it and technology makes such action possible. Tapani Vaahtoranta, author of the last selection in this chapter, argues that change-oriented groups, the self-interestedness of states, and available technology will all be necessary to make inroads into the problems facing mankind. But, as his case studies show, it remains unclear whether even these three factors will be enough. The question for incrementalists is whether ad hoc actions will merely be "too little, too late."

In the years ahead, we will see more and more international efforts to deal with the problems that preoccupy world order advocates. We will also get a chance to test the validity of their assumptions, their projections, their transition strategies, and their proposed solutions.

# The Selections

The first three readings will allow you to delve into some of the very best writings by world order proponents, while the last selection raises the prospects for reform within a moderated international system. After you have drawn your initial conclusions about the strengths and weaknesses of the world order perspective, you might want to read some of the more critical works listed in the bibliography.

You might also devise a response to the world order perspective from the vantage of one or more of the mainstream views. You should also compare and contrast the world order and radical worldviews. How would a radical respond to this perspective? Finally, unlike the mainstream worldviews, commitment to a world order perspective will entail significant changes in the way you live your life and the purposes that guide your life.

# 23. Louis Rene Beres
## *From Conflict to Cosmopolis: The World Order Imperative*
## 1984

In this selection, Louis Rene Beres attacks the basic premise of American foreign policy—"that a balance of power produces peace"—and advocates a foreign policy based upon a new definition of the national interest.

During the last year of his tenure as Secretary of State, Henry Kissinger remarked to the Council of Ministers of the Central Treaty Organization: "The fundamental principles of U.S. foreign policy have been constant for the past 30 years, through all administrations—and they will remain constant. The American people have learned the lessons of history."[1] This statement is markedly self-contradictory, for if the American people have indeed learned the "lessons of history," they would surely prevail upon their leaders to *undo* the constancy of American foreign policy.

These lessons, if they teach us anything at all, point up the futility of America's strategy of realpolitik, a strategy founded upon the very principles that have ensured the oblivion of other great states. To suggest otherwise is to ignore the fact that policies of power politics have never succeeded in producing either justice or security. Unless these policies are now rapidly and completely transformed, they will produce the most intolerable conditions the United States and the world have ever known.

To transform these policies in a manner that reflects genuine learning from lessons of the past, we must first recognize the false premises that continue to shape our search for a durable and just peace in world affairs. Differences in rhetoric and style notwithstanding, these premises, articulated by Henry Kissinger in 1976, are still at the core of U.S. foreign policy:

> Peace rests fundamentally on an equilibrium of strength. The United States will stand by its friends. It accepts no spheres of influence. It will not yield to pressure. It will continue to be a reliable partner to those who defend their freedom against foreign intervention or intimidation.[2]

Each of these premises is entirely untrue:

> There is absolutely no logical argument or historical evidence to support the contention that a "balance of power" produces peace.[3]

> The United States will certainly not "stand by its friends" if such support is apt to produce devastating military consequences, a distinct possibility in today's apocalyptic age.

> The United States has always accepted the idea of "spheres of influence" and cannot afford to reject this idea within the existing structure of world power.

> The United States will necessarily yield to pressure if the probable benefits of this course are judged to exceed the probable costs. To suggest otherwise would be to suggest irrational national leadership in the U.S. foreign policy establishment.

The United States will prove a "reliable partner" in defense of "freedom" only where such action is deemed consistent with the realpolitiker's assessment of national interest.

The United States, therefore, must begin to fashion its foreign policy behavior on a new set of premises, one consonant with the constraints of planetary conditions and the exigencies of national survival. Underlying these principles must be the understanding that this nation coexists with others on this endangered planet in a perilously fragile network of relationships. Racked by insecurities, poverty, and inequality, this network can no longer abide the conflictual dynamics that have shaped international relations since the sixteenth and seventeenth centuries.

Unless the United States, while it is still a preeminent (if not ascendant) power in the world, begins to understand that its own national interest must be defined from the standpoint of what is best for the world system as a whole, that interest will not be sustained. Instead, it will crumble along with the rest of a foreign policy edifice that is oblivious to its own self-destructive tendencies. Consider the following:

The nuclear arms race cannot last forever. In a world already shaped by some 6,000 years of organized warfare, it is hard to imagine that nuclear weapons will remain dormant amidst steadily accelerating preparations for nuclear war. Rather, the apocalyptic possibilities now latent in these weapons are almost certain to be exploited, either by design or by accident, by minsinformation or by miscalculation, by lapse from rational decision or by unauthorized decision.

Since the dawn of the Atomic Age, the search for security through destructive weaponry has led only to increased insecurity. Although the world's stockpile of nuclear weapons now represents an explosive force more than 5,000 times greater than all the munitions used in World War II, the expansion of superpower arsenals continues at a frantic pace. And in the United States this expansion is undertaken from a policy perspective that ties successful deterrence to a capacity to "fight" a nuclear war that might be "protracted."

The situation is further undermined by the ever-hardening dualism of U.S.-USSR relations and by the associated American tendency to cast all such relations in zero-sum terms. Although the period from the Cuban missile crisis (1962) to the present was marked by a conscious commitment, to avoid direct confrontations with the Soviet Union, there now seems to have developed an increased U.S. willingness to accept such confrontations as an essential requirement of rational competition in a decentralized world system. Moreover, wars have been increasing in frequency since 1945, from an average of nine a year in the 1950s to fourteen a year so far in the 1980s, a development that contributes to the likelihood of a direct conflict between the superpowers.[4]

There are also very serious problems with current U.S. foreign policy on human rights. Apart from this policy's disregard for moral and legal obligations, it is also contrary to our national interests. While this policy is cast in pragmatic terms, it should be apparent from the persistent failure of antecedent U.S. policies that it can never succeed.

In making anti-Sovietism the centerpiece of its policy on human rights, the United States has accepted an orientation to global affairs that is inherently self-defeating. During the next several years, the victims of U.S.-supported repression throughout the world will begin to overthrow their oppressors, creating successor governments with unquestionably anti-American leanings. In the fashion of Vietnam, Cuba, Nicaragua, and Iran, these governments will join the ever-expanding legion of states opposed to the United States. Sadly, this development will have been avoidable if only this country had remained true to its doctrinal foundations, opposing not only "leftist thugs" (President Reagan's characterization of the regime overthrown in Grenada) but all tyrannical regimes (that is, rightist thugs as well).

There has been no learning from lessons of the past. Although it is now perfectly clear that the Vietnam War might have been avoided if the United States had only understood the forces of revolutionary nationalism in the Third World, there is still no attempt to understand these forces. While it is now quite likely that early support for a still pro-American Ho Chi Minh rather than for his colonial masters might have created an ally instead of an adversary, the United States continues to advance its visceral counterrevolutionary ethos. What can this country hope to accomplish by standing alongside such pariah states as Chile and South Africa while unleashing forces to "destabilize" less repressive regimes? Whatever their deficiencies, these "totalitarian" regimes are spotless models of Jeffersonian democracy in contrast to the governments of our most "authoritarian" allies.

In considering these problems of United States foreign policy on nuclear strategy and human rights, we must also understand that they are interrelated. In one of the dominant ironies of the current situation, the presumed U.S. imperative to ignore human rights in anti-Soviet states as a requirement of national security makes nuclear war more likely. By its policy to align itself with right-wing juntas and other reactionary regimes, the United States enlarges the prospects for confrontation with the Soviet Union, either directly or by escalating involvement with surrogate forces. In Central America, for example, U.S. policies portend a transnational civil war, with authoritarian regimes and counterrevolutionary guerrillas backed by the United States fighting against leftist insurgents and revolutionary regimes backed by the Soviet Union.

With an understanding of these problems, this [essay] points the way from America's realpolitik orientation to foreign policy making toward a new definition of national interest. The United States must now do away with its long-standing adherence to an ethic of social Darwinism in world affairs. To accept this imperative would be to indicate genuine learning from lessons of the past. To do otherwise would be to capitulate to a developing planetary predicament with literally catastrophic qualities.

What is this developing planetary predicament? In the most general terms, it is a condition of widespread insecurity, poverty, alienation, injustice, ecological spoliation, and economic inequality. More specifically,

The global arms race continues at a very fast pace while the security of nations continues to erode.

The governments of the developing nations spend as much on military programs as on education and health care combined.

The United States and the Soviet Union, although still pre-eminent in terms of the instruments of violence, are steadily losing real *power*. They also lag behind many other nations in terms of principal indicators of social well-being.

The use of torture and other forms of repression by governments against selected segments of their populations continues to grow.

The rich states are getting richer while the poor states are getting poorer.

The global environment is being depleted and poisoned all the time.

The normative expectations of international law remain widely unsupported by the foreign policy conduct of virtually all major states.

This is only the tip of the iceberg. Should we begin to penetrate the anesthetized universe of international relations scholarship, we would discover an almost measureless degree of human pain and despair, a configuration of suffering that demands an indictment of the entire system of world political processes. Such an indictment is an essential precondition for creative planetary renewal.

How might such renewal actually be accomplished? To answer this question, we must first try to answer the following antecedent question;

What should be the future goal of American foreign policy?

Our goal must be nothing less than the erection of a new pattern of thinking that defines national interests in terms of strategies that secure and sustain the entire system of states. By supplanting competitive self-seeking with cooperative self-seeking, the United States can move forward to the kind of global renaissance that is so desperately needed. By building upon the understanding that it is in America's best interest to develop its foreign policy from a systemic vantage point, our national leaders can begin to match the awesome agenda of world order reform with viable strategies of response. We require, in the final analysis, a policy that is based on the reaffirmation of humane purposes and the creation of a respected framework of international cooperation.

Such a policy has never been tried. With its membership in the United Nations, the United States has done little to move beyond the Westphalian dynamics of competition and conflict. Although it is certainly true that the UN Charter goes much further than the League of Nations Covenant in formalizing the replacement of self-help with the centralized determination and application of sanctions, this change has had no meaningful effect on the calculations and preference-maximizing behavior of states. For all intents and purposes, law continues to follow power in the United Nations and the organization itself remains an institutional reflection of the prevailing pattern of influence. The state of nations is still the state of nature.

Even so, much can be done to improve upon this condition. For the United States as well as for the rest of the world, survival requires a renunciation of the "everyone for himself" principle. It is no longer possible to describe as "realistic" a foreign policy that is at cross-purposes with the spirit of systemic well-being. The impersonal logic of possessive individualism is at odds with the imperatives of national and international life.

To illustrate the argument for transforming competitive inclinations to foreign policy into cooperative ones, consider the following analogy: The nations in world politics coexist in the fashion of herdsmen who share a common pasture and who feel it advantageous to increase the size of their respective herds. Although these herdsmen have calculated that it is in their own best interests to augment their herds, they have calculated incorrectly. This is the case because they have failed to consider the *cumulative effect* of their calculations, which happens to be an overgrazed commons and economic ruin.

In the manner of herdsmen in this analogy, American foreign policy elites continue to act as if the security of the state is coincident with national military power. Like the herdsmen, these elites fail to understand the cumulative effects of such reasoning, leading the nation and the rest of the world away from the intended condition of peace and security. Blithely unaware that its outmoded strategy of realpolitik is strikingly unrealistic, the American search for an improved power position inevitably generates a pattern of antagonisms that hinders rather than helps the search for an improved world order.

Consider still one more analogy. The nations in world politics are prone to act in the manner of an audience in a crowded movie theater after someone has yelled "Fire!" Confronted with a sudden emergency, each member of the audience calculates that the surest path to safety is a mad dash to the nearest exit. The cumulative effect of such calculations, however, is apt to be far worse than if the members of the audience had relied on some sort of cooperative plan for safety.

In the fashion of the movie audience, the United States continues to misunderstand that its only safe course is one in which its own well-being and security are determined from the standpoint of what is believed best for the world system as a whole. The path to security that is founded upon the presumed benefits of preeminence is destined to fail. If we want peace, then we must prepare for peace, not for war.

How might such preparations be accomplished? Most importantly, the United States must cease its tendency to identify national security with conditions that undermine the entire system of states. This tendency is itself derived from an underlying and overwhelming egoism, a national incapacity to imagine the total annihilation of the United States.

E.M. Cioran, who speaks in the tradition of Kierkegaard, Nietzsche, and Wittgenstein, said, "Nature has been generous to none but those she has dispensed from thinking about death." In this he is only partly correct. Although it is true, as Freud noted, that "It is indeed impossible to imagine our own death,"[5] it is an effort that must be attempted. While some repression of the fear of death may be essential to happiness and well-being, it can—where it is too "successful"—make extinction more imminent. Similarly, states can impair their prospects for survival by insulating themselves from reasonable fears of collective disintegrations.

American leaders must take heed. There are more things in heaven and earth than are dreamt of in their philosophy.

But what, exactly, are these "things"? What can actually be done to bring about the desired condition? How can the United States reroute its narrowly self-interested mode of foreign policy activity to a more promising global orientation? How can American leaders begin to build upon the understanding that it is in this country's own best interests to develop strategies of international interaction from a systemic vantage point?

Heraclitus tells us that: "Men who love wisdom must enquire into very many things" (Fragment 49). Following this advice, the United States must begin to inquire into the ways in which a more secure and just system of world order might be obtained. Ultimately, this inquiry must direct our national leaders to an appropriate reversal of current policy directions on the major issues of world politics: the issues of nuclear strategy and human rights.

Should we fail in the obligation to sustain and dignify human life on this planet, it will be because of a failure to recognize *ourselves* as the proper locus of responsibility. The idea that humankind produces its own misfortunes has endured for millennia. Aeschylus, Homer, and Hesiod were convinced that humankind's disregard for wisdom accounts for its history as a continuous bath of blood. Such disregard, at the core of human wrongdoing, spawns a sea of ruin, fathomless and impassable. In such a sea, comments the King of Argos in *The Spanish Maidens*, "Nowhere is there a haven from distress."

The Greek idea of fate does not imply the absence of human control over events but an inevitable penalty for failing to cultivate justice and peace. Understood in terms of the American responsibility for a more harmonious system of planetary political life, this idea suggests a willingness to seize the initiative for survival while there is still time. Vitalized by genuine knowledge rather than the desolate clairvoyance of realpolitik, the United States could then confront the dying world of apocalyptic militarism and repression with wisdom and hope. . . .

Today the leaders of the United States are not content with despising the spirit of the Age of Reason, the spirit that gave birth to their country. They also find it necessary to execrate it as a source of impiety. As a result they have fostered a spirit of realpolitik that goes far beyond the bounds of an earlier ancient pattern of reluctant pragmatism. In this spirit the perceived interests of the United States *are* the ultimate value, even though their lack of congruence with worldwide interests renders them self-destructive. A stand-in for the deity, this nation is now taken as a Godhead of which everything is anticipated, a self-proclaimed overseer of an unrelated global society.

Before this situation can be changed, the United States must begin to act upon entirely different principles of international relations, principles that are based not on the misdirected ideas of geopolitical competition but upon the spirit of cooperation. To make this possible, our leaders will need to understand that realpolitik proves its own insubstantiality, that it is an unrealistic principle whose effects are accentuated by the steady sacralizing of the state.

To begin to act in its own interests as well as in the interests of the world as a whole (since they are inextricably intertwined), the United States should draw upon the wisdom of Hugo Grotius, the seventeenth century classical writer on international law. Accepting the existence of law outside and above the state, Grotius understood that purposeful international relations cannot be based on relations of pure force. Although coexisting without an all-powerful authority above them, states must learn to regard themselves as members of a true society, one warranted by the overriding imperatives of justice and natural law. These principles are of the highest utility, and the community of states can never be preserved in their absence.

In the *Leviathan*, Chapter 13, Hobbes offers his well-known description of interstate relations:

> Kings and persons of sovereign authority, because of their independency, are in continual jealousies, and in the state and posture of gladiators; their forts and garrisons, and guns upon the frontiers of their kingdoms, and continual spies upon their neighbors; which is a posture of war.

It need not follow from this description, however, that to improve upon its position in this dreadful condition of war (by which Hobbes does not necessarily mean actual fighting, but rather "the known disposition thereto . . ." or cold war), each state must act in disregard of the common interest. Although there exists no "common power" to harmonize relations between them, states can learn to understand that their safety and long-term interests are tied to compliance with certain norms of global cooperation. There is, moreover, nothing utopian about such an idea; rather, as Grotius understood, a cooperative legal system amid the conditions of juristic equality is not only imaginable, but essential: "That as soon as we recede from the Law, there is nothing that we can certainly call ours."

With this understanding, states are urged to act on the basis of binding obligations in their relations with each other *in their own interests*. The United States must not be paralyzed by uncertainty over the probable reciprocity of the other states, by the fear that its own compliance with the normative obligations concerning peace and human rights will not be paralleled by other members of the community of states. This is the case . . . because the benefits of cooperative action in this community are no longer contingent on the expectation of a broad pattern of compliance. Since the prospect of a catastrophic end within the extant dynamic of realpolitik is so very likely, U.S. action according to world order imperatives would meet the criteria of rational action whatever the expected responses of other major states.

We should not assume, however, that U.S. initiative toward world order would most likely go unimitated. If we can assume that leaders of other major states are also aware of the urgency of planetary conditions, their rational response to U.S. initiatives might well be far-reaching acts of reciprocity. Should such acts begin to take place, a new and infinitely more hopeful pattern of interaction could supplant the lethal lure of primacy, a pattern that could serve U.S. interests and ideals simultaneously. Should such acts fail to materialize, the net effect of U.S. initiatives would still be gainful, since nothing could be more futile than continuing on the present collision course.

In the beginning, in that primal promiscuity wherein the swerve toward power politics occurred, the forerunners of modern states established a system of struggle and competition that can never succeed. Still captivated by this system, the United States allows the spirit of realpolitik to spread, further and further, like a gangrene upon the surface of the earth. Rejecting all standards of correct reasoning, this spirit cannot impose limits upon itself. It continues to be rife despite its rebuffs; it takes its long history of defeats for conquests; it has never "learned" anything.

The United States now has a last opportunity to confront the spirit of realpolitik as a long-misguided design for action and to witness the eclipse of this spirit with jubilation. In the absence of such a confrontation, the time will come when future civilizations, such as they might be, will examine the skeletal remains of the last prenuclear war epoch with a deserved sneer. Thrashing about in the paleontology of international relations, they will get the impression that the flesh of this epoch was fetid upon its advent, that in any meaningful sense it never existed at all, that it was a cosmetic disguise that masked nothing.

## NOTES

1. Speech at opening of CENTO meeting, May 26, 1976, London, p. 1.
2. Ibid., p. 3.
3. Although the balance of power appears to have offered two relatively peaceful periods in history, the ones beginning with the Peace of Westphalia and the Congress of Vienna, the hundred-year interval between the Napoleonic Wars and the First World War was actually a period of frequent wars in Europe. The fact that the balance of power has been disastrously ineffective in producing peace during our own century hardly warrants mention. Moreover, the current preoccupation with "balance" in nuclear forces between the superpowers is certainly misconceived, since balance has nothing to do with credible deterrence. Historically, of course, a balance-of-power system was ushered in with the Peace of Westphalia in 1648, and has been with us ever since. The basic dynamics of this system were reaffirmed at the Peace of Utrecht in 1713, the Congress of Vienna in 1815, and the two World War settlements. Strictly speaking, neither the League of Nations nor the United Nations can qualify as a system of collective security. Rather, both are examples of international organization functioning within a balance-of-power world. As for world government, even the case of Imperial Rome does not, strictly speaking, fulfill the appropriate criteria, since the extent of its jurisdiction was coextensive with only a portion of the entire world.
4. These assessments are supported by recent empirical work in the field. For example, in his very refined deductive theory about war, Bruce Bueno de Mesquita offers data that suggest a strong relationship between the level of risk that national leaders are willing to accept and the consequent likelihood of war. See his book *The War Trap* (New Haven, Conn.: Yale University Press, 1981).

5. See Freud's "Thoughts for the Times on War and Death," in James Strachey, ed., *The Complete Psychological Works of Sigmund Freud*, standard ed. (London, The Hogarth Press, 1953), vol. 14, p. 289.

## 24. Richard Falk
### *Toward a New Order: Modest Methods and Drastic Visions*
### 1975

In 1975, Richard Falk published *A Study of Future Worlds*, the most comprehensive world order scheme to have appeared in the postwar period. This selection is drawn from a bare bones abridgement of Falk's ideas, which appeared in Saul Mendlovitz's anthology, *On the Creation of a Just World Order: Preferred Worlds for the 1990s*.[20] If this excerpt whets your appetite, you might want to read Falk's 485-page book!

## INTRODUCTORY COMMENTS

The basic objective of this essay is to put forward a vision of a new, improved system of world order that could come about by the end of the century.

These proposals are not predictions. On the contrary, we seek to provide an intellectual framework capable of guiding efforts to realign the predicted future with a specifically depicted preferred future. At this time in human history a world-order movement is needed to overcome the basic drift of the present world-order system, based on the primacy of sovereign states, toward positions of danger, a general deterioration, and an uncertain prospect of disaster. We believe the sooner such a movment built around these concerns takes shape in the principal societies of the world, the better the prospects for constructive human interventions in the decades ahead.

At present, world-order reform movements must operate mainly within the limited arenas of principal states and select regions, building transnational and global links in only the most preliminary and haphazard fashion. Only now do we see the first glimmerings of a genuinely global movement for world-order reform, one impetus for which is arising from the continuing efforts of the World Order Models Project (WOMP). Such a movement requires an agreed ideology, and the United States section of WOMP (WOMP/USA) hopes to provide such an ideological statement. It should be noted here that ideology is being used in an affirmative sense to denote a body of thought relevant to the pursuit of a series of explicit social, political, and economic goals.

The label world order causes difficulties. To some it is too idealistic, suggesting a kind of dreamy utopianism; hence, in this view, world-order studies are irrelevant to practical men of action and influence in the real world. To others, for almost opposite reasons, the phrase is mere rhetoric, associated with appeals for world order that are routinely worked into Law Day proclamations by power-wielders who scarcely bother to disguise their hypocrisy. To still others, talk of world order sounds uncomfortably similar in spirit to domestic promises of law and order; it is the serious talk of the powerful who seek higher budgets for police departments to keep the poor and the weak in line, to find instruments to control disorder, and to discourage demands for change.

In WOMP we support major reforms of the world political system capable of contributing to the prospects for peace, social and economic well-being, human dignity, and environmental quality. This conception of world-order reform concentrates upon a search for political, social, and economic arrangements that will achieve these four goals as fully as possible. In this phase of WOMP we have emphasized the prospects for *structural reform* that might reasonably be achieved *by the end of the century.* WOMP/USA has shaped its inquiry to avoid some weaknesses of world-order studies in the past. In this regard three features of our inquiry may be identified: *systemic scope, normativity,* and *orientation to the future.*

## SYSTEMIC SCOPE

By systemic scope we mean a genuinely global orientation that serves as a basis for disciplined inquiry; we do not propose a transplant of national governmental structures into a global setting. Hence it is possible and desirable to consider a range of structural arrangements in relation to our world-order goals. Indeed, throughout this effort we seek to reconcile notions of planetary guidance as the nexus of a new system of world order, with wide dispersals of power and authority based on minimum bureaucratic build-ups and maximum human participation at every level of social organization.

## NORMATIVITY

The success or failure of a world-order system—whether past, present, or future—depends on its capacity to promote the realization of the four WOMP goals. In this sense a world-order system is not necessarily valued because it achieves peace unless it also makes sufficiently important contributions to the reduction of poverty, repression, and pollution. We seek a system of world order that is peaceful, just and protective of the ecosphere, and in this search we are concerned with man's relations over various time horizons as well as across national boundaries. A world-order system must hence heed the claims of future generations, especially in relation to the use of scarce and finite resources, but also with respect to the preservation of our cultural and natural heritage.

## ORIENTATION TO THE FUTURE

World-order inquiry needs to be concerned with grasping the predicted and probable future; a careful study of trend projections is part of the developing field of world-order studies. At the same time, futurology should not be regarded as a substitute for speculation and appraisal, nor should the work of futurology be conducted according to the characteristics of computers and other high-status technological apparatus. We need to *envision* the future as well as to *project* it, and hence the energies of the imagination are at least as relevant as the printouts of the computer.

The essence of our project for global reform involves shifts in political consciousness (value change), mobilization of energies for action (active politics), and the transformation of structures (building the preferred world order of the future). In very schematic terms we can correlate these three phases with time zones:

1970s: The Decade of Consciousness Raising [$t_1$]

1980s: The Decade of Mobilization [$t_2$]

1990s: The Decade of Transformation [$t_3$]

Of course the three stages are not so mutually exclusive or temporally precise as this sequence seems to suggest. Consciousness-raising needs to persist throughout the entire transition process, transformation begins now for certain issues such as ocean resources and environmental protection, and mobilization will have to go on during the whole process. Nevertheless, we believe it helpful to suggest a model of transition based on a series of stages, provided that each stage is understood as a matter of tactical priority and that its duration of a decade is understood more as a metaphor than a prediction.

We should also make it plain that the work of world-order reform will never end. We are seeking a substantially improved system of world order by 2000, not its perfection. Indeed, the integrity of any human society depends on its capacity to keep re-envisioning a preferred future; human fulfillment presupposes an ongoing *process* of moral growth that influences individual and collective aspects of existence. Past conceptions of a preferred system of world order have seemed dreary, in part because they tend to presuppose a stoppage of history, a perfection so complete that no improvement thereafter was needed or sought, in effect the creation of a *closed political system*. The WOMP/USA models of future systems of world order are decisively *open*, and a sense of political realism indicates to us that even the most successful world-order movement can do no more than begin the work of realizing the planetary potential for human development by devising beneficial arrangements of organizing power and authority as our generation now perceives them.

A first step toward commitment to drastic and mainly nonviolent world-order reform is to build a consensus about the properties of a preferred world-order system that could be attained by relatively peaceful means in the next few decades, quite conceivably by 2000. Thus, we need representative statements of world-order positions—the shape of a preferred world and the tactics and strategies of transition—from different ideological, regional, development, cultural and personal perspectives. It is very likely that at the present time such representative statements can be most usefully prepared by those without deep-seated attachment to the existing world order.

Those with views and values at variance with the prevailing world-order consensus need to be particularly imaginative and dedicated to obtain a fair hearing. Governmental efforts all over the world to induce media to conform to official ideology suggest the difficulty facing those who seek to promote changes in the state system by peaceful means. Without communication within the large states and across their boundaries, it is very difficult to offset the official manipulation of human desires and beliefs and thereby loosen the regressive hold of vested economic, political, and social interests on the human imagination. We therefore attach great importance to securing national and international protection for civil liberties to facilitate the internal and transnational mobility of ideas.

In this connection also, prospects for consciousness-raising depend on the degree to which a new conception of world order begins to attract domestic and transnational support. In the years ahead a primary priority for world-order education is to assure that domestic, change-oriented, progressive elites understand the relevance of the larger world setting to their more specific and local programs of reforms. Thus movements associated with the status of women, minority rights, labor reform, population policy, environmental protection, and consumer protection need to be linked to an interpretation of the total world order and its dangers and deficiencies, and to be made part of the emergent debate about a direction and program of response. Such a domestic emphasis—complemented because of the nature of interdependence by a transnational emphasis—reflects the judgment that proposals for reform of the world-order system should take account of the present realities of power and authority. The continuing global dominance of national governmental actors, reinforced by domestic economic and social leaders, is the proper starting-point for any analysis of prospects for world-order reform. *Without substantially changing the orientation of these leadership groups (governmental and nongovernmental) there is no realistic hope either for adjustments (except in a post-catastrophe period) to the hazards of the present world order or for use of the opportunities for transition and reform. . . .*

In world-order speculation we also, as a traveller with a tight schedule and a fixed budget and some keen curiosities, have constraints and biases that condition our approach. To orient the approach, we enumerate those biases that seem relevant:

We should like to bring the new system into being by the year 2000 or shortly thereafter.

We should like to reach our destination without relying on violence or intimidation.

We should like to make the shifts in organization and priorities result from preference rather than necessity.

On a more concrete level such a world-order budget places a premium on limiting expectations. We cannot hope to achieve all our goals by the year 2000, assuming survival without catastrophe until then, even if developments are very favorable. We might however reach a world-order destination that overcomes the worst features of the present situation and initiates a process of change that builds momentum in the direction of further positive developments.

The first leg of the journey is long and difficult, beset with dangers, uncertainties, and adversaries; the odds of getting through do not seem high. World-order expectations involve a comprehensive response to rising danger and deepening decay in the present context. Our concerns can be enumerated:

The planet is too crowded and is getting more so.

The war system is too destructive, risky, and costly and is getting more so.

An increasingly large number of people live at or below the level of subsistence.

Pressure on the basic ecosystem of the planet is serious and growing, as is the more tangible pollution of air, water, and land.

Governing groups in many socieites are repressing their own people in an intolerable manner.

Human and material resources of the planet are wasted and depleted in a shortsighted way, and at increasing rates.

Technologies are not adequately managed to assure planetary and human benefit.

On the basis of these concerns we seek by the end of the century, a world system that:

achieves and moves beyond the norm of zero population growth;

moves toward dismantling the war system, including putting into effect a plan for drastic disarmament;

moves toward a world economic system in which each individual is assured the right to the minimum requirements of body, mind, and spirit and in which food, clothing, housing, education, health, and work are regarded as collective as well as personal responsibilities;

moves toward an integrated and coherent system of dynamic equilibrium so far as human impacts on the biosphere are concerned;

achieves and moves beyond a minimum bioethical code based on human survival, planetary habitability, and species diversity;

moves toward a conservation policy that is sensitive to the life chances of future human generations and protective of natural wonders and species diversity;

achieves an effective system of global oversight on the side-effects of technological innovation.

Although these objectives are extremely ambitious, they are mainly designed to plug leaks and improve man's prospects of survival. These reforms are designed to overcome the worst features and tendencies of the present world system and stabilize the results without discouraging further world-order reform. We expect the shape of the relevant utopia for the first generation of reformers of the twenty-first century, assuming prior realization of WOMP goals, will involve liberating people from various sorts of bondage—work, mores, anxieties—so that more and more of them can participate more fully in a life of dignity, joy, and creativity that mobilizes the full energies of self-development. Putting this sense of potentiality differently, we believe that on the average human beings are now able to make use of 5 percent or so of their potential for development and that our preferred world-order system might reasonably expect to raise the average to 20 percent or so, but the challenge and opportunity will remain immense after our initial program of world order reform has been completed. In this first phase, WOMP/USA is seeking to deal only with the establishment of *minimum preconditions* for tolerable human existence, free from high risks of catastrophe and misery.

Our focus is on the *organizational framework* of collective human existence. We believe it will be necessary to modify the present structure of world order, but that it will be possible only after a considerable effort of persuasion, planning, and mobilization in the principal parts of the planet. One ingredient of this effort involves the design of the sort of organizational framework that will realize our minimum goals and support the continuing pursuit of the objectives of personal development.

To economize on space and focus response we shall rely on some visual representations of design structures for new world-order systems. The rationale of our preferred system will become clearer in the exposition of the transition strategy in the next section, but at least its principal properties may be indicated at this point in the discussion.

We begin with several general considerations:

First, conventional world-order thinking has tended to proceed on the basis of a stark alternative between virtual anarchy and virtual world government. We seek to explore the *numerous* intermediate world-order *options*, as well as the many variants of world government and anarchy.

Second, our design of a system is put forward as a tentative sketch that will be frequently revised as the world-order building process unfolds. It is therefore misleading and trivial to make highly detailed institutional proposals, which would exhibit *the fallacy of premature specification.*

Third, our design of a preferred world system is not confined to *external linkages* of principal actors but also encompasses the *internal linkages* of national governments to substructures and to the population as a whole, thereby reflecting the hypothesis that a progressive world order is not reconcilable with regressive systems of domestic order, at least in principal societies.

Fourth, our design is intended to convey a sense of *organizational pattern* rather than embody *precise measurements* of relative actor roles and capability.

Fifth, preferred organizational solutions will involve simultaneous dialectical movements towards *centralization* and *decentralization* of authority within and among states. . . .

## WOMP/USA: THE PREFERRED MODEL

In Figure 7.1 we indicate the table of organization for the central guidance system that is entrusted with general functions of coordination and oversight. The specific allocation of institutional roles is discussed elsewhere, but it should be emphasized that the degree of bureaucratic complexity apparent in the diagram does not entail either a highly bureaucratized or hierarchical arrangement of functions and powers. Instead, the high degree of differentiation among institutions seeks to combine considerations of efficiency arising from specialization with the diffusion of authority designed to invigorate a network of checks and balances within the central guidance framework. The institutional arrangement seeks to embody the value priorities underlying proposals for world-order reform as put forward by WOMP/USA.

The basic conception of our preference model is that considerations of what is possible by 2000 suggests a dual emphasis on macrofunctional potentialities and on the trade-off between global managerial build-ups and partial dismantling of national bureaucracies. In essence we anticipate the centralized administration of many realms of human activity—health, environmental protection, money, business operations, ocean and space use, disarmament, disaster relief, peace-keeping and peaceful settlement, and resource conservation. These superagencies will enjoy competence only in relation to their functional domain. Augmented international political institutions less tied to the state system will attempt to assure that normative priorities are upheld and that various functional activities are coordinated. As is any other political mechanism, it will be vulnerable to whatever deficiencies exist with regard to the intensity and clarity of the underlying consensus shaped around WOMP values during the transition process.

Constitutional mechanisms will attempt to mediate between concerns for efficiency and dignity. There will be checks and balances, as wide a participation in decisional processes as feasible, procedural opportunities for review, a code of restraints designed to safeguard diversity, autonomy, and creativity, and a minimization of the bureaucratic role.

The WOMP/USA preference model also allocates authority between the

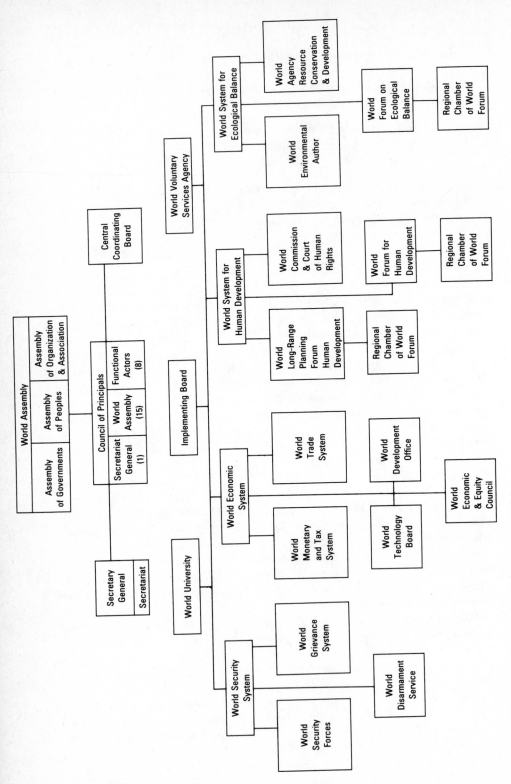

Figure 7.1 Central guidance in the preference model.

global and regional levels to a considerable extent. This allocation reflects a commitment to diversify control arrangements, to limit centralizing tendencies to real functional requirements, and to offset the decline of the state system in as balanced a fashion as possible.

# THE PLAN FOR TRANSITION TO WOMP/USA

The idea of planned transition during $t_1$ [the 1970s] should be approached as systematically as possible. We indicate a $t_1$ framework as well as a series of suitable proposals. Here again our effort is to illustrate and provisionally prescribe in relation to a commitment to realize $S_{2(WOMP/USA)}$. In essence, we are suggesting first steps. One of the features of this kind of world-order analysis is that it takes action possibilities as seriously as it takes intellectual speculation. There must be a continuous audit of action initiatives and a corresponding willingness to revise the concept and substance of planned transition and of the preference model. Although we locate $S_0$ late in $S_1$ we do not believe that the world setting is at all conducive as yet to voluntary or contractual transition procedures designed to bring about any positive variant of $S_2$, including our preferred arrangement $S_{2(WOMP/USA)}$.

In $t_1$ our emphasis is on changing value priorities within existing centers of decision and control, especially with respect to government operation in principal national societies. Such an undertaking depends on some degree of ideological space in the domestic arena. It may not be possible now to envision relevant reorientations of consciousness in the more *closed* societies of the world, and we may expect even the more *open* socieities to experience pressure as a consequence of value challenges. The Nixon Administration's efforts to intimidate the media were partly a defensive reaction against a very fundamental set of pressures for change. We believe, however, that until principal domestic arenas are significantly more receptive to WOMP goals, the prospects for planned transition to $S_2$ by voluntary means are minimal. In this setting of uncertainty and limited opportunity there are several critical forms of activity that bear on transition prospects during this initial phase of $t_1$. These activities are approached from the time-space locus of the United States in the mid-1970s and are organized around our broader conception of the transition path to WOMP/USA: Consciousness $\rightarrow$ Mobilization $\rightarrow$ Transformation. As we are dealing with early efforts in $t_1$, the most important payoffs are likely to involve consciousness-raising activities.

To depict the range of our interests we provide some illustrations, some consciousness-raising tactics and programs:

*1. World-Order Education.* There is a surge of energy in many settings to provide a more convincing account of man's place in the world and of the relation between national well-being and global community. There is a decline of interest in conceiving of world politics purely as an arena for power manipulation and in thinking of global idealism purely in terms of peace. There has evolved a more richly conceived interpretation of social, political, and economic factors that encourages a more comprehensive view of global reform. Many distinct orientations toward world-order studies are being developed. We are already at the stage of allowing a hundred flowers to bloom. Many of these initiatives share globalist, futurist, and reformist goals and thereby share an opposition to an earlier kind of consensus built around nationalism and the war system. As $t_1$ proceeds, this kind of education revolution is likely to produce a consensus in many national societies and transnational arenas on what is wrong, what is to be done, and what are the most efficient and humane means available. World-order education in all its forms is likely to provide the entire base for the consciousness-raising enterprise of $t_1$ and to incorporate within itself other notable coordinate developments.

2. *Apollo Vision.* Informing images shape and orient consciousness. To the extent that the Apollo program portrays the earth as an island spinning in space, it conveys a sense of the earth's wholeness and finiteness. By comparison, state boundaries seem artificial and unnatural, although existentially more relevant categories of neighborhood, nationality, race, or religion might not. In $t_1$ the growth of cross-cutting personal affiliations across and within sovereign states could help shape identity patterns receptive to $S_{2(WOMP/USA)}$. An Apollo-type space program usefully connects developments on the technological frontier with at least covert support for a new globalism. Despite the end of the Apollo program, space activities have enormous educational potency with respect to earth activities. Space probes of various sorts provide a dramatic focus of human endeavor, which can be shared through satellite TV by the whole world. Unlike more obvious consciousness-raising efforts, the Apollo world-view penetrates the living-rooms of mainstream America. We may yet discover that the real payoff from American tax dollars devoted to the Apollo program arises from their contribution to the growth of a human identity that is both planetary and species-wide and accepts as fundamental the solidarity of all humans, rather than to deepening cosmological insights derived from samplings of moon dust.

3. *The Drift of the Counter-Culture.* It is difficult at this time to assess the impact, the duration, or even the eventual main orientations of counter-cultural tendencies such as expressed in "The Woodstock Nation," the drug culture, *The Greening of America*, the Jesus People, women's liberation, gay liberation, and the new utopians. These youth-dominated reevaluations of American culture stand in stark contrast to statist values, especially as embodied in the governing ideology of the Nixon era. The essence of the counter-cultural resistance is antagonism to technocracy, statism, and moralism. In this sense, the counter-culture leads toward self-definition, self-evolved and experimental personalities, communes, communities, and communication. Implicit in this movement—which has many factions and cross-currents—is a reverence for nature and an antipathy toward artifact and artifice. Also implicit in its embrace of Oriental cultural forms is a significant transnationalism, shaping new belief systems dissociated from the history and traditions of any single nation and especially alien to the ethos of a western industrial nation. Whether the counterculture takes sufficient hold to stimulate a second effort to assert its central claims remains an open question, but the potentiality is there to infuse

those who reject the technocratic and necrophilic drift of American society for a much more life-oriented vision of a new world order. This counter-cultural constituency might yet become an important activist force in promoting a movement for $S_{2(WOMP/USA)}$.

4. *The Limits-to-Growth Debate.* In 1972 publication of two studies caused a major stir: *Blueprint for Survival* by the editors of the British magazine *The Ecologist*, and *The Limits to Growth* by an team of scholars from the Massachusetts Institute of Technology headed by Dennis Meadows and commissioned by the Club of Rome. Both documents emphasized the incompatibility between the growth dynamics of industrial civilization and the prospects for human survival at tolerable levels. Neither document reflected world-order thinking, although the clear implication of the limits-to-growth hypothesis is the need for an increased capacity for planetary coordination and management, which in turn presupposes either centralized domination or a more modest capacity for central guidance combined with globalist orientations in principal state actors.

The limits-to-growth debate has stimulated widespread controversy about the viability of the existing system of world order. The alarmist interpretation of growth dynamics has not yet prevailed, but it has eroded conventional wisdom about the desirability of indefinite and unregulated growth and, more importantly, has set the stage for the presentation of further evidence that pressures on the limited capacities of the earth are crossing dangerous, possibly irreversible, thresholds. Just as the breakup of the Torrey Canyon in 1967 was the Hiroshima of the ecological age, further disasters of an environmental character will strengthen sentiments supporting a movement for drastic world-order reform.

5. *Free-Flow Ethos: Ideas and Men.* The technology of broadcasting, the ease of travel, the moderation of great-power rivalry, and the universal endorsement of minimum human rights and cultural exchange programs are among the factors favorable to the free flow of ideas and people. We believe that the freest possible mobility of ideas and people will diminish further nationalist inhibitions about world-order reform. The virtual abandonment of passport and customs control in intra-European travel represents a further significant reduction in the symbolic and substantive relevance of national boundaries and hence in national identities. In general, diffusion of reformist thinking might help stimulate convergent demands from distinct regions of the globe, providing the sort of premobilization consensus that must accompany the passage from $t_1$ to $t_2$ [the 1980s].

6. *The Prometheus Project.*[1] The physicist Gerald Feinberg has pointed to the need for a major attempt to reinvigorate ethical inquiries in response to some very fundamental technological developments—artificial (computer) intelligence and genetic engineering, for example. Feinberg argues that these developments will have a profound impact on human nature and social organization and that we should try to forecast these probable impacts to be in a position to control them.

From a somewhat different perspective Van Rensellaer Potter argues that a new code of behavior based on a bioethical orientation that regards human survival as the prime ethical value is needed.[2] Potter's argument rests on the belief that society is now organized in a bioethically regressive manner as a consequence of various outmoded patterns of belief and behavior.

A still different ethical perspective derives from the Nuremberg idea. This perspective rests on the view that all individuals and groups everywhere have a responsibility to oppose governmental crimes of war. In a sense the Nuremberg precedent arising from the World War II war-crimes trials is inverted. Instead of serving accusatory purposes as it has in the past, it becomes the foundation for individual responsibility. Even the war-crimes circumference is not a rigid boundary. One can easily imagine the Nuremberg idea expanded to provide an ethical underpinning for citizen resistance to all forms of governmental wrongdoing wherever they occur. This idea builds transnational bonds, e.g Canadian citizens and officials have a responsibility to oppose American crimes of war in Indochina. Olaf Palme, Prime Minister of Sweden, assumed a measure of such responsibility when, in defiance of intergovernmental decorum, he denounced U.S. policies of warfare in Indochina as ecocidal at the UN Conference on the Human Environment held in Stockholm in June 1972.

These new directions in personal ethics are part of a broader questioning of traditional patterns of authority and belief. To the extent that this questioning is intensified by the crisis of legitimacy experienced by the state it is part of an inchoate movement for the kind of world-order reform WOMP supports, even if such ethical reevaluation is not so understood by its adepts.

7. *Progressive Governmental Actors.*    In $t_1$ the main consciousness-raising contexts will be nongovernmental, if not antigovernmental in character; there may be indirect, unintentional contributions to transition within main governmental arenas as considered in Step 2 in relation to the Apollo vision. In general, however, principal governmental actors will feel threatened by programs of drastic world-order reform and those reorientations of political consciousness heavily influenced by WOMP priorities.

An exception to this pattern may be governments in small to medium-sized countries that have enjoyed a considerable period of stable rule, have been independent over a long span of time, and have largely eliminated domestic social injustice. Sweden, Norway, and Canada are typical states in this category. A second exception may be some governments in the Third World which have not betrayed their idealistic vision of human and societal potentiality: although there is room for controversy as to a partiuclar case, China and Tanzania seem to belong in this category. These classifications are provisional, as governments and their outlooks may change rapidly in either direction under the pressure of events, including policy conflicts within their own ruling groups.

The main point, however, is that these kinds of governmental actors may themselves assess the need for world-order reform in realistic terms and begin to challenge ingrained patterns of statist logic by their words and deeds within the principal international arenas of the world. Should these challenges coincide with the domestic liberalization of governmental outlook in Japan, the Soviet Union, the United States, and Western Europe, they might create a significant awareness of and support for a program of international reforms responsive to WOMP values, especially with respect to the war system. In this regard governmental arenas might become agents of transition rather than centers of resistance. In the years ahead it is important to disseminate a credible conception of planned transition to $S_2$ so that leaders of opinion in moderate and progressive states are encouraged to consider world-order reform as a practical project for politics and politicians.

   *8. Multinational Corporate Globalism.*   Many large multinational corporate actors are seeking to establish an *anational* or global identity for themselves. The search for such an identity is connected with, first, an effort to avoid neoimperialist stigmatization associated with foreign capital; second, creation of a global milieu as supportive as possible of corporate expansion; third, avoidance of regulatory and safety standards of rich countries, as well as their wage and employment policies. Thus, the self-interest of multinational actors seems to support a globalist thrust, a movement for world-order reform that diminishes the role of state actors. . . .

   As we have suggested, there are two contrary tendencies in multinational corporate development. The large multinational corporation may seek to mobilize the apparatus of the state to protect its foreign investments. The 1972–73 disclosures in the U.S. of the efforts by International Telegraph and Telephone (ITT) in attempted conjunction with the Central Intelligence Agency (CIA) to prevent President Allende's electoral accession to power in Chile suggests the statist facet of multinational corporate behavior. ITT became at the very least an abettor of covert intervention in a foreign society to implement a program designed to foment strife and stifle national self-determination. ITT-CIA links illustrate coalition possibilities among regressive elements in the corporate and statist structures.

   Even the globalist aspirations of multinational corporations should not necessarily be confused with a commitment to $S_{2(WOMP/USA)}$. Global mechanisms of coordination and management guided by considerations of market efficiency are not in any sense assurances of support for fairer patterns of economic distribution, for nonrepressive governance, or for the protection of environmental quality. The bulk of available evidence suggests that corporations are responsive to social values only if forced by regulatory and populist pressures.

## MOBILIZATION CONTEXTS IN $t_1$

In contrast to the consciousness-raising contexts of $t_1$ we illustrate in this section mobilization-for-action contexts that might become significant during $t_2$ [the 1980s]. We do not anticipate any transformation of vital structures or patterns of behavior, but we do foresee the active political pursuit of reform programs incorporating WOMP or closely analogous value priorities.

   *1. Change-Oriented Domestic Reform Movements.*   Militant minority groups, the women's liberation movement, and progressive factions in political parties and the labor movement are among those groups in domestic society seeking major reforms by mounting a very direct attack on prevailing values. These groups do not in general include world-order issues within their reform platforms, but their outlook and goals are compatible with WOMP, and their access to power or influence would improve greatly the prospects for consciousness-raising. These groups are already mobilized for action, and it is important that efforts be made to encourage their formulation of world-order extensions of their most immediate goals.

2. *Peace-Activist Groups.*   There are groups mobilized for action around war/peace issues. These groups often have no general world-order ideology beyond an opposition to current levels of defense spending, to foreign commitments and bases, and to militarization of foreign policy. Their contributions consist of challenging the dominant groupings of power and wealth within domestic arenas. Such groups can relate strongly to specific antiwar causes (e.g., Vietnam) and exert considerable short-term and special-purpose influence. Their institutional proposals—as for a Department of Peace or a peacekeeping force—are usually well-intentioned but innocuous and unlikely to be realized (and, if realized, likely to evolve in a form enveloped in restrictions emanating from statist guidelines). The fate of the U.S. Arms Control and Disarmament Agency is instructive; its bureaucracy combines an acute sense of inferiority with a very low degree of bureaucratic independence.

3. *Transnational Promotion of Human Rights.*   There is a growing realization that human rights are not domestic questions. Transnational campaigns on behalf of political prisoners are symbolically and substantively important in relation to the growth of the idea of a human community that takes precedence over statist prerogatives. Amnesty International has given some organizational focus to the progressive view that severe deprivations of human rights are not matters of domestic jurisdiction. International psychiatric associations have been protesting Soviet uses of medical detention as a way of quarantining and punishing dissenters. These developments help create patterns of behavior and belief that support planned transition to $S_2$.

4. *Congressional Initiative.*   The Cranston/Taft initiatives to increase the role and effectiveness of the International Court of Justice suggest an effort in the U.S. Senate to encourage governments to seek peaceful settlement of international disputes; as such, it derives from a posture opposed to statist prerogatives with respect to war and peace. Efforts to impose responsibility on public officials for war crimes by legislative enactment move in the same direction.

Action by Congress is not necessarily likely to be progressive from a world-order perspective, although its representative character makes it the most neutral governmental organ to express the outlook and policies of a grassroots or populist movement for global reform. The Senate has so far failed to ratify the Genocide Convention of 1950 and for years a series of human-rights treaties have either not been ratified or not been submitted to the Senate for advice and consent. Congress enacted the so-called Hickenlooper Amendment, which extended capitalistic views of the sanctity of private property into the assessment of expropriation disputes with foreign governments, even requiring the

President to terminate foreign aid if American investors are not fully reimbursed for any expropriated assets, regardless of the extent of their pre-expropriation profits.

5. *The Honeywell and Gulf Campaigns.*    There is a fairly extensive set of organized efforts to make corporate management moderate its profit-making by taking account of certain fundamental international policies, such as prohibition of war crimes in the case of the Honeywell firm and repudiation of apartheid in the case of Gulf. These efforts are directed against both ethically responsive shareholders (churches, charitable organizations, universities) and against the corporate managers themselves (shareholder protests, proxy fights, and so on). The goals of protest are not explicitly associated with world-order reform, but the demands reflect a sense of transnational accountability (to the Indochinese or African victims) based on ethical notions of human worth and equality. Such a mobilization context tends to embody an antistatist outlook and could easily be widened to accommodate a comprehensive plan for world order reform such as is embodied in $S_{2(WOMP/USA)}$.

6. *No-First-Use Proposal.*    A majority of members of the UN have voted in favor of absolute prohibition of nuclear weapons. A great step forward would involve a renunciation by the nuclear powers of a first-use option in the event of armed conflict. China has unilaterally made such a pledge. It seems important to urge such a policy on the United States government. A no-first-use policy would help denuclearize international politics and establish a measure of reciprocity in arms-control initiatives between nuclear and nonnuclear countries. More significantly, a renunciation of the nuclear option would entail a renunciation of that most absolute of statist claims, the discretion to eradicate civilian populations in the event that a foreign government is perceived as acting in a provocative or unacceptable manner.

7. *Urban Separatism and Secessionism.*    The city as the bearer of progressive values is a familiar theme. The city as the victim of an exploitative tax structure and an insensitive political approach is a central affliction of American life. Singapore as a model city-state might encourage other cities to disengage and secede formally from their suburban and rural hinterland. The 51st-state movement in New York City, although feeble, may be the early signal of an emerging set of claims associated with an urban separatist movement. In any event, it seems critical for world-order reform efforts to become more sensitive to and associated with more drastic conceptions of urban reform, especially given the magnitude of the movement of people from the countryside to the city throughout the world.

## TRANSFORMATION CONTEXTS

As indicated, we do not anticipate significant world order *transformations* in $t_1$. There are likely to be a large number of international arrangements designed to stabilize economic competition, to cut costs in the arms race, and to make the over-all system less accident-prone. Such arrangements are not, in one sense, transition steps at all, but are rather contributions to the durability of $S_1$. However, to the extent that the durability of $S_1$ lengthens the interval between $S_0$ and the collapse of $S_1$ through catastrophe, it provides a longer interval within which to effectuate planned transition to a benevolent variant of $S_2$.

Some institutional reforms are of a forward-looking character that can be conceived of as direct contributions to transition. Some illustrations follow:

1. *UN Seabed Authority.*    There is a possibility that the UN will be given an independent institutional role in relation to ocean resources. Such a role may be modest at first, but it is likely to expand over time until the authority acquires significant status as a world actor. Such an actor might fund other international institutions as well as establish itself as a quasi-autonomous actor within the world system.

2. *European Supranationalism.*    By late $t_1$ the institutions of the EEC may possess a significant element of supranationality. A major, genuinely regional participant in the world-order system may thus have importance for transition purposes. Such a regional actor could either stabilize a new phase of $S_1$ or encourage transition to one of a number of variants of $S_2$.

3. *Special-Purposes Functional Regimes.*    One can envision in $t_1$ a series of institutional developments on a global level dealing with narcotics flow, air piracy, satellite broadcasting, and environmental quality that in their over-all effect will diminish the status of governmental actors in $S_1$. The need for functional mechanisms on an international plane may reinforce consciousness-raising and mobilization efforts in $t_1$ and thereby hasten the advent of $t_2$.


## CONCLUSION

The main objective of this essay has been to suggest new directions of response to the principal challenges of the modern world. These new directions are concerned with three sorts of issues: how to think, what to hope, and what to do. These issues are approached from the perspective of world order, specifically from a conviction that the existing system does not deal adequately with individual and social problems and will become even less capable of meeting minimum human and planetary needs in the future. The existing order is breaking down at a very rapid rate, and the main uncertainty is whether mankind can exert a positive role in shaping a new world order or is doomed to await collapse in a passive posture. We believe a new order will be born no later than early in the next century and that the death throes of the old and the birth pangs of the new will be a testing time for the human species. In this testing time we should not entrust our destiny to the wisdom of national governments, at least as most of them are presently oriented. These state institutions came into being and were generally shaped by much that is obsolescent in the existing world system. We urgently need a spontaneous mass movement for world-order reform that is committed to promoting the four world-order values of peace, economic well-being, environmental quality, and social and political justice, and is skeptical of experts and bureaucrats but reluctant to promise any kind of quick fix for the ills of the planet.

## NOTES

1. This rubric is borrowed from Gerald Feinberg, who develops a persuasive rationale for "the Prometheus Project" in his stimulating book *The Prometheus Project: Mankind's Search for Long-Range Goals* (Garden City, N.Y.: Doubleday, 1968).
2. See Van Rensselaer Potter, *Bioethics: Bridge to the Future* (Englewood Cliffs, N.J.: 1971); cf. also Garrett Hardin's provocative book *Exploring New Ethics for Survival* (New York: Viking, 1972).

## 25. Saul H. Mendlovitz
### *Struggle for a Just World Peace: A Transition Strategy*                  1989

A pioneer in the world order movement, Saul Mendlovitz is codirector of the World Order Models Project and a professor of international law at Rutgers University. In this selection, Mendlovitz writes in his capacity as editor of *Alternatives*, a journal dedicated to the exploration of issues related to Third World development and world order issues. In the previous selection, Richard Falk presented a three-stage transition process that obviously did not meet its target deadlines. Mendlovitz assesses the global situation from a world order perspective at the end of the 1980s and puts forth new targets along with an assessment of their feasibility.

## COMMITMENT AND CALL

"There is a great disorder under heaven."[1] It is not clear whether this condition is good or evil, but it is clear that major changes are taking place in the global political system and in the domestic structures of the majority of the states of the world, including the most powerful. The emergence of global civilization at a period of unprecedented growth rate in human population combined as it is with intensive communicative interaction amongst various societies, the demands and claims of people everywhere to tolerable material satisfaction—basic human needs, the right to be free from authoritarian abuse by governments and perhaps even to participate meaningfully in decisions which affect one's own life, are now part of the political environment of all societies and the global society. Meanings and practices of democracy and sovereignty are being challenged and questioned. Transformation—meaning fundamental change in human society—appears to be taking place and some form of global polity comprehending interdependence, integration and interpenetration is evolving.

Whether that polity will be preceded by a "Dark Age" or Lebanonisation of the globe, whether it will be organized and run by a relatively small powerful group of individuals and states who in the name of order will impose a system, or whether the polity will be for the benefit of the vast bulk of humanity, is open. Precisely because of this openness we believe it is a moment for people who are committed to peace and justice to mobilize a transnational social movement: The Movement For A Just World Peace.

This is a commitment and call to individuals, groups, organizations, and leadership of progressive governments throughout the globe to join in a common effort in the *struggles* for a more just world peace. We are very much aware that war, hegemonic imperialism, authoritarianism, poverty, social injustice, ecological instability and alienation are problems faced by human beings throughout the globe; that the interaction of these problems produces a global political system in which militarism is deeply rooted and there is an almost unquestioned component of the ideological and political doctrines of the state system. It is against this background that we commit ourselves to a set of interrelated values: peace, social justice, economic well-being, ecological balance and positive identity. We know that straight line projection or, more concretely, present structures prevent realization of these values for some 40 percent of humanity; this is intolerable.

We also know and take heart in the fact that there are a growing number of people throughout the entire globe who are concerned and ready to act to change these straight line projections and structures; there are literally hundreds, indeed thousands, of struggles attempting to create local communities and a global society providing acceptable conditions for material living, appropriate social and political participation, an ecologically sound environment and polity free from militarism. We recognize that the nation-state in the Third World has been a progressive force and does provide some protection and some security against imperial hegemony or domination by stronger powers. Yet it must be acknowledged that the nation-state system as it is presently constituted is incapable of dealing with a series of global crises. The structure of the present system now operates to produce the straight line projections we have just noted.

It is against this background that we announce our intention to join in the formation of the Movement For A Just World Peace. This movement must be rooted in the existential circumstances of people struggling against oppression for justice and dignity in concrete political and social conditions throughout the globe. At the same time the social reality in which we participate at this moment in history is one which involves global penetration by Western civilization and an awareness by almost everyone—no matter how confined and isolated to one's own area—that they are a part of the human society and the globe. It is the recognition of immediate struggles and the power of global political, economic, and social forces that lead us to characterize present circumstances as many worlds/one world.

Within this context it is important to establish some principles for selection of specific political and social objectives. These principles as well as objectives are intended to promote the realization of the values of peace, social justice, economic well-being, ecological balance and positive identity. Here we propose some principles which we believe would be useful as the basis for this selection.

# PRINCIPLES, PROGRAM AND PRAXIS

To begin with, we must be willing, in fact invite, the possibility of transcending the images, norms, and concerns of the nation-state system as we have known it for the past 500 years. Furthermore, we must take into account the vast variety and disparity, in income, power, and influence among the many territorial groupings of human beings throughout the globe. It is important, therefore, to identify struggles, programs and projects which develop simultaneously in the following fashion:

1. To the maximum extent possible, attempt to form decentralized units of production, consumption and community participation; these units must be informed by universalist as well as local existential values and some right of appeal to some outside unit should be made part of this formation.
2. The development of unique and creative forms of transnational cooperation to promote the values of the movement.
3. Wide participation in the creation and management of global institutions for global problems.

Within a framework of these principles, images, and norms we recommend the following criteria in the selection of transformative projects:

1. Engage only in those political, social and cultural projects which benefit humanity. If that criterion proves to be too difficult, select only those projects which directly benefit the lowest 40 percent of humanity in terms of material well-being and meaningful participation in decision-making.
2. System transformation rather than system reform should guide selection of projects.
3. Select projects which have the capacity of organizing somewhere between 5–15 percent of the polity in which you expect the project to take place.
4. The use of violence should be avoided, if at all possible. If used, it should be used only against targets which are themselves the direct source of oppression and the decision to use violence should be subjected not only to "local" people but wherever possible to a transnational group of like-minded indivdiuals.

The images, principles and concerns just noted suggest the following actions to achieve short, intermediate, and long-run targets for a Movement For A Just World Peace.

## Short-run: Targets for 1991–93

- Establishment of cadres (national and sectoral) for a Movement For A Just World Peace (see below, Organization Program).

- Establishing links with like-minded individuals in other societies for the purpose of setting up a network for a transnational social movement.
- Establishing peace and justice agendas for local and national politics.
- Debt relief.
- Targeting human rights violations (most egregious state behavior, i.e., Iran, Iraq, Afghanistan, etc.).
- A democratic Union of South Africa.
- Initiating an annual process of five reductions in defense budgets over a ten-year period with savings being allocated for basic needs, domestically and globally. If necessary, initiate tax resistance movements.

## Intermediate-run: Targets for 2001–03

- Establishment of a small but permanent peacekeeping force for the UN with the authority of humanitarian intervention in civil wars.
- Establishment of a global food agency to implement the right to food.
- Vigorous implementation of Forward Looking Strategies of the 1985 UN Conference on International Women's Decade.
- Promotion of individuals for office, whether electoral or appointive, who announce a commitment to global policy as a framework in which national and local society must operate.
- Acceptance of a global code of conduct for multinational corporations, state trade associations of the socialist bloc, and the various state-owned enterprises of the Third World which would be accountable to the values of a just world peace as well as the test of profitability.
- Submission to the compulsory jurisdiction of the International Court of Justice for all treaties concluded during and after the decade of 1990.
- Establishment of a court to deal with individuals who commit crimes against humanity.

## Long-run: Targets for 2011–13

- Global tax scheme to establish and maintain a basic needs regime for global society.
- Complete and general disarmament with alternative security system in place.
- Political decision-making authority to be given to an ecological regime.
- A constitutional framework for global institutions on global matters with appropriate authoritative linkages for transnational cooperative enterprises based on the principle of maximum decentralization of production, consumption, and community participation in decision-making.
- Regional and global human rights regime with compulsory jurisdiction.

It should be noted that the 2011–13 targets are set out so as to provide standards for evaluating the work that is being done on a yearly basis from 1991–93. It should also be pointed out that, in the main, work on all of these targets would begin now; that is to say, in order to accomplish the 2001–03 and 2011–13 targets, some groups would have to begin working immediately on these tasks.

This set of targets will need to be reviewed constantly and opportunities not already mentioned can fit in while others which seem impossible to bring about in the period suggested will have to be dropped. But the first question is, can we agree—even among a small number of people who are committed to both reflection and action—on some such set of targets as these?

If that is possible, then we should move to the next question. How do we organize ourselves, catalyze, and join with others in the Movement For A Just World Peace?

# ORGANIZING A GLOBAL TRANSFORMATION CADRE (GTC) FOR THE UNITED STATES

## Some Preliminary Thoughts

We consider essential to the validity and success of the movement that it be a transnational effort—both in practice as well as image. It is for that reason we have included transnational linkages in our short-run targets and in an organizational program. At the same time, it is important, perhaps crucial, to specify concretely the way to organize in one's own society. The exercise that follows should be undertaken by individuals in all regions of the world; that is to say some specification on the matter in which struggle movements in one's own society can relate to global processes is indispensable. It is in this spirit that we direct our attention to the United States. There is one very important additional reason to concern oneself with the United States; it is the fact that this polity is still one of the major actors in the globe. Thus, what we do or do not do in the United States will have a significant impact on the success or failure of the Movement For A Just World Peace.

The overriding organizational thrust is to develop a critical mass of individuals who are committed and dedicated to global transformation. I will call this group the Global Transformation Cadre (GTC).

The implementation of this concept should probably be initiated in the following manner: Bring together a group of intellectuals and social activists, perhaps no more than 25–35 people, whose task it would be to articulate the concerns and issues of both a political ideology and practical action program for the movement. It would be critical to ask, is the time ripe for participating in an articulate, announced social movement to bring about global transformation for the realization of a just world peace? In addition to a close scrutiny of whether or not such a movement is sensible at this time, we should probably go over some carefully prepared documents relating to all the matters noted above, i.e., theoretical, ethical, and praxis aspects for the movement.

It is difficult to assess how long it will take to reach consensus on these matters. Assume, however, that after two to ten meetings with a group of anywhere from 20 to 100 people we have worked through an ideological position and a set of targets for the next 15–20-year period, we can then move on to the organization of the movement.

Implicit in these comments is the awareness that there already exist in the United States many movements (i.e., ideological and political left; community organizing, neighborhood empowerment groups; ecological and life style change; interpersonal transformation; and spiritual transformation).[2] These movements tend to share the same values, but have differing conceptions of praxis and somewhat competing visions of the good world. The movement, to be effective, should engage in interaction with all of these movements.

It will have to appeal as well to individuals in all categories of occupations, professions, bureaucracies. That is, we want the young executive of IBM or the associated partner in a major Wall Street firm or the foreman of a Ford Motor Company or the worker in a vineyard in California, conceiving of themselves as carrying forward the movement by the activity they are engaged in. There would have to be constant interaction between the thinking and action parts of our programming. Whether this should be done through cell meetings or through some broad-scale educational movement or through some new social invention or through some combination of these and other ways is something we need to discuss at length.

A few words about structure. As an initial matter we should make the distinction among cells, cadres, and coalitions. Cells would be groups of individuals who choose to live together and do so in such a way as to exemplify in their daily living as well as their political action the manner in which a just world peace might be brought into being and would be operated. I have in mind here such groups as the Berrigans, the Movement for a New Society, and some of the environmental, feminist, and religious communes which have been set up in various parts of the United States. Cadres are individuals who, while not living together, form a group which set up an organizational structure with concrete political targets, specific functions and responsibilities, and submit themselves to monitoring and review of their achievements with regard to these objectives by a cadre. Coalitions are broader scaled political alliances, more opportunistic and pragmatic in terms of allies around particular issues.

Undoubtedly, the GTC will have to be concerned on how much interaction and engagement it should have in coalition politics. There is, of course, a wide variety of individuals, associations, and organizations who have developed single issue, reformist, and multiple issue programs. The questions of linkages and the problems they raise may be addressed in the early stages of organization or can be left for consideration after we have developed our own cadres.

## Some Additional Thoughts Concerning Organization

Perhaps it might be useful to jot down some specific organizational projects we might engage in initiating the movement.

1. First, we should attempt to ferret out the "closet" globalists in the United States. This would consist not only of the lapsed World Fed-

eralist, Planetary Citizens, as well as individuals who have been associated with the UNA, World Affairs Councils and the like, but people who, once they were asked to respond to a genuine global movement, would come out of the closet and identify themselves. The particular techniques for identifying and ferreting out these people need a good deal of discussion.

2. In addition to picking up individuals who have an inherent global policy attitude, we must begin to establish linkages at the grass-roots, local, and sectoral levels of the United States. More specifically, we need to find people in activist movements, for example, supporters of the Rainbow Coalition, other poverty and minority actors, feminists, ecologists, and show the connection between the problems they are trying to solve and the global political system. At the same time, there are many difficult analytical and ethical issues involved in relating local and sectoral (labor, education, agriculture, religion) levels which will need a good deal of thought. The religious community should be one of our main targets in all of this.

3. It might be important to initiate a political process now with two kinds of specific actions: First, we should identify perhaps a half dozen Congressional candidates like Alan Cranston of California, Mark Hatfield of Oregon, and Patricia Schroeder of Colorado, who might be willing to run on a Just World Peace platform or more minimally use this kind of rhetoric in their 1990s campaigns. We should be prepared to discuss with them the movement's participation in their campaign, identifying all the risks and opportunities involved.

   Second, we should make certain that people running for office at all levels of the society—and the various sectors—be questioned on their feelings towards global policy. There is no reason why we should not be asking candidates for governors, state legislators, mayors, town council people, school board people, and presidents of community colleges, heads of utility companies, chief executive officers of large industries at their annual board meetings, how they feel about disarmament policies, apartheid in South Africa, environmental spoilation, and the like.

4. It is crucial that we have a transnational link visibly operating and prepared to permit us to join them in appropriate ways in their own society. More concretely, as soon as possible we should invite a half dozen people from various parts of the world to become involved in the movement and to think through the strategy of their being part of the movement.

Finally, I should make clear that the targets which are listed for the years 1991–93, 2001–03, and 2011–13 are intended seriously and illustratively. That is to say, these are the targets and processes I would argue for within the GTC. At the same time, they are illustrative in the sense that I do not consider this particular set of projects as the only ones a social movement for A Just World Peace could center around. It is crucial, however, I believe, to attempt to set up a process which articulates concrete political goals and particular kinds of actions to achieve those goals.

## NOTES

1. Ambassador, People's Republic of China, UN General Assembly 1974: his statement then went on to say, "and it is good."
2. See Chadwick Alger and Saul H. Mendlovitz, "Grass-Roots Activism in the United States: Global Implications?", *Alternatives*, Vol. IX, No. 4, 1984, pp. 447–474.

## 26. Tapani Vaahtoranta
### *Atmospheric Pollution as a Global Policy Problem*                1990

A major issue between world order proponents and their critics involves the prospects for reform within the existing nation-state system. Or, as the author of this selection puts it, "Is the establishment of a new world order necessary for averting ecocatastrophe?" Tapani Vaahtoranta, a senior research fellow at the Finnish Institute of International Affairs, develops the issues involved in this controversy and examines the conditions that led states to take action to alleviate atmospheric pollution.

Vaahtoranta argues that nations will take action on global issues whenever certain conditions exist—mutual vulnerability to the ill-effects of the problem, available technology to alleviate the problem, and public pressure on policy makers. To evaluate Vaahtoranta's position, you might compile a list of issues that world order advocates place on their agenda and assess the extent to which these conditions are present.

## 1. INTRODUCTION

Atmospheric pollution is a process whereby chemicals emitted from human activities cause damage to the man-made and natural environment. It is not uncommon for wind currents to transmit harmful agents across national boundaries, especially because of the construction of high smokestacks designed to lessen the local impact of pollutants. Thus, atmospheric pollution has become too broad in geographical scope to be dealt with effectively by national governments on their own. It is an international or even a global policy problem whose control requires collaborative efforts by states (Soroos, 1986). During the 1980s, three problems associated with atmospheric pollution caused widespread concern: acid precipitation, ozone depletion, and the greenhouse effect.

Can international pollution be controlled in a world where the scope of the problem is not congruent with the structure of the international system? Though mankind faces common ecological problems, the international system lacks a central authority which could articulate the common interest and act upon it. As a result, the interests that shape collective measures for dealing with common problems are national rather than international or global.

From the perspective of political realists, international anarchy fosters competition and conflict and inhibits co-operation among states. If there is little prospect of co-operation on security and economic issues, why should effective environmental action be any more feasible? As a matter of fact, since the early 1970s, grave concern has characterized not only forecasts regarding the man-nature relationship, but also the political ability of mankind to manage environmental degradation.

The objective of this article is to call attention to the potential for environmental co-operation on the control of atmospheric pollution. It is noteworthy that five multilateral agreements have been signed to control atmospheric pollution. We shall examine the factors which induce states to strive for international environmental action.


## 2. THE ENVIRONMENTAL REVOLUTIONISM OF THE 1970s

The 1970s were marked by grave concern about the possibilities for effective protection of the global environment. This concern is based on two propositions. First, mankind will face an ecological disaster unless there is a fundamental change in the man-nature relationship. Second, such a change is not feasible in the current anarchic international system.

The authors of the famous *The Limits to Growth* study warned of ecological disaster in the first of the basic conclusions from their analysis:

> If the present growth trends in world population, industrialization, pollution, food production, and resource depletion continue unchanged, the limits to growth on this planet will be reached sometime within the next one hundred years. The most probable result will be a rather sudden and uncontrollable decline in both population and industrial capacity (Meadows et al., 1972, p. 29).

In two other conclusions the authors of the study pointed out that it was possible to avoid disaster by radically altering the growth trends. They considered it necessary to start striving to establish a condition of ecological and economic stability as soon as possible (ibid., p. 29). This solution was generally interpreted to mean zero growth.

One of the limitations of the *The Limits to Growth* was its exclusive focus on the physical aspects of the global environmental predicament (Ronge, 1978, pp. 216–218). Social, economic, and political factors that would further complicate the problems mankind faces were not included in the model on which the conclusions were based. Nor did the authors elaborate on how the hoped-for change could be made (Meadows et al., 1972, p. 185).

Other scholars, including Richard Falk (1971) and William Ophuls (1977), have explored the political dimensions of global environmental problems. These 'environmental revolutionists', as I shall refer to them, supplemented the analysis of *The Limits to Growth* with the realities posed by power and national interest, claiming that basic changes in the man-nature relationship were impossible without simultaneously altering the underlying structure of the international system.[1]

The following description of the political reasons for considering structural change necessary does not necessarily correspond to the thinking of any individual scholar. Its aim is to point to the apparent obstacles to a sufficient degree of environmental co-operation.

The perceived need for structural change takes account of the realist assumptions of international relations: anarchy, national egoism, and the difficulty of co-operation.

First, the incongruence between the ecological unity of the earth and the fragmentation of the state system is regarded as the main political source of the problem. Falk (1975) suggests:

> . . . the state system encourages irresponsible environmental policies on a world level. Each government seeks to maximize its economic product and to shift some of the costs of waste disposal to areas outside its boundaries of responsibility (p. 46).

In other words, sovereign states are concerned primarily about the quality of their own territory and national wealth, regardless of the effect their activities have on the global environment. It is also believed that the anarchic international system will prevent the solution of environmental problems. Despite the need for environmental co-operation, the self-help system dictates that states 'compete with one another for power, wealth, and prestige, and jealously guard their sovereign prerogatives'. Thus, state behavior 'generates conflict, waste, and distrust' (Falk, 1971, p. 2).

The environmental revolutionists fear that environmental degradation and resource depletion will heighten conflict rather than encourage co-operation. In the words of William Ophuls (1977):

> . . . the disappearance of ecological abundance seems bound to make international politics even more tension ridden and potentially violent than it already is. Indeed, the pressures of ecological scarcity may embroil the world in hopeless strife, so that long before ecological collapse occurs by virtue of the physical limitations of the earth, the current world order will have been destroyed by turmoil and war (p. 214).

Both the 'deadlock' of national interests (Oye, 1985, pp. 6–7) and the 'dilemma of common interests' (Stein, 1982, pp. 304–308) are assumed to hinder environmental co-operation. With regard to the deadlock of interests. Falk (1971, p. 245) observed that it is difficult to have international action because the impact of environmental problems 'does not fall equally or at the same time upon states and because some states are under far greater immediate pressures than others'.

Even if mutual interests exist, they do not necessarily lead to co-operation due to the dilemma of common interests. Garrett Hardin's (1968) 'tragedy of the commons' is an example of this dilemma. Hardin applied its logic not only to resource depletion, but also to pollution. He observed that because the adverse effects of the pollution of a common environment are shared by all actors, stopping production or purifying wastes before releasing them is more expensive to the individual polluters than discharging wastes into a commons. There is also the concern that others will not impose corresponding emission regulations, as they yield to the temptation to be a free-rider. But all will be adversely affected if the ecological balance of the environment is destroyed.

As a result, it is believed that a sufficient level of environmental cooperation is unlikely. It is even suggested that states cannot agree on

> . . . any common approach beyond the endorsement of lofty aspirations and, possibly, the creation of machinery to gather information on general environmental trends and to respond quickly to certain kinds of international disasters (e.g., tanker collision, oil blowout, space accident) (Falk, 1975, p. 68).

Despite the convergences of environmental revolutionism and political realism in describing international relations, there are two characteristics that distinguish the two schools of thought. First, the environmental revolutionists contend that since the essential features of the existing international system have been rendered obsolete, structural change is necessary. Because the system is assumed to be incapable of fulfilling the basic goals of man on the earth, it is logical to conclude that 'the conditions of human existence could become safer and the quality of human life could be improved by inducing certain changes in the organization of world society' (Falk, 1971, p. 8). Second, they believe in the possibility of such change.

Realists, however, question whether such change is possible. They are also reluctant to conclude that there are other ways of organizing power and authority in the world than the anarchic state system that would enable mankind to better manage common problems.

Thus, is the establishment of a new world order necesary for averting ecocatastrohpe? It is noteworthy that with the signing of the air pollution control agreements a beginning has been made to protect the global atmosphere. Clearly, under some circumstances states are able to agree upon reciprocal emission reductions. Thus, perhaps the views of the 1970s are too gloomy. This may even have been the purpose of the environmental revolutionists. It is possible that they overdid their dire predictions in order to call attention to the need for environmental protection.

# 3. PROGRESS ON ATMOSPHERIC POLLUTION CONTROL

Atmospheric pollution as an international issue is still a rather recent phenomenon. The first multilateral agreements which specifically oblige states to reduce the atmospheric pollution caused by peaceful human activities were reached in this decade. As for acid precipitation, 21 states signed the Helsinki Protocol in 1985, committing themselves to reduce sulfur dioxide emissions by 30% by 1993, using 1980 levels as the basis for reductions. The Protocol is a follow-up treaty to the 1979 Convention on Long-Range Transboundary Air Pollution negotiated in the United Nations Economic Commission for Europe. The Helsinki Protocol was the first multilateral treaty on specific emissions of air pollutants. Its main shortcoming is that three major sulfur emitters—United States, United Kingdom, and Poland—have not signed it yet. The Helsinki Protocol came into force in 1987. A protocol to freeze emissions by nitrogen oxides at the levels of 1987 by 1995 was signed by 25 states in Sofia in 1988.

Another important step was taken in Montreal in 1987, when states agreed upon controlling the production of pollutants believed to be depleting the ozone layer. The Montreal Protocol, which came into force in 1989, obliges states to reduce the production and consumption of five chlorofluorocarbons (CFCs), first by 20% by 1993–1994 and then by 30% by 1998–99, and to freeze the production and consumption of three halons by 1994.

The Montreal Protocol is important for two reasons. First, both the principal industrial states, which are the major producers of the harmful substances, and some developing countries agreed on limiting their economic activity to protect the global environment. No less-developed country signed the protocols on sulfur and nitrogen emissions. Second, it was successfully negotiated even though there are as yet few concrete manifestations of the adverse consequences of ozone depletion. Thus, not only do states seem capable of reducing atmospheric pollution after damage has occurred, as in the case of acid rain, but they can also take measures that anticipate future environmental damage.

These agreements demonstrate that co-operation to reduce atmospheric pollution is politically possible. This is not to say, however, that the environmental revolutionists were entirely wrong, since the protocols are not as such sufficient to effectively address the acid precipitation or ozone depletion problems. Critics of the Montreal Protocol argue that CFC emissions have to be reduced by 85–95% if the ozone layer is to be saved. Similarly, critics point out that an overall 80% cut in sulfur and a 75% cut in nitrogen emissions are needed to combat acid rain.

Fortunately, further tightening of the regulations is possible. In issuing the Helsinki Declaration of May 1989, the representatives of 81 countries and the European Community agreed to a total phase-out of CFCs by the year 2000. Also, several states aim at reducing suflur emissions by more than the Helsinki Protocol requires, and twelve states declared at Sofia that they are reducing nitrogen emissions by 30% within ten years.

What accounts for the co-operation on the control of atmospheric pollution? Looking at the negotiations on acid precipitation and ozone depletion, one can see that the environmental revolutionists were to a certain extent correct in pointing to how the different ways in which states are effected by environmental problems pose an obstacle to effective environmental co-operation. As in other issue-areas of international relations, states may still fail to co-operate on environmental protection, not because they cannot surmount the prisoners' dilemma, but because they are in deadlock and do not perceive common interests in the first place (Jervis, 1988, pp. 322–324). However, it is suggested next that there are three changes in particular—two systemic ones and one unit-level one—that cause states to perceive a sufficient amount of common interest in the international control of air pollution and, more specifically, make the agreements on reducing sulfur and CFC emissions possible.

# 4. THREE INCENTIVES FOR CONTROLLING ATMOSPHERIC POLLUTION

## 4.1 Systemic Process Changes

To understand the impact of systemic changes, it is useful to distinguish between two dimensions of international relations: structure and process (Keohane & Nye, 1987, pp. 745–749). The international structure, as conceived by Kenneth Waltz (1979), is an important factor in explaining state behavior and its outcomes on the system level. Two characteristics of the existing international structure are important: first, its anarchic nature in view of the lack of an overarching governmental authority and, second, the unequal distribution of capabilities which causes variations of state behavior.

But structure seems insufficient for understanding systemic changes without attention being given to process. Waltz's structural theory leaves a great number of important changes unaccounted for and seems to be too static. Process refers to the ways in which units relate to each other. In addition to the distribution of power, states experience constraints and opportunities because of changes in levels of world economic activity, technological innovation, and alterations in international norms and institutions (Nye, 1988, pp. 243–244, 249–250).

Two systemic process changes have contributed to the emergence of restrictions on atmospheric pollution. First, due to growing ecological interdependence, states now perceive the need for environmental protection more often than was acknowledged in the 1970s. Second, technological development is providing states with more advanced means of reducing harmful emissions.

For some time it has been apparent that national interest could be harnessed to the cause of environmental protection if environmental protection if environmental problems became sufficiently exacerbated. The more serious international environmental problems become, the more they would threaten the core of national interest, namely national security. To reduce environmental damage, states would have to make adaptive changes in their foreign policies. These changes, in turn, offer opportunities for co-operation (Shields & Ott, 1974, pp. 642–647).

Accordingly, the growing severity of international atmospheric pollution is a process change. It is increasingly difficult for an individual state to protect its environment through unilateral action in a world of ecological and economic interdependence. A state's own emission reductions, even though achieved at great expense, will correct only part of the problem if others do not introduce corresponding regulations. Thus, international atmospheric pollution stimulates a strong 'demand' for international co-operation among states, especially those most vulnerable to pollution from foreign sources (Keohane, 1982).

Technological developments are another process change which is part of the reason for stepped-up environmental co-operation. In the 1970s it seemed that all technological development and economic growth invariably accelerated resource depletion, generating more pollution. In the 1980s, however, there was an increasing tendency for new technologies to use resources more efficiently and in doing so to produce fewer harmful discharges.

As a matter of fact, in several technologically advanced countries—Denmark, France, the Federal Republic of Germany, Sweden, the United Kingdom, and United States—the environmental impact of economic activity tends to be decreasing despite the growth of GNP. In Japan, the environmental impact is not growing as fast as the gross national product (Simonis, 1988, pp. 14–17). In short, new technologies seem to enable states to continue to progress economically with less adverse impacts on the environment.

## 4.2 Public Pressure

Growing public pressure on policy-makers is a third factor contributing to international efforts to deal with atmospheric pollution. While policy-makers have traditionally concentrated on raising production to legitimize their position, citizens have increasingly been suffering from the adverse impacts of production on the environment. Thus, it has become apparent that in many countries the citizenry has been ahead of its government in perceiving the need for stricter environmental policies. A recent international survey in fourteen countries found that over 75% of the people believe that stronger government action is needed to protect against the harmful effects of pollution. Most governments were given poor or mediocre grades on dealing with environmental matters (UNEP, 1989, p. 4).

Wealth and vulnerability shape the attitudes of individuals on environmental issues. In the most advanced countries the value priorities of people are undergoing a shift from an emphasis on material goals to a concern with postmaterial values. Postmaterial attitudes on the environment are reinforced by personal experiences with pollution problems (Rohrschneider, 1988). For example, people in the industrialized world increasingly recognize that the health of the environment and of the economy are linked. Surveys show that the majority of respondents give top priority to environmental protection or consider that environmental protection and economic growth are simultaneously possible. Most people in developing countries are believed to give priority to economic growth, sometimes at the expense of environmental conservation. A common feature in both developed and developing countries is the sharp heightening of public concern following a significant hazardous environmental incident (UNEP, 1988, pp. 15–18).

Concern about the environment is not by itself sufficient to change policies, but the impact of public opinion also depends on two elements of the political system. First, the opportunity for political mobilizing is an important factor.

Second, the decision-making system must be responsive to active public opinion. In general, public pressure for environmental protecton has the greatest impact in Western democracies (Gottweis, 1988, pp. 10–12).

## 5. THE FEDERAL REPUBLIC OF GERMANY AS AN EXAMPLE

The recent enthusiasm of the FRG for controlling atmospheric pollution is perhaps the most remarkable development in the negotiations on environmental problems during the 1980s. Earlier, the FRG resisted international efforts to control acid rain and preserve the ozone layer, but recently it has actively promoted effective international regulations. It is noteworthy that unlike other states that 'push' such rules, notably Canada, the Netherlands and the Nordic states, the FRG is one of the world's greatest emitters of air pollution. Ecological vulnerability, the availability of new technologies, and public pressure seem to have contributed to the FRG's change of policy for the environment.

First, in regard to acid rain, the area of central Europe consisting of the FRG, Belgium, the Netherlands, the German Democratic Republic, Poland, and Czechoslovakia has the highest acidity of precipitation in Europe. Half of West German forests are seriously affected by acid rain, more than is reported in any other European country (Kauppi et al., 1987, p.28). Only in the Netherlands is severe forest damage more widespread than in the FRG ('ECE Report', 1987).

Though the damage to the West German forests dates back to the 1960s, *Waldsterben* (forest death) did not cause public alarm until the beginning of the 1980s when the phenomenon spread dramatically. This awareness coincides with the change of the FRG's policy toward new international targets for sulfur dioxide emission reductions. The sudden about face of the FRG was first evident at a conference in Stockholm in 1982, when it abandoned the camp of 'drag' states and declared that it was supporting the establishment of an international program for controlling sulfur dioxide throughout Europe (Prittwitz, 1986, pp. 64–67).

There are still three states—United States, United Kingdom, and Poland—that are major source states of sulfur dioxide which have not signed the Helsinki Protocol. One of the principal reasons for the opposition of the United States and the United Kingdom is their relatively low vulnerability to foreign emissions, while much of their own emissions are transported beyond their borders (Elsom, 1987, pp. 259, 271). Poland is badly affected by acid rain from both internal and foreign sources of pollution, but it simply cannot afford the cost of reducing emissions.

Second, the ability to produce new compounds for CFCs seems to explain the change in German policy on ozone depletion. The FRG first opposed proposals offered by the Nordic countries, the Netherlands, and Canada for large reductions in CFC production. In 1987, however, West German officials issued a statement that the FRG would aim at a nearly total elimination of CFC production and emissions by the year 2000. The government would begin the reduction by concentrating on the aerosol industry. The aerosol industry was willing to abide by the plan, having already gone a long way toward the elimination of all but essential aerosol uses of CFCs, with further reductions in sight (Dickman, 1987).

Similarly, the United States continued to oppose international regulations on other than aerosol uses for CFCs until it began to strive for ending all uses in 1986–87. About the same time, the first reports about the development of new substitutes for CFCs appeared in the press. Dupont, a United States based company that is the largest producer of CFCs, announced in 1988 that it would be able to produce a substitute for CFCs in a few years and accordingly supported 'an orderly transition to a total phaseout' of the most harmful CFCs ('Ozone: A Close Call', 1988). Both the European Community and Japan expressed concern during the negotiations that the US companies, with their successes in developing substitutes, might enjoy a significant competitive advantage if drastic international regulations were adopted. The ability to produce alternative compounds seems also to explain why the United Kingdom agreed in 1989 on a complete ban on ozone-depleting emissions (Crawford, 1988; Upton, 1989).

Third, public pressure on policy-making could explain why vulnerability and new technological development so quickly affected German foreign policy on the environment. Through the opportunity to vote for the Green Party, citizens have been able to make environmental protection a salient political issue and ultimately to influence the decision-making process. The Greens have not had as much political influence in any other country (Rädig, 1985).

## 6. CONCLUSIONS

This article has suggested that three factors—vulnerabilty to pollution, technological ability to reduce emissions, and public pressure on policy-making—explain why some states are more willing than others to work for international control of air pollution. The growing number of push states in the negotiations on reducing acid rain and protecting the ozone layer has altered the pessimism of the 1970s on the prospects for international environmental protection.

However, it is evident that not all states are equally vulnerable to pollution; their level of technological development varies and their political systems differ considerably. As a result, if these factors shape the receptivity of states to curbs on international pollution control, conflicts of interests are inevitable when stronger measures to address acid rain, ozone depletion, and global warming are discussed. It is therefore important to develop ways of influencing states that have been reluctant to effectively reduce air pollution.

If their reluctance is caused by lack of awareness of the problems that are looming, more information about the state of the environment must be made available. Co-operation between national environmental movements and the activity of NGOs may also facilitate environmental diplomacy. Also, there is a need for both positive and negative inducements as ways of influencing the drag states. Peace research can assist in devising the most effective means.

## NOTE

1. Martin Wright divided international relations thinkers into three groups: the Machiavellians (the realists), the Grotians (the rationalists), and the Kantians (the revolutionists). According to his definition, the revolutionists reject the realist and rationalist view that international relations is about conflict and co-operation among states. At the deeper level it is about relations among the human beings (Bull, 1976, pp. 105–106). The environmental revolutionist is used here in a broader meaning to refer to all scholars who believe that in order to protect the global environment the state system has to be superseded by other types of world order.

## REFERENCES

Bull, Hedley, 1976. 'Martin Wight and the Theory of International Relations,' *British Journal of International Studies*, vol. 2, no. 2, July, pp. 101–116.
Crawford, Mark, 1988. 'EPA: Ozone Treaty Weak'. *Science*, vol. 242, 7 October, p. 25.
Dickman, Steven, 1987. 'West Germany Strides towards CFC Elimination by 2000'. *Nature*, vol. 327, 14 May, p. 93.
'ECE Report: European Forest Damage', 1987, *Acid News*, no. 3, p. 6.
Elsom, Derek, 1987. *Atmospheric Pollution: Causes, Effects and Control Policies.* Oxford: Blackwell.
Falk, Richard A., 1971. *This Endangered Planet: Prospects and Proposals for Human Survival.* New York: Random House.
Falk, Richard, 1975. *A Study of Future Worlds.* New York: Free Press.
Gottweis, Herbert, 1988. 'Politik in der Risikogesellschaft'. *Österreichische Zeitschrift für Politikwissenschaft*, vol. 17, no. 1, pp. 3–15.
Hardin, Garrett, 1977 [1968]. 'The Tragedy of the Commons', ch. 13 in Garrett Hardin & John Baden, eds., *Managing the Commons.* San Francisco: Freeman.
Jervis, Robert, 1988. 'Realism, Game Theory and Co-operation'. *World Politics*, vol. 40, no. 3, April pp. 317–349.
Kauppi, Pekka; Kaarle Kenttämies; Seppo Oikarinen & Raisa Valli, 1987. *Happamoituminen Suomessa: Maa ja metsätalousministeriön ja ympäristöministeriön Happamoitumisprojektin yleiskatsaus*, Sarja A., no. 57. [*Acidification in Finland: Overview of Hapro's Secretariat.* Series A, no. 57. Ministry of the Environment.] Ympäristöministeriö, Ympäristön- ja luonnonsuojeluosasto. Helsinki: Helsingin Printing.
Keohane, Robert O., 1982. 'The Demand for International Regimes'. *International Organization*, vol. 36, no. 2, Spring, pp. 325–355.
Keohane, Robert O. & Joseph S. Nye, Jr., 1987. 'Power and Interdependence Revisited'. *International Organization*, vol. 41, no. 4, Autumn, pp. 725–753.
Meadows, Donella H.; Dennis L. Meadows; Jørgen Randers & William W. Behrens III, 1972. *The Limits to Growth: A Report for the Club of Rome's Project on the Predicament of Mankind.* New York: New American Library.

Nye, Joseph S., Jr., 1988. 'Neorealism and Neoliberalism'. *World Politics*, vol. 40, no. 2, January, pp. 235–251.

Ophuls, William, 1977. *Ecology and the Politics of Scarcity*. San Francisco: Freeman.

Oye, Kenneth A., 1985. 'Explaining Cooperation under Anarchy: Hypotheses and Strategies'. *World Politics*, vol. 38, no. 1, October, pp. 1–24.

'Ozone: A Close Call', 1988. *International Herald Tribune*, March 29, p. 4.

Prittwitz, Volker, 1986. 'Die Luft hat keine Grenzen: Das Problem der weiträumige Luftverschmutzung', pp. 61–70 in Peter Cornelius Mayer-Tasch, ed., *Die Luft hat keine Grenzen: Internationale Umweltpolitik, Fakten und Trends*. Frankfurt am Main: Fischer.

Rohrschneider, Robert, 1988. 'Citizens Attitudes toward Environmental Issues: Selfish or Selfless?' *Comparative Political Studies*, vol. 21, no. 3, October, pp. 347–367.

Ronge, Volker, 1978. 'Staats- und Politikkonzepte in der sozio-ökologischen Diskussion', pp. 213–248 in Martin Jänicke, ed., *Umweltpolitik: Beiträge zur Politologia des Umweltschutzes*. Opladen: Leske & Budrich.

Rüdig, Wolfgang, 1985. 'Die grüne Welle: Zur Entwicklung ökologischer Parteien in Europa', *Aus Politik und Zeitgeschichte*, Beilage 45 zur Wochenzeitung Das Parlament, pp. 3–18.

Shields, Linda P. & Marvin C. Ott, 1974. 'The Environmental Crisis: International and Supranational Approaches', *International Relations*, vol. 4, no. 6, November, pp. 629–648.

Simonis, Udo E., 1988. *Ecological Modernization of Industrial Society*. FS II 88–401. Berlin (West): Wissenschaftszentrum Berlin für Sozialforschung.

Soroos, Marvin S., 1986. *Beyond Sovereignty: The Challenge of Global Policy*. Columbia, SC: University of South Carolina Press.

Stein, Arthur, 1982. 'Coordination and Collaboration: Regimes in an Anarchic World', *International Organization*, vol. 36, no. 2, Spring, pp. 299–324.

UNEP, 1988. *The State of the Environment 1988: The Public and the Environment*. Nairobi: United Nations Environment Program.

UNEP, 1989. *North America News*, vol. 4, no. 4, August.

Upton, Kaija, 1989. 'Kenia puhui kehitysmaiden puolesta: Rikkaiden tuki tarpeen freonien vähentämisessä. [Kenya Talked on Behalf of LDCs: The Assistance of Rich Countries Necessary for Reducing Freons.] *Uusi Suomi*, 6 March, p. 13.

Waltz, Kenneth N., 1979. *Theory of International Politics*. Reading: Addison-Wesley.

# COMPREHENSION CHECKPOINT

What is the significance of the following?

| | | |
|---|---|---|
| WOMP | realpolitik | greens |
| genuine leaders | zero growth | technocracy |
| Apollo vision | Montreal Pact | functional regimes |
| social Darwinism | analogy of the commons | |
| limits to growth debate | Westphalian State System | |

Can you answer the following questions?

1. World order advocates propose approaching international issues in ways that are systemic, normative, and futuristic. Sketch out how this approach might be used to tackle a global issue such as world hunger, nuclear proliferation, or the greenhouse effect.

2. According to Louis Rene Beres, "power politics have never succeeded in producing either justice or security. Unless these policies are now rapidly and completely transformed, they will produce the most intolerable conditions the United States and the world have ever known." Can you think of evidence that supports and rebuts these statements?

3. According to Richard Falk, world order advocates "do not propose a transplant of national global structures on to a global setting." If this is ture, what exactly are world advocates proposing, and what evidence is there that what they are proposing will work?

4. What are the major areas of agreement and disagreement between Vaahtoranta and the authors of the first three selections—Beres, Falk, and Mendlovitz?

5. According to Vaahtoranta, what factors led states to take action in the area of atmospheric pollution? To what extent do these conditions exist in the areas of population, world hunger, nuclear proliferation, ocean dumping, and human rights?

6. Refer to the chart of reassertionist and neorealist polarities presented on page 135. Where would the world order perspective fall along the polarities? Sketch out a set of world order responses to the quotation by Hart and the particular policy proposals that follow the quotation. What similarities and differences do you find between the answers that flow from the world order perspective and the three mainstream worldviews? What accounts for these similarities and differences?

## For Further Consideration

*Periodicals and journals* that contain essays reflecting world order perspectives: *Alternatives, Bulletin of the Atomic Scientists, Future Society, The Journal of Conflict Resolution, Journal of Peace Research, The Nation, Peace and Change, Political Psychology, The Progressive, Third World Quarterly, World Policy Journal.*

*Leading scholars, authors, activists:* Louis Rene Beres, Elise Boulding, Kenneth Boulding, Richard Falk, Johan Galtung, Robert Irwin, Robert Johansen, George Lopez, Saul Mendlovitz, Richard Smoke, Carolyn Stephenson.

# FOR FURTHER READING

Beres, Louis Rene. *Reason and Realpolitik: U.S. Foreign Policy and World Order*. Lexington, MA: D.C. Heath and Company, 1984. A critique of American foreign policy during the Carter and early Reagan years from a world order perspective. Beres directs his attack against U.S. nuclear strategy and human rights policies. He concludes that the current foreign policies of the United States are "designs for the end of the world" [p. 154].

Brock-Utne, Brigit. *Educating for Peace: A Feminist Perspective*. New York: Pergamon Press, 1985. A feminist perspective on the pursuit of world peace. According to Brock-Utne, peace will not come until fathers instill feminist values in their sons and women who do not act like men get into positions of power. The book contains a rich bibliography of feminist writings.

Brown, Lester, *et al. State of the World 1990: A Worldwatch Institute Report on Progress Toward a Sustainable Society*. New York: W. W. Norton & Company, 1990. An annual and invaluable audit of the state of the world in global issue areas—global warming, water resources, world hunger, air quality, the oceans, global poverty.

Cousins, Norman. *The Pathology of Power*. New York: W. W. Norton & Company, 1987. A plea for world government by one of the nation's founding world federalists. In this book, Cousin highlights the great waste in military spending and the threat which, he believes, our burgeoning military establishment poses to our liberty and our prosperity.

Falk, Richard. *The Promise of World Order*. Philadelphia: Temple University Press, 1987. A collection of addresses and essays on such current issues as human rights, nuclear weapons, and technology. In essays directed to American foreign policy, Falk proposes that U.S. officials renounce the first use of nuclear weapons as well as covert or military intervention in Third World struggles. He also urges American support for global management of the world economy. This book illustrates how world order perspectives can be used to assess current issues of foreign policy.

Farer, Tom, Jr. "The Greening of the Globe: A Preliminary Appraisal of the World Order Models Project." *International Organization*, Vol. 31 (Winter 1977), pp. 129–47. A withering and dismissive attack on the conception, goals, and execution of the World Order Models Project (WOMP) by a neorealist professor of international law at Rutgers University.

Galtung, Johan. *There Are Alternatives: Four Roads to Peace and Security*. Chester Springs, PA: Dufour Editions, 1984. A leading European peace researcher looks at four alternative security policies from a global perspective. He advocates "transarmament from offensive to defensive defense," nonalignment, and greater self-reliance.

Goodwin, Neva R. "Introduction." *World Development*, Vol. 19, No. 1 (January 1991), pp. 1–15. This "introduction" frames the essays in a special volume of *World Development* dedicated to examining post–cold war global issues from a world order perspective. Regulating access to global resources, minimizing or mediating conflicts over those resources among nations and groups, increasing equity of access, and moving toward sustainable development are Goodwin's goals. The agents to ensure these goals will be newly trained "civic corps" who speak and work for humanity against states, private transnational actors, and bureaucrats, both national and international. Goodwin addresses difficult questions forthrightly and realistically. This essay should be read with the selections by Falk and Mendlovitz in mind.

Gurtov, Melvin. "Open Borders: A Global Humanist Approach to the Refugee Crisis." *World Development,* Vol. 19, No. 5 (May 1991), pp.485–97. Gurtov uses the principles he developed in his book, *Global Politics in the Human Interest* (cited above), to reduce and more effectively deal with the increasing number of global refugees.

Hardin, Garrett. "The Tragedy of the Commons," Ch. 13 in Garrett Hardin & John Baden (eds.), *Managing the Commons.* San Fransisco: Freeman, 1977. Anyone who rejects the world order perspective must come to grips with Hardin's thesis, as Vaahtoranta tries to do in Selection 27.

Helman, Udi. "The Environment: A Research Survey." *The Washington Quarterly,* Vol. 13, No. 4 (Autumn 1990), pp. 233–65. An analytical survey of the growing literature on (1) environmental change and national security, (2) the relationship between economics and energy, (3) the north-south dimensinos of environmental issues, and (4) approaches and obstacles to international cooperation. Helman presents an overview of basic facts and issues in each of these areas and concludes that tackling environmental issues will require international coordination and control "unprecedented in the history of diplomacy." This essay is the first source to consult in building a bibliography on international politics and the environment.

Irwin, Robert A. *Building a Peace System: A Book for Activists, Scholars, Students, and Concerned Citizens.* Washington, DC: ExPro Press, 1989. Anyone who wants to get involved in the world order movement should buy this invaluable resource book. Irwin, a professor of sociology at Brandeis University, presents the world order perspective, explains the world order studies methodology, and examines strategies for change. The book contains extensive annotated bibliographies, study guides, and instructions for setting up and running world order study groups. The bibliographies contain major works by mainstream as well as non-mainstream authors.

Johansen, Robert C. *Jimmy Carter's National Security Policy: A World Order Critique.* Working Paper Number 14. World Order Models Project. New York: Institute for World Order, 1980. This 46-page paper is a skillfully executed analysis of the gap between Carter's globalist values and his failure to act upon them. Readers will learn how world order advocates do their research and construct world order critiques.

Johansen, Robert. *The National Interest and the Human Interest.* Princeton: Princeton University Press, 1980. Johansen evaluates American foreign policy during the Nixon and Carter years in four areas: strategic arms limitations, foreign aid to India, the human rights policies in Chile, and American policy toward the international control of marine pollution. In addition to evaluating American policies against "global humanist values," Johansen compares official rhetoric with actual behavior in each area. Although a bit dated, *The National Interest and the Human Interest* is well worth reading both for an understanding of the world order perspective and the wealth of information it contains. Johansen should update this book or write a sequel.

Kothari, Rajni, and Richard Falk, Mary Kaldor, and Giri Deshingkar. *Towards a Liberating Peace.* New York: New Horizons Press, 1989. This book, written under the United Nations Programme on Peace and Global Transformation, examines four major dimensions of the world order agenda—military, economic, ecological, and sociocultural. The authors present their preferred visions, propose strategies for change, and identify agents who will carry out those strategies.

Mendlovitz, Saul (ed.). *On the Creation of a Just World Order: Preferred Worlds for the 1990s*. New York: The Free Press, 1975. This book provides summaries of world order schemes written by an international array of scholars under the auspices of the World Order Models Project or WOMP, for short. In addition to Falk's essay (Selection 25), selections are presented by an African, Ali A. Mazrui, an Indian, Rajni Kothari, a Chilean, Gustavo Lagos, and a Japanese, Yoshikazo Sakamoto, as well as others. This book is well worth reading for the variety of visions and insights that it contains.

Michalak, Stanley J., Jr. "Richard Falk's Future World: A Critique of WOMP-USA. *The Review of Politics*, Vol. 24, No. 1 (January 1980), pp. 3–18. A comprehensive critique of Richard Falk's *A Study of Future Worlds*, a summary of which appeared as Selection 25. The article is followed by a thirteen-page response from Falk and a four-page response by Michalak.

Oakes, Guy and Kenneth Stunkel. "In Search of WOMP." *Journal of Political & Military Sociology*, Vol. 9, No. 1 (Spring, 1981), pp. 83–99. A highly critical review of the six volumes produced as part of the World Order Models Project. The authors argue that the world order advocates have no relevant audience for their ideas, no credible transition strategy, and no coherent research program.

Streeten, Paul. "Global Prospects in an Interdependent World." *World Development*, Vol. 19, No. 1 (January 1991), pp. 122–33. After outlining some emerging trends in the post–cold war world, Streeten sketches out some fairly detailed world order regimes based on the values of plurality and equality in the following issue-areas: recycling trade surpluses in the interests of Third World development, Third World debt, commodity price stabilization; international taxation, energy policy, corporate monopolies and oligopolies, and environmental protection. Streeten's essay is a good supplement to the selections by Falk and Beres.

Waters, Maurice. "The Law and Politics of a U.S. Intervention: The Case of Grenada." *Peace and Change*, Vol. 14, No. 1 (January 1989), pp. 65–106. A critique of the American invasion of Grenada from a world order perspective.

Wesley T. Wooley. *Alternatives To Anarchy: American Supranationalism since World War II*, Bloomington, IN: Indiana University Press, 1988. An excellent history of American world order movements since the end of World War II—the world federalist movement in the late forties and early fifties, the Atlantic Unionists from the mid-fifties to the mid-sixties, and the world order advocates of the 1970s.

## NOTES

1. Richard Falk, "Toward a New World Order: Modest Methods and Drastic Visions," in Saul Mendlovitz, *On the Creation of a Just World Order* (New York: The Free Press, 1975), pp. 221–22.
2. Mel Gurtov, *Global Politics in the Human Interest* (Boulder, CO: Lynne Rienner Publishers, 1988), pp. 4–5. Italics inserted.
3. Lester R. Brown, et al., *State of the World 1990* (New York: W. W. Norton & Company, 1990), p. xi.

4. Louise Rene Beres, *Reason and Realpolitik: U.S. Foreign Policy and World Order* (Lexington, MA: D.C. Heath and Company, 1984), p. 5.

5. Dante's *On Monarchy*, which proposed uniting Christian Europe under the Pope, appeared in 1313, over 300 years before the Peace of Westphalia in 1648.

6. Richard Falk, *A Study of Future Worlds* (New York: The Free Press, 1975), p. 68.

7. All of these quotations are taken from Saul Mendlovitz, "Struggle for a Just World Peace: A Transition Strategy," *Alternatives*, XIV (1989), pp. 363–69.

8. Beres, *Reason and Realpolitik*, p. 2.

9. All of these contrasting values are drawn from a list of "Alternative Norms and Structures" that Mel Gurtov presents in his *Global Politics in the Human Interest*, pp. 15–16.

10. Beres, *Reason and Realpolitik*, p. 5.

11. Robert A. Irwin, *Building A Peace System: A Book for Activists, Scholars, Students, and Concerned Citizens* (Washington, DC: Expro Press, 1989), p. 38.

12. Falk, *A Study of Future Worlds*, p. 39. Of the 531 members of the United States Congress, Saul Mendlovitz estimates that only about "haf a dozen" might be willing to run on a just world peace program. See his "Struggle for a Just World Peace," p. 369.

13. Richard Falk, "Toward a New World Order: Modest Methods and Drastic Visions," p. 252. Falk cites the following as exceptions to this statement: governments of some small- to medium-sized countries such as Sweden, Norway, and Canada, and "some governments in the Third World which have not betrayed their idealistic vision of human and societal potentiality," such as China and Tanzania.

14. Gurtov, *Global Politics in the Human Interest*, p. 170.

15. See Falk, "Toward a New World Order: Modest Methods and Drastic Visions," p. 249.

16. Richard Falk, *The End of World Order* (New York: Holmes & Meier Publishers, 1983), p. 22.

17. Mendlovitz, "Struggle for a Just World Peace: A Transition Strategy," *Alternatives*, XIV (1989), p. 363.

18. For example, the whole May 1990 issue of the *Journal of Peace Research* was dedicated to methods for studying global issues.

19. Falk, "Toward a New World Order: Modest Methods and Drastic Visions," p. 212.

20. Richard Falk, "Toward a New World Order," in Saul Mendlovitz (ed.), *On the Creation of a Just World Order: Preferred Worlds for the 1990s* (New York: The Free Press, 1975).

# Chapter
## 8
# New World,
# New Worldviews?

*N*ot since 1919 has the nation enjoyed such an opportunity for making fundamental choices in the area of foreign policy. With the end of the cold war and the dissolution of the Soviet bloc, citizens and foreign policy makers alike must address the following questions.

- Having attained its cold war goals of self-determination in Eastern Europe and the end of Soviet imperialism, can the nation now retreat from world power and pursue a less active, if not neo-isolationist, role in world affairs?
- Or should the United States work with the Soviet Union and other great powers in building a new system of world order as embodied in the United Nations Charter?
- Or should the United States play a more traditional great power role—working alone or with other like-minded nations in securing stable balances of power in Europe and Asia and maintaining order in other areas?

Essays addressing these questions have been appearing with increasing frequency in scholarly journals, magazines of opinion, and the editorial pages of the nation's newspapers. In fact, as the cold war wound down at the turn of the decade, symposiums and articles on the future of our foreign policy became a new mini-industry. In the spring of 1990, for example, *Policy Review* ran a symposium of leading conservatives and neoconservatives on what America's foreign and domestic goals should be for the rest of the century. Explicitly following *Policy Review*'s example, *The Progressive* ran its own symposium of nineteen perspectives from the left end of the political spectrum in its November issue. In its Fall 1990 issue, the *National Interest* ran a symposium on "America's Purpose Now," which featured the views of ten American and European notables whose political orientation ranged from the left to the right. Other magazines such as *The Atlantic, Foreign Affairs, Foreign Policy, Harper's, The Nation, The New Republic*, and *The Washington Quarterly* have also been running articles that explore and propose future foreign policy alterna-. tives for the nation.

As there were maximalists and minimalists during the cold war, there are maximalist and minimalist positions in the post–cold war era. Thus, the alternatives range from a policy of isolationism to one of leadership in building a new world order. Despite the array of alternatives, which includes some familiar faces, there is considerable agreement about the nation's immediate foreign policy agenda and the nature of the emerging international system. On the following propositions, there is a consensus:

1. The cold war is over and there is no turning back for the Soviet Union. There is little dissent from the belief that the Soviets have neither the desire nor the capacity to return to an ideologically driven superpower competition. As the neoconservative Irving Kristol expressed it,

> Focusing on overall developments within the Soviet system, all [political analysts of Soviet affairs] concur that the Cold War is indeed over. They agree that the Soviet Union today is simply impotent, lacking in political energy, to sustain an intention of aggressive expansion. Moreover, it no longer even desires to. The classical and long-dominant Soviet intention, which properly alarmed much of the world, has withered away.[1]

Clearly, the wisdom of George Kennan's three-stage strategy has been vindicated. Containment did succeed in keeping Soviet power from expanding into Kennan's vital industrial areas of Britain, Western Europe, and Japan. In addition, containment provided the security that allowed those areas to regain their economic strength and political confidence. Secondly, as the Soviet bloc expanded, the power of nationalism led to its fragmentation just as Kennan predicted. And finally, after decades of frustration, the Soviet conception of international politics has changed—no longer do Soviet leaders equate international politics with an ideological class struggle. In sum, the Soviet Union has returned to the status of a European great power.

2. Although the cold war is over, it needs to be wound up and wound up well. At a minimum, all agree that the United States and the Soviet Union should quickly agree on drastic reductions in strategic nuclear weapons and conventional military forces in Europe. Many also agree that the United States should not leave Europe until a new security system is in place, although there are many different ideas about what such a system should look like and how it should come about.[2]

3. Militarily and strategically, the international system has become unipolar. With the Soviet Union increasingly turning inward, the United States has become by default the preeminent military power with a capability for rapid global deployment, as seen in the Persian Gulf crisis.

4. However, despite this unipolarity, the utility of America's military power and the deference that others will give to it, might be much less than during the cold war era. According to Earl Ravenal, "Predictably, the United States will remain the leading power, but it will not be able to translate that primacy into much usable political-military influence beyond its own region."[3]

5. Having lost its global and bipolar East-West fault lines, international

politics will dissolve into regional orbits in the future. According to Harvard University professor Stanley Hoffman:

> Security concerns and balances are more likely to be regional rather than global; and while the United States, because of its military preeminence and its capacity to project might abroad, might see itself as the "sun" at the center of the solar system, there is no obvious need for the "planets" to turn around it in such a fragmented system—now that the somewhat artificial and never totally effective unity imposed by the Cold War is waning. In this system, nuclear states and states with an abundance of conventional forces will be powers of importance in each region.[4]

6. With the end of the cold war, former clients of the superpowers will be less restrained in pursuing local and regional objectives. Thus, regional powers with hegemonic ambitions may begin to act unilaterally, as Hussein did in Kuwait. In addition, long-festering and unresolved conflicts are likely to open into skirmishes, guerrilla war, or open warfare.[5] And, after decades of heavy arms sales and generous military assistance programs, we can expect some of these regional conflicts to be horribly destructive. According to General Carl Vuono, chief of staff of the army:

> Regional rivalries supported by powerful armies have resulted in brutal and devastating conflicts in the Third World. The proliferation of advanced military capabilities has given an increasing number of countries in the developing world the ability to wage sustained mechanized land warfare.[6]

The Iran-Iraq war serves as an omen of what we might expect in an international system where regions are the dominant centers of activity. From 1980 to 1987, the Iranian army averaged 617,000 men and reached a peak of 900,000 in 1987, while Iraq's military forces averaged around 378,000 from 1980 to 1983 and climbed to a high of over 650,000 in 1985 and 1986. In terms of casualties, Iran, with a population of 50 million, suffered 300,000 dead, 500,000 wounded, and 50,000 prisoners of war. Iraq, with a population of 17 million, suffered 150,000 dead, 300,000 wounded, and 70,000 prisoners of war. In the course of their ten-year war, both sides secured over $50 billion in arms from 28 different governmental and private arms suppliers.[7]

If the Iran-Iraq war is a precedent, the post–cold war era may be much more violent and unstable than the cold war era that preceded it—an era that historian John Lewis Gaddis referred to as "the long peace."[8] But even if regional conflicts do not replicate the scale of the Iran-Iraq war, almost all observers expect a much more disorderly international system in the years ahead. In summarizing the characteristics of the emerging international system, Earl Ravenal wrote in the winter of 1990–91 issue of *Foreign Policy* that "the first [characteristic] is the high probabilty of troubles such as embargoes, expropriations, coups, revolutions, externally supported subversions, and thrusts by impatient irredentist states."[9]

7. As the East-West conflict evaporates, economic competition will increase among the developed democracies, and conflicts over trade issues may sharpen. But rather than a "state-to-state" or "government-to-government" competition, this economic competition will increasingly take place among private individ-

uals and enterprises within an international economic system of "supranational capitalism." According to Stanley Hoffmann, "Key decisions about the world economy are made not in the political realm of states, but by private agents— investors, corporations, firms, banks, speculators, merchants, mafias—either without much control by state authorities or with enough influence to manipulate them."[10]

Increasingly, global production, investment, finance, and communications have become internationalized by private agents. Herbert Stein clearly perceived the nature of this newly emerging international economic order when he served as chairman of the Council of Economic Advisers under presidents Richard Nixon and Gerald Ford:

> The world economic order was to be universalist and private. We were floaters and free traders. In a strict sense, there would be no economic relations between countries. There would be economic relations between individuals who happened to live in different countries but who operated in a world market that didn't distinguish between friend or foe.[11]

8. The increasing integration of nations into this private international economic order makes it more difficult for governments to maintain economic security and affluence for their own citizens—full employment, stable prices, job and pension security, and widely shared rising standards of living.

9. Finally, there is amidst all of these trends a growing "people's power" or "populism" that is shaping and breaking even totalitarian governments. Perhaps the first hints of this new force appeared with the rise of the Ayatollah Khomeini and the consequent fall of the Shah and with the persistence of the Solidarity movement in Poland during the early 1980s. But, by the end of the 1980s, a decade of fallen dictators indicated a new force to be reckoned with. The increasing accessibility of a wide variety of information is making it much more difficult for governments to control the minds of their peoples and shape their images about life beyond their borders.

Scholars are still trying to characterize and figure out both the meaning and direction of this new force. Whether it will be a force for democracy, as in Eastern Europe, or a new instrument for populist demagogues, as in Iran, is uncertain.[12] But so far, this new "people's power" seems to be running against governments that have begun to lose their legitimacy. As Robert Bartley put it, "All Mikhail Gorbachev's intercontinental missiles could not impose his will on Eastern Europe, and probably in the long run not even on Lithuania."[13]

## THE NEW WAR OF THE WORLDVIEWS

Of the worldviews considered in this book, the world order perspective has been least affected by the collapse of Communism and the Soviet empire. For world order advocates, the end of the cold war means that the United States, in particular, and the developed world, in general, can turn their attention to building "a workable system of collective security through a structure of world interdependence."[14] However, a world order policy of "disinterested global-ism"—a policy that follows international majorities or universal principles with-out regard to particular American national interests—has no support within the mainstream.[15]

The radical worldview, on the other hand, has obviously been affected by the events of the late 1980s. In fact, one might say that the collapse of Communism has meant the collapse of at least half of the radical worldview. The future, it appears, did not work. Only in Castro's Cuba is the banner of "socialism" unabashedly waved. And, with the economic storms that lie ahead for that country, it is uncertain whether even as charismatic a leader as Fidel Castro can stem the worldwide rejection of Communist authoritarianism. Among radical scholars, then, there is also a reassessment taking place.

But the other half of the radical perspective has not been affected by the collapse of Communism—that half which seeks to explain American foreign policy in terms of the needs of corporate and international capitalism. Thus, radical scholars are busily at work seeking to assess the debate within the mainstream and predict the future of American foreign policy, as the selection in this chapter by Michael Klare indicates.

# THE DEBATE WITHIN THE MAINSTREAM

The bulk of the debate about America's role in the world is taking place among former mainstream contenders. The major fault line lies between neo-isola-tionists and internationalists. Then, within each of these categories, there are further subdivisions.

## Neo-isolationists and Internationalists

Neo-isolationists or noninterventionists eschew any involvement in creating geopolitical structures designed to preserve global or regional balances of power. They also oppose foreign policies designed to foster democracy, promote capitalism, or secure human rights abroad. For them, the guiding light for America should be the precept of John Adams quoted in Chapter 5: "America does not go abroad in search of monsters to destroy. She is the well-wisher of the freedom and independence of all. She is the champion and vindicator only of her own." This noninterventionist posture rests upon a set of assumptions that echo many of the arguments made by neo-isolationists in the past:

- The Soviet Union has lost its will and capacity to challenge the nation's security, and no other great power rival appears looming in the future.
- Even if such a challenger does appear, nuclear weapons will provide a sure deterrent against nuclear attacks, and strong defensive forces can deter, or easily defeat, any conventional invasion.
- Our former allies are capable of providing for their own defense and securing their national interests in such volatile regions as the Middle

East, Africa, and Asia. If they fail in such efforts, no vital American interests would be jeopardized.

- Interests will prevail over ideology, be that ideology Marxism or Islamic fundamentalism, and America's access to markets and resources would not be imperiled by an America that is a well-wisher to all.
- The United States can do little to control, channel, or resolve the innumerable kinds of instabilities and conflicts that exist or will arise in the Third World.
- Potential negative impacts of such chronic instability and conflict for any tangible American interests can be managed by domestic measure plus a judicious strategy of seeking multiple suppliers of any goods and raw materials that America truly needs.
- The world is not tightly interrelated in a political and military sense.
- The American public would acquiesce in, if not actively support, a policy that ignored the fate of our former allies and left the field of international leadership to anyone or to no one, whichever the case may be.

Because it prescribes a policy of nonintervention, neo-isolationism has little need for stock characters and scripts except negative ones—no more Koreas, no more Vietnams, no more Somozas, no more foreign aid, no more El Salvadors. The metaphors are those of "the city on the hill" and "America come home."

Internationalists, on the other hand, reject most of the neo-isolationist tenets and believe that the United States should be involved in the world for geopolitical, security, and environmental purposes. Their response to neo-isolationists can be summarized in a set of counterpropositions:

- While the Soviet Union has lost its will and capacity to challenge the nation's security, the United States still has an interest in the future evolution of Europe and Asia.
- Given the high probability of increasing regional disorders, America's power does bring responsibility, especially since no other country possesses America's interventionary capacity. Thus, given its power, the United States does have an obligation to help secure the weak from the predatory and to support and maintain orderly procedures for peaceful international change, as in South Africa and the Middle East.
- Many internationalists also believe that since America can no longer turn its back upon the liberal international economic order, the security of that order will require the nation to act with others, and at times perhaps even unilaterally, to keep that order secure, especially in the volatile Middle East.

Internationalists are well aware that the American public will not support long and costly military interventions. At the same time, they do not believe that the American people would support a policy that ignored the fate of the weak, left the fate of Europe and Asia to others, and discarded the mantle of leadership. Nor do internationalists believe that Americans would long be indifferent to the nature of the world within which they live. Thus, internationalists favor efforts to foster a global environment in which our acknowledged values of freedom, human rights, and economic enterprise can flourish. Contrary to neo-isolationists, internationalists believe that the United States can be a force for good in the world. While America may not always succeed, it can at least help to increase the amount of order, liberty, security, freedom, and prosperity in the world.

## Divisions Among Neo-isolationists

Post–cold war neo-isolationists include a mix of neorealist liberals and former reassertionists. While all agree that our military strategy should be confined to defending against direct threats to the nation's physical security, they disagree on the extent to which the United States should continue to enmesh itself in the increasingly supranational international economic order.

Liberal neo-isolationists, such as Michael Tonelson, favor insulating the nation somewhat from the international economic order, regaining greater control over our economy, and directing more attention to pressing domestic needs. Integration into an open world economy, such neo-isolationists argue, has increasingly led to dependencies upon foreign sources for vital products and commodities—dependencies that entail the kinds of "international interests" that might lead the nation back into an interventionist foreign policy. In addition, they also believe that economic integration opens the nation to forces beyond its control. According to Tonelson, a policy of economic openness ignores "the need to preserve certain industries suffering from even fair competition because they are vital either to the country's defenses or to its economic health in general."[16]

Harvard economist Charles Reich, no isolationist by any means, has expressed well the liberal neo-isolationist fears that our international economic policies are leading to a two-class nation. In the years ahead, Reich foresees an economy where our elites will compete effectively and flourish within the international economy while the vast majority will descend increasingly into low-paying, dead-end jobs in services and retailing. The following comments are taken from an interview with Reich which appeared in the magazine, *Society:*

> If you examine it closely, there is no longer an "American economy." There is no longer a monolithic issue called "U.S. competitiveness." There is no longer a "we." The top twenty percent of Americans are competing quite well in the international economy. . . . [This] top twenty percent are cosmopolitan. Their fates are linked to the fate of the global economy, not uniquely to that of the national economy. If present trends continue there will be a widening gap between rich and poor or, more accurately, between the rich and everybody else in this country. That will create grave problems.[17]

Conservative isolationists disagree. In their opinion, the economic insularity advocated by "storm shelter isolationism," is neither desirable nor possible. According to Ted Galen Carpenter, director of foreign policy studies at the Cato Institute in Washington, D.C., "The necessary curtailing of security commitments must not lead to a headlong plunge into economy autarky or intolerant nationalism."[18] Such neo-isolationists stress enhancing the nation's competitiveness and adjusting to, and taking advantage of, international market forces. In opposition to the "new nationalism" of Tonelson, Paul Weyrich wrote in *The National Interest* that "mercantilist governments basically exploit their own citizens and these policies will be unsustainable in an information age. The main lesson for elites to teach, and learn, is that unlike military competition, economic competition is a win-win game."[19]

## Divisions Among Internationalists

As indicated above, all internationalists share a commitment to maintaining a stable and peaceful international system and to fostering an environment in which liberal values may flourish and expand. Disagreements among them involve *the extent* of the nation's involvement and the *how* of that involvement.

**Multilateral Internationalism**   The changed Soviet conception of international politics now makes it possible for the five permanent members of the Security Council to revitalize the United Nations and make that organization work as its framers originally intended. In fact, when President Bush worked through the United Nations in response to the Iraqi invasion of Kuwait, the early results surprised even the most avid supporters of the world organization.

Consequently, many observers now favor giving a central role to the United Nations and other international institutions in all of the global issue areas— security, development, human rights, and the environment. In the opinion of one such multilateralist, America should work with other democracies in "the construction of a peaceful world order through multilateral cooperation and effective international organizations."[20]

**Contingent Multilateralism**   Yet, cooperations has its costs, and the most important of these is freedom of action. As Elie Kedourie put it, "The consequence of speaking as though [Desert Shield] is simply the executant of U.N. decrees is to allow those who have ventured neither blood nor treasure in the cause to claim the right to offer advice and to bestow (or deny) a strictly gratuitous approval."[21] Working through international institutions would require the United States to compromise, to persuade, to cajole, and to concede. Very early in the effort to build an international coalition against Iraq, for example, people began asking what "price" the United States had to pay to get certain countries to support its resolutions in the Security Council.[22] And, of course, a multilateral policy has to mean that the United States will not get what it wants at times.

Thus, many internationalists are skeptical of the entanglement, the risks, and the loss of freedom that multilateral internationalism would entail. For such internationalists, the United Nations should be an instrument of American diplomacy, an instrument to be used when it serves our interests but ignored or avoided whenever serious national interests are at stake. The argument of these more unilateral internationalists is a simple one: As a great power, the United

States has worldwide interests, and it cannot allow the security of those interests to be decided by, if not held hostage to, a coterie of nations who may not share, and may even oppose, those interests. Peace and the balance of power in the world, more unilaterally prone internationalists argue, will depend upon what the great powers decide to do or not do.

The differences between these two groups of internationalists are, of course, matters of degrees. Liberal internationalists do not oppose unilateral action when global action is impractical or impossible. Their presumption, however, is in favor of multilateral action and leadership, especially in regional conflicts. More unilateral internationalists favor multilateral approaches for dealing with such issues as global warming and world hunger. On security issues, however, they are most skeptical of multilateral approaches, especially those that rely upon the United Nations.

**Globalists and Regionalists**    Internationalists also divide on the extent to which the United States should concern itself with regional balances of power. Some internationalists believe that the United States should concern itself with the balance of power among the major powers and leave regional conflicts to international institutions or other powers. Other internationalists believe that America has vital interests in almost all of the regions of the world. Therefore, they favor a policy of opposing potentially hostile regional powers and, if unilateral uses of force are necessary to maintain those balances, they would not shrink from action. The orientation of these internationalists stems from a reading of nineteenth-century European diplomacy, and especially British diplomacy. The essays by Nitze and Katz develop each of these internationalist positions.

# The Selections

*The essays that follow provide a small sample of post–cold war musings from the perspectives outlined above. As you read these selections, you will note strong continuities with the worldviews presented in earlier chapters. By recasting these essays into worldview profile sheets, you will be able to compare and evaluate them better. The bibliography that follows has been carefully selected to allow a deep immersion into some of the best writings that have appeared.*

## 27. Paul H. Nitze
### *America: An Honest Broker*                                    1990

In this essay, one of the nation's most distinguished diplomats and strategists calls for multilateral internationalism. "In a world of growing interdependence, where the problems of distant neighbors are increasingly our own," Nitze writes that "it is not now time for the United States to retreat from the world stage." In addition to making the case for multilateralism, Nitze's essay is especially valuable for its succinct historical overview of American foreign policy since the end of World War II. Nitze's career spans the entire cold war period, ranging from his work in the State Department during the founding years of containment to his service as an arms control negotiator for Ronald Reagan.

Each of us has experienced the phenomenal central European revolution of 1989, its preliminaries in Poland and its continuing aftermath, particularly in Germany and the Soviet Union. But each has done so from his or her own window on the world.

Having spent much of my life as a policy planner, I tend to focus on the future, on what lies ahead, on what is desirable and perhaps practical, and on what policies would most successfully help to bring about these aims. I also tend to translate this forward-looking perspective into American terms: What should we in this country view as our role in collaboration with others in moving the world toward this desired future?

In charting a road to the future, it is sometimes wise to look back on relevant turning points of the past. For over forty years the foreign and defense policies of the United States have been guided by a central theme, a well-defined basic policy objective. That goal, throughout the Cold War, was for the United States to take the lead in building an international world order based on liberal economic and political institutions, and to defend that world against communist attack.

The political-strategic situation is now changed. We are in an important period of transition. Our postwar policies appear to have achieved their principal objective, and a new conception of our foreign and defense policies is required as we face a future less dominated by an ideologically driven U.S.S.R. Before we can formulate a new strategy, however, it is first in order that we review our postwar policy of containment, its origins and rationale, and where and the degree to which it has succeeded.

## II

In the summer and fall of 1943 fragments of discussion could be heard in Washington about U.S. postwar relations with the Soviet Union. Much of World War II remained to be fought, but for the first time Hitler's eventual defeat seemed probable. It was not too early to think about what kind of peace and relations among the leading powers we wished to see established in the postwar world.

By the war's end a majority of Washington's policymakers favored a three-point plan. The first objective was to support the United Nations and its associated agencies and to make them operational. The second objective was to work out methods of collaboration with Stalin and his associates; this was seen as a prerequisite for the smooth and successful operation of the United Nations and its organs. The third objective was to rely on the British to deal with the wide array of political problems arising from the chaos of a world destroyed by two wars just twenty years apart. Only a minority at this point thought that the principal problems of the postwar period would be caused by the Soviet Union, which had borne a major share of the burden of defeating Hitler.

A key participant in this debate was of course George F. Kennan, who while serving in our embassy in Moscow sent to Washgton in February 1946 a compelling analysis of Stalinist policy, its origins, its evils and its dangers, in what became known as the "long telegram." Stalin's expansionism, he informed Washington, was becoming more aggressive as it fed upon its successes. He elaborated in the well-known "Mr. X" article published in *Foreign Affairs* in July 1947 as follows:

> The United States has it in its power to increase enormously the strains under which Soviet policy must operate, to force upon the Kremlin a far greater degree of moderation and circumspection than it has had to observe in recent years, and in this way to promote tendencies which must eventually find their outlet in either the breakup or the gradual mellowing of Soviet power. For no mystical, Messianic movement—and particularly not that of the Kremlin—can face frustration indefinitely without eventually adjusting itself in one way or another to the logic of that state of affairs.

Kennan recommended a policy of containment until such time as the Soviet people awoke to the destruction of their heritage and withdrew their support from Stalinesque policies. His recommendations were not immediately accepted by the Truman administration, which was still hoping for a cooperative relationship with Moscow. The evidence, however, soon became overwhelming that Stalin and Molotov had no intention of collaborating with the West to work out a just and equitable arrangement in Europe.

Other pillars of our postwar policy were failing as well. The Soviet Union's continuing opposition and frequent use of its veto power in the Security Council turned the United Nations largely into a forum for public debate and diminished its influence on matters where East and West disagreed. Additionally, the third pillar of American policy, reliance on Britain to maintain global political stability, became untenable when in February 1947 the British government informed President Truman that it could no longer sustain the burden of supporting Greece and Turkey in their struggle against Soviet pressure and Soviet-supported guerrilla units. This decision by Britain brought the postwar crisis to a head; if assistance to Greece and Turkey were to continue, it would have to come from the United States.

Truman's response was immediate: the United States would come to the aid of both countries. This historic and crucial decision not only implied approval of the containment policy and the European Recovery Program but, more generally, it represented America assuming leadership of a new postwar world order. We pledged our efforts to the creation of a world made in the mold of the best that Western culture had to offer, with full freedom for others to participate in its benefits if they wished to cooperate while doing so.

## III

The next 15 weeks saw a whirlwind of activity. Truman announced the Greek-Turkish aid program and the Truman Doctrine, declaring U.S. willingness to consider such aid as could prudently be made available to any country subject to aggression or intimidating pressure and prepared to act in its own defense. Under Secretary of State Dean Acheson outlined in a Mississippi speech the rationale for a general program of European economic aid, and Secretary of State George C. Marshall set forth the concept of the Marshall Plan in June 1947 in a commencement speech at Harvard University.

Surprisingly, bipartisan support for this ambitious program developed in Congress, which approved all necessary authorizations and appropriations. Congress then passed the 1947 National Security Act, establishing the Department of Defense and the Joint Chiefs of Staff, providing for an air force independent of the army and creating the Central Intelligence Agency. Legislation authorizing the Marshall Plan cleared Congress in 1948, and shortly thereafter negotiations began on the North Atlantic Treaty, and then NATO. Concurrently, we began working to bring both Germany and Japan back to economic self-sufficiency and, step by step, into the community of nations.

The detonation of a Soviet nuclear device in September 1949 gave further impetus to the U.S. policy of containment, as the Soviet threat acquired a new and more ominous dimension. That event, together with the consolidation of communist rule on the Chinese mainland, suggested that we were on the verge of what the communists would call "a shift in the correlation of forces" in their favor. The question was what Moscow would do and how Washington should react.

A crucial aspect of the problem was whether the United States should move forward with the development of a thermonuclear weapon, the hydrogen bomb. Truman appointed a special committee of the National Security Council composed of the secretaries of state and defense and the chairman of the Atomic Energy Commission to study the problem and make recommendations. A heated debate led to the question of whether the Soviets themselves had the potential to develop a thermonuclear device. When he was told in January 1950 that the Soviet Union did indeed have the necessary capabilities, Truman authorized an accelerated program to test the possibility of a thermonuclear reaction, though he did not make a decision to proceed beyond a test. What we did not know was that the Soviet Union had initiated development of the hydrogen bomb a full three months earlier.

Truman ordered the National Security Council to reexamine the aims and objectives of our national security policy in light of the possibility that thermonuclear weapons were technically feasible. Acheson and Defense Secretary Louis Johnson were given joint responsibility for the review. On the State Department side, the policy planning staff and I, as director, were responsible for the review work. From this study evolved NSC-68, which was eventually approved by the president in September 1950, after the North Koreans attacked South Korea.

This report was highly classified until 1975, when it was released to the public, finally shedding the mystique that had gathered around its long years of official secrecy. NSC-68 did not call for as sharp a departure in U.S. policy as was commonly believed. It reaffirmed conclusions of NSC-20/4, an already approved policy paper regarding relations with the Soviet Union prepared in 1948 by Kennan. The major change recommended in NSC-68 was a stepped-up effort to counter recent global developments, specifically a significantly increased Soviet military capability, with emphasis on strengthening our own military capabilty. NSC-68 stressed the thesis that U.S. and allied power, including military power, had become fundamentally important to the successful pursuit of our foreign policy objectives and to the defense of our national interests.

In this respect NSC-68 differed from NSC-20/4, which reaffirmed the fundamentals of "containment," only in the method of implementation; Kennan did not attach the same degree of importance to the role of military power in the pursuit of foreign policy objectives.

Sustaining the policy of containment for the time necessary to achieve its objective—almost four decades as it turned out—required great perseverance on the part of the nation. It was necessary during the Korean War for us to expand our military budgets; likewise, in the Eisenhower years we had to expand significantly our strategic nuclear capabilities in order to offset extraordinary efforts by the Soviet Union to obtain nuclear superiority.

Efforts on arms control began immediately after World War II with the Baruch Plan. They continued thereafter in international forums under the aegis of the United Nations. But the actual limitation of offensive and defensive systems foundered on efforts, largely by the Soviets, to use the negotiations as a platform for worldwide propaganda.

The United States and the Soviets agreed by 1969 to initiate bilateral negotiations to limit offensive systems, as well as the defensive systems designed to counter them. For different reasons both sides were interested from the beginning in equal limitations on antiballistic missile systems. With respect to offensive systems, however, the Soviets believed time was on their side and insisted on advantages that the United States could not permanently accept.

Two arms control agreements were entered into in 1972. The first was the Antiballistic Missile Treaty, evenhanded in its terms but containing a number of ambiguities, not all of which have yet been fully resolved. The second was an Interim Agreement on offensive systems, which it was agreed would be superseded by a comprehensive permanent treaty to be arrived at through prompt subsequent negotiations. Eighteen years later, such a comprehensive treaty has still not been achieved or ratified, and inventories of offensive nuclear weapons have continued to grow.

By 1981 both the United States and the Soviet Union had shifted their primary focus in negotiations to the issue of elimination, or at least control, of intermediate-range nuclear forces (INF). This issue was of crucial importance to the European members of the NATO alliance. The United States had agreed with its NATO partners to deploy Pershing II and ground-launched cruise missiles in Europe in order to offset the Soviet Union's earlier deployment on the continent of longer-range nuclear missiles with multiple warheads. The Soviet aim in these negotiations was now to block the U.S. deployment, without giving up their own missiles. If successful in this objecive, the Soviets would have shattered the NATO alliance and isolated the United States.

NATO did not flinch, however, despite a concerted Soviet propaganda campaign and Moscow's walkout from the INF talks. This check to Soviet policy was a crucial point in the long, continuous Western effort to contain Soviet expansionism. It provided clear evidence to a new generation of Soviet leaders that old tactics of intimidation would not work. Led by Mikhail Gorbachev, the Soviets were now prepared to reconsider their former policies and methods.

In a meeting in Moscow in 1987 with Secretary of State George Shultz, Gorbachev recalled that when he first became general secretary of the Communist Party he did not begin from a standing start. He and Nikolai Ryzhkov were appointed to the Politburo in 1982 and, Gorbachev recounted, it was then that they exchanged views on the serious internal problems facing the Soviet state— the political structure of the party, the backwardness of the economy, the excessive allocation of resources to defense, and more. After these discussions, Gorbachev said, they appointed a hundred teams composed of the brightest minds they could find to analyze these problems and come up with suggestions for solutions.

When I heard these statements by Gorbachev, it seemed to confirm that our policy of containment had indeed achieved its basic aim; Soviet leaders were forced to look inward, and they did not like what they saw.

Containment has thus been largely successful, the Cold War is waning and communist ideology may well be in its final decline, much as Nazism and fascism were at the end of World War II. The non-Soviet part of the Warsaw Pact has now lost its strategic significance. It is time therefore to reexamine containment, our longstanding central policy objective, with the goal of making a transition to a new conception of U.S. policy, one better suited to a changing future.

## IV

A time of transition is bound to be a period of uncertainty; old guideposts are gone or quickly fading and new landmarks need to be sorted out and established. The United States cannot possibly ensure that global stability will follow this period of transition. The most we can do is to use our influence to move world events in a direction of peace.

We first need to break down the problem into its relevant parts—political, economic, military, regional, environmental, etc.—and reach tentative conclusions about sensible policy in each category, testing from time to time the coherence of an overarching line of policy that integrates these various components. Thus while thinking through the long-term measures that we hope will lead to global stability, we must also deal concurrently with the immediate problems before us. It is only by successfully handling these problems that we keep our long-range planning from losing touch with the practical world as it is evolving.

What are our current issues?

- First, should we continue to focus our policy toward the Soviet Union on helping Gorbachev preserve his base of power, or should we focus more on our longer-term relations with whatever regime may emerge in control of the Russian people and those willing to remain associated with them?

    We need to walk a fine line on this question. It is in the U.S. interest that Gorbachev remain in charge. He is a known quantity and his policies, with all their faults, are probably preferable to those we could currently expect from any likely successor.

    On the other hand, we should not tie ourselves so closely to Gorbachev that we undermine our ability, should he lose power, to work with those who will follow. We made that mistake with Chiang Kai-shek in China and the shah in Iran. We cannot afford to repeat it with Gorbachev in the Soviet Union.

- Should we seek a prompt conclusion to the Strategic Arms Reduction Talks (START) along the lines suggested in the communiqué at the U.S.-Soviet summit in June 1990, or should we reassess the possibility and desirability of a deeper set of stabilizing reductions?

I believe it is in our interest to seek deeper and more stabilizing cuts in strategic forces than those contemplated by the summit communiqué. These cuts should focus on land-based missiles with multiple warheads, particularly the Soviets' heavy intercontinental ballistic missiles (ICBMS). As long as these missiles exist, their great destructive capability will poison our political and military relations with the Soviet Union. These missiles will cause us to take costly and undesirable countermeasures to assure that there is no possibility of the Soviet Union exploiting their enormous potential. It would be far better for all if the Soviet Union were to eliminate its heavy ICBMS as part of an agreement under which both it and the United States eliminated land-based, multiple-warhead missiles and placed equal ceilings on remaining strategic nuclear warheads.

Specifically, I suggest the draft START treaty be amended as follows:

- to ban land-based missiles with multiple warheads;
- to relax or even eliminate the limit of 1,600 on the number of weapon systems for each side, as this would remove the necessity for either to deploy destabilizing, multiple-warhead systems;
- to limit the weight of individual warheads to 200 kilograms or less in order to prevent the deployment of new large special-function nuclear warheads, such as those the Soviets are suspected of planning to deploy on their new SS-18 Mod 6; and

- to reduce the number of existing strategic warheads by at least twice that contemplated by START, i.e., by approximately 75 percent as opposed to approximately 35 percent.

If all ground-based, multiple-warhead nuclear missiles were banned, the remaining systems permitted to each side would be highly survivable against a first-strike nuclear attack. These remaining systems would include single-warhead, fixed or mobile, ground-based nuclear missiles; submarine-launched nuclear ballistic missiles and nuclear cruise missiles; long-range air-launched nuclear cruise missiles; and bombers armed only with gravity bombs and short-range attack missiles limited to less than 600 kilometers.

If the nuclear systems permitted to each side were inherently highly survivable and unable to attack more than a single target, there would be no point in either side's attempting to improve its position by initiating an attack on the strategic forces of the other. Three to five thousand such systems on each side would suffice to make undetected cheating or the capabilities of other nuclear powers—now and in the foreseeable future—insufficient to upset the inherent stability this type of arrangement would bring to the nuclear relationship between the United States and the U.S.S.R.

I believe the opportunity for a radical and mutually beneficial solution is better now than it would be if the issue were postponed. We should therefore insist now on a truly stabilizing treaty, rather than being satisfied with the half-measures currently proposed.

- Should we encourage Lithuania and the other Baltic states seeking greater independence to postone or scale back their demands in order to relieve the pressure on Gorbachev, or should we support our long-held position that the absorption of these states by Stalin through an unsavory deal with Hitler was improper?

This is of course one of the issues important to Gorbachev's prospects. In the case of the Baltic states, however, I believe other considerations must prevail. The United States has never recognized the propriety of Soviet annexation of the Baltic states, and to change our position now would be inconsistent with our values and counterproductive in the long term. It is thus sensible to encourage negotiations between Moscow and the Baltic states, but we should allow the Baltic governments to decide for themselves what negotiating position to take.

- What should our attitude be toward a united Germany and NATO?

The United States and NATO continue to have an important role in maintaining stability on the European continent and contributing to stability elsewhere on the globe. Other organizations, such as the 35-nation Conference on Security and Cooperation in Europe (CSCE), may play useful supporting roles, but could not possibly substitute for NATO, at least as far as the United States is concerned. It is important that NATO include the powerful political, economic and military forces that a unified Germany will represent. I also believe that Soviet security interests will be better served by a Germany united within NATO than by a neutral Germany. Recent negotiations suggest that Gorbachev has also come around to this view. Clearly, an isolated Germany is potentially more dangerous than one cooperating as a valued member of a community of nations.

- What are our primary economic concerns and what should we do about them?

Economic problems abound worldwide, from the collapse of the Soviet economy, to the struggles of the East European countries to convert to free-market economies, to the ordeal of Third World nations seeking to emerge from overwhelming debt. In considering the panoply of global economic problems and possible solutions, I think we must first concentrate on getting our own house in order. The U.S. budget deficit, coupled with our balance-of-payments problems, is limiting our ability to aid the new democracies of Eastern Europe and Central America, to help fund solutions to global environmental problems and to otherwise bring our economic clout to bear on world problems of great interest to everyone. If we are to suggest sacrifices by others attempting to shift to market economies, pay off their debts and remedy sources of ecological damage, then we must also be prepared to reduce excessive consumption and heal our economy

The United States must also deal with other domestic problems currently exacerbating international difficulties. A stepped-up campaign against drug use should be undertaken in an effort to reduce the U.S. demand that is such a major factor in the worldwide drug trade. Separately, strict enforcement of the clean air law is necessary to help reduce the U.S. emissions that are major contributors to worldwide environmental deterioration.

- How should we deal with problems that transcend national boundaries, such as global environmental decay?

Many problems we now face cut across national boundaries and affect many cultures. Economic and environmental problems are but two categories; others include terrorism and drugs. Still other problems that face many individual nations, such as hunger, can best be addressed through concerted international efforts.

These types of problems can generally be handled more efficiently and effectively by supranational institutions than by individual governments acting in the absence of some central coordinating body. Any grant of authority to a supranational body, however, implies some loss by nations of sovereign choice. We must therefore be careful to balance the gains of centrally directed efforts against the costs of reduced freedom of choice for individual nations. The gains to be derived from a supranational authority most clearly outweigh the costs in environmental issues. One nation's efforts to reverse the growing damage to the world ecology can easily be undercut by the negligence of other countries. A coordinated international effort is certainly required if we are to save our environment.

# V

Returning to the question of an overall policy line, a strategic concept to guide our approach to the panoply of issues we face and to give our individual policies larger coherence. The new strategic concept I propose is captured in the following four sentences:

- The central theme of the policy of the United States should be the accommodation and protection of diversity within a general framework of world order.
- Our aim should be to foster a world climate in which a wide array of political groups are able to exist, each with its own and perhaps eccentric ways.
- Supranational institutions, such as the United Nations and its organs, NATO, the European Community, CSCE and the Organization for Economic Cooperation and Development, should be given the role of providing stability and forward movement on important global and regional issues that transcend national or ethnic boundaries.
- The United States, with inherent political, economic, cultural and military strengths, and no territorial or ideological ambitions of its own, can and should play a unique role in bringing its powers to the support of order and diversity among the world's diffuse and varied groups.

The emphasis on diversity derives from one of the most important lessons of the past few years: the near impossibility of erasing cultural ties, ethnic identities and social practices in a world where communications and ideas cannot be suppressed. Despite the efforts by communist leaders for decades to impose a common culture and society on their subjects, a Europe with a rich mix of nationalities and cultures is once again reviving. A similar process is occurring on other continents as well. Not only are the aspirations of individuals and ethnic groups once again being realized, but this constellation of the cultures promises to enrich us all.

While there is much to learn from the ways of others, diversity also creates problems. The tensions that diversity had generated in the past have arisen once more—between Hungarians and Romanians, Bulgarians and Turks, Serbs and Albanians, and among the many nationalities throughout the Soviet Union. Such tensions may be the primary threat to peace in the years ahead.

Diversity therefore presents us with mixed blessings. As a democratic nation that honors freedom, we protect the right to dissent and to be different, as well as the rights of minorities from discrimination, and thus the United States supports this movement toward greater diversity. As a people who can learn from the ways of others, we welcome the opportunity to do so. As students of history, we understand that the aspirations of various peoples to realize their heritage cannot in any event be long suppressed.

As realists, however, we must recognize and try to contend with the dangers that accompany excessive nationalism and threaten to destroy the general peace. The assertion that the United States has no ideological ambitions does not mean we are without strong values; it means only that we should not impose these values on others. Just as we can learn from other peoples, they too can learn much from us, but we must realize that cooperative efforts among nations are generally more effective in achieving this end. The central element of my theme is thus the accommodation and protection of diversity within a framework of global order.

# VI

The emphasis on a global role for the United States is perhaps controversial. Many Americans argue that the current mood favors a withdrawal from a leading role in international affairs. Their reasoning is that a great threat is no longer evident, and the United States is therefore free to turn inward and tend to its domestic concerns.

This outlook is shortsighted. As the issues I have addressed above indicate, there remain numerous international problems that deeply affect American interests. New problems of this same nature are bound to arise. The United States remains uniquely capable of contributing in conjunction with others to the effective solution of these problems. No other nation can do the job as well.

The Soviet Union, for example, even with the reductions I have advocated for a START treaty, will retain thousands of nuclear warheads and remain a potential threat to the United States and its allies. The current instability in that country only exacerbates the problem; no one can be sure into whose hands these weapons may eventually fall. No other country is capable of relieving the United States of the burden of deterring the use of these weapons, and none is likely to be able to do so in the future. Nor would we want any other country to deploy the nuclear arsenal needed to assume that role alone.

Similarly, should nationalist tensions in Europe erupt into civil or cross-border conflicts, no other country would seem as well qualified to play the role of honest broker in facilitating, with others, a peaceful resolution of these differences and terminating hostilities. In the absence of the United States from Europe, Germany would seem to have the greatest military, political and economic power on the continent, and thus leadership would fall to it in such a situation. Germany, however, is not well suited for such a role. Suspicion of German intentions, justified or not, remains too high among the nations of Europe for Germany to be effective in the role of honest broker.

The United States therefore must remain in a position to contribute to the continent's stability should European nations, including Germany, wish us to do so. This does not necessarily mean the continued presence of large numbers of American troops in Europe; we will only keep such forces there as are wanted and only for such a time as they are wanted. A constructive U.S. role in European affairs can be derived from more than simply the number of troops deployed; potential power can be symbolized even by the presence of forces of limited size.

Similar examples of problems meriting a U.S. role exist in other regions of the world. In the Middle East, the strategic importance of which is obvious, the United States is currently actively supporting the peace process, attempting to work with Israel, Egypt and the Palestine Liberation Organization. It is not evident that any other country has the clout necessary to assume this role effectively.

In time our leading role in the Far East could perhaps be assumed by Japan. But this would raise considerable concern among other Asian nations, especially those who have fallen under Japanese domination in the past. It is further doubtful that the Japanese would find it feasible to consider the interests of others comparable to their own.

All of these cases argue for the American role I have proposed. But let me also make clear the constraints on this role. I am proposing active U.S. participation in cooperative efforts with varying groups of sovereign nations to deal constructively with common problems; I am not proposing unilateral U.S. action. I am suggesting we act internationally where the common interest can be served; I am not suggesting unduly impinging upon the sovereignty of others. Our engagement on the world scene should therefore be carefully selective, based on our new objective of tolerating and strengthening diversity around the globe.

## VII

As we advance further into this difficult period of transition, the West will find new opportunities to resolve the longstanding problems. The United States must remain alert to signs of conflict and creative in analyzing new means of cooperative efforts among nations interested in resolving these conflicts without unnecessarily impinging upon national sovereignties or individual rights. We must be ready to bring our unique levers of influence to bear when they are able to play a constructive role in world events.

In a world of growing interdependence, where even the problems of distant neighbors are increasingly our own, it is not now the time for the United States to retreat from the world stage. It is, rather, the time for prudent leadership to bring America's extraordinary potential to bear on today's problems so that the many benefits promised by a free and diverse world can soon be realized by all. In order to create the public foundation for such action, however, we need to build a broad consensus on a new concept for America's foreign and defense policy and, to build upon that, a new national resolve.

## 28. Alan Tonelson
## *A Manifesto for Democrats*                      1989

In this selection, Alan Tonelson, a former associate editor of *Foreign Policy*, presents the case for a more insulationist and nationalist foreign policy. Tonelson argues that the Democratic party has a strong interest in adopting a more insular foreign policy because its major supporters—factory workers, minorities, and the poor—have been most hurt by America's postwar internationalist foreign policies. Thus, he calls upon the Democratic party "to abandon internationalism and its no longer affordable strategy of grounding American security and prosperity in a congenial world environment of liberal democracies, collective security, and free trade."

Foreign policy certainly did not lose the 1988 presidential election for the Democrats, but it clearly did not help, either. And a party that has lost the White House in five of its last six tries, and that considers Michael Dukakis' ten-state haul an encouraging showing, needs all the help it can get.

Nineteen eighty-eight once again revealed the Democrats' inability to meet a triple foreign policy challenge—convincing the public that they can be tough national security managers (still essential in the Gorbachev era, as the Bush victory shows), championing the interests of working-class and other economically squeezed voters, and differentiating themselves from the Republicans.

To pass these political tests and to cope with the foreign policy agenda of the 1990s and beyond, the Democrats need a complete overhaul in their foreign policy thinking. Specifically, they are going to have to abandon internationalism and its no longer affordable strategy of grounding American security and prosperity in a congenial world environment of liberal democracies, collective security, and free trade. Instead, the party needs an approach that emphasizes the restoration of U.S. military and economic strength; that is more discriminating about foreign military commitments and more willing to use force unilaterally to secure truly important interests; that advocates tougher trade policies with the country's leading economic partners; and that seeks greater self-sufficiency in strategically important reosurces and manufactures. What the Democrats need—with apologies to Progressive-era intellectual Herbert Croly—is a New Nationalism.

In his classic *The Liberal Tradition in America* (1955), historian Louis Hartz wrote that Lockeian liberalism so pervaded American political life that we forget that it is an ideology rather than the natural order of things. The same can be said for internationalism in American foreign policy since 1945.

As a foreign policy approach that has commanded the loyalty of every postwar American president (Ronald Reagan was only a partial exception), internationalism has taken on a bewildering variety of forms. Indeed, in the Winter 1985–86 issue of *Foreign Policy*, Carnegie Endowment president Thomas L. Hughes, a perceptive chronicler of internationalism's fortunes, described it as a "disposition, mindset, or world view" rather than a coherent school of thought; a phenomenon that was, "like the Church of England . . . doctrinally inexplicable, but how it did go on." But all of its variants—as Hughes describes them, sensitive cooperationism, insensitive interventionism, soft inclusionism, hard exclusionism, the internationalism of the barracks, the officer's club, the counting house, and the diplomatic circuit, the culture of security and the culture of equity—have shared very specific and distinguishing beliefs.

First and foremost is the conviction that the United States will never know true security, lasting peace, and genuine prosperity unless the rest of the world is secure, peaceful, and prosperous as well. Second is the belief that these favorable conditions depend on the creation and enforcement of worldwide norms of behavior. Third, internationalists insist that the United States, as the free world's strongest military and economic power, still has no choice but to shoulder the largest share of the burden for keeping the resulting global systems intact. . . .

In a complicated, diverse world, anything purporting to be a foreign policy "doctrine" should be viewed skeptically. But the following principles could help point the Democrats towards a New Nationalist synthesis that combines the best of the ideas now scattered among the party's various wings.

*First,* the purpose of American foreign policy is not to promote peace, stability, and development throughout the world; to spread American values; to get on the right side of history (something no one can identify with any confidence); to obey and strengthen international law; to contain the expansion of Soviet power everywhere; or to compete internationally with the Soviets or anyone else for global influence. The purpose of American foreign policy is to do whatever is necessary to defend America's security and domestic freedoms, and to sustain or increase its material welfare.

*Second,* for any country whose material resources are limited physically or by competing domestic priorities—that is to say, any country—the only way to accomplish these tasks is to identify a finite set of countries or regions whose geographic position, resources, or markets make their defense or cooperation important. Hinging American security or prosperity on the creation or maintenance of a congenial international environment, and especially emphasizing a central U.S. role in this task, is a recipe for spending the country into the ground. For this approach forces on U.S. policy-makers the conclusion that every effort to prop up the system is worth the candle, no matter how costly. Foreign policies that attempt to create conditions that have never before existed—like democracy in most of the Third World—are especially likely to become exorbitantly expensive.

In addition, the more realistic a country's set of foreign policy priorities, the more effectively and the more credibly that country can defend them. Since the United States lost its military preponderance, pretensions of omnipotence have been difficult to carry off. Moreover, a foreign policy that ignores costs for the sake of indiscriminate abstractions like "democracy" or "free trade" is unlikely to guarantee that sufficient resources are available for the truly important international challenges.

*Third,* the United States is not powerful enough to remake the world in its own image. But it is powerful enough to survive and prosper without serving as the noncommunist world's defender, banker, and market of last resort, as well as its chief social worker. The United States is militarily strong, geopolitically secure, immensely wealthy and economically dynamic, and more self-sufficient economically than any significant power on earth except for the Soviet Union.

Further, geography still counts, even in the nuclear age. And as long as they possess a survivable nuclear deterrent, American strategists no longer need to worry about the bogeyman of an invasion by an Old World hegemon. Not only would any attacking force have to travel thousands of miles across the oceans, but nuclear weapons could easily vaporize any enemy armada seconds after it left port—if not while troops were being massed. In the economic field, access to the U.S. market and American technology is still the world's top prize.

In other words, other countries need the United States far more than the United States needs them, and U.S. foreign policy should start reflecting the leverage this country enjoys. In particular, the United States need not run around the world begging other countries to let it protect them, or selling them arms for the privilege of talking with them (à la Reagan's ill-fated Iran initiative). Nor must it retreat in trade negotiations when its economic partners threaten retaliatory responses to protectionist U.S. policies. It is time for the United States to start demanding much more favorable quid pro quos.

*Fourth,* beyond the core security concerns of national survival, independence, and territorial integrity, all the major issues of U.S. foreign policy must be subjected to a strict cost-benefit calculus. The expenses of various foreign military commitments, aid programs, and trade postures should be compared with anticipated concrete benefits—whether measured in terms of sales for American companies, income from U.S. overseas investments, the value of critical foreign supplies of manufactures or commodities, or the importance of denying adversaries control over certain worldwide centers of production and technology.

Under such a regimen, of course, a policy that costs more than it brings in within some finite, measurable time frame cannot be justified. This has particularly big implications for the most expensive items in the American national security budget—the defense of Western Europe and Japan. The former costs somewhere in the neighborhood of $150 to $175 billion annually; the latter approximately $40 to $50 billion. However important the economic relationships that these expenditures preserve, they cannot by definition be worth the bankruptcy of the U.S. economy—which could well result if they are not reduced soon.

These U.S. expenditures become even more difficult to justify against the backdrop of chronic American trade deficits with all of these major allies—for 1988, $12.5 billion with Western Europe and $52 billion with Japan. And the economic rationale for the U.S. defense commitment to Western Europe could be strained to the breaking point by the scheduled achievement of a single West European internal market in 1992, a development that could eventually shut out many U.S. exports. America's major defense commitments make considerable strategic and economic sense as genuine alliances. They make no sense as the protectorates they are now.

*Fifth,* free trade can bring enormous benefits to the United States, but as many Democrats of all stripes have observed, free trade must be fair. Even the party's most strident economic nationalists, however, define the obstacles to creating the proverbial "level playing field" too narrowly. These obstacles include much more than tariffs, dumping, quotas, or administrative and regulatory nontariff barriers. They include the security costs of maintaining the liberal international order that all countries benefit from, but which fall disproportionately on the United States. They also include the anti-union policies of many of America's Third World trade partners; the official winking at copyright and patent infringement; and the mercantilist economic priorities of many of America's trade partners, encompassing export-led growth strategies and policies of dampening domestic consumption through high interest rates, high taxes, or other devices. When, during the early primaries, Gephardt scolded South Korea for imposing higher tariffs on imported American cars than America imposes on South Korean autos, he—and his critics—missed the point. South Korea's primary objective is less to discriminate against Americans or any other foreign countries than to hold down South Korean spending on all consumer goods, including domestic products.

*Sixth*, as implied above, because the United States trades with a group of countries whose own characteristics are diverse and whose value to us varies, using one set of trade rules to govern all these relationships makes little sense from the standpoint of U.S. interests. As former U.S. trade negotiator Clyde Prestowitz has observed in his 1988 book *Trading Places*, the liberal, multilateral, nondiscriminatory post-World War II trade regime assumed that the parties would be "like-minded" countries. But this has not been the case for decades, if ever, and the United States needs to adopt its policies accordingly. Washington should feel much freer to depart from the multilateral trade regime when its interests dictate.

*Seventh*, in a world in which countries must still work hard to safeguard their security and cannot rely on others to have their best interests at heart, economic self-sufficiency and the freedom of action it can bring are intrinsic goods. They are even often worth paying for with higher prices for domestic alternatives to imports. Obviously, the United States cannot simply abandon efficiency as a goal of foreign economic policy. But it must strike a much better balance between efficiency and self-reliance. Finding or developing domestic supplies, natural substitutes, or synthetic alternatives to critical imports should be a much higher U.S. priority. And reducing U.S. dependence on foreign energy supplies through means such as conservation, a gasoline tax, and greater reliance on natural gas, nuclear power, coal, and renewable energy sources must be emphasized as well.

*Eighth*, when the United States does have to depend on foreign supplies of critical materials, it should try to depend on countries that are either stable and friendly already, or located nearby enough to make defending or coercing them feasible. This means that American foreign policy should be more "hemispherist," to borrow from the mid-century isolationists.

The U.S.-Canadian free trade agreement was an excellent first step in this direction, and Democrats should advocate the creation of special bilateral economic relationships with Mexico as well. In fact, Washington should be prepared to bend over backwards to make the Mexicans comfortable with such an arrangement. If Americans can't control their appetite for foreign oil, better to get it from Campeche than from Kuwait.

*Ninth*, to those concerned that such non-internationalist policies would turn

America into an amoral nation, two responses. In the first place, keeping out of trouble, and thereby reducing the human and financial costs of U.S. foreign policy to the American people, is an eminently moral goal. There should be no shame whatever attached to a policy that seeks to enable Americans to live as peacefully and as happily as they can. In the second place, domestic development—the rebuilding of the country's cities and transportation networks, the revitalization of its schools, the further extension of economic opportunity, the promotion of scholarship and the arts—is an aspiration second to none in nobility. And unlike most of the developing world, the United States has the political and legal systems and the social cohesion needed to give such efforts reasonable promise of success, especially if enough resources are mobilized. Those still concerned about an altruistic world role should recall that no tradition is more deeply rooted in American foreign policy than that of leading the world by example.

Since the Vietnam War, the three major wings of the Democratic party have struggled to restore their foreign policy credibility with the American people and to develop positions that serve the interests of their chief constituencies. But they have been frustrated continually by their acceptance of internationalism's universal definition of vital U.S. interests and its addiction to an active, outsized U.S. world role. Worse, lingering internationalism has vitiated the potentially valuable non-internationalist insights that each faction has stumbled across.

Thus the Right has confused the clear need to be strong militarily and to use military strength when necessary or optimal with a broadly interventionist policy of crusading for freedom and righting the world's wrongs. It fails to understand that these policies would squander the very strength whose importance they recognize and pauperize the middle-income voters whose patriotism they hope to enlist. The Left evidently believes that the only way to justify the equally clear need to reallocate resources to pressing domestic problems—and the far more questionable need to strive for international economic justice—is to push a utopian view of international politics as well as a hopelessly romantic picture of the globe's Have-Nots. They fail to understand that no responsible national leadership can count exclusively on foreign policy approaches, such as diplomacy, accommodation, and aid that have never succeeded without credible, usable military power—and that most of the electorate will not trust in the foreseeable future.

A New Nationalism based on the above principles would combine the best of both the Nunn and Jackson approaches in a way that is strategically sound and politically potent. It is a policy that realistically assesses U.S. objectives, the strengths America can use to achieve them, and the obstacles that must be overcome. It is also a strategy in tune with new public attitudes that can be expected to shape electoral politics for many years to come—chiefly, a determination to remain powerful militarily coupled with a strong reluctance to use that power unless American security is directly threatened; sharply rising worries about economic security and America's ability to retain control of its economic future; and growing resentment of the burden of protecting wealthy allies.

Finally, the New Nationalism would create strengths out of current Democratic vulnerabilities on what George Bush has so eloquently called "the vision thing." Dukakis's loss occasioned grumbling that his campaign was more appropriate for a town hall than for the White House. And the continuing recent pattern of Republican presidents and Democratic Congresses suggests to many that voters see the Democrats more as ombudsmen for local, immediate interests than as statesmen who will keep broad national concerns in view.

The American public has shown signs of interest in a fundamentally new international role, to a future dedicated primarily to the creation of a more perfect union, not to the pipedream of world order, whether in its hard-headed Nunnian or big-hearted Jacksonian versions. And this future will look ever more appealing as Bush's first term wears on, and economic constraints sharpen the competition between foreign policy-related and domestic spending. But political leaders and parties are needed to turn popular discontents into a cohesive and viable political program. Can the Democrats rise to the challenge?

## 29. Patrick Buchanan
### *America First—and Second, and Third*    1990

In this selection, the conservative syndicated columnist, Patrick Buchanan, calls upon the American people to wind up the cold war and "go home." Buchanan argues that American can scale its military establishment back to strong defensive naval and air forces while still leading the world.

On the birthday of Thomas Jefferson, dead half a decade, the President of the United States raised his glass, and gave us, in a six-word toast, our national purpose: "The Union," Old Hickory said, "it must be preserved."

It was to "create a more perfect Union" that the great men came to Philadelphia; it was to permit the Republic to grow to its natural size that James K. Polk seized Texas and California; it was to preserve the Union—not end slavery—that Lincoln invaded and subjugated the Confederate states.

"A republic if you can keep it," Franklin told the lady in Philadelphia. Surely, preservation of the Republic, defense of its Constitution, living up to its ideals—that is our national purpose. "America does not go abroad in search of monsters to destroy," John Quincy Adams said. "She is the well-wisher of the freedom and independence of all. She is the champion and vindicator only of her own."

Yet, when the question is posed, "What is America's national purpose?", answers vary as widely as those who take it. To Randall Robinson of TransAfrica, it is the overthrow of South Africa; to Jesse Jackson, it is to advance "justice" by restoring the wealth the white race has robbed from the colored peoples of the earth; to AIPCA, it is to keep Israel secure and inviolate; to Ben Wattenberg, America's "mission" is a crusade to "wage democracy" around the world. Each substitutes an extra-national ideal for the national interest; each sees our national purpose in another continent or country; each treats our Republic as a means to some larger end. "National purpose" has become a vessel, emptied of original content, into which ideologues of all shades and hues are invited to pour their own causes, their own visions.

In Charles Krauthammer's "vision" (in the Winter issue of *The National Interest*), the "wish and work" of our nation should be to "integrate" with Europe and Japan inside a "super-sovereign" entity that is "economically, culturally, and politically hegemonic in the world." This "new universalism," he writes, "would require the conscious depreciation not only of Amerian sovereignty but of the notion of sovereignty in general. This is not as outrageous as it sounds."

While Krauthammer's super-state may set off onanistic rejoicing inside the Trilateral Commission, it should set off alarm bells in more precincts than Belmont, Massachusetts. As national purpose, or national interest, like all of the above, it fails the fundamental test: Americans will not fight for it.

Long ago, Lord Macaulay asked:

> And how can man die better
> Than facing fearful odds
> For the ashes of his fathers,
> And the temples of his gods?

A nation's purpose is discovered not by consulting ideologies, but by reviewing its history, by searching the hearts of its poeple. What is it for which Americans have always been willing to fight?

Let us go back to a time when the establishment wanted war, but the American people did not want to fight.

In the fall of 1941, Europe from the Pyrenees to Moscow, from the Arctic to North Africa, was ruled by Hitler's Third Reich. East of Moscow, Stalin's gulag extended across Asia to Manchuria, where it met the belligerent Empire of the Rising Sun whose domain ran to mid-Pacific. England was in her darkest hour. Yet, still, America wanted to stay out; we saw, in the world's bloody conflict, no cause why our soldiers should be sent overseas to spill a single drop of American blood. Pearl Harbor, not FDR, convinced America to go to war.

The isolationism of our fathers is today condemned, and FDR is adjudged a great visionary because he sought early involvement in Britain's war with Hitler. But even the interventionists' arguments were, and are, couched in terms of American national interest. Perhaps we did not see it, we are told, but our freedom, our security, our homes, our way of life, our Republic, were at risk. Thus do even the acolytes of interventionism pay tribute to the true national interests of the United States, which are not to be found in some hegemonic and utopian world order.

When Adams spoke, he was echoing Washington's Farewell Address that warned his fickle countrymen against

> inveterate antipathies against particular nations, and passionate attachments for others. . . . The Nation which indulges toward another an habitual hatred or an

habitual fondness, is in some degree a slave. It is a slave to its animosity or to its affection, either of which is sufficient to lead it astray from its duty and its interest.

For a century after Washington's death, we resisted the siren's call of empire. Then, Kipling's call to "Take up the white man's burden" fell upon the receptive ears of Bill McKinley, who came down from a sleepless night of consulting the Almighty to tell the press that God had told him to take the Philippines. We were launched.

Two decades later, 100,000 Americans lay dead in France in a European war begun, as Bismarck predicted it would begin, "because of some damn fool thing in the Balkans."

"To make the world safe for democracy," we joined an alliance of empires— British, French, and Russian—that held most of mankind in colonial captivity. Washington's warning proved prophetic. Doughboys fell in places like the Argonne and Belleau Wood, in no small measure to vindicate the Germanophobia and Anglophilia of a regnant Yankee elite. When the great "war to end war" had fertilized the seed bed that produced Mussolini, Hitler, and Stalin, Americans by 1941 had concluded a blunder had been made in ignoring the wise counsel of their Founding Father.

After V-E Day and V-J Day, all America wanted to "bring the boys home," and we did. Then they were sent back, back to Europe, back to Asia, because Americans were persuaded—by Joseph Stalin—that the Cold War must be waged, because Lenin's party had made the United States the "main enemy" in its war against the West. As the old saw goes, you can refuse almost any invitation, but when a man wants to fight you have to oblige him.

If the Cold War is ending, what are the terms of honorable peace that will permit us to go home? Are they not: withdrawal of the Red Army back within its own frontiers; liberation of Central Europe and the Baltic republics; reunification of Germany; and de-Leninization of Moscow, i.e., overthrow of the imperialist party that has prosecuted the Seventy Years War against the West?

Once Russia is rescued from Leninism, its distant colonies, Cuba and Nicaragua, must eventually fall, just as the outposts of Japan's Empire, cut off from the home islands, fell like ripe apples into the lap of General MacArthur. Withdrawal of the Red Army from Europe would remove from the hand of Gorbachev's successor the military instrument of Marxist restoration.

The compensating concession we should offer: total withdrawal of U.S. troops from Europe. If Moscow will get out, we will get out. Once the Red Army goes home, the reason for keeping a U.S. army in Europe vanishes. Forty years after the Marshall Plan, it is time Europe conscripted the soldiers for its own defense.

As the Austrian peace treaty demonstrates, troop withdrawals are the most enduring and easily verifiable form of arms control. If we negotiate the 600,000 troops of the Red Army out of Central Europe, they cannot return, short of launching a new European war.

There is another argument for disengagement. When the cheering stops, there is going to be a calling to account for the crimes of Tehran, Yalta, and Potsdam, where the Great Men acceded to Stalin's demand that he be made cartographer of Europe. In the coming conflicts—over Poland's frontiers east and west, over Transylvania, Karelia, Moldavia, the breakup of Yugoslavia—our role is diplomatic and moral, not military.

In 1956, at the high water mark of American power, the U.S. stood aside as Soviet tanks crushed the Hungarian revolution. With that decision, Eisenhower and Dulles told the world that, while we support freedom in Central Europe, America will not go to war with Russia over it. The year of revolution, 1989, revealed the logical corollary: From Berlin to Bucharest to Beijing, as Lord Byron observed, "Who would be free, themselves must strike the first blow."

Would America be leaving our NATO allies in the lurch? Hardly. NATO Europe contains fourteen states, which, together, are more populous and three times as wealthy as a Soviet Union deep in an economic, social, and political crisis. Moreover, NATO would have a new buffer zone of free, neutral, anticommunist nations between the Soviet and German frontiers. Our job will have been done.

To conquer Germany, the Red Army would have to cross a free Poland of 500 miles and 40 million people, before reaching the frontier of a united Reich of 80 million, whose tradition is not wholly pacifist. In the first hours of invasion, Moscow would see her economic ties to the West severed, and a global coalition forming up against her, including Germany, France, Britain, China, Japan, and the United States. As the Red Army advanced, it would risk atomic attack. To what end? So the Kremlin can recapture what the Kremlin is giving up as an unwanted and unmanageable empire?

The day of the realpoliticians, with their Metternichian "new architectures," and balance-of-power stratagems, and hidden fear of a world where their op-ed articles and televised advice are about as relevant as white papers from Her Majesty's Colonial Office, is over.

Why seek a united Germany? Because it is consistent with our values, our promise to the German people, and our national interest. Moreover, the Germans desire it, and will attain it. "Conditions" set down by President Bush and Secretary Baker will prove as ineffectual as they are insulting. (If the Germans decide to unite, what, exactly, would we do to stop them: Occupy Munich until they yield to our demand that they stay in NATO?)

A free, united Germany in the heart of Europe, inoculated against Marxism by forty-five years of the disease, would be a triumph of American policy, a pillar of Western capitalism, and the first line of defense against a resurgent Russian imperialism. For the United States to permit itself to be used by London, Paris, and Moscow to impede reunification is to reenact, seventy years later, the folly of Versailles. Deny Germans the unity they rightly seek, and we shall awake one morning to find the Russians have granted it.

But, disengagement does not mean disarmament.

Still the greatest trading nation on earth, the U.S. depends for its prosperity on freedom of the seas. The strength of the U.S. navy should be non-negotiable; and, when the President is invited to enter naval arms control negotiations, the answer should be no, even if it means Moscow walks out.

With the acquisition of ballistic missiles by China, Iran, Iraq, Syria, and

Libya, with atomic weapons work being done in half a dozen countries of the Third World, the United States needs—nay, requires—a crash research and development program for missile defense, to protect our homeland, our warships, our bases. No arms control agreement is worth trading away SDI.

An island-continent, American should use her economic and technological superiority to keep herself permanent mistress of the seas, first in air power, first in space. Nor is the cost beyond our capacity. For, it is not warships and weapons that consume half our defense budget; it is manpower and benefits. When defense cuts are made, they should come in army bases no longer needed for homeland defense, and ground troops no longer needed on foreign soil.

As U.S. bases close down in Europe, we should inform Moscow we want all Soviet bases closed in the Caribbean and Central America, all Soviet troops out of the Western hemisphere. They have no business here. This is our hemisphere; and the Monroe Doctrine should be made again the cornerstone of U.S. foreign policy.

As the U.S. moves off the mainland of Europe, we should move our troops as well off the mainland of Asia. South Korea has twice the population and five times the economic might of North Korea. She can be sold the planes, guns, missiles, and ships to give her decisive superiority; then, U.S. troops should be taken out of the front line.

We are not going to fight another land war in Asia; no vital interest justifies it; our people will not permit it. Why, then, keep 30,000 ground troops on the DMZ? If Kim Il Sung attacks, why should Americans be first to die? If we must intervene, we can do so with air and sea power, without thousands of army and marine dead. It is time we began uprooting the global network of "trip wires" planted on foreign soil to ensnare the United States in the wars of other nations, to back commitments made and treaties signed before this generation of American soldiers was born.

The late Barbara Tuchman wrote of the Kaiser that he could not stand it if somewhere in the world a quarrel was going on and he was not a party to it. Blessed by Providence with pacific neighbors, north and south, and vast oceans, east and west, to protect us, why seek permanent entanglement in other people's quarrels?

The beginning of the end of the Cold War is surely time for that "agonizing reappraisal" of which Dulles only spoke. As Chesterton said, one ought not tear down a wall until you know why it was put up, but we must begin asking why some walls were built, and whether maintaining them any longer serves *our* interests.

As we ascend the staircase to the twenty-first century, America is uniquely situated to lead the world. Japan has a population older and not half so large as ours; her land and resources cannot match California's. Even united, the two Germanies have but a third of our population, a fifth of our GNP, and a land area smaller than Oregon and Washington. Neither Japan nor Germany is a nuclear power; neither has a navy or air force to rival ours; even their combined GNP is dwarfed by ours. While the Soviet Union has the size, resources, and population to challenge us as a world power, she is a prison house of nations whose ethnic hatreds and unworkable system mean a decade of turmoil. Who is left? The corrupt, bankrupt China of Deng Xiaoping? It will not survive the decade. Nakasone was right: The twentieth century was the American century. The twenty-first century will also be the American century.

But America can only lead the world into the twenty-first century if she is not saddled down by all the baggage piled up in the twentieth.

For fifty years, the United States has been drained of wealth and power by wars, cold and hot. Much of that expenditure of blood and treasure was a necessary investment. Much was not.

We cannot forever defend wealthy nations that refuse to defend themselves; we cannot permit endless transfusions of the life blood of American capitalism into the mendicant countries and economic corpses of socialism, without bleeding to death. Foreign aid is an idea whose time has passed. The communist and socialist world now owe the West a thousand billion dollars and more, exclusive of hundreds of billions we simply gave away. Our going-away gift to the globalist ideologues should be to tell the Third World we are not sending the gunboats to collect our debts, but nor are we sending more money. The children are on their own.

Americans are the most generous people in history. But our altruism has been exploited by the guilt-and-pity crowd. At home, a monstrous welfare state of tens of thousands of drones and millions of dependents consumes huge slices of the national income. Abroad, regiments of global bureaucrats siphon off billions for themselves, their institutions, their client regimes.

With the Cold War ending, we should look, too, with a cold eye on the internationalist set, never at a loss of new ideas to divert U.S. wealth and power into crusades and causes having little or nothing to do with the true national interest of the United States.

High among these is the democratist temptation, the worship of democracy as a form of governance and the concomitant ambition to see all mankind embrace it, or explain why not. Like all idolatries, democratism substitutes a false god for the real, a love of process for a love of country.

When we call a country "democratic," we say nothing about whether its rulers are wise or good, or friendly or hostile; we only describe how they were chosen, a process that produced Olaf Palme, Lopez Portillo, Pierre Trudeau, Sam Nujoma, Kurt Waldheim, and the Papandreous, *pére et fils*, as well as Ronald Reagan.

Raul Alfonsín, elected president, led Argentina to ruin; while General Pinochet, who seized power in a coup, rescued Chile from Castroism, and leaves her secure, prosperous, and on the road to freedom. Why, then, celebrate Alfonsín, and subvert Pinochet?

As cultural traditions leave many countries unsuited to U.S.-style democracy, any globalist crusade to bring its blessings to the natives everywhere must end in frustration; and will surely be marked by hypocrisy. While the National Endowment for Democracy meddles in the affairs of South Africa, the State Department props up General Mobutu. Where is the consistency?

Democracies, too, place their own selfish interests first. India, the world's largest, supported Moscow's genocidal war of annexation in Afghanistan, while General Zia, an autocrat, died aiding the resistance. Who was the true friend of liberty?

In 1936, Franco rescued Spain from a corrupt "democracy"; in 1937, Hitler received a "democratic" mandate from the German people; in 1941, Britain declared war on Finland, a democracy, at the behest of Stalin; in 1942, we deprived our own fighting men of needed weapons to send them to the USSR, the most contemptuous enemy democracy has ever known.

How other people rule themselves is their own business. To call it a vital interest of the United States is to contradict history and common sense. And for the Republic to seek to dictate to 160 nations what kind of regime each should have is a formula for interminable meddling and endless conflict; it is a textbook example of that "messianic globaloney" against which Dean Acheson warned; it is, in scholar Clyde Wilson's phrase, a globalization of that degenerate form of Protestantism known as the Social Gospel.

"We must consider first and last," Walter Lippman wrote in 1943, "the American national interest. If we do not, if we construct our foreign policy on some kind of abstract theory of rights and duties, we shall build castles in the air. We shall formulate policies which in fact the nation will not support with its blood, its sweat, and its tears." Exactly.

What do Tibetans, *mujabeddin*, UNITA rebels, and *contras* have in common? Not belief in a bicameral legislature, or in separation of church and state, but love of liberty and a hatred of communism. Is it not that spirit of patriotism that brought down the vassal regimes of Central Europe, that today threatens to tear apart the Soviet Empire?

"Enlightened nationalism" was Mr. Lippmann's idea of a foreign policy to protect America's true national interest. What we need is a new nationalism, a new patriotism, a new foreign policy that puts America first, and, not only first, but second and third as well.

## 30. Mark N. Katz
### Beyond the Reagan Doctrine: Reassessing U.S. Policy Toward Regional Conflicts  1991

In this selection, Mark Katz proposes that the United States play the role of a balancer against changing regional hegemons through the Third World. According to Katz, a professor of political science at George Mason University, "U.S. interests would be hurt if any power, not just the Soviet Union, came to dominate certain regions of the Third World such as the Persian Gulf, the Middle East, Southeast Asia, Latin Ameica, or any of the world's most important sea lanes." While he recommends the use of military force and unilateral action only as a last resort, the course Katz proposes would heavily involve the United States in the politics among regional actors throughout much of the third world. Katz's essay provides a well-constructed rationale for the Bush Administration's actions during the Kuwait crisis.

The retreat of Soviet influence . . . does not mean that international relations will be marked by inevitable progress toward democracy, the peaceful resolution of all outstanding disputes under Soviet-U.S. direction, and increasing harmony among nations generally. Some serious threats to stability exist in regions of the developing world where certain states pursue hegemonic ambitions.

Even at the height of Soviet expansionism, the Soviet Union was by no means the only expansionist power in the Third World. While Moscow may have become disillusioned with expansionism, others have not. For while no one power poses the same threat of global expansionism as the Soviet Union once did, the behavior of several indicates that they are actively or potentially seeking hegemony within certain regions. And U.S. interests would be hurt if any power, not just the Soviet Union, came to dominate certain regions of the Third World such as the Persian Gulf, the Middle East, Southeast Asia, Latin America, or any of the world's important sea lanes.

**The Persian Gulf**   An Iranian victory in the Iran-Iraq war could have resulted in Iranian dominance over the entire Gulf region. The United States, eager to prevent Iran from gaining control over even more of the Gulf's oil reserves, worked to prevent this. The threat of Iranian hegemony over the region has subsided, but the threat of Iraqi hegemony arose when Saddam Hussein's forces overran Kuwait and menaced Saudi Arabia. The United States and its allies certainly have no interest in allowing Iraq to gain greater control over the Gulf, on which the West depends so heavily for its oil, or to obtain greater influence in the Middle East, which is already volatile enough. Iraq now poses and Iran has posed (and may again pose) a far greater threat of such hegemony than the Soviet Union, and they are thus greater threats than Moscow to U.S. interests in this vital region.

**Southeast Asia**   In Southeast Asia, U.S. and Western interests would suffer if any power were in a position to dominate the economically prosperous states of the Association of Southeast Asian Nations (ASEAN). During the 1970s and 1980s, the United States and ASEAN saw an aggressive Vietnam, backed by the Soviet Union, as posing the greatest threat to regional security. In consequence, both worked with China to thwart Soviet and Vietnamese efforts to dominate Cambodia. The U.S. motive was not the strategic importance of Cambodia, but fear of what the Soviet Union and Vietnam would do next in the region if they succeeded in dominating that country.

Now, however, Vietnam has withdrawn its troops from Cambodia and neither Hanoi nor Moscow appears interested in pursuing an expansionist policy in the region. Yet, despite this change, China continues to provide substantial quantities of arms to the genocidal Khmer Rouge. In addition to being concerned about how the Khmer Rouge would behave if they returned to power, the United States and its allies ought to be concerned about China's motives. Why is China not satisfied with the decline of Soviet and Vietnamese influence in Cambodia? Does China seek to dominate Cambodia? If it succeeds in doing so, how will it behave toward ASEAN? Unlike the government of the Soviet Union, the ruling party in China has become increasingly authoritarian. If ASEAN was worth protecting from Soviet influence, it is surely worth protecting from Chinese influence too. And although the threat of expanding Soviet and Vietnamese influence in the region may not have disappeared, it is receding while the threat of expanding Chinese influence is growing.

**The Indian Ocean**    The United States and its allies have a strong interest in maintaining maritime access to the Indian Ocean, if only to secure the flow of oil from the Gulf. For years the Soviet Union attempted to constrain that access through proposing various "zone of peace" formulas. Moscow never really expected the West to accept them, but apparently hoped that the states of the region would, thereby limiting Western naval access.

Although the Soviets did not succeed in rousing the region's enthusiasm for this goal, and their efforts in pursuing it have notably flagged, one important nation—India—enthusiastically advocated limiting the naval presence of outside parties in the Indian Ocean. New Delhi may well pursue this goal because, if it could be achieved, India would have the largest naval presence in the region. How would India behave if it achieved naval dominance in the Indian Ocean? Could the West depend on India to safeguard its access to Gulf oil? India's often belligerent attitude toward its weaker South Asian neighbors appears to indicate a desire to dominate where it can. If India achieved greater influence in South Asia, how would it behave in the broader Indian Ocean region? Although India can hardly be said to pose as serious a threat of regional expansionism as Iraq or China, New Delhi's policies are definitely a potential problem. Washington should be no less concerned about India's efforts to limit or exclude Western access to the Indian Ocean than it was about Moscow's.

**Latin America**    The United States has a strong interest in preventing any hostile power from gaining predominant influence in Latin America. This concern, the basis of the Monroe Doctrine, long predates the Cold War. Under Gorbachev, Soviet support for revolution in Latin America has declined markedly. But Cuban support for revolutions against U.S.-supported governments continues, especially in Central America. What is Fidel Castro's goal in seeking to promote revolution? Does he aspire to some form of regional hegemony? Even if his actions are not supported by the Soviet Union, his efforts to extend his influence at the expense of the United States are clearly undesirable from Washington's point of view.

## HEGEMONY AND U.S. FOREIGN POLICY

The United States has a strong interest in seeing that states aspiring to hegemony do not succeed. Hegemonic powers could cause serious problems for U.S. interests, and not just by constraining or excluding a regional U.S. presence. Even in regions that are remote or have little strategic value to the

United States, a hegemon could threaten U.S. interests in other more important regions.

U.S. concern for the future of the Third World, then, is in one sense similar to its past concern: to prevent regional hegemony. The difference is that while the United States was primarily concerned about preventing Soviet efforts to achieve hegemony in various regions in the past, it should now be concerned to prevent any regional hegemony. Continued pursuit of the Reagan Doctrine is inappropriate for achieving this goal because, although its main objective—halting Soviet expansionsim—has already been achieved, it does not address the task of halting the expansionism of regional hegemons.

To pursue this goal successfully, the United States will have to make considerable changes in its foreign policy. During the Cold War, it enjoyed the certainty of having one prime enemy and a relatively constant set of allies. Further, this one enemy was clearly threatening, and the U.S. government could usually (but not always) rouse the public to support defense expenditures against it.

In the future, the United States probably will not enjoy the certainty of having either permanent friends or permanent enemies in the Third World. A case in point is that while Iraq was an ally in preventing Iranian regional hegemony during the latter part of the Iran-Iraq war, that ally has now become an aspiring hegemon itself. Similarly, the alliance between China and the United States was based on the common fear of Soviet expasnion, but now that this danger has receded, China may be pursuing hegemonic ambitions of its own.

Although the United States should oppose their aspirations to hegemony, it must be prepared to cooperate with Iraq and China once again if Iran, Vietnam, or some other country more aggressively and effectively pursues hegemonic ambitions in the future.

Some may object that for the United States to cooperate with China after it suppressed the democracy movement in 1989 or Iraq after it invaded Kuwait would be immoral, unthinkable, and unacceptable to the American public. But in a world where there may be many potential sources of expansionism in addition to the ones that are most threatening at any one time, the U.S. government should avoid public demands to vilify its current opponents completely so that cooperation with them is impossible. If President Bush had acceded to congressional and public insistence on isolating Beijing after Tiananmen Square, China might have vetoed the United Nations resolutions against Iraq for invading Kuwait simply to thwart the United States. The Bush administration's insistence on maintaining a high-level dialogue with Beijing may have been largely responsible for avoiding a Chinese veto, which could have made rallying worldwide support for sanctions and other measures against Iraq more difficult to achieve.

There can be no cooperation with Iraq while it is pursuing an expansionist course, but it must be noted that Iraq has the same regime now as it had when Iran threatened to defeat it in the latter part of the Gulf war. Cooperating with Saddam Hussein to prevent Iranian expansion was a worthwhile goal. Indeed, the United States and the world must be careful that their efforts to thwart Saddam Hussein do not lead to a power vacuum in Iraq into which Iran could easily move.

Similarly, if Iraqi or Chinese actions become even more threatening to regional balances of power, the United States will not be able to afford the luxury of treating Iran and Vietnam as permanent enemies just because their governments bested Washington in the 1970s and may need actively to cooperate with them to maintain the balance of powers.

The cold war pattern in which the United States supported a relatively permanent set of friends against a permanent enemy is not likely to serve as a useful guidepost for U.S. foreign policy toward the Third World in the future. Instead, the U.S. role vis-à-vis the Third World may resemble that of the British vis-à-vis Europe in the eighteenth, nineteenth, and first half of the twentieth centuries: the balancer that sought to prevent any state or alliance from gaining or threatening to gain hegemony. The British acted to frustrate the ambitions of any and all hegemons, not just one special enemy; so too should the United States.

How can the United States effectively act as a balancer in various regions of the Third World? As the British did when they played this role, the United States should employ diplomatic means primarily and employ military means only as a last resort. Indeed, the United States will want to do its utmost diplomatically to prevent conflict from breaking out in order to avoid the drain on U.S. resources and public tolerance that would result from frequent intervention. Rallying other nations to support economic sanctions against regional aggressors is especially important; greater world economic integration means that fewer nations can afford to be isolated economically from the rest of the world.

Playing the role of balancer, though, will also involve a military dimension. Some of the same military policies Washington pursued in order to thwart Soviet hegemonism can also be employed to thwart regional hegemonies. These include providing security assistance for defensive purposes to countries being threatened, diplomatic efforts aimed at denying military aid to aggressive nations, supplying weapons to nations in conflict with hegemonic powers, or preventing hegemonic powers from interrupting the sea lines of communication on which the targets of their aggression depend (just as the United States and others protected Kuwaiti oil shipping against Iranian attack).

A serious problem is posed by the buildup of substantial military forces by aspiring hegemons with which vulnerable neighbors cannot cope militarily. The United States will face certain dilemmas in such cases. When and how should it become directly involved militarily to protect weaker nations against threatening states? It is far from certain that Americans would tolerate direct involvement in a protracted conflict to prevent regional hegemony if they did not perceive themselves as directly threatened or their allies as worth defending.

In the past, the United States has relied on the threat of nuclear attack to deal with a militarily robust opponent in Europe, but this strategy does not translate easily to the developing world. There are several reasons: the U.S.

public would be unlikely to support such a policy; aspiring hegemons might not believe the United States would actually employ nuclear weapons, or they would pursue their aims in a more piecemeal way against which nuclear retaliation would be less appropriate or credible; and some potential hegemons already or may soon possess nuclear weapons and might be able to deter U.S. use of nuclear weapons because they could retaliate against U.S. interests, or the United States itself.

There may also be obstacles to deterring regional hegemons with the threat of military intervention by conventional forces. The example of U.S. military withdrawal from Indochina in 1973 and from Lebanon in 1984 may lead some states to doubt the credibility of U.S. threats to intervene against them. A well-armed aggressor may calculate that the U.S. Congress and public will not be willing to pay the human costs of intervention against it—or at least not pay them for very long. If the United States is perceived as continuing to suffer from the "Vietnam syndrome," some hegemons might be willing to engage it in protracted conflict. In some cases, then, conventional deterrence may not be possible; some form of intervention may be necessary.

Is this an exaggerated portrait of the real security dilemmas the United States faces in the Third World? Perhaps not. Kuwaiti armed forces were obviously unable to deter or prevent Iraq from conquering their country. The large number of troops that the United States and other countries have sent to defend Saudi Arabia is indicative of the enormous effort needed to defend weaker states against regional aggressors.

Iraq is not the ony example. If there is war between India and Pakistan, and if India emerges a militarized winner (and especially if the war has a nuclear component), who in the region will not fear the consequences? What if an expansionist Khmer Rouge regime is ensconced in Cambodia and backed by China, and turns its attention toward Thailand? What if several attempts to achieve regional hegemony occur simultaneously?

U.S. interests would be best served by the emergence of regional balances of power rather than acute threats to achieve hegemony because the requirements for maintaining stability will be far less than those of restoring stability once it has been upset by an ambitious and well-armed regional military power. The United States cannot achieve this goal alone. Cooperation with its Western allies on problems of regional security is growing more important, not less. Support for beleaguered third world allies would be easier to muster, and the isolation of aspiring hegemons easier to achieve, if the United States, Europe, and Japan acted in concert than if the United States acted alone. Such cooperation would signal to those contemplating aggressive behavior that they could not play off the Western powers against each other—a danger that may grow when Western nations no longer fear a common Soviet threat. Maintaining regional balances of power would be more difficult if the Western allies disagreed over whether a particular nation was pursuing a hegemonic policy, or if some sold weapons to an aggressive state while others sought to deny them. Close collaboration among the Western allies will be necessary to ensure that such scenarios do not arise.

# WHAT ROLE FOR THE SOVIET UNION?

U.S. efforts to play the role of regional balancer will be affected not just by the attitudes of its Western allies, but also by the policy of the Soviet Union. Even a weakened Soviet Union could thwart U.S. efforts by either selling or giving weapons from its huge surplus arsenal to aggressive states. On the other hand, U.S.-Soviet cooperation in maintaining regional balances of power in the Third World could be highly effective in deterring or thwarting hegemonic aspirations. Indeed, if the United States, the Soviet Union, and the Western allies all worked together, even the most aggressive state would probably see that the prospects for achieving its ambitions were extremely poor. Although Western actions were not coordinated with the Soviet Union, their parallel efforts during the Iran-Iraq war to protect oil shipping in the Gulf may have been instrumental in convincing Tehran that it could not stop the conservative Gulf monarchies from providing substantial economic assistance to Iraq and that its efforts to defeat Iraq were futile. Iran might not have come to this conclusion so soon, or even at all, if it had not seen all the great powers working against it in the Gulf. Similarly, Saddam Hussein's threat to the Arabian Peninsula would have been far more difficult for the United States to contain if it had occurred during the cold war era and Moscow had acted to insulate Iraq from economic and military sanctions.

The West and the Soviet Union could undertake several actions jointly to deter or defuse threats to regional balances of power elsewhere. If the great powers could agree that a particular nation was purusing a hegemonic policy, they could act jointly to halt arms transfers to it. Arms, of course, can be obtained from other sources; many countries have large stocks of Soviet or Western weapons, and increasing numbers of countries make their own. It is doubtful, however, that other potential arms suppliers would be willing to transfer large quantities of weapons on concessionary terms as the United States and the Soviet Union have done in the past. Even if an aspiring hegemon could pay hard currency, it probably could not obtain from other sources the sophisticated systems available from the great powers. And if the great powers acted to cut off arms to a hegemonic power while they supplied arms to neighboring states, these actions alone might serve to deter aggressive policies.

The great powers could also undertake joint diplomatic initiatives to defuse regional conflicts. The primary importance of these initiatives would be to show states contemplating aggressive behavior that they cannot exploit differences between the Soviet Union and the West in order to gain support for expansionism. Rivalry among the great powers in the past has made it easier for smaller powers to pursue regional imperialism.

The great powers could also work together to find democratic solutions to regional conflicts. The Soviet Union has opposed such solutions in the past. Since 1989, however, Moscow has accepted the results of free elections in Eastern Europe and Nicaragua. Increasingly open elections are occurring within the Soviet Union itself. Soviet and Western support for the principle of free elections provides a face-saving means for accepting the victory of a contestant previously opposed by one or more of the great powers. Elections may also lay the basis for more lasting solutions to regional conflicts.

Finally, if all else fails, the joint use of force (or threat to use force) by the great powers at various levels, from maintaining freedom of navigation to intervention, would be far more effective than if the United States attempted such activity on its own.

This type of Soviet-U.S. or Soviet-Western cooperation on regional conflicts is not a proposal for a Northern condominium over the South. An attempt to achieve such a condominium would unite the South against the North, would be extremely costly to maintain, and would not be supported domestically in the North. Instead, this is a proposal for Soviet-U.S. cooperation to prevent some developing countries from exercising condominium over others and thereby threatening the security interests of the majority of states in both the North and South.

Is such Soviet-Western cooperation possible? Is it desirable?

To begin with the question of possibility: Why would the Soviet Union cooperate with the United States and the West in countering attempts to achieve regional hegemony? Certain efforts to achieve regional hegemony would hurt Soviet interests as much or more than they would hurt U.S. interests, especially in areas near the Soviet borders. Particularly at a time when Soviet power is declining, Moscow has no interest in seeing Chinese power grow too strong. Soviet interests would suffer if China became so powerful in Southeast Asia that Beijing was able to pressure Hanoi into refusing Moscow's continued access to naval facilities in Vietnam. This would result in reduced Soviet ability to secure its vital sea line of communication between the western Soviet Union and Vladivostok and perhaps encourage China to press its substantial territorial claims against the Soviet Union. For fear of similar consequences, Moscow would not want India or any other power to constrain Soviet naval access to the Indian Ocean. Nor would Moscow want to see a regional hegemon emerge in the Middle East that could undermine Soviet control of its own increasingly fractious Moslem republics. The Soviets, then, may have considerable incentive to oppose attempts to achieve hegemony in the regions near their borders.

Yet, even if Moscow were willing to cooperate with the West, would this be desirable? The danger U.S. conservatives point out is that the Soviet union may be able to expand its own power to the West's disadvantage under the guise of cooperating with the West in countering regional hegemons. This is clearly a danger, and the West must guard against it. The United States and its Western allies must make it clear to the Soviet Union that mutually beneficial cooperation in East-West relations generally will not be possible if the Soviet Union reverts to pursuing its own unilateral advantage in the Third World. Although possible, this is less likely now as a result of voluntary Soviet withdrawal from Eastern Europe and parts of the Third World, in addition to the steps taken toward democratization inside the Soviet Union. There is far greater risk to the West in insufficiently countering the rising hegemonic ambitions of regional powers through overzealously guarding against the declining threat of Soviet expansionism.

Although Soviet cooperation with the West in countering expansionism by regional powers may be both possible and desirable, it is still doubtful that Washington will convince Moscow to undertake such cooperation so long as the United States pursues the Reagan Doctrine. U.S. interests would hardly be served if the Soviets decided Washington was deliberately attempting to deprive their country of its superpower status and so retaliated by increasing their aid to expansionist states such as Iraq, Libya, and Cuba. Western security will not be advanced if Washington's zeal to punish Moscow for its now exhausted and abandoned expansionism distracts both Washington and Moscow from countering new, vigorous expansionisms, that, if unchecked, could threaten both.

## CONCLUSION

As the effort to counter Saddam Hussein's aggression has demonstrated, the United States cannot undertake the task of halting regional expansionism alone. Cooperation with other states in the region, regional organizations, other Western states, and even the Soviet Union as well as others is required. Preventing or countering regional expansionism successfully in the future will depend on U.S. ability to maximize the number of other states participating in a united front to oppose it. Achieving this goal will depend on minimizing differences with those states with which Washington may have serious disagreements, but which are not actively pursuing expansionism either.

In addition, U.S. intelligence must be alert to the need to judge whether an ally in opposing one state's hegemonism is itself becoming a threat to the balance of power in a given region. U.S. diplomacy must also be flexible enough to promote new united fronts against new aggressors that might arise. The conquest of Kuwait should serve as an object lesson as to what can happen when potential aggression is not identified soon enough or actions to counter it are insufficient. Finally, care must be taken to ensure that actions to counter aggression by one state do not result in a situation that allows another state to pursue expansionism more easily and effectively.

Instead of a new age of peace in the Third World, the post–cold war era may well witness the pusuit of expansionist policies by several regional powers. As Iraqi aggression has shown, the hegemonic ambitions of even relatively small states can have extremely serious repercussions throughout the world as well as in a particular region. No one regional power's expansionism poses the same worldwide threat as Soviet expansionism did in the past. But because regional hegemonism does pose serious threats to U.S. security interests, and because there are numerous potential hegemons in the developing world, the task of deterring and countering regional expansionism will require a more flexible and sophisticated U.S. foreign policy in the post-cold war era than did countering Soviet expansionism in the past.

# 31. Michael T. Klare
## *Policing the Gulf—And the World*     1990

In this selection, Michael Klare, associate professor of peace and security studies at Hampshire College and the *Nation's* defense correspondent, provides a radical assessment of President Bush's intervention in the Persian Gulf. According to Klare, the issue in the Gulf was neither the ambitions of Saddam Hussein nor his subjugation of Kuwait. Hussein's subjugation of Kuwait, in Klare's opinion, was merely a convenient pretext that allowed the Bush administration to implement a previously devised long-term policy for the post–cold war era.

Klare argues that before the Gulf crisis, the Bush administration was considering two alternative long-term strategies: a geo-economic strategy designed to restore economic competitiveness and independence and a geopolitical strategy of "guarding the Western world's principal trade routes and sources of raw material against insurgency, sectarian violence and regionalism of the sort practiced by Saddam Hussein." Klare concludes that Bush's action in the Gulf reveals his selection of the geopolitical strategy.

"In the life of a nation," President Bush declared on August 8, "we're called upon to define who we are and what we believe." Those words, spoken as the first detachments of U.S. soldiers were arriving in Saudi Arabia, are perhaps the most revealing yet uttered on the Persian Gulf crisis. More than anything else—more than the price of oil, or the configuration of power in the Middle East—the decision to send troops concerns the nature of America's national identity; specifically, America's role as a global power in the post–cold war environment. If Bush and his associates have their way, the United States will emerge from the present crisis as the industrial world's enforcer, ready to provide troops and shed blood in the name of global economic stability.

This yearning for a refurbished national identity is closely associated with anxiety over the durability of America's status as a global superpower. "Do we want to remain a superpower?" Chief of Naval Operations Adm. Carlisle Trost asked in April. The answer, he said, "is a resounding 'yes.'" Similarly, on the eve of the U.S. invasion of Panama, Gen. Colin Powell, Chairman of the Joint Chiefs of Staff, reportedly avowed, "We have to put a shingle outside our door saying 'Superpower Lives Here,' no matter what the Soviets do, even if they evacuate from Eastern Europe."

The desire to retain our status as a superpower, no matter what the cost, represents the underlying motive for U.S. intervention in the Persian Gulf. By supplying most of the troops for the so-called multinational force, America demonstrates that it, and it alone, has the will and capacity to serve as the world's policeman. Former Assistant Secretary of Defense Richard Armitage affirmed on August 16 that the gulf crisis demonstrates "there is absolutely no substitute for decisive, clearheaded American leadership." Those pundits who until recently were predicting the decline of America "must now ackowledge that the United States alone possesses sufficient moral, economic, political and military horsepower to jump-start and drive international efforts to curb international lawlessness."

But while such assertions may arouse great enthusiasm in some Washington circles (as suggested by the Congressional aide who told a reporter for *Newsweek*, "There's nothing like a good war to make people feel important"), this obsession with being a superpower, as an end in itself, forebodes great peril and distress for America. Not only can we not afford the mammoth costs of such folly—the estimated "add-on" costs of Operation Desert Shield are $1 billion per month—but we place our very freedom and democracy at risk. History suggests that democratic and civil rights cannot survive in a society that is organized for the purpose of sustaining unending and unethical military adventures abroad. At stake in the gulf, therefore, is the very soul of American society. Will we jettison our fundamental civil values in return for the dubious benefit of acting as a global superpower?

Anxiety of America's superpower status accelerated last autumn, when the rupture of the Berlin wall signaled the end of the cold war era. For forty years, America had reveled in its role as undisputed "leader of the Free World," the principal bulwark against Soviet aggression around the world. This messianic self-image allowed Americans to "stand tall," even when the costs of such praetorianism began to erode our economic primacy. Thus, with the end of the cold war, America faced an acute crisis of confidence: With our "leadership" role threatened, Washington would have to compete for world influence on an equal footing with economic superpowers like Germany and Japan.

This identity crisis produced some extraordinary soul-searching in Washington. "It may sound like an odd thing to say," Senator David Boren observed in April, "but I don't think that we fully understand [that] the decline of the Soviet Union might lead to our decline as well." Why is that so? Because, Boren explained, the European nations and Japan were willing to accept American leadership only when the international climate made it advantageous to do so. "As long as there was an external Soviet threat, as long as there was a threat from the Warsaw Pact, as long as we were providing the shield of military protection for them . . . they needed the United States." But now, with the disappearance of those threats, will they be as willing to follow the lead of the United States? Boren's answer: "I don't think so."

Because the thought of losing this commanding international role is anathema to American leaders of the cold war generation, U.S. strategists have been working overtime to devise new policies that will insure U.S. dominance in the post-cold war era. While many variations can be discerned, most of these proposals follow one of two basic models: the geo-economic and the geostrategic.

The first, advocated by a broad spectrum of political and financial interests, calls for a scaled-back U.S. military establishment and a greater U.S. investment in science, technology, education and trade development. If we are to compete successfully in world markets, this position holds, we must become more like Germany and Japan—that is, we must spend less on military forces and more on domestic industrial revolution.

Expressions of this view can be found in *Foreign Affairs,* the journal of the Council on Foreign Relations, and in other mainstream publications. A good example is an essay in the Summer 1990 issue of *Foreign Affairs* by former presidential counsel Theodore Sorensen on "Rethinking National Security." Unless we can restore our economic effectiveness and independence, Sorensen writes, America's freedom of action—its national security—will be progressively erased by growing subservience to Japanese and European lenders. If we are to avert this peril, we must recognize the importance of industrial modernization to national security, and "the folly of continuing to devote federal funds for research and development almost exclusively to military and space uses."

Although popular on Wall Street, the geo-economic model is not attractive to the political and corporate forces that have long associated U.S. power and prosperity with a strong defense and a significant military presence abroad. Those groups have responded with an alternative, geostrategic model for America's post-cold war posture: a model that entails a conspicuous U.S. role in guarding the Western world's principal trade routes and sources of raw materials against insurgency, sectarian violence and regional adventurism of the sort practiced by Saddam Hussein.

Characteristic of this perspective is a January 1990 essay by Senator John McCain, a conservative Republican and a member of the Senate Armed Services Committee. "If anything, the global conditions that led us to make these uses of force [in Korea, Vietnam and Grenada] are likely to be even more important in the future," he wrote in *Armed Forces Journal.* "'Glasnost' does not change the fact that there has been an average of more than 25 civil and international conflicts in the developing world every year since the end of World War II," nor that "the U.S. economy is critically dependent on the smooth flow of world trade." Our allies are even more dependent on trade with the Third World, and thus, in the absence of any other suitable choice, the United States must assume responsibility for the protection of vital trade routes and raw-material suppliers. "The U.S. may not be the 'world's policeman,'" McCain noted, "but its power projection forces will remain the free world's insurance policy."

Debate over the relative merits of the geo-economic and geostrategic positions was the order of the day in elite Washington circles between January and July, with partisans of both camps circulating articles, reports, position papers and other missives to promote their respective models. And however genteel this struggle may appear, its outcome entails extraordinary consequences for all concerned. At issue are such questions as (1) who will control America's foreign policy establishment in the years ahead; (2) which of the giant federal bureaucracies will prosper and which will fall into decline; (3) which of our states and communities will be the beneficiaries of government spending and which will be deprived; and, likewise, (4) which giant corporations will receive lucrative government contracts and which will not.

At issue in this contest, in other words, is the relative power, wealth and prestige of America's top movers and shakers. To give just a small indication of the stakes involved, consider this suggestion by Sorensen: "The National

Security Council, originally intended to integrate military and nonmilitary analysis, will need to expand its capacity for the latter, relying on fewer generals and Kremlinologists and more economists." However attractive this proposal may appear to professional economists, it is not likely to win support from the generals and Kremlinologists who have controlled the national security state since 1945; the latter are doing everything in their power to insure the failure of such endeavors.

In the short term, the most important issue in the debate over America's future international role is the size and configuration of the defense budget. At stake here is not only the total volume of dollars that will flow to the Defense Department in the years ahead but also their proportional distribution among the four military services—and, within the services, among the units devoted to nuclear, conventional and low-intensity conflict. Advocates of the geo-economic approach believe all of the services should be cut back, with the heaviest cuts coming from the nuclear weapons sector and from the ground and air forces committed to NATO. Advocates of the geostrategic position are willing, out of economic necessity, to accept modest cuts in nuclear and NATO-oriented forces, but insist on the preservation (if not expansion) of America's "power projection" forces—that is, those air, ground and sea forces designed for rapid deployment to distant trouble spots in the Third World. Such forces, Senator William Cohen wrote in April, "will grow significantly" more important in the 1990s than they were during the cold war period.

In the past year the prospect of significant reductions in Pentagon spending has prompted the individual military services to fight with one another over the smaller pile of dollars coming their way, and to denigrate the capabilites of their fellow services in order to strengthen their own case for continued funding. But beginning in March and April a remarkable consensus emerged among the service chiefs on the military's role in the post-cold war era. The substance of this consensus was that America must gear up for "mid-intensity conflicts" or combat against emerging Third World regional powers like Iraq.

The clearest expression of this outlook is found in a statement by Gen. Carl Vuono, the Chief of Staff of the Army. "Because the United States is a global power with vital interests that must be protected throughout an increasingly turbulent world," he wrote in April, "we must look beyond the European continent and consider other threats to our national security." This, in turn, compels us to consider the threat posed by emerging Third World powers:

> Regional rivalries supported by powerful armies have resulted in brutal and devastating conflicts in the Third World. . . . The proliferation of advanced military capabilities has given an increasing number of countries in the developing world the ability to wage sustained, mechanized land warfare. The United States cannot ignore the expanding military power of these countries, and the Army must retain the capability to defeat potential threats wherever they occur. *This could mean confronting a well-equipped army in the Third World.* [Emphasis added.]

To prepare for such encounters, Vuono argues, the Army must be reconfigured from a static, NATO-oriented force into a mobile "contingency force" capable of defeating powerful Third World armies.

Not to be outdone by the Army, the other military services have issued statements regarding the threat of mid-intensity conflict in the Third World. In developing this common outlook, all the military chiefs have agreed on one fundamental point: The United States and its closest industrial allies are becoming increasingly dependent on markets and raw materials located in volatile areas of the Third World, and so military action is essential to protect these vital interests. As Commandant of the Marine Corps Gen. A.M. Gray wrote in May, "If we are to have stability in these regions, maintain access to their resources, protect our citizens abroad, defend our vital installations, and deter conflict, we must maintain within our active force structure a credible military power projection capabilitiy with the flexibility to respond to conflict across the spectrum of violence throughout the globe."

In this revealing passage, General Gray spells out the guiding vision of the geostrategic model: As the sole Western power still capable of using force to protect economic "assets" abroad, the United States retains an indispensable international mission as the industrial world's enforcer. "Our position as a world leader," Gray explained, is a direct result of "our willingness to maintain credible force levels to protect our interests and those of our friends."

This outlook is shared by General Powell and, through Powell's influence, by the President himself. Thus, in his August 2 speech in Aspen, Colorado, Bush said, "Notwithstanding the alteration in the Soviet threat, the world remains a dangerous place with serious threats to important U.S. interests wholly unrelated to the earlier patterns of the U.S.-Soviet relationship." Because these threats include aggressive action by well-equipped regional powers, the United States must retain military forces with a high degree of strength and readiness.

As noted, the partisans of the geostrategic model had developed and articulated their positions prior to the Iraqi invasion of Kuwait on August 2 [see Klare, "The U.S. Military Faces South," *The Nation*, June 18, 1990]. However, as soon as the scale of the invasion became obvious, President Bush saw a golden opportunity to discredit the geo-economic model and to insure the triumph of the geostrategic approach. Thus, in seeking to evict Iraqi forces from Kuwait, Bush is also attempting to mobilize public support for a permanent U.S. commitment to the role of global gendarme. "Recent events have surely proven that there is no substitute for American leadership," Bush crowed in his nationally televised September 11 speech. "Let no one doubt our American credibility and reliability. Let no one doubt our staying power."

For those familiar with the postwar era, this seizure of a purely temporal, local crisis to implement a previously devised, long-term strategy will seem uncannily like the sequence of events occasioned by the outbreak of the Korean War. The strategic planners of the Truman Administration never viewed Korea as a critical cold war battlefield, but they used the anxieties aroused by that conflict to secure Congressional approval of a massive U.S. commitment to the defense of NATO—the real goal of Truman's advisers (as evidenced in N.S.C.-68, the secret strategy document prepared by Paul Nitze in early 1950), and one that had previously been opposed by an economy-minded Republican-controlled Congress.

As was the case with the Korean War, advocates of the new U.S. global posture conceal their imperial objectives under the mantle of international peace and order. Here, for instance, is Nitze providing, in 1990 as in 1950, the intellectual scaffolding for a policy of global military engagement: "The United States, with first-class military potential, inherent political, economic, and cultural strengths and no territorial or ideological ambitions, can play a unique role in bringing its latent power to the support of order and diversity" among groups and nations.

Similar comments have been made by President Bush and Secretary of State James Baker. The Persian Gulf crisis "offers a rare opportunity to move toward an historic period of cooperation," Bush affirmed in his September 11 speech. "Out of these troubled times," he noted, "a new world order can emerge: a new era, freer from the threat of terror, stronger in the pursuit of justice, and more secure in the quest for peace."

But rather than pursue noble objectives like peace, tolerance and cooperation for their own sake, American policy-makers see them as rationales for a continuing U.S. role as the world's reigning superpower. To achieve this objective—which will insure the continued prominence of the national security establishment at the expense of economic renewal—leaders are prepared to risk the lives of U.S. soldiers in recurring "contingency operations" abroad. How else after all, do we demonstrate America's "credibility and reliability," to use Bush's words? The answer, Defense Secretary Dick Cheney explained in March, "is that we're willing to put U.S. troops on the ground. The message, to friends and enemies alike, is that *Americans are willing to risk their lives to insure the security of our friends and allies.*" [Emphasis added by Klare.]

Is this the sort of future we want? To be perennially risking the lives of our young people so that generals and spymasters can retain their positions of power in Washington and so that our economic rivals will be guaranteed a steady supply of cheap oil? Americans who are concerned about the restoration of our economic health and the preservation of our democratic values cannot consent to such a prospect. We must reject the global military role advocated by President Bush and adopt a new foreign policy based on U.S. partnership with, not leadership over, other international actors.

---

## COMPREHENSION CHECKPOINT

What is the significance of the following?

| | | |
|---|---|---|
| Truman Doctrine | Marshall Plan | geo-economic model |
| "messianistic globalony" | NSC-68 | geostrategic model |

Can you answer the questions and do the tasks that follow?

1. What are Nitze's policy proposals in the following areas: helping Gorbachev, strategic arms reductions, and a united Germany? What does he mean when he writes that American foreign policy should seek "the accommodation and protection of diversity within a general framework of world order?" What does Klare claim that Nitze means by this statement? Why does Nitze reject isolationism?

2. Why does Tonelson believe that the United States should drop its internationalist strategy "of grounding American security and prosperity in a congenial world environment of liberal democracies, collective security, and free trade." What are the major components of his "New Nationalist synthesis"? How would Tonelson respond to the criticism that it would be immoral for America to turn its back upon the beleaguered nation of Israel or the victims of human rights abuses in China and South Africa?

3. How would Buchanan distinguish between national interests and extranational interests? While proposing a noninterventionist foreign policy, Buchanan argues that America is uniquely qualified to lead the world in the years ahead. What does he mean by leadership? How will it be undertaken, and for what ends?

4. What possible threats does Mark Katz see to American interests in the Persian Gulf, Southeast Asia, the Indian Ocean, and Latin America? How would Katz reply to Jeane Kirkpatrick's statement that "we have virtually no experience in protecting and serving our interests in a multipolar world in which diverse nations and groups of nations engage in endless competition for marginal advantage?"[23]

5. According to Klare, what are the stakes in the conflict between the geo-economic and geostrategic models? What evidence does Klare present in support of his position that Bush has adopted the geostrategic strategy? Why would Bush would choose the geostrategic over the geo-economic strategy?

6. Refer to the chart on page 135, which delineates the major differences between reassertionists and neorealists. Using this chart as a starting point, construct a new chart that delineates the differences among the post–cold war worldviews. What overlap is there between the old and the new chart? What new items appear? How do you account for the similarities and differences?

7. Which post–cold war worldview do you prefer? Why? Which of the mainstream worldviews presented in this chapter accords most closely with Klare's assessment? Which alternative do you think the American people will favor?

8. Fill in the matrix that appears on the following page.

WORLDVIEW

| Component | Insular isolationism | Involved isolationism | Multilateral internationalism | Unilateral internationalism | Post–cold war radicalism |
|---|---|---|---|---|---|
| 1. Top agenda items | | | | | |
| 2. Emerging axes of conflict | | | | | |
| 3. Significance of conflicts | | | | | |
| 4. Degree of relatedness | | | | | |
| 5. Major metaphors | | | | | |
| 6. Major stock characters and nations | | | | | |
| 7. "Lessons of history" | | | | | |
| 8. Major scripts | | | | | |

# FOR FURTHER READING

"American Foreign Policy in the 1990s." *SAIS Review.* Vol. 10, No. 1 (Spring 1990), pp. 15–52. Thirteen foreign policy experts respond to the following questions: "Which one current international development . . . holds the greatest significance for U.S. national interests in the 1990s? How should the U.S. react to this development?" Among the respondents are Richard Barnet, William Cline, Richard Feinberg, Senator Nancy Landon Kesselbaum, Senator Richard G. Lugar, and Joseph S. Nye, Jr.

"America's Purpose Now." *The National Interest.* 21 (Fall 1990). A symposium of ten foreign policy notables, ranging from neo-isolationists to internationalists and from liberals to conservatives. Among the contributors are neoconservatives Jeane Kirkpatrick, Nathan Glazer, and Ben Wattenberg, the libertarian noninterventionist Ted Carpenter, and the liberal democratic congressman Stephen Solarz.

Art, Robert J. "A Defensible Defense: America's Grand Strategy After the Cold War." *International Security*. Vol. 15, No. 4 (Spring 1991), pp. 5–54. Art holds the Christian A. Herter Chair of International Relations at Brandeis University. In this essay, he sketches out a "grand strategy" for the post–cold war era that is designed to secure five specific national interests—(1) protection of the homeland from destruction, (2) continued prosperity based on an open international economic order, (3) sure access to Persian Gulf oil, (4) prevention of war among the great powers in Europe and Asia and assured security for Israel and South Korea, and (5) "where feasible, the promotion of democratic governments and the overthrow of governments engaged in mass murder of their citizens." Art's discussion is notable for its discussion of how these interests have been secured in the past.

Chipman, John. "Third World Politics and Security in the 1990s." *The Washington Quarterly*. Vol. 14, No. 1 (Winter 1991), pp. 151–68. A comprehensive survey of the kinds of conflicts among Third World states that the United States will face in the era of regional international politics. Chipman's conclusion: "It will be almost impossible to construct overarching themes to guide policy in an age where regional conflict is *sui generis*, interests are variable, and the distribution of power and influence so diffuse." This essay can be seen as a counterpoint to the selection by Katz.

Chomsky, Noam. "The Dawn, So Far, Is in the East." *The Nation*. January 29, 1990, pp. 130–33. Chomsky believes that the collapse of Bolshevism and the decline of "state capitalist democracy" may make possible "the revival of libertarian socialist and radical democratic ideals. . . .".

"Defining the New World Order: What Is It? Whose Is It?" *Harper's*, May 1991, pp. 59–66. *Harper's* asked three notable foreign policy experts to address the questions posed in this article's title. The respondents are Owen Harries, editor of *The National Interest*, Ian Buruma, foreign editor of *The Spectator* in London, and Richard Barnet, co-founder of the Institute for Policy Studies in Washington, D.C. The three short responses are full of insights—some sobering, some novel, some depressing—from a variety of worldviews. This forum is essential reading.

Fuentes, Carlos. "Time for Our Sinatra Doctrine." *The Nation*. February 12, 1990, cover page and pp. 198–203. A leading Mexican novelist calls upon the United States to follow the Soviet example in Eastern Europe by ceasing its involvement in internal struggles in Latin America.

Gaddis, John Lewis. "Coping With Victory." *The Atlantic Monthly*. May 1990, pp. 49–60. A leading historian of the cold war raises and answers some major questions on the foreign policy agenda—should we welcome the decline and possible breakup of the Soviet Union; how will NATO, the Warsaw Pact, and a reunified Germany fit together; what happens after Gorbachev?

Gaddis, John Lewis. "Toward the Post–Cold War World." *Foreign Affairs*. Vol. 70, No. 2 (Spring 1991), pp. 102–22. After rejecting an isolationist alternative, Gaddis sketches out the essentials of an internationalist foreign policy designed to fit the "new geopolitical cartography" of the post–cold war era. For those interested in making projections about future trends in the international system, this essay should be read in conjunction with those of Chipman, Krauthammer, Hoffmann, Pfaff, and Ravenal included in this bibliography.

Gardner, Richard N. "The Comeback of Liberal Internationalism." *The Washington Quarterly.* Vol. 13, No. 4 (Summer 1990). Gardner, a distinguished diplomat and professor of Law and International Organization at Columbia University, calls for a return to liberal internationalism of the type envisioned by FDR at the end of World War II. In rejecting isolationism, unilateral nationalism, balance of power politics, and disinterested or utopian world order politics, Gardner argues that the United States should work with other liberal democracies, "in the construction of a peaceful world order through effective international organizations." While he recognizes that the United States might have to act unilaterally at times, Gardner argues that such action should always be "inside" the United Nations Charter. This important essay complements the selection by Paul Nitze.

Hoffmann, Stanley. "What Should We Do in the World?" *The Atlantic Monthly.* October 1989, pp. 84–96. A brilliant assessment of the forces at work in the emerging post–cold war era by one of the nation's leading foreign policy analysts. Hoffmann proposes a multilateral foreign policy designed to secure "more order and justice in the world."

Hoffmann, Stanley. "The Case for Leadership." *Foreign Policy.* 81 (Winter 1990–91), pp. 20–39. Hoffmann calls on the United States to take the lead in building a new security system in Europe.

Huntington, Samuel P. "America's Changing Strategic Interests." *Survival.* Vol. XXXIII, No. 1 (January/February 1991), pp. 3–17. One of the nation's leading political scientists assesses the impact of the changing international environment on "three major strategic interests of the U.S."—meeting the Japanese economic challenge, maintaining the European balance of power, and protecting concrete Third World interests.

Hyland, William. "America's New Course." *Foreign Affairs.* Vol. 69, No. 2 (Spring 1990), pp. 1–13. Hyland, the editor of *Foreign Affairs,* makes a careful assessment of the questions the United States will face in the post–cold war era and proposes a middle course between "indiscriminate isolationism" and "indiscriminate internationalism."

Kirkpatrick, Jeane. "Beyond the Cold War." *Foreign Affairs: America and the World 1989/90.* Vol. 69, No. 1, pp. 1–17. Kirkpatrick argues that with the end of the cold war the United States can shed its superpower status and become "a normal nation."

Kissinger, Henry. "False Dreams of a New World Order." *The Washington Post,* February 26, 1991. Kissinger rebuts the opinion of the Bush Administration that the success of the United Nations in meeting the Kuwait crisis signalled the birth of a new world order. Only particular interests of the key nations involved, Kissinger argues, led to the concerted action. Rejecting the alternatives of a new world order or American hegemony, Kissinger concludes that "we come back to a concept much maligned in much of America's intellectual history—the balance of power."

Klare, Michael. "The New World War." *The Progressive.* November 1990, pp. 14–16. Klare expands upon the analysis he presented in "Policing the Gulf—And the World." According to Klare, America will remain the developed world's policeman against radical or nationalist Third World states that seek national control over their oil and other economic assets.

Kolko, Gabriel. "The Logic of U.S. Geopolitics: An Interview with Gabriel Kolko." *Multinational Monitor.* September 1989, pp. 27–31. A leading radical scholar assesses the nationalist forces that will increasingly confront American capitalism in the Third World.

Krauthammer, Charles. "The Unipolar Moment." *Foreign Affairs: America and the World 1990/91*. Vol. 70, No. 1 (1991), pp. 23–34. Krauthammer argues that the United States should pursue a unilateral world order foreign policy in the post–cold war era. The goal of this policy would be to deter and defeat, if necessary, hostile regional powers which Krauthammer defines as Weapons States. Krauthammer's position is close to that proposed by Mark Katz.

Kristol, Irving. "Defining Our National Interest." 21 (Fall 1990), pp. 16–26. A leading neoconservative calls for a more restrained foreign policy in the post–cold war era.

Maynes, Charles William. "A Necessary War?" *Foreign Policy*. 82 (Spring 1991), pp. 159–78. In this essay written before the outcome of the war against Iraq was known, Maynes rebuts four major arguments made in support of the Bush administration's policy—oil, international order, U.S. security, and the security of Israel.

McNamara, Robert S. *Out of the Cold War: New Thinking for American Foreign and Defense Policy*. New York: Simon and Schuster, 1989. The former Secretary of Defense and former President of the World Bank proposes joint codes of conduct through which the United States and the Soviet Union would agree to renounce the use of force, cut military weapons substantially, refrain from intervention in regional conflicts, and resolve disputes through the United Nations.

Mead, Walter Russell. "On the Road to Ruin: Winning the Cold War, Losing the Economic Peace." *Harper's Magazine*. March 1990, pp. 59–64. Mead, a senior fellow in international economics at the World Policy Institute, argues that America's pursuit of victory in the cold war cost the nation its economic vitality. If the United States fails to regain its economic competitiveness and economic leadership, Mead fears the world will break up into three rival trading blocs where all will be losers.

Mearsheimer, John. "Why We Will Soon Miss the Cold War." *The Atlantic*. August 1990, pp. 35–52. A sobering projection of the kinds of instabilities and disarray that the United States might face in Europe after the cold war.

Morss, Elliott R. "The New Global Players: How They Compete and Collaborate. Global Prospects in an Interdependent World." *World Development*, Vol. 19, No. 1 (January 1991), pp. 122–33. According to Morss, the information revolution and the demise of the United States as the dominant world power has led to increased influence for three new global players—transnational corporations, international organizations, and private special interest groups. Morss believes nation-states are increasingly losing control over these new forces. This essay supplements and supports points made by Robert Reich (cited above) and deserves a very careful reading by anyone who wants to know how the information revolution and the globalization of business are affecting our nations and our personal lives.

Muravchik, Joshua. *Fulfilling America's Destiny*. Washington, DC: The AEI Press, 1991. Muravchik rejects balance of power politics, isolationism, and what he terms "pacifist idealism" as alternatives for the post-cold war era. Instead, he proposes a policy of democratic idealism which would foster the development of democratic governments around the world.

*The National Interest*. Beginning with its Winter 1989/90 issue (Number 18), *The National Interest* began running a series of essays on what the nation's purpose should be during the rest of the century. The selection by Patrick Buchanan was taken from this series.

"Nineteen Perspectives for the Left." *The Progressive*. November 1990, pp. 17–38. As the title indicates, nineteen radicals and progressives indicate where they think America should be going both domestically and internationally in the post–cold war era. Among the contributors are Richard Barnet, Jesse Jackson, Francis Moore Lappé, Saul Landau, Harry Magdoff, and Howard Zinn.

Nixon, Richard. "Should We Help Gorbachev? Not If You Take History Seriously." *The American Spectator*. March 1990, pp. 18–21. Nixon's answer is contained in the title.

Nixon, Richard. "A War Called Peace: The Victory of Freedom." *Vital Speeches*, April 1, 1991, pp.357–60. In this address delivered to the Republican Congressional Committee in December of 1990, former President Nixon takes his audience on a tour of the world and sketches out a post–cold war foreign policy. According to Nixon, "the world is still a dangerous place and the United States must continue to play a leading role on the world stage . . . because there is no one else to take our place." In addition, he presents a set of domestic priorities that would make America an example for others to follow.

Nye, Joseph S., Jr. "The Misleading Metaphor of Decline." *The Atlantic Monthly*. March 1990, pp. 86–94. Harvard Government Professor Joseph Nye rebuts the recently fashionable belief that America is in decline as a world power. Nye argues that analogies with past great powers are misleading. In his opinion, America can play a leading role in the world and strengthen its economy at home.

Odum, William E. "Why Helping Gorbachev Could Backfire." *U.S. News and World Report*. May 21, 1990. Odum argues that the United States should support self-determination for the republics within the Soviet Union.

Pfaff, William. "Redefining World Power." *Foreign Affairs: America and the World 1990/91*. Vol. 70, No. 1 (1991), pp. 34–49. A leading journalist critically examines both uniploar and multilateralist internationalism. In so doing, Pfaff projects possible futures for Europe and the Soviet Union.

Pines, Burton Yale. "A Primer for Conservatives." *The National Interest*. 23 (Spring 1991), pp. 61–8. A senior vice-president of the Heritage Foundation presents his set of ten conservative foreign policy principles for the post–cold war era. Pines concludes that "Americans no longer need to conduct a foreign policy that automatically imposes great costs, great risks, and great distortions in the power relationships between the American people and their government." Pines proposes particular policies for particular governments.

Ravenal, Earl C. "The Case for Adjustment." *Foreign Policy*. 21 (Winter 1990–91), pp. 3–20. Ravenal characterizes emerging trends in the international system and makes the case for a noninterventionist foreign policy.

Reich, Robert B. *The Work of Nations: Preparing Ourselves for 21st-Century Capitalism*. New York: Alfred A. Knopf, 1991. Reich, a professor at Harvard University's Kennedy School, explores in great detail the impact of the international economic order upon our national economy. According to Reich, "Nations can no longer substantially enhance the wealth of their citizens by subsidizing, protecting, or otherwise increasing the profitability of "their" corporations; the connection between corporate profitability and the standard of living of a nation's people is growing ever more attenuated." (p. 153) The validity of Reich's thesis and its foreign policy implications will be debated for years to come, but undoubtedly , *The Work of Nations* will be one of the most important books of the 1990s.

"Rethinking the Left: The Road to Reconstruction." *The Nation.* April 22, 1991, pp. 512–25. The collapse of communism in Eastern Europe has created an intellectual crisis for many radical and leftist thinkers. In his symposium, four leading scholars from "the left and the liberal side of the spectrum" seek to start a dialogue on the future of the left in both domestic and foreign policy matters. These essays by Marcus Raskin, Aryeh Neier, Mary Kaldor, and Gar Alperovitz merit careful reading.

Rizopoulos, Nicholas X. (ed.) *Sea-Changes: American Foreign Policy in a World Transformed.* New York: Council on Foreign Relations, 1990. Brief assessments by the nation's leading foreign policy analysts on the impact of the end of the cold war for the major regional and functional areas of international politics. This book is essential reading.

Russet, Bruce and James S. Sutterlin. "The U.N. in a New World Order." *Foreign Affairs.* Vol. 70, No. 2 (Spring 1991), pp. 69–84. Russett, Dean Acheson Professor of International Relations and Political Science at Yale, and Sutterlin, former Director of the Executive Office of the U.N. Secretary General, provide a careful and realistic assessment of the possible roles the United Nations can play in the post–cold war era and the requisite conditions to make those roles a reality. In making their assessments, Russett and Sutterlin draw heavily on the Korean War and the Persian Gulf crises.

Sorensen, Theodore C. "Rethinking National Security." *Foreign Affairs.* Vol. 69, No. 3 (Summer 1990), pp. 1–19. Sorensen argues that the United States should puruse human rights and economic competitiveness in the post–cold war era.

"Stopping the War." *The Nation.* March 4, 1991, pp. 255–57, 271. *The Nation* asked four foreign policy experts—Charles William Maynes, Peter Weiss, Robert C. Johansen, and Richard Falk—to present possible diplomatic solutions to the war in the Gulf.

Streeten, Paul. "Global Prospects in an Interdependent World." *World Development,* Vol. 19, No. 1 (January 1991), pp. 122–33. Streeten identifies emerging trends in the post-cold war international system, namely, the demise of the United States as the hegemonic international actor and the rise of new global issues. He then critically assesses three possible future systems that might arise to deal with those trends—global, world order systems, a world divided into trading blocs, and a system of global coordination among oligarchs—the United States, Germany, and Japan. Streeten prefers the global, world order approach, but believes that a benign bloc system would be a good second best.

Sweezy, Paul M. "Revolution of 89: Is This Then the End of Socialism?" *The Nation.* February 26, 1990, first page, 276–78. A leading Marxist thinker assesses the implications of the dissolution of the Soviet bloc for the future of socialism as an ideal and a reality. His answer: "I believe that socialism has exactly the same chance of surviving and realizing its potential as does the human species."

Sweezy, Paul M. "U.S. Imperialism in the 1990s." *Monthly Review.* Vol. 41, No. 5 (October 1989), pp. 1–17. Sweezy argues that American capitalism will increasingly be placed on the defensive by the aggressive, competing imperialisms of its allies in the developed countries.

Thompson, E.P. "E.N.D. and the Beginning: History Turns on A New Hinge." *The Nation.* January 29, 1990, pp. 117–22. Thompson, a distinguished British historian and peace advocate, argues that it was the European Peace Movement and not the West's containment policy that brought an end to the cold war.

Tonelson, Alan. "The End of Internationalism? Gorbachev Spells the Doom of the Foreign Policy Industry." *The New Republic.* February 13, 1990, pp. 23–5. Tonelson argues that Gorbachev's new foreign policy has made all strands of internationalism obsolete, from reassertionism to the disinterested world order position of people like Falk, Beres, and Gurtov.

VanEvera, Stephen. "The Case Against Intervention." *The Atlantic Monthly.* July 1990, pp. 72–80. An MIT political scientist argues that neither the United States nor the Soviet Union has any significant strategic interests in the Third World. He calls on the Bush administration to end its support for proxy wars in El Salvador, Angola, Cambodia, and Afghanistan.

VanEvera, Stephen, "Why Europe Matters, Why the Third World Doesn't: American Grand Strategy After the Cold War." *Journal of Strategic Studies.* Vol. 13, No. 2 (June 1990), pp. 1–51. An in-depth and carefully argued presentation of a neorealist strategy for the post–cold war era.

Yankelovich, Daniel and Richard Smoke. "America's 'New Thinking.'" *Foreign Affairs.* Vol. 67, No. 1 (Fall 1988). This essay reports the responses of a 1988 public opinion survey on a wide range of foreign policy issues. Comparisons are made with earlier surveys.

# NOTES

1. Irving Kristol, "Defining our National Interest," *The National Interest,* 21 (Fall 1990), p. 17.
2. For a sample of proposed approaches, see Zbigniew Brzezinski, "Beyond Chaos: What the West Must Do," *The National Interest,* 19 (Spring 1990), pp. 3–13; Marshall Brennan, "Reaching Out to Moscow," *Foreign Policy,* 80 (Fall 1990) pp. 56–11; Peter Corterier, "Transforming the Atlantic Alliance," *The Washington Quarterly,* Vol. 14, No. 1 (Winter 1991), pp. 27–39; Stanley Hoffmann, "The Case for Leadership," *Foreign Policy,* 81 (Winter 1990–91), pp. 20–39; Gregory Lynn and David J. Scheffer, "Limited Collective Security," *Foreign Policy,* 80 (Fall 1990), pp. 77–102; and Paul H. Nitze, "America: An Honest Broker," *Foreign Affairs,* Vol. 69, No. 4 (Fall 1990), pp. 1–15.
3. Earl C. Ravenal, "The Case for Adjustment," *Foreign Policy,* 81 (Winter 1990–91), p. 11.
4. Stanley Hoffmann, "A New World and Its Troubles," in Nicholas X. Rizopoulos (ed.), *Sea Changes* (New York: Council on Foreign Relations, 1990), pp. 278–79.
5. On the issue of Central America especially, see John J. Mearsheimer, "Why We Will Soon Miss the Cold War," *The Atlantic Monthly* (August 1990), pp. 35–50.
6. Cited in Michael Klare, "The Superpower Trip: Policing the Gulf—And the World," *The Nation,* October 15, 1990, p. 418.
7. These figures are taken from the Arms Control and Disarmament Agency, *World Military Expenditures and Arms Transfers 1988* (Washington, DC: U.S. Government Printing Office, 1989).
8. See his book, *The Long Peace* (New York: Oxford University Press, 1987).

9. Earl Ravenal, "The Case for Adjustment," p. 12.
10. Stanley Hoffmann, "A New World and Its Troubles," p. 279.
11. Cited in Alan Tonelson, "A Manifesto for Democrats, *The National Interest*, 16 (Summer 1989), p. 38.
12. For differing views on this new force see Robert Bartlett, "A Win-Win Game," *The National Interest*, 21 (Fall 1990), pp. 26–28; Stanley Kober, "Idealpolitik," *Foreign Policy*, 79 (Summer 1990), pp. 3–25; and Stanley Hoffmann, "A New World and Its Troubles," pp. 280–81.
13. Bartlett, "A Win-Win Game," p. 27.
14. Norman Cousins, "Need of the 90s: Structured Interdependence," *The Christian Science Monitor*, January 2, 1990.
15. The phrase is Jeane Kirkpatrick's. See her article in "A Normal Country in a Normal Time," in *The National Interest*, 21 (Fall 1990), p. 42.
16. Alan Tonelson, "A Manifesto for Democrats," p. 38.
17. Robert Reich, "American Society in a Global Economy," *Society*, November/December 1990, p. 67.
18. Ted Galen Carpenter, "An Independent Course," *The National Interest*, 21 (Fall 1990), p. 30.
19. "A Populist Policy," *The National Interest*, 21 (Fall 1990), p. 26.
20. Richard N. Gardner, "The Comeback of Liberal Internationalism," *The Washington Quarterly*, Vol. 13, No. 4 (Autumn 1990), p. 23.
21. Elie Kedourie, "Hamlet in Kuwait," *The New Republic*, December 24, 1990, p. 14.
22. See, for example, the questions raised by the editors of *The New Republic* about the prices extracted by Ethiopia and Zaire for their support in the Security Council in "Tough Duty," *The New Republic*, December 10, 1990, p. 8.
23. Jeane Kirkpatrick's "A Normal Country in a Normal Time," p. 40.

# Acknowledgments

Grateful acknowledgment is made for the use of the following material*:

George F. Kennan (X), "The Sources of Soviet Conduct," Parts II and III. Reprinted by permission of *Foreign Affairs* (Spring 1987). Copyright (1987) by the Council on Foreign Relations, Inc.

Hans Morgenthau, "The Real Issue between the United States and the Soviet Union," from *In Defense of the National Interest* (New York: Alfred A. Knopf, 1951), pp. 69–81. Reprinted by permission of Matthew Morgenthau and Susanna Morgenthau.

Charles Wolf, Jr., "Extended Containment," from Aaron Wildavsky (ed.), *Beyond Containment* (San Franscisco: ICS Press, 1983). Reprinted by permission of ICS press.

Jeane Kirkpatrick, "The Reagan Reassertion of Western Values," from *The Reagan Phenomenon and Other Speeches on Foreign Policy* (Washington, DC: American Enterprise Institute, 1983), pp. 28–36. Reprinted with the permission of the American Enterprise Institute, Washington, DC.

William E. Odom, "How to Handle Moscow," from *The Washington Post*. March 12, 1989. Reprinted by permission of William Odom.

Hans Morgenthau, "U.S. Misadventure in Vietnam," from *Current History* (January 1968), pp. 29–31, 34. Reprinted with permission from *Current History* magazine, copyright © 1968, Current History Inc.

Tom Farer, "Searching for Defeat," from *Foreign Policy*, 40 (Fall 1980), pp. 155–74. Reprinted by permission of *Foreign Policy*, copyright owned by the Carnegie Endowment for International Peace.

Richard E. Feinberg and Kenneth A. Oye, "After the Fall: U.S. Policy Toward Radical Regimes," from *World Policy Journal* (Fall 1983), pp. 201–25. Reprinted by permission of *World Policy Journal*.

Robert Mueller, "Enough Rope: The Cold War was Lost, Not Won," *The New Republic*, July 3, 1989, pp. 14–16. Reprinted by permission of *The National Republic*.

Albert J. Beveridge, "Pitfalls of a League of Nations," from *The North American Review* (March 1919), pp. 312–14. Reprinted by permission of *The North American Review* and the University of Northern Iowa.

Christopher Layne, "The Real Conservative Agenca" from *Foreign Policy*, 61 (Winter 1985–86), pp. 73–93. Reprinted by permission of *Foreign Policy*, copyright owned by the Carnegie Endowment for International Peace.

Earl Ravenal, "An Alternative to Containment" excerpted from Earl Ravenal, "Containment, Nonintevention, and Strategic Disengagement," in Terry L. Diebel and John Lewis Gaddis (eds.), *Containing the Soviet Union* (Washington,

---

*Authors listed in order of their appearance in book.